Study Guide
Chapters 1-15

College Accounting

Twenty-first Edition

James A. Heintz, DBA, CPA
Professor of Accounting
School of Business
University of Kansas

Robert W. Parry, Jr., Ph.D.
Professor of Accounting
Kelley School of Business
Indiana University

SOUTH-WESTERN
CENGAGE Learning

Australia • Brazil • Japan • Korea • Mexico • Singapore • Spain • United Kingdom • United States

For product information and technology assistance, contact us at **Cengage Learning Academic Resource Center, 1-800-423-0563.**

For permission to use material from this text or product, submit all requests online at **www.cengage.com/permissions.** Further permissions questions can be emailed to **permissionrequest@cengage.com.**

ISBN-13: 978-1-285-41889-6
ISBN-10: 1-285-41889-1

South-Western Cengage Learning
5191 Natorp Boulevard
Mason, OH 45040
USA

Cengage Learning is a leading provider of customized learning solutions with office locations around the globe, including Singapore, the United Kingdom, Australia, Mexico, Brazil, and Japan. Locate your local office at: **international.cengage.com/region.**

Cengage Learning products are represented in Canada by Nelson Education, Ltd.

For your course and learning solutions, visit **www.cengage.com.**

Purchase any of our products at your local college store or at our preferred online store **www.CengageBrain.com.**

Printed in the United States of America
1 2 3 4 5 6 7   16 15 14 13

Table of Contents

CHAPTER 1
INTRODUCTION TO ACCOUNTING

LEARNING OBJECTIVES

Chapter 1 is designed to introduce you to accounting—its purpose, process, and career opportunities. Businesses that keep good accounting records benefit in many ways. Users of accounting information are able to make sound decisions, which will affect the business's future. Accounting offers many career opportunities, some of which are entry level and task oriented and others that involve decision making and planning.

Objective 1.   Describe the purpose of accounting.
   Accounting is the process by which businesses keep track of daily transactions and determine how the business is doing. Accounting provides needed information for its many users, from owners to government agencies and others.

Objective 2.   Describe the accounting process.
   The accounting process contains six major steps.
   Step 1 Analyzing: Looking at information available and figuring out what to do with it. This first step in the accounting process usually occurs when the business receives some type of information, such as a bill, that needs to be properly entered into the business's records. This first step also involves deciding if the piece of information should result in an accounting entry or not.
   Step 2 Recording: Entering the information, manually or via a computer, into the accounting system.
   Step 3 Classifying: Grouping like items together.
   Step 4 Summarizing: Aggregating many similar events to provide information that is easy to understand.
   Step 5 Reporting: Communicating the results, such as profit or loss, commonly using tables of numbers to tell the financial status of the business.
   Step 6 Interpreting: Examining the financial statements to evaluate the financial health of the business.

Objective 3.   Define GAAP and describe the process used by FASB to develop these principles.
   Generally accepted accounting principles (GAAP) are the rules that businesses must follow when preparing financial statements. The Securities and Exchange Commission (SEC) has the legal power to make these rules for firms listed on one of the U.S. stock exchanges. However, the SEC has delegated this responsibility to the Financial Accounting Standards Board (FASB).

FASB takes the following steps to develop an accounting standard:
   1. The issue is placed on FASB's agenda.
   2. After researching an issue, FASB issues a Preliminary Views document to offer the pros and cons of the accounting alternatives and to invite others to comment.
   3. To gather additional views on the issue, the Board often holds public hearings around the country.
   4. Following these hearings, the Board issues an exposure draft. This document explains the rules that FASB believes firms should follow in accounting for this event.
   5. After considering feedback on the exposure draft, the Board issues an Accounting Standards Update which amends the FASB Accounting Standards Codification.

Objective 4.   Define three types of business ownership structures.
   Businesses can be classified according to who owns them and the specific way they are organized. A sole proprietorship is owned by one person who assumes all risks for the business and makes all business decisions. A partnership is owned by two or more persons who share the risks and decision making. Corporations have many owners (shareholders) whose risk is limited to their investment and who have little influence in business decisions.

Objective 5.   Classify different types of businesses by activities.

Businesses also can be classified by the type of service or product they provide. A service business provides a service, a merchandising business purchases a product from another business to sell, and a manufacturing business makes a product to sell.

Objective 6.   Identify career opportunities in accounting.

Accounting has varied and diverse opportunities, depending on the education and experience of the worker, the type of business, and the accounting processes used within the business.

Accounting clerks record, sort, and file accounting information. Bookkeepers supervise clerks, help with daily accounting work, and summarize information. Para-accountants provide many accounting, auditing, or tax services under the direct supervision of an accountant.

Public accountants offer services such as auditing, tax advice, management advisory services, and forensic accounting services. Under the Sarbanes-Oxley Act, however, they may not provide audit and management advisory services to the same company. Further, audit and tax services may be provided to the same company only if preapproved by the audit committee of the company.

Managerial accountants offer services to private businesses, such as designing accounting information systems, general accounting, cost accounting, budgeting, tax accounting, and internal auditing. Government and not-for-profit organizations also employ accountants.

Accounting is a professional field, which includes organizations and certifications for those who pass examinations and have relevant work experience.

REVIEW QUESTIONS

Instructions: Analyze each of the following items carefully before writing your answer in the column at the right.

Question	Answer

LO 1 **1.** The purpose of accounting is to provide current information to users. For each user below, briefly describe what type of information is needed.

    a. Owners (present and future)

    b. Managers who make decisions for the business

    c. Creditors (present and future)

    d. Government agencies (state, local, and national)

LO 5 **2.** A travel agency is an example of this type of business. .... _____

LO 4 **3.** The ownership structure where owners share risks and decision making is called a(n) _____. .... _____

LO 5 **4.** A(n) _____ business makes a product to sell. .... _____

LO 5 **5.** A business that purchases a product from another business to sell to customers is called a(n) _____ business. .... _____

LO 4 **6.** Under the _____ ownership structure, the owner's personal assets can be taken to pay creditors. .... _____

LO 3 **7.** The Financial Accounting Standards Board develops procedures and guidelines called _____ to be followed in the accounting process. _____

LO 3 8. The following actions are taken by FASB when developing an accounting standard. Indicate the proper sequence of events by placing a 1 through 5 in the space provided.

Step

_____ The Accounting Standards Update is issued which amends the FASB Accounting Standards Codification.

_____ Public hearings are held.

_____ An exposure draft is issued.

_____ The issue is placed on FASB's agenda.

_____ A Preliminary Views document is issued.

LO 4 9. The owners' risk is usually limited to their initial investment in this type of ownership structure. .... _____

LO 6 10. Is a public accounting firm permitted to provide audit and tax services to a publicly held company?.. _____

LO 6 11. By meeting education and experience requirements and passing an examination, a public accountant can achieve recognition as a(n) _____. _____

LO 6 12. The segment of accounting practice that includes fraud detection, fraud prevention, litigation support, business valuation, expert witness services, and other investigative activities is known as _____. .... _____

LO 2 13. The six major steps of the accounting process are listed in the box at the right. In front of each term, write the letter that identifies the correct description provided in the column on the left.

a. The process of entering financial information about events affecting the business

b. Aggregating similar events to provide information that is easy to understand

c. The process of sorting or grouping like things together, rather than merely keeping a simple, diary-like narrative record of numerous and varied transactions

d. The process of determining the effect of various events on the business

e. The process of deciding the importance of the information in various reports

f. The process of communicating the results of operation

_____	Analyzing
_____	Recording
_____	Classifying
_____	Summarizing
_____	Reporting
_____	Interpreting

Name _____

CHAPTER 2
ANALYZING TRANSACTIONS:
THE ACCOUNTING EQUATION

LEARNING OBJECTIVES

Chapter 2 continues the introductory discussion of accounting—its elements, equation, and transactions. The accounting equation provides a structure for analyzing transactions. After all transactions have been analyzed, the financial statements—income statement, statement of owner's equity, and balance sheet—are prepared. Let's look at each of these learning objectives in detail.

Objective 1.   Define the accounting elements.

Accounting elements are the parts that make up the accounting equation: assets, liabilities, and owner's equity. **Assets** are items *owned* by the business that will provide future benefits. **Liabilities** are debts *owed* by the business and will require a future outflow of assets. **Owner's equity** (also called net worth or capital) is the difference between assets and liabilities. **Revenues** represent the amount a business charges customers for products sold or services provided. Revenues create an inflow of assets. **Expenses** represent an outflow of assets (or increase in liabilities) as a result of the efforts made to generate revenues.

Objective 2.   Construct the accounting equation.

The accounting equation shows the relationship among assets, liabilities, and owner's equity (the accounting elements).

$$\text{Assets} = \text{Liabilities} + \text{Owner's Equity}$$

When given two of the numbers for the equation above, you can calculate the missing number by adding or subtracting.

The accounting equation may be expanded to include revenues, expenses, and drawing. Although drawing is not considered a major element in the accounting equation, it is a very special type of owner's equity account. It represents the withdrawals of assets from the business by the owner.

ASSETS (Items Owned)			LIABILITIES (Amts. Owed)		OWNER'S EQUITY				
					(Owner's Investment)		(Earnings)		
Cash	+	Delivery Equipment	=	Accounts Payable	+	Damon Williams, Capital	− Damon Williams, Drawing	+ Revenues	− Expenses

Objective 3.   Analyze business transactions.

Analyzing is the first step in the accounting process. Three questions must be answered: (1) What happened? (2) Which accounts are affected, and what kind of accounts are they (asset, liability, owner's equity)? (3) How is the accounting equation affected? (Accounts will increase or decrease, but the equation always remains in balance.)

Objective 4.   Show the effects of business transactions on the accounting equation.

Each transaction will affect asset, liability, owner's equity, revenue, or expense accounts. For example, when an owner invests cash in the business, the asset account called *Cash* increases, and the owner's equity account *Capital* also increases.

For each transaction, you must decide what accounts are affected and whether the accounts increase or decrease. After each transaction, the equation must still be in balance.

Objective 5.   Prepare and describe the purposes of a simple income statement, statement of owner's equity, and balance sheet.

After the transactions are completed, the financial statements are prepared to show the results of those transactions. As shown on page 7, all financial statements have a heading that indicates the name of the firm, title of the statement, and time period or date covered by the statement. The income statement reports revenues, expenses, and the net income for the period. The statement of owner's equity shows the beginning balance of the owner's capital account, plus investments and net income, less withdrawals to compute the ending capital balance. The balance sheet reports all assets, liabilities, and the owner's capital on a certain date and confirms that the accounting equation has remained in balance.

Note that net income computed on the income statement is transferred to the statement of owner's equity to compute Patty V's capital at the end of the month. Patty V's capital on December 31, 20--, is then transferred to the balance sheet to compute total liabilities and owner's equity.

Objective 6.   Define the three basic phases of the accounting process.

The three basic phases of the accounting process are input, processing, and output. The inputs to the accounting process are the business transactions. These transactions are processed to recognize their effects on the assets, liabilities, owner's equity, revenues, and expenses of the business. The results of these events are then reported as outputs of the accounting process in the financial statements.

Patty V's Consulting Income Statement For Month Ended December 31, 20--		
Revenues		$10,000
Consulting fees		
Expenses		
Wages expense	$5,000	
Rent expense	1,500	
Telephone expense	500	
Total expenses		7,000
Net income		$ 3,000

Patty V's Consulting Statement of Owner's Equity For Month Ended December 31, 20--		
		$ —
Patty V, capital, December 1, 20--		20,000
Investment in December		$20,000
Total investment		
Net income for December	$3,000	
Less withdrawals for December	1,000	
Increase in capital		2,000
Patty V, capital, December 31, 20--		$22,000

Patty V's Consulting Balance Sheet December 31, 20--			
Assets		Liabilities	
Cash	$ 500	Accounts payable	$ 6,500
Accounts receivable	8,000		
Computer equipment	20,000	Owner's Equity	
		Patty V, capital	22,000
		Total liabilities and	
Total assets	$28,500	owner's equity	$28,500

REVIEW QUESTIONS

Instructions: Analyze each of the following items carefully before writing your answer in the column at the right.

Question	Answer

LO 2 1. The entire accounting process is based on one simple equation called the _____. .... _____

LO 1 2. An individual, association, or organization that engages in business activities is called a(n) _____. .... _____

LO 1 3. An item owned by a business that will provide future benefits is a(n) _____. .... _____

LO 1 4. Something owed to another business entity is a(n) _____. .... _____

LO 1 5. A(n) _____ is an unwritten promise to pay a supplier for assets purchased or a service rendered. .... _____

LO 2 6. The amount by which assets exceed the liabilities of a business is called _____. .... _____

LO 1 7. According to the _____ concept, nonbusiness assets and liabilities are not included in the business entity's records. .... _____

LO 2 8. Assets – Liabilities = _____. .... _____

LO 2 9. Assets – Owner's Equity = _____. .... _____

LO 2 10. Assets = Liabilities + _____. .... _____

LO 4 11. The outflow of assets (or increase in liabilities) as the result of efforts to produce revenue is called a(n) _____. .... _____

LO 4 12. When total revenues exceed total expenses, the difference is called _____. .... _____

LO 4 13. When expenses are greater than revenues, the difference is called _____. .... _____

LO 4 14. Any accounting period of 12 months' duration is called a(n) _____. .... _____

LO 4 15. Withdrawals, or _____, represent a reduction in owner's equity because the owner takes cash or other assets for personal use. .... _____

LO 5 16. The financial statement that reports the profitability of the business for a period of time is the _____. .... _____

LO 5 17. The financial statement that shows investments and withdrawals by the owner, as well as profit or loss generated by the business, is the _____. .... _____

LO 5 18. The financial statement that reports the assets, liabilities, and owner's equity on a specific date is the _____. .... _____

Name _____

LO 5 19. On the balance sheet, assets are listed in order of _____, or the ease with which they can be converted to cash. .... _____

EXERCISES

Exercise 1 (LO 2) THE ACCOUNTING EQUATION

Using the accounting equation provided below, compute the missing amounts.

	ASSETS	=	LIABILITIES	+	OWNER'S EQUITY
(a)	_____	=	$4,000	+	$20,000
(b)	$25,000	=	$8,000	+	_____
(c)	$50,000	=	_____	+	$10,000

Exercise 2 (LO 2/4) THE EXPANDED ACCOUNTING EQUATION

Using the accounting equation provided below, compute the missing amounts.

	ASSETS (Items Owned) Cash	=	LIABILITIES + (Amts. Owed) Accounts Payable	+	OWNER'S INVESTMENT Capital	–	Drawing	+	EARNINGS Revenues	–	Expenses
(a)	_____	=	$60,000	+	$20,000	–	$10,000	+	$80,000	–	$60,000
(b)	$80,000	=	_____	+	$35,000	–	$5,000	+	$70,000	–	$55,000
(c)	$90,000	=	$25,000	+	_____	–	$2,000	+	$57,000	–	$50,000
(d)	$60,000	=	$20,000	+	$30,000	–	$5,000	+	_____	–	$40,000
(e)	$40,000	=	$25,000	+	$40,000	–	$5,000	+	$30,000	–	_____
(f)	$75,000	=	$20,000	+	$50,000	–	_____	+	$40,000	–	$25,000

Exercise 3 (LO 5) STATEMENT OF OWNER'S EQUITY

If owner's equity was $38,000 at the beginning of the period and $45,000 at the end of the period, compute the net income or loss for the period. (There were no investments or withdrawals during the period.)

Exercise 4 (LO 2) ACCOUNTING EQUATION

If Irma Elkton, a dentist, owns office equipment amounting to $3,500, laboratory equipment amounting to $10,000, and other property that is used in the business amounting to $4,620, and owes business suppliers a total of $5,000, what is the owner's equity in the business?

Exercise 5 (LO 2) ACCOUNTING EQUATION

This is an extension of Exercise 4. One year later, the amount of Dr. Elkton's business assets has increased to a total of $22,000, and the amount of business liabilities has increased to a total of $6,000. Assuming that Dr. Elkton has not made any additional investments or withdrawals, compute the following:

(a) Owner's equity at year-end $ _____

(b) Net income or loss for the year $ _____

Exercise 6 (LO 3/4) EFFECTS OF TRANSACTIONS (BALANCE SHEET ACCOUNTS)

Rich Brite has started his own business. During the first month, the following transactions occurred:

(a)   Invested $15,000 cash in the business, which was used to open a bank account.
(b)   Purchased office equipment for cash, $4,000.
(c)   Purchased a computer on account for $9,000.
(d)   Paid $2,000 on account for the computer.

Using the lines provided below, show the effect of each transaction on the basic elements of the accounting equation: assets, liabilities, and owner's equity. Compute the new amounts for each element after each transaction to satisfy yourself that the accounting equation has remained in balance.

	ASSETS	=	LIABILITIES	+	OWNER'S EQUITY
(a)	_____		_____		_____
Bal.	_____		_____		_____
(b)	_____		_____		_____
	_____		_____		_____
Bal.	_____		_____		_____
(c)	_____		_____		_____
Bal.	_____		_____		_____
(d)	_____		_____		_____
Bal.	_____		_____		_____

Exercise 7 (LO 3/4) EFFECTS OF TRANSACTIONS (REVENUE, EXPENSE, WITHDRAWALS)

In late May, Glen Ross opened a business by investing $20,000 cash and purchasing office equipment on account for $8,000. These events were properly entered in the accounting records. In June, the following transactions took place:

(a)   Received $4,000 from a client for professional services rendered.
(b)   Paid $1,200 office rent for the month.
(c)   Paid $200 to the power company for the month's utility bill.
(d)   Withdrew $600 cash for personal use.

On the first Balance (Bal.) line provided on the following page, record the amount of assets, liabilities, and owner's equity as the result of Ross's investment and purchase of office equipment in May. Then, record the effect of transactions (a) to (d) on the expanded accounting equation: Assets = Liabilities + Owner's Equity (Capital – Drawing + Revenues – Expenses). Following transaction (d), compute the new balances for each category to satisfy yourself that the accounting equation has remained in balance.

Chapter 2 Sg-11

Name _____

Exercise 7 (Concluded)

ASSETS (Items Owned)	= LIABILITIES + (Amts. Owed)	OWNER'S EQUITY (Owner's Investment)		(Earnings)		
Cash	Accounts Payable	Glen Ross, Capital	– Glen Ross, Drawing	+ Revenues	– Expenses	Description
Bal.						
(a)						
(b)						
(c)						
(d)						
Bal.						

Exercise 8 (LO 3/4) EFFECTS OF TRANSACTIONS (ALL ACCOUNTS)

Judith Moore started her own business. During the month of July, the following transactions occurred:

(a) Invested $10,000 cash in the business.
(b) Purchased office equipment for $5,500 on account.
(c) Received $900 cash from a client for services rendered.
(d) Purchased computer equipment for cash, $6,000.
(e) Received $1,500 cash from a client for services rendered.
(f) Paid $800 office rent for the month.
(g) Paid the telephone bill for the month, $75.
(h) Paid $100 on account, for office equipment previously purchased.
(i) Withdrew $500 for personal use.

Required:

1. Record the effect of each of the transactions listed above on the accounting equation provided in the chart on the following page. Following transaction (i), compute the new balances for the accounts to satisfy yourself that the equation has remained in balance.

© 2014 Cengage Learning. All Rights Reserved. May not be scanned, copied or duplicated, or posted to a publicly accessible website, in whole or in part.

Exercise 8 (Concluded)

	ASSETS (Items Owned)		= LIABILITIES + (Amts. Owed)	OWNER'S EQUITY (Owner's Investment)			(Earnings)		
	Cash	Office + Equipment =	Accounts Payable	J. Moore, + Capital	J. Moore, – Drawing	+ Revenues	– Expenses	Description
(a)								
(b)								
(c)								
(d)								
(e)								
(f)								
(g)								
(h)								
(i)								
Bal.								

2. After recording the transactions in part (1), compute the following:

Total assets .... $ _____

Total liabilities .... $ _____

Owner's equity .... $ _____

Owner's equity in excess of original investment .... $ _____

Total revenues .... $ _____

Total expenses .... $ _____

Net income .... $ _____

Exercise 9 (LO 5) PREPARATION OF AN INCOME STATEMENT

Based on the transactions reported in Exercise 8, prepare an income statement for Judith Moore Enterprises for the month ended July 31, 20--, in the space provided below.

Exercise 10 (LO 5) PREPARATION OF THE STATEMENT OF OWNER'S EQUITY

Based on the transactions reported in Exercise 8, prepare a statement of owner's equity for Judith Moore Enterprises for the month ended July 31, 20--, in the space provided below.

Exercise 11 (LO 5) PREPARATION OF A BALANCE SHEET

Based on the transactions reported in Exercise 8, prepare a balance sheet as of July 31, 20--, in the space provided below.

PROBLEMS

Problem 12 (LO 2) THE ACCOUNTING EQUATION

Dr. Abe Miller is a general practitioner. As of December 31, Miller owned the following assets related to the professional practice:

Cash	$3,300	X-ray equipment	$7,000
Office equipment	4,500	Laboratory equipment	4,000

As of that date, Miller owed business suppliers as follows:

General Office Equipment Inc.	$2,000
Young Medical Supply Company	1,500
Buck Gas Company	1,200

Required:

1. Compute the amount of assets, liabilities, and owner's equity as of December 31.

    ASSETS   =   LIABILITIES   +   OWNER'S EQUITY

    _____   _____   _____

2. Assuming that during January there is an increase of $4,600 in Dr. Miller's business assets and an increase of $2,500 in business liabilities, compute the resulting accounting equation as of January 31.

    ASSETS   =   LIABILITIES   +   OWNER'S EQUITY

    _____   _____   _____

3. Assuming that during February there is a decrease of $1,500 in assets and a decrease of $1,200 in liabilities, compute the resulting accounting equation as of February 28.

    ASSETS   =   LIABILITIES   +   OWNER'S EQUITY

    _____   _____   _____

4. Assuming that Dr. Miller made no additional investments or withdrawals, compute the net income or loss for each month.

Problem 13 (LO 3/4) EFFECT OF TRANSACTIONS ON ACCOUNTING EQUATION

Susan Cole started her own consulting business in October 20--. During the first month, the following transactions occurred:

(a) Invested $12,000 cash in the business.
(b) Purchased office equipment for $7,500 on account.
(c) Purchased computer equipment for cash, $800.
(d) Received $700 cash from a client for services rendered.
(e) Paid $600 office rent for the month.
(f) Paid student assistant wages for the month, $150.
(g) Paid one-year insurance premium, $200.
(h) Paid $3,000 on account for the office equipment purchased in transaction (b).
(i) Withdrew cash for personal use, $100.

Problem 13 (Concluded)

Required:

1. Record the effect of each of the transactions from the previous page on the accounting equation chart provided below. Following transaction (i), compute the new amounts in the accounts.

| | ASSETS | | | = LIABILITIES + | OWNER'S EQUITY | | | | |
| | (Items Owned) | | | (Amts. Owed) | (Owner's Investment) | | (Earnings) | | |
	Cash	+ Office Equip.	+ Prepaid Insur.	= Accounts Payable	+ S. Cole, Capital	− S. Cole, Drawing	+ Revenues	− Expenses	Description
(a)									
(b)									
(c)									
(d)									
(e)									
(f)									
(g)									
(h)									
(i)									
Bal.									

2. After recording the transactions, compute the following:

Total assets.. $ _____

Total liabilities .... $ _____

Owner's equity.. $ _____

Change in owner's equity from original investment................. $ _____

Total revenues .... $ _____

Total expenses.. $ _____

Net income (loss) .... $ _____

Problem 14 (LO 5) INCOME STATEMENT

Based on the transactions in Problem 13, prepare an income statement for Susan Cole Consulting Services for the month ended October 31, 20--, in the space provided below.

Problem 15 (LO 5) STATEMENT OF OWNER'S EQUITY

Based on the transactions in Problem 13, prepare a statement of owner's equity for Susan Cole Consulting Services for the month ended October 31, 20--, in the space provided below.

Problem 16 (LO 5) BALANCE SHEET

Based on the transactions in Problem 13, prepare a balance sheet as of October 31, 20--, in the space provided below.

Problem 17 (LO 3/4/5) ANALYZE THE EFFECTS OF BUSINESS TRANSACTIONS ON THE ACCOUNTING EQUATION AND PREPARE FINANCIAL STATEMENTS

Stuart Cassady is opening a typing service. During the first month (April 20--), the following transactions occurred:

(a) Invested $10,000 in the business.

(b) Purchased office supplies for $200 cash.

(c) Purchased office supplies for $800, $400 on account and $400 in cash.

(d) Received typing fees of $300 cash.

(e) Paid the rent, $600.

(f) Withdrew $100 for personal use.

(g) Earned typing fees of $600, $200 in cash and $400 on account.

(h) Made partial payment for office supplies in transaction (c) of $200.

(i) Received $200 cash for typing fees earned on account in transaction (g).

Required:

1. Record the effect of each transaction on the accounting equation below. Following transaction (i), compute new amounts for each account.

	ASSETS			= LIABILITIES +		OWNER'S EQUITY				
	(Items Owned)			(Amts. Owed)	(Owner's Investment)		(Earnings)			
	Cash	+ Accounts Receivable. +	Office Supplies =	Accounts Payable +	S. Cassady, Capital −	S. Cassady, Drawing +	Revenues −	Expenses	Description
(a)									
(b)									
(c)									
(d)									
(e)									
(f)									
(g)									
(h)									
(i)									
Bal.									

Name _____

Problem 17 (Concluded)

2. Based on the transactions in part (1) of Problem 17, prepare an income statement, statement of owner's equity, and balance sheet for Stuart Cassady Typing Service.

Income Statement

Statement of Owner's Equity

Balance Sheet

CHAPTER 3
THE DOUBLE-ENTRY FRAMEWORK

LEARNING OBJECTIVES

Objective 1.   Define the parts of a T account.

The **T account** gets its name from the fact that it resembles the letter *T*. There are three major parts of an account. The title of the account is on top. The left side of the T account is the debit side, and the right side is the credit side.

Objective 2.   Foot and balance a T account.

To determine the balance of a T account, simply total the dollar amounts of the debit and credit sides. These totals are known as **footings.** The difference between the footings is called the *balance* of the account. The balance is written on the side with the larger footing.

Objective 3.   Describe the effects of debits and credits on specific types of accounts.

Assets are on the left side of the accounting equation. Thus, increases are entered on the left, or debit, side; and decreases are entered on the right, or credit, side. The normal balance of an asset account is a debit.

Liabilities and owner's equity are on the right side of the equation. Thus, increases are entered on the right, or credit, side; and decreases are entered on the left, or debit, side. The normal balance of a liability and owner's capital account is a credit.

Revenues increase owner's equity. Thus, increases in revenue are recorded as credits. The normal balance of a revenue account is a credit.

Expenses decrease owner's equity. Thus, increases in expenses are recorded as debits. The normal balance of an expense account is a debit.

Withdrawals of cash and other assets by the owner for personal reasons decrease owner's equity. Thus, an increase in drawing is recorded as a debit. The normal balance of a drawing account is a debit.

The following figure should be helpful in developing your understanding of debits and credits and the accounting equation:

Objective 4.   Use T accounts to analyze transactions.

There are three basic questions that must be answered when analyzing a transaction: (1) What happened? (2) Which accounts are affected? and (3) How is the accounting equation affected? After analyzing the transaction, in every instance, debits will equal credits.

Objective 5.   Prepare a trial balance and explain its purposes and linkages with the financial statements.

There are two very important rules in double-entry accounting: (1) The sum of the debits must equal the sum of the credits. This means that at least two accounts are affected by each transaction. (2) The accounting equation must remain in balance.

A **trial balance** is a list of all accounts showing the title and balance of each account. The total debits and credits must be equal. A trial balance is not a formal statement or report. It can be used as an aid in preparing the financial statements.

REVIEW QUESTIONS

Instructions: Analyze each of the following items carefully before writing your answer in the column at the right.

Question	Answer
Question	**Answer**

LO 1   1.   A form or record used to keep track of the increases and decreases in each type of asset, liability, owner's equity, revenue, and expense is known as a(n) _____. ....

_____

LO 1   2.   The left side of a T account is called the _____ side. ....

_____

LO 1   3.   The right side of a T account is called the _____ side. ....

_____

LO 2   4.   The process of entering totals in the debit and credit sides of a T account is referred to as _____. ....

_____

LO 2   5.   The amount of the difference between the debits and credits recorded in a T account is called the _____. ....

_____

LO 3   6.   An increase in the asset Cash is recorded by a(n) _____. ....

_____

LO 3   7.   An increase in the liability Accounts Payable is recorded by a(n) _____. ....

_____

LO 3   8.   The normal balance of a revenue account is on the _____ side. ...

_____

LO 3   9.   A decrease in the liability Accounts Payable is recorded by a(n) _____. ....

_____

LO 3   10.   The normal balance of a liability account is on the _____ side. ...

_____

LO 4   11.   The fact that each transaction has a dual effect on the accounting elements provides the basis for what is called _____. ....

_____

LO 5   12.   A list of all of the accounts showing the title and balance of each account is called the _____. ....

_____

EXERCISES

Exercise 1 (LO 1) DEFINING PARTS OF THE T ACCOUNT

Provided below are T accounts for the six types of accounts discussed to this point. Identify the debit and credit side of each type of account by writing debit on the debit side and credit on the credit side.

Assets	Liabilities	Owner's Capital	Owner's Drawing	Expenses	Revenues

Exercise 2 (LO 3) EFFECTS OF DEBITS AND CREDITS

Indicate whether each of the following types of accounts would normally have a debit or credit balance by circling either debit or credit in the column at the right:

Type of Account	Normal Balance (Circle one)	
(a) Assets.	Debit	Credit
(b) Liabilities.....................................	Debit	Credit
(c) Owner's capital	Debit	Credit
(d) Revenues	Debit	Credit
(e) Expenses......................................	Debit	Credit
(f) Drawing.......................................	Debit	Credit

Exercise 3 (LO 3) INCREASING AND DECREASING ACCOUNTS WITH DEBITS AND CREDITS

Provided below are T accounts representing the six types of accounts discussed. Indicate how each account would be increased and decreased by placing a (+) or (−) on the debit and credit side of each account.

Assets	Liabilities	Owner's Capital	Owner's Drawing	Expenses	Revenues

Exercise 4 (LO 4) USING T ACCOUNTS TO ANALYZE TRANSACTIONS

The following transactions were completed by Jacque Hamon, an educational consultant. Analyze each transaction and enter the amounts in the proper debit and credit positions in the T accounts at the right.

(a) Invested $3,000 cash in the business.

Cash	Jacque Hamon, Capital

(b) Received $1,000 in cash for consulting services rendered.

Cash	Professional Fees

(c) Bought office equipment from Gusse Supply Co. on account, $500.

Office Equipment	Accounts Payable

(d) Paid electric bill, $75.

Cash	Utilities Expense

Exercise 4 (Concluded)

(e)   Paid Gusse Supply $200 on account.

Cash	Accounts Payable

(f)   Received $300 in cash for consulting services rendered.

Cash	Professional Fees

(g)   Borrowed $1,000 from bank by signing a note.

Cash	Notes Payable

(h)   Paid the telephone bill, $50.

Cash	Telephone Expense

Exercise 5 (LO 4) USING T ACCOUNTS TO ANALYZE TRANSACTIONS (BALANCE SHEET ACCOUNTS)

Connie Sung has started her own typing business. During the first month, the following transactions occurred:

(a)   Invested $12,000 cash in the business, and the money was deposited in a bank account.
(b)   Purchased a new computer and printer on account from Stahl Electronics for $8,000.
(c)   Paid the premium on a one-year insurance policy on computer equipment, $75 cash.
(d)   Secured a bank loan by signing a note for $5,000.
(e)   Made payment of $3,000 to Stahl Electronics on account.

Required:

Record the above transactions in the T accounts provided below.

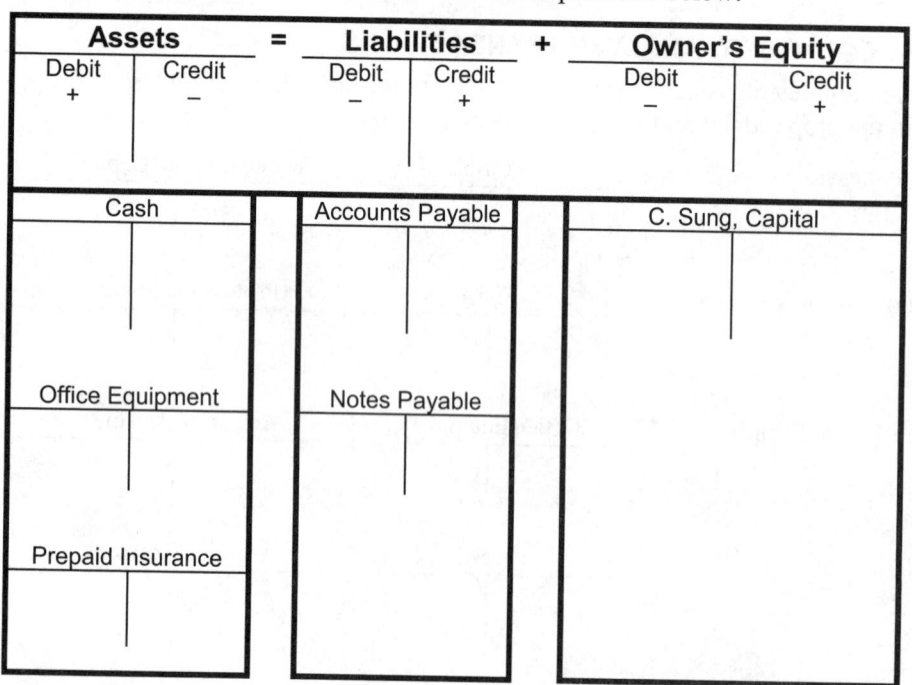

Exercise 6 (LO 4) USING T ACCOUNTS TO ANALYZE TRANSACTIONS (ALL ACCOUNTS)

In late April, Frazier Baar opened a psychiatry practice by investing $9,000 cash and purchasing a couch, chair, and leather-covered note pad on account for $2,500. These events were properly entered in the accounting records. In May, Dr. Baar began seeing patients and entered into the following transactions:

(a) Received $500 for counseling services rendered.
(b) Paid $100 for *Psychology Today* and other magazines for patients to read in the waiting room.
(c) Paid $1,200 office rent for the month.

Required:

1. Enter the balances as of May 1 in the following accounts: Cash, Office Furnishings, Accounts Payable, and F. Baar, Capital.

2. Record the May transactions in the accounts listed below.

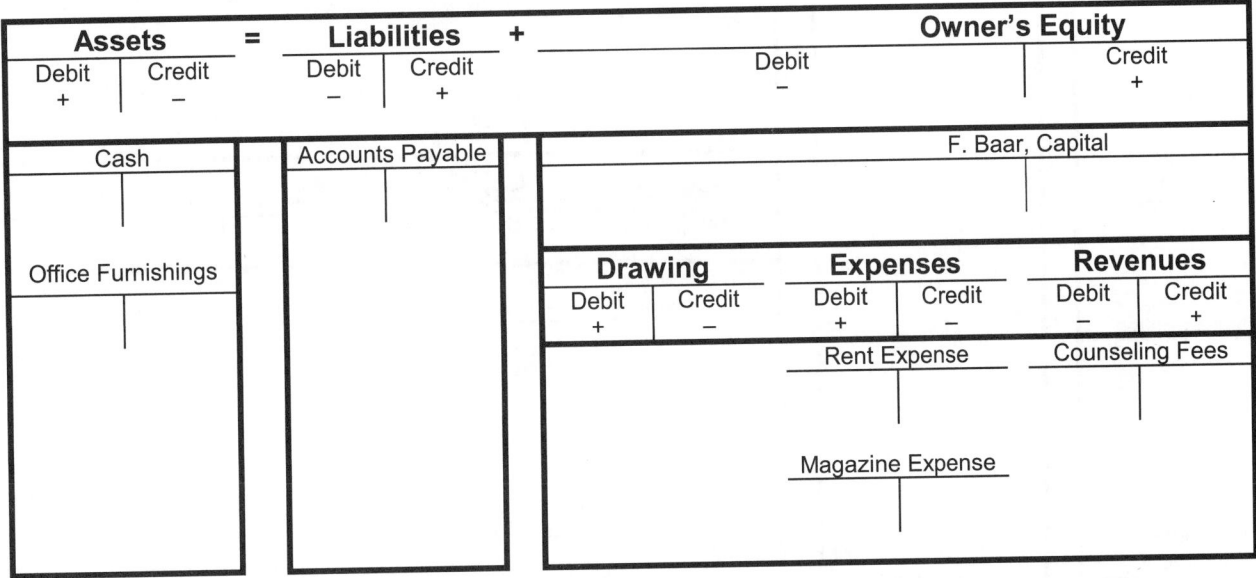

Exercise 7 (LO 2/4) USING T ACCOUNTS TO ANALYZE TRANSACTIONS, FOOTING AND BALANCING T ACCOUNTS

In January 20--, Blanca Estavez, CPA, started her own accounting practice. The following is a list of transactions for the first month:

(a) Invested $20,000 cash in the business.
(b) Purchased office supplies, $500 cash.
(c) Purchased office furniture, $6,000 cash.
(d) Purchased a computer and printer for $9,000: $5,000 cash and $4,000 on account.
(e) Paid $800 for accounting software programs.
(f) Performed accounting services and earned fees totaling $1,800: $1,200 in cash and $600 on account.
(g) Paid $700 rent for the month.
(h) Withdrew $200 for personal use.
(i) Paid $2,000 on account for the computer.

Exercise 7 (Concluded)

Required:

1. Record the transactions in the T accounts that follow.
2. After all transactions have been entered, foot and balance the T accounts.

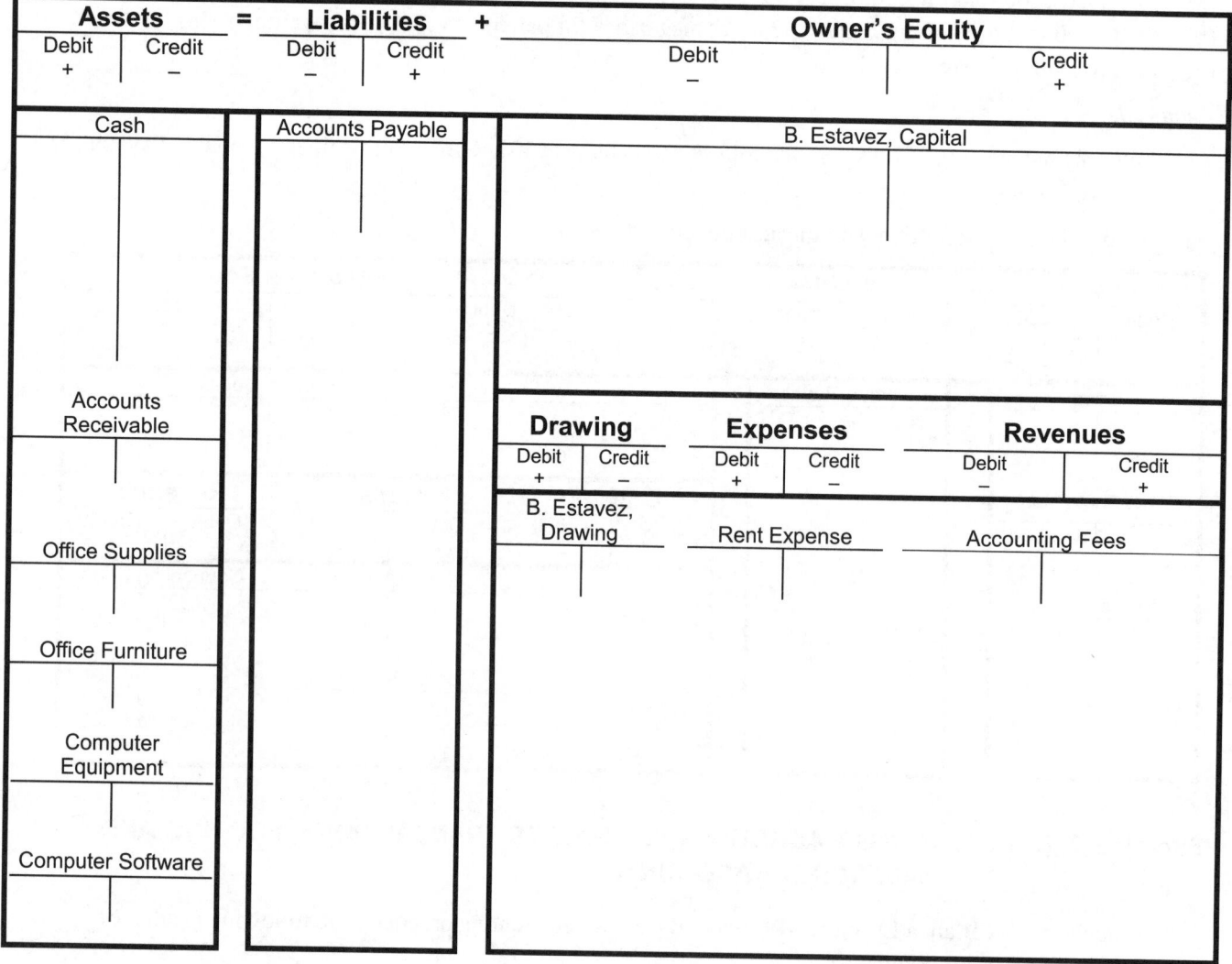

Exercise 8 (LO 5) PREPARE A TRIAL BALANCE

Based on the transactions recorded in Exercise 7, prepare a trial balance at the end of the first month of operations using the form provided below.

ACCOUNT	DEBIT BALANCE	CREDIT BALANCE

PROBLEMS

Problem 9 (LO 2/4/5) ANALYZING TRANSACTIONS WITH T ACCOUNTS, FOOTING AND BALANCING ACCOUNTS, AND PREPARING A TRIAL BALANCE

Jali Abdul has decided to offer his services as a promoter for local rock-n-roll bands. Following is a narrative of selected transactions completed during January, the first month of J. A. Productions' operations:

(a) Invested $10,000 in the business and opened a checking account.

(b) Purchased office furniture on account at a cost of $5,000.

(c) Purchased computer equipment for $4,500. Abdul paid $1,500 cash and promised to pay the balance over the next three months.

(d) Purchased office supplies for cash, $350.

(e) Sent letters to numerous performing groups throughout the region explaining the services available through J. A. Productions. Postage of $200 was paid in cash.

(f) Began arranging performances throughout the region after securing contracts with several groups. The telephone bill came to $300 and was paid in cash.

(g) Earned promotion revenue of $2,500: $2,000 in cash and $500 on account.

(h) Paid part-time receptionist $600.

(i) Withdrew $1,000 for personal use.

(j) Paid $2,500 on account for the office furniture purchased in part (b).

(k) Collected $250 for promotional fees earned on account.

© 2014 Cengage Learning. All Rights Reserved. May not be scanned, copied or duplicated, or posted to a publicly accessible website, in whole or in part.

Problem 9 (Continued)

Required:

1. Record the transactions in the T accounts provided.
2. Foot and balance the accounts.
3. Prepare a trial balance of the accounts as of January 31, 20--, using the form provided.

1. and 2.

Assets	=	Liabilities	+	Owner's Equity	
Debit + / Credit −		Debit − / Credit +		Debit −	Credit +

Cash

Accounts Payable

J. Abdul, Capital

Accounts Receivable

Drawing		Expenses		Revenues	
Debit +	Credit −	Debit +	Credit −	Debit −	Credit +

Office Supplies

J. Abdul, Drawing

Wages Expense

Promotion Fees

Office Furniture

Telephone Expense

Computer Equipment

Postage Expense

Problem 9 (Concluded)

3. _____

ACCOUNT	DEBIT BALANCE	CREDIT BALANCE

Problem 10 (LO 5) REVIEW: ACCOUNTING EQUATION AND FINANCIAL STATEMENTS

Based on the transactions recorded in Problem 9, select the information needed to fill in the blank space in the following statements:

(a) Total revenue for the month _____

(b) Total expenses for the month _____

(c) Net income for the month _____

(d) Abdul's original investment in the business _____

　　　+ Net income for the month _____

　　　– Owner's drawing _____

　　　Increase in capital

　　　= Owner's equity at the end of the month _____

(e) End-of-month accounting equation:

Assets	=	Liabilities	+	Owner's Equity
_____		_____		_____

Problem 11 (LO 5) REVIEW: PREPARATION OF FINANCIAL STATEMENTS

Refer to the trial balance in Problem 9 and to the analysis of the change in owner's equity in Problem 10.

(a) Prepare an income statement for J. A. Productions for the month ended January 31, 20--.

(b) Prepare a statement of owner's equity for J. A. Productions for the month ended January 31, 20--.

(c) Prepare a balance sheet for J. A. Productions as of January 31, 20--.

(a)

Problem 11 (Concluded)

(b)

(c)

Name _____

CHAPTER 4
JOURNALIZING AND POSTING TRANSACTIONS

LEARNING OBJECTIVES

Chapter 3 introduced the double-entry framework and illustrated the impact of debits and credits on the accounting equation and T accounts. In Chapter 4, business transactions are entered into the general journal and posted to general ledger accounts.

Objective 1.   Describe the flow of data from source documents to the trial balance.

The flow of financial data from the source documents through the accounting information systems follows the steps listed below.

1. Analyze what happened by using information from source documents and the firm's chart of accounts.
2. Enter business transactions in the general journal.
3. Post entries to accounts in the general ledger.
4. Prepare a trial balance.

INPUT   PROCESSING

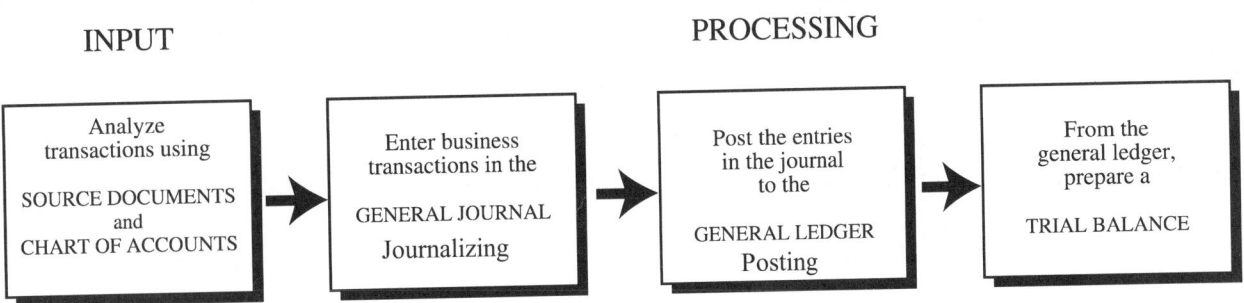

Objective 2.   Describe and explain the purpose of source documents.

A **source document** provides objective information needed to record a transaction. Examples include check stubs, receipts, cash register tapes, sales invoices, and memos. Source documents are analyzed to determine which accounts should be increased or decreased.

Objective 3.   Describe the chart of accounts as a means of classifying financial information.

The **chart of accounts** lists in numerical order all of the accounts being used by a business. Assets are listed first (begin with "1"); liabilities are second (begin with "2"); owner's equity accounts are third (begin with "3"); revenues are fourth (begin with "4"); and expenses are last (begin with "5"). In a three-digit account numbering system, for example, Cash may be account number 101 and Accounts Receivable may be account number 122. Spacing numbers this way permits easy addition of new accounts as the business grows.

Objective 4.   Journalize transactions.

Journalizing is the process of entering information into the journal, or book of original entry. This simply means the journal is the first place a transaction is recorded. The general journal has space to enter the date of the transaction, the name of the accounts being debited and credited, the account numbers, and the amounts of the debits and credits. A brief description follows each journal entry stating the reason for the entry.

Objective 5.   Post to the general ledger and prepare a trial balance.

Once the transactions are entered into the general journal, they must be **posted** to (copied to) the individual accounts, which are located in the general ledger. The accounts are in the general ledger in the chart of accounts order. That is, the assets are first, followed by liabilities, owner's equity, revenue, and expense accounts.

In this chapter, the general ledger accounts are in the form of four-column accounts. This is better than the T account because a running balance is maintained.

The **trial balance** is a listing of account balances at the end of the month—after all the transactions have been posted from the general journal to the general ledger accounts. The total of the debit balances must equal the total of the credit balances.

Objective 6.   Explain how to find and correct errors.

Finding errors can be a long and frustrating process. But there are some methods to reduce the time and effort needed. The first thing to do is double check your calculations and the accuracy of the posting activities. Common errors include sliding ($230 could become $23 or $2,300) and transposing numbers ($326 could become $236). Taking the difference between the debits and credits and dividing by 9 or by 2 may help locate the error.

There are two methods of correcting errors. The **ruling method** may be used before the transaction has been posted. Under this method, you draw a line through the incorrect title or amount and write in the correct information above the ruling. The **correcting entry method** is used after an entry has been posted to the general ledger. The correcting entry increases and decreases accounts in a manner that corrects the errors made in previous transactions.

REVIEW QUESTIONS

Instructions: Analyze each of the following items carefully before writing your answer in the column at the right.

Question	Answer
LO 1/2 1. A document that provides information about a business transaction is called a(n) _____ .	_____
LO 3 2. A list of all the accounts used by a business enterprise is called a(n) _____ .	_____
LO 3 3. Accounts that begin with the number "3" are _____ .	_____
LO 3 4. Expenses are accounts that begin with which number?	_____
LO 4 5. A document that provides a day-by-day listing of transactions of a business is called a(n) _____ .	_____
LO 4 6. A journal is commonly referred to as a(n) _____ because it is here that the first formal accounting record is made.	_____
LO 4 7. Transactions affecting more than two accounts are called _____ .	_____
LO 4 8. The act of entering transactions into a journal is called _____ .	_____
LO 4 9. In a journal, debits are entered first; then credits are entered and indented _____ (how much space).	_____
LO 5 10. A complete set of all accounts used by a business is known as the _____ .	_____

LO 5 11. A(n) _____ account allows the accountant to keep a running balance. .... _____

LO 5 12. The process of copying debits and credits from the journal to the ledger accounts is called _____. .... _____

LO 5 13. Posting from the journal to the ledger is done _____ or at frequent intervals. .... _____

LO 5 14. The information in the Posting Reference columns of the journal and the ledger accounts provides a link known as a(n) _____. .... _____

LO 5 15. A(n) _____ is taken after transactions are posted to the general ledger accounts to be sure that debit and credit balances in the ledger are equal. .... _____

LO 6 16. A(n) _____ error occurs when you move a number a decimal place to the right or left. .... _____

LO 6 17. A(n) _____ error occurs when you use the right numbers but in the wrong order. .... _____

LO 6 18. Drawing a line through the incorrect amount or account title and writing correct information above it is an example of the _____ method. .... _____

LO 6 19. When an incorrect entry has been journalized and posted, a(n) _____ entry is required. .... _____

EXERCISES

Exercise 1 (LO 4) REVIEW: TRANSACTION ANALYSIS

Before a transaction is recorded in the journal, it should be analyzed to determine the following:

(a) What accounts are affected by the transaction.
(b) Whether each affected account is to be increased or decreased.
(c) Whether the increase or decrease is to be accomplished by a debit or credit.

In the following list of transactions for Abbott Service Co., indicate the names of the accounts to be debited and credited. Place a check mark in either the plus (+) or minus (−) column to indicate whether the account has been increased or decreased. The first transaction is entered as an illustration.

Transaction	Account		(+)	(−)
1. J. A. Abbott invested cash in a business enterprise.	Debit:	Cash	✓	
	Credit:	J. A. Abbott, Capital	✓	
2. Received cash for services provided.	Debit:			
	Credit:			

Transaction	**Account**	**(+)**	**(−)**
3. Paid cash for rent on the office.	Debit: _____	_____	_____
	Credit: _____	_____	_____
4. Purchased office equipment on account.	Debit: _____	_____	_____
	Credit _____	_____	_____
5. Paid cash to a creditor for a debt previously owed.	Debit: _____	_____	_____
	Credit: _____	_____	_____
6. Paid the telephone bill for the month.	Debit: _____	_____	_____
	Credit: _____	_____	_____
7. Paid supplier for office equipment purchased in transaction (4) above.	Debit: _____	_____	_____
	Credit: _____	_____	_____
8. Paid cash for a car for the owner's personal use.	Debit: _____	_____	_____
	Credit: _____	_____	_____
9. Paid temporary secretary's wages.	Debit: _____	_____	_____
	Credit: _____	_____	_____
10. Performed services that will be paid for later.	Debit: _____	_____	_____
	Credit: _____	_____	_____

Exercise 2 (LO 4) JOURNALIZING TRANSACTIONS

Susan Poe started a business, Poe's Connections. She provides resource referral services whereby she helps businesses locate vendors of specialty products and vice versa. She charges a referral fee to her clients who may be businesses or vendors. She has a part-time clerk who enters information into a database to match requests with potential users or suppliers. Her chart of accounts is as follows:

Assets
101 Cash
122 Accounts Receivable
182 Office Furniture

Liabilities
202 Accounts Payable

Owner's Equity
311 Susan Poe, Capital
312 Susan Poe, Drawing

Revenues
401 Referral Fees

Expenses
511 Wages Expense
521 Rent Expense

Exercise 2 (Continued)

Required:

Enter the following transactions in the two-column journal provided on the next page.

20--

May	1	Susan invested $5,000 cash to start the business.
	5	Purchased office furniture on account, $3,000.
	9	Paid office rent for the month, $450.
	10	Received fees for referral services, $500.
	15	Made payment on account (for office furniture), $100.
	20	Earned referral fees: $125 cash and $175 on account.
	25	Paid wages to clerk for part-time work, $400.
	28	Withdrew cash for personal use, $100.
	29	Received cash for referral services previously rendered, $150.

Exercise 2 (Concluded)

GENERAL JOURNAL

	DATE		DESCRIPTION	POST. REF.	DEBIT	CREDIT	
1							1
2							2
3							3
4							4
5							5
6							6
7							7
8							8
9							9
10							10
11							11
12							12
13							13
14							14
15							15
16							16
17							17
18							18
19							19
20							20
21							21
22							22
23							23
24							24
25							25
26							26
27							27
28							28
29							29
30							30
31							31
32							32
33							33
34							34
35							35
36							36
37							37

Name _____

Exercise 3 (LO 5) POST TO THE GENERAL LEDGER

Post the transactions from Exercise 2 to the general ledger accounts provided as follows. Be sure to enter the appropriate cross-reference information in the Posting Reference columns of the general ledger accounts and the general journal.

GENERAL LEDGER

ACCOUNT: Cash   ACCOUNT NO. 101

DATE	ITEM	POST. REF.	DEBIT	CREDIT	BALANCE DEBIT	BALANCE CREDIT

ACCOUNT: Accounts Receivable   ACCOUNT NO. 122

DATE	ITEM	POST. REF.	DEBIT	CREDIT	BALANCE DEBIT	BALANCE CREDIT

ACCOUNT: Office Furniture   ACCOUNT NO. 182

DATE	ITEM	POST. REF.	DEBIT	CREDIT	BALANCE DEBIT	BALANCE CREDIT

ACCOUNT: Accounts Payable   ACCOUNT NO. 202

DATE	ITEM	POST. REF.	DEBIT	CREDIT	BALANCE DEBIT	BALANCE CREDIT

Exercise 3 (Concluded)

GENERAL LEDGER

ACCOUNT: Susan Poe, Capital   ACCOUNT NO.   311

DATE	ITEM	POST. REF.	DEBIT	CREDIT	BALANCE	
					DEBIT	CREDIT

ACCOUNT: Susan Poe, Drawing   ACCOUNT NO.   312

DATE	ITEM	POST. REF.	DEBIT	CREDIT	BALANCE	
					DEBIT	CREDIT

ACCOUNT: Referral Fees   ACCOUNT NO.   401

DATE	ITEM	POST. REF.	DEBIT	CREDIT	BALANCE	
					DEBIT	CREDIT

ACCOUNT: Wages Expense   ACCOUNT NO.   511

DATE	ITEM	POST. REF.	DEBIT	CREDIT	BALANCE	
					DEBIT	CREDIT

ACCOUNT: Rent Expense   ACCOUNT NO.   521

DATE	ITEM	POST. REF.	DEBIT	CREDIT	BALANCE	
					DEBIT	CREDIT

Exercise 4 (LO 5) REVIEW: PREPARE A TRIAL BALANCE

After the transactions are posted in Exercise 3, prepare the trial balance.

ACCOUNT TITLE	ACCT. NO.	DEBIT BALANCE	CREDIT BALANCE

PROBLEMS

Problem 5 (LO 4/5) JOURNALIZING AND POSTING TRANSACTIONS FOLLOWED BY PREPARATION OF A TRIAL BALANCE

Della Jordan started her own business, D. J. Parties. For about $50 per hour, Della and a group of part-time associates serve as disc jockeys for parties held at the client's home. As part of the service, Della provides a lighting system, stereo equipment, CDs, and two disc jockeys working as a team for each party. A wide range of music is offered, and the client may provide additional CDs to be played. A chart of accounts is provided below.

D. J. Parties
Chart of Accounts

Assets
101 Cash
122 Accounts Receivable
181 Stereo Equipment
182 Office Furniture
183 CDs
184 Lighting Equipment
185 Van

Liabilities
202 Accounts Payable

Owner's Equity
311 Della Jordan, Capital
312 Della Jordan, Drawing

Revenue
401 Disc Jockey Fees

Expenses
511 Wages Expense
521 Rent Expense
525 Telephone Expense
538 Gas Expense

Problem 5 (Continued)

The following transactions occurred during May, the first month of operation:

20--

May	1	Jordan invested $30,000 cash in the business. The funds were deposited in a business checking account.
	3	Purchased stereo equipment and speaker systems from Big Al's Discount Stereo for $7,000: $3,000 cash and $4,000 on account.
	4	Purchased compact discs and tapes for $2,500.
	4	Purchased lighting equipment for $2,000.
	5	Purchased office furniture on account, $500.
	7	Purchased a van to be used to haul the equipment to the clients' homes, $9,500.
	18	Earned fees for services rendered, $3,800: $800 cash and $3,000 on account.
	20	Paid part-time associates for work performed, $600.
	21	Made payment on account for stereo equipment bought on May 3, $1,500.
	25	Paid for gas for the van, $40.
	27	Paid telephone bill, $80.
	28	Received cash for services previously rendered, $1,500.
	29	Paid part-time associates, $1,100.
	30	Paid rent, $500.
	30	Made payment on account for stereo equipment bought on May 3, $1,200.
	30	Jordan made withdrawal for personal use, $1,000.

Required:

1. Enter the transactions in the two-column journal provided on pages 45–46. Use journal page 1 for transactions through May 20. Enter the remainder on page 2.

2. Post the transactions from the journal to the general ledger accounts on pages 47–50.

3. Prepare a trial balance.

Name _____

Problem 5 (Continued)

1. *[Instructor: Account numbers in Post. Ref. column are entered when completing requirement 2.]*

GENERAL JOURNAL

PAGE 1

	DATE	DESCRIPTION	POST. REF.	DEBIT	CREDIT	
1						1
2						2
3						3
4						4
5						5
6						6
7						7
8						8
9						9
10						10
11						11
12						12
13						13
14						14
15						15
16						16
17						17
18						18
19						19
20						20
21						21
22						22
23						23
24						24
25						25
26						26
27						27
28						28
29						29
30						30
31						31
32						32
33						33

Problem 5 (Continued)

GENERAL JOURNAL

	DATE	DESCRIPTION	POST. REF.	DEBIT	CREDIT	
1						1
2						2
3						3
4						4
5						5
6						6
7						7
8						8
9						9
10						10
11						11
12						12
13						13
14						14
15						15
16						16
17						17
18						18
19						19
20						20
21						21
22						22
23						23
24						24
25						25
26						26
27						27
28						28
29						29
30						30
31						31
32						32
33						33

Name _____

Problem 5 (Continued)

2.

GENERAL LEDGER

ACCOUNT: Cash   ACCOUNT NO. 101

DATE	ITEM	POST. REF.	DEBIT	CREDIT	BALANCE	
					DEBIT	CREDIT

ACCOUNT: Accounts Receivable   ACCOUNT NO. 122

DATE	ITEM	POST. REF.	DEBIT	CREDIT	BALANCE	
					DEBIT	CREDIT

ACCOUNT: Stereo Equipment   ACCOUNT NO. 181

DATE	ITEM	POST. REF.	DEBIT	CREDIT	BALANCE	
					DEBIT	CREDIT

Problem 5 (Continued)

ACCOUNT: Office Furniture

ACCOUNT NO. 182

DATE	ITEM	POST. REF.	DEBIT	CREDIT	BALANCE	
					DEBIT	CREDIT

ACCOUNT: CDs

ACCOUNT NO. 183

DATE	ITEM	POST. REF.	DEBIT	CREDIT	BALANCE	
					DEBIT	CREDIT

ACCOUNT: Lighting Equipment

ACCOUNT NO. 184

DATE	ITEM	POST. REF.	DEBIT	CREDIT	BALANCE	
					DEBIT	CREDIT

ACCOUNT: Van

ACCOUNT NO. 185

DATE	ITEM	POST. REF.	DEBIT	CREDIT	BALANCE	
					DEBIT	CREDIT

ACCOUNT: Accounts Payable

ACCOUNT NO. 202

DATE	ITEM	POST. REF.	DEBIT	CREDIT	BALANCE	
					DEBIT	CREDIT

Name _____

Problem 5 (Continued)

ACCOUNT: Della Jordan, Capital — ACCOUNT NO. 311

DATE	ITEM	POST. REF.	DEBIT	CREDIT	BALANCE DEBIT	BALANCE CREDIT

ACCOUNT: Della Jordan, Drawing — ACCOUNT NO. 312

DATE	ITEM	POST. REF.	DEBIT	CREDIT	BALANCE DEBIT	BALANCE CREDIT

ACCOUNT: Disc Jockey Fees — ACCOUNT NO. 401

DATE	ITEM	POST. REF.	DEBIT	CREDIT	BALANCE DEBIT	BALANCE CREDIT

ACCOUNT: Wages Expense — ACCOUNT NO. 511

DATE	ITEM	POST. REF.	DEBIT	CREDIT	BALANCE DEBIT	BALANCE CREDIT

ACCOUNT: Rent Expense — ACCOUNT NO. 521

DATE	ITEM	POST. REF.	DEBIT	CREDIT	BALANCE DEBIT	BALANCE CREDIT

Problem 5 (Concluded)

ACCOUNT: Telephone Expense   ACCOUNT NO. 525

DATE	ITEM	POST. REF.	DEBIT	CREDIT	BALANCE	
					DEBIT	CREDIT

ACCOUNT: Gas Expense   ACCOUNT NO. 538

DATE	ITEM	POST. REF.	DEBIT	CREDIT	BALANCE	
					DEBIT	CREDIT

3.

ACCOUNT TITLE	ACCT. NO.	DEBIT BALANCE	CREDIT BALANCE

Problem 6 (LO 5) REVIEW: PREPARATION OF FINANCIAL STATEMENTS

From the information in Problem 5, prepare an income statement, a statement of owner's equity, and a balance sheet.

Problem 6 (Concluded)

Problem 7

1. (LO 6) CORRECTION OF ERRORS: The Ruling Method

The following journal entries were made but not posted. On January 1, $500 cash was withdrawn by the owner for personal use (R. J. Hammond) but was charged to Wages Expense. On January 2, $230 was paid on account. Make corrections using the ruling method.

GENERAL JOURNAL

PAGE

	DATE		DESCRIPTION	POST. REF.	DEBIT	CREDIT	
1	20-- Jan.	1	Wages Expense		5 0 0 00		1
2			Cash			5 0 0 00	2
3			Paid R. J. Hammond				3
4							4
5		2	Accounts Payable		3 2 0 00		5
6			Cash			3 2 0 00	6
7			Payment on account				7
8							8

Problem 7 (Concluded)

2. (LO 6) CORRECTION OF ERRORS: The Correcting Entry Method

On January 10, Office Equipment was debited for $800 when the debit should have been to Office Supplies. Since the entry has been posted, show the appropriate correcting entry made in the general journal on January 15.

GENERAL JOURNAL   PAGE _____

	DATE	DESCRIPTION	POST. REF.	DEBIT	CREDIT	
1						1
2						2
3						3
4						4
5						5
6						6
7						7
8						8

CHAPTER 5
ADJUSTING ENTRIES AND THE WORK SHEET

LEARNING OBJECTIVES

We are coming to the end of the accounting cycle, and certain things must be done at the end of the period that are not done during the regular accounting period. In Chapter 5, adjusting entries and the work sheet are presented.

Objective 1.   Prepare end-of-period adjustments.

In Chapters 2 through 4, we learned how to account for business transactions—events based primarily on arm's length exchanges with other parties. During the accounting period, however, other changes occur which affect the financial condition of the business. For example, supplies are being used, equipment is wearing out, insurance is expiring, and employees may have earned wages that have not yet been paid. It is important for information reported on the financial statements to accurately reflect the results of business transactions with outside parties <u>and</u> other activities taking place inside the business. Therefore, adjustments must be made at the end of the accounting period to properly report assets and liabilities on the balance sheet and to comply with the revenue recognition and matching principles. The **revenue recognition principle** states that revenues should be recognized when earned, regardless of when cash is received from the customer. Revenues are considered earned when a service is provided or a product sold. The **matching principle** requires the matching of revenues earned during an accounting period with the expenses incurred to produce the revenues. This approach offers the best measure of net income.

Objective 2.   Post adjusting entries to the general ledger.

After the adjusting entries are journalized, the next step is to post them to the general ledger. The word "Adjusting" is written in the Item column in the general ledger, and each adjustment is posted to the proper general ledger account.

Objective 3.   Prepare a work sheet.

The work sheet is a tool used by accountants to help organize work done at the end of the accounting period. This document is not a formal part of the accounting system. Therefore, information recorded here has no effect on the accounts or financial statements. The main purposes of the work sheet are to prepare the adjusting entries and accumulate information that will be used in the preparation of the financial statements. Five steps are taken to prepare a work sheet.

Step 1	Prepare a trial balance to ensure that the general ledger is in balance before adjusting the accounts.
Step 2	Analyze and enter the adjusting entries in the Adjustments columns of the work sheet. Every adjustment must have an equal debit and credit; and upon completion, the total debits and credits must be equal in the Adjustments columns.
Step 3	Prepare the adjusted trial balance. Every account appearing in the Trial Balance columns will be extended to the Adjusted Trial Balance columns and include any changes due to the adjusting entries. Upon completion, the total of the debits and credits in the Adjusted Trial Balance columns must be equal.
Step 4	Extend the balances in the adjusted trial balance to either the Income Statement or Balance Sheet columns. All revenue and expenses are extended to the Income Statement columns. All other accounts (assets, liabilities, owner's capital, owner's drawing) are extended to the Balance Sheet columns.

Step 5   Complete the work sheet. Initially, the totals of the Income Statement columns will not be equal. Similarly, the totals of the Balance Sheet columns will not be equal. If the Income Statement Credit column exceeds the Income Statement Debit column, the difference represents net income. If the Income Statement Debit column exceeds the Income Statement Credit column, the difference represents net loss. The difference in the Balance Sheet columns will be exactly the same as the difference in the Income Statement columns. The amount of net income should be added to the Income Statement Debit column and the Balance Sheet Credit column for total debits to equal total credits for all four columns. If there is a net loss, this amount should be added to the Income Statement Credit column and the Balance Sheet Debit column.

Partial Work Sheet

	For Net Income					For Net Loss			
	Income Statement		Balance Sheet			Income Statement		Balance Sheet	
	Debit	Credit	Debit	Credit		Debit	Credit	Debit	Credit
Net Income	2,500	3,200	6,200	5,500	Net Loss	3,000	2,500	7,000	7,500
	700			700			500	500	
	3,200	3,200	6,200	6,200		3,000	3,000	7,500	7,500

Apart — Together

Objective 4.   Describe methods for finding errors on the work sheet.

The following tips may help in finding errors on the work sheet:

1. Check the addition of all columns.
2. Check the addition and subtraction required when extending to the Adjusted Trial Balance columns.
3. Make sure the adjusted account balances have been extended to the appropriate columns.
4. Make sure that the net income or net loss has been added to the appropriate columns.

Objective 5.   Journalize adjusting entries from the work sheet.

Once the adjustments have been "penciled in" on the work sheet, the next step is to journalize the adjusting entries. "Adjusting Entries" is written in the Description column in the general journal, and the adjusting entries are copied from the work sheet into the general journal.

Objective 6.   Explain the cash, modified cash, and accrual bases of accounting.

The *accrual basis* of accounting recognizes revenues when earned, regardless of when cash is received from the customer. Likewise, expenses are recognized when incurred, regardless of when they are actually paid. The *cash basis* is used by some small businesses and by individuals for income tax purposes. With the cash basis, no revenue or expenses are recognized until cash is actually received or paid.

The *modified cash basis* is a combination of the accrual and cash methods. Revenues and most expenses are recorded only when cash is received or paid (like the cash basis). However, when cash is paid for assets with useful lives greater than one accounting period, exceptions are made. Cash payments like these are recorded as assets, and adjustments are made each period as under the accrual basis. Figure 5-25 in the text compares these methods in different types of transactions.

REVIEW QUESTIONS

Instructions: Analyze each of the following items carefully before writing your answer in the column at the right.

Question	Answer

LO 1 1. The revenue recognition principle requires revenues to be recognized when _____. .... _____

LO 1 2. The matching principle in accounting requires the matching of _____ and _____. .... _____

LO 1 3. The asset account Supplies is adjusted to the income statement account entitled _____. .... _____

LO 1 4. The asset account Prepaid Insurance is adjusted to the income statement account entitled _____. .... _____

LO 1 5. The adjustment to Wages Expense will also affect a liability account called _____. .... _____

LO 1 6. The period of time a plant asset is expected to help produce revenues is called its _____. .... _____

LO 1 7. The purpose of _____ is to spread the cost of a plant asset over its useful life. .... _____

LO 1 8. A plant asset's original cost less salvage value is called _____. _____

LO 1 9. A _____ has a credit balance and is deducted from the related asset account on the balance sheet. .... _____

LO 1 10. The depreciation adjusting entry consists of a debit to Depreciation Expense and a credit to _____. .... _____

LO 1 11. The difference between the original cost of a plant asset and its accumulated depreciation is called _____. .... _____

LO 3 12. A _____ is helpful in preparing end-of-period adjustments and financial statements. .... _____

LO 3 13. The first two monetary columns of a work sheet are called the _____ columns. .... _____

LO 3 14. To which columns of the work sheet are asset and liability accounts extended? .... _____

LO 3 15. To which columns of the work sheet are revenue and expense accounts extended? .... _____

LO 3 16. To which columns of the work sheet are the capital and drawing accounts extended? .... _____

LO 3 17. If the total of the Income Statement Credit column exceeds the total of the Debit column, the business has earned _____. ....

               _____

LO 6 18. In the _____ basis of accounting, revenues are recorded when earned and expenses are recorded when incurred, regardless of when cash is received or paid. ....

               _____

LO 6 19. In the _____ basis of accounting, revenues are recorded only when cash is received and expenses are recorded only when cash is paid. ....

               _____

LO 6 20. The _____ basis of accounting uses the cash basis for revenues and most expenses. ....

               _____

LO 6 21. Many small professional _____ businesses use the modified cash basis of accounting. ....

               _____

EXERCISES

Exercise 1 (LO 1) PREPARING END-OF-PERIOD ADJUSTMENTS: SUPPLIES

The beginning balance of the supplies account was $300. During the year, additional supplies costing $600 were purchased and entered as debits to the supplies account. An end-of-period inventory determined that $200 worth of supplies are still on hand.

Required:

1. Determine the balance of the supplies account just prior to making any end-of-period adjustments. _____

2. When preparing the balance sheet, what should be reported for Supplies at the end of the year? _____

3. Determine the balance of the supplies expense account just prior to making any end-of-period adjustments. _____

4. When preparing the income statement, what should be reported for Supplies Expense? (What was the cost of the supplies used?) _____

5. What adjustment must be made to the supplies and supplies expense accounts? _____

Exercise 2 (LO 1) PREPARING END-OF-PERIOD ADJUSTMENTS: DEPRECIATION

Office equipment with an expected life of 10 years and no salvage value was purchased on January 1 for $5,000. Assume the business has no other office equipment and straight-line depreciation is used.

Required:

1. What is the balance of the office equipment account at the end of the year? _____

2. What expense amount should be reported on the income statement for the use of the office equipment? _____

3. What book value should be reported on the balance sheet for the office equipment at the end of the first year? _____

4. What adjustment must be made at the end of the year to report information about the office equipment on the income statement and balance sheet? _____

Exercise 3 (LO 1/2) PREPARING, JOURNALIZING, AND POSTING ADJUSTING ENTRIES: SUPPLIES

The Maddie Hays modeling agency began the current period with office supplies that cost $1,225. During the period, additional supplies costing $4,545 were purchased. At the end of the accounting period, December 31, 20--, only $800 in supplies remain.

Required:

1. Enter the appropriate adjusting entry in a two-column journal.
2. Post this entry to the ledger accounts provided on the next page.

Exercise 3 (Concluded)

1.

GENERAL JOURNAL

PAGE 5

	DATE	DESCRIPTION	POST. REF.	DEBIT	CREDIT	
1						1
2						2
3						3
4						4
5						5

2.

GENERAL LEDGER

ACCOUNT: Supplies

ACCOUNT NO. 141

DATE		ITEM	POST. REF.	DEBIT	CREDIT	BALANCE DEBIT	BALANCE CREDIT
20--							
Jan.	1	Balance	✔			1 2 2 5 00	
Feb.	12		J2	4 5 4 5 00		5 7 7 0 00	

ACCOUNT: Supplies Expense

ACCOUNT NO. 524

DATE	ITEM	POST. REF.	DEBIT	CREDIT	BALANCE DEBIT	BALANCE CREDIT

Exercise 4 (LO 1/2) PREPARING, JOURNALIZING, AND POSTING ADJUSTING ENTRIES: DEPRECIATION

The Billy Willis Detective Agency began the accounting period by purchasing three cars that cost a total of $75,000. The estimated useful life of these cars is only two years with no salvage value.

Required:

1. Enter the appropriate adjusting entry at the end of the first year in a two-column journal. Willis uses straight-line depreciation.
2. Post this entry to the ledger accounts provided on the next page.

Exercise 4 (Concluded)

1.

GENERAL JOURNAL   PAGE 5

	DATE	DESCRIPTION	POST. REF.	DEBIT	CREDIT	
1						1
2						2
3						3
4						4

2.

GENERAL LEDGER

ACCOUNT: Automobiles   ACCOUNT NO. 185

DATE	ITEM	POST. REF.	DEBIT	CREDIT	BALANCE DEBIT	BALANCE CREDIT
20-- Jan. 2		J1	75 0 0 0 00		75 0 0 0 00	

ACCOUNT: Accumulated Depreciation—Automobiles   ACCOUNT NO. 185.1

DATE	ITEM	POST. REF.	DEBIT	CREDIT	BALANCE DEBIT	BALANCE CREDIT

ACCOUNT: Depreciation Expense—Automobiles   ACCOUNT NO. 541

DATE	ITEM	POST. REF.	DEBIT	CREDIT	BALANCE DEBIT	BALANCE CREDIT

Exercise 5 (LO 1/2) PREPARING, JOURNALIZING, AND POSTING ADJUSTING ENTRIES: PREPAID INSURANCE AND WAGES PAYABLE

On June 1, the Straw Basket Herb Farm purchased a one-year liability insurance policy for $600.

As of June 30, an additional $120 was earned by the employees but not yet paid.

Required:

1. Enter the appropriate adjusting entries at the end of June in the following general journal.
2. Post the entries to the ledger accounts provided.

1.

GENERAL JOURNAL
PAGE 6

	DATE	DESCRIPTION	POST. REF.	DEBIT	CREDIT	
1						1
2						2
3						3
4						4
5						5
6						6
7						7

2.

GENERAL LEDGER

ACCOUNT: Prepaid Insurance   ACCOUNT NO. 145

DATE	ITEM	POST. REF.	DEBIT	CREDIT	BALANCE DEBIT	BALANCE CREDIT
20-- June 1		J2	6 0 0 00		6 0 0 00	

ACCOUNT: Wages Payable   ACCOUNT NO. 219

DATE	ITEM	POST. REF.	DEBIT	CREDIT	BALANCE DEBIT	BALANCE CREDIT

Exercise 5 (Concluded)

ACCOUNT: Wages Expense   ACCOUNT NO. 511

DATE		ITEM	POST. REF.	DEBIT	CREDIT	BALANCE	
						DEBIT	CREDIT
20-- June	14		J5	5 0 0 00		5 0 0 00	
	28		J5	5 0 0 00		1 0 0 0 00	

ACCOUNT: Insurance Expense   ACCOUNT NO. 535

DATE	ITEM	POST. REF.	DEBIT	CREDIT	BALANCE	
					DEBIT	CREDIT

Exercise 6 (LO 6) CASH BASIS OF ACCOUNTING

In the space provided, indicate which account is debited and which account is credited, using the **cash basis** of accounting. If no entry is made, write "NO ENTRY."

1. Paid rent, $500.

_____

_____

2. Purchased typewriter (office equipment) for $300.

_____

_____

3. Revenue for week: $300 cash, $200 on account.

_____

_____

4. Purchased fax machine (office equipment) for $400, on account.

_____

_____

5. Made payment on fax machine, $100.

_____

_____

Exercise 7 (LO 6) MODIFIED CASH BASIS OF ACCOUNTING

In the space provided, indicate which account is debited and which account is credited, using the **modified cash basis** of accounting. If no entry is made, write "NO ENTRY."

1. Paid electricity bill, $50.

_____

_____

2. Purchased office equipment for $500, on account.

_____

_____

3. Revenue for week: $500 cash, $200 on account.

_____

_____

4. Wages earned but not paid, $500.

_____

_____

5. Made payment on office equipment previously purchased, $25.

_____

_____

Exercise 8 (LO 6) ACCRUAL BASIS OF ACCOUNTING

In the space provided, indicate which account is debited and which account is credited, using the **accrual basis** of accounting. If no entry is made, write "NO ENTRY."

1. Purchased supplies (prepaid asset), $500, on account.

_____

_____

2. Revenue for week: $400 cash, $250 on account.

_____

_____

3. Wages earned but not paid, $250.

_____

_____

Exercise 8 (Concluded)

4. Made payment on account, $50, for supplies previously purchased.

_____

_____

5. Depreciation on long-term assets, $300.

_____

_____

PROBLEMS

Problem 9 (LO1/3) PREPARING ADJUSTMENTS AND THE WORK SHEET

Kim Ho offers employment counseling to middle managers unemployed due to corporate downsizing. On January 1 of the current year, Ho purchased office equipment with an expected life of 12 years and no salvage value. Computer equipment with an expected life of four years and no salvage value was purchased on July 1 of the current year. Ho uses straight-line depreciation. Office supplies on hand at year-end amounted to $150. Employees earned $300 in wages that have not yet been paid. Provided are the general ledger accounts as of December 31, prior to adjustment.

Required:

1. Using the ledger accounts, complete the Trial Balance columns of the year-end work sheet provided.

2. Prepare the necessary year-end adjustments.

3. Complete the work sheet.

GENERAL LEDGER

ACCOUNT: Cash   ACCOUNT NO. 101

DATE		ITEM	POST. REF.	DEBIT	CREDIT	BALANCE DEBIT	BALANCE CREDIT
20-- Dec.	1	Balance	✔			2 4 0 0 00	
	21		J20	10 8 0 0 00		13 2 0 0 00	
	27		J20		4 2 0 0 00	9 0 0 0 00	

ACCOUNT: Office Supplies   ACCOUNT NO. 142

DATE		ITEM	POST. REF.	DEBIT	CREDIT	BALANCE DEBIT	BALANCE CREDIT
20-- Dec.	1	Balance	✔			2 0 0 00	
	6		J20	3 0 0 00		5 0 0 00	

Problem 9 (Continued)

ACCOUNT: Office Equipment   ACCOUNT NO. 181

DATE		ITEM	POST. REF.	DEBIT	CREDIT	BALANCE DEBIT	BALANCE CREDIT
20-- Dec.	1	Balance	✔			6 0 0 0 00	

ACCOUNT: Accumulated Depreciation—Office Equipment   ACCOUNT NO. 181.1

DATE	ITEM	POST. REF.	DEBIT	CREDIT	BALANCE DEBIT	BALANCE CREDIT

ACCOUNT: Computer Equipment   ACCOUNT NO. 187.

DATE		ITEM	POST. REF.	DEBIT	CREDIT	BALANCE DEBIT	BALANCE CREDIT
20-- Dec.	1	Balance	✔			8 0 0 0 00	

ACCOUNT: Accumulated Depreciation—Computer Equipment   ACCOUNT NO. 187.1

DATE	ITEM	POST. REF.	DEBIT	CREDIT	BALANCE DEBIT	BALANCE CREDIT

ACCOUNT: Accounts Payable   ACCOUNT NO. 202

DATE		ITEM	POST. REF.	DEBIT	CREDIT	BALANCE DEBIT	BALANCE CREDIT
20-- Dec.	1	Balance	✔				3 0 0 00
	6		J20		2 0 0 00		5 0 0 00
	27		J20	1 0 0 00			4 0 0 00

Problem 9 (Continued)

ACCOUNT: Wages Expense   ACCOUNT NO.   511

DATE		ITEM	POST. REF.	DEBIT	CREDIT	BALANCE	
						DEBIT	CREDIT
20--							
Dec.	1	Balance	✔			7 0 0 0 00	
	31		J20	1 5 0 0 00		8 5 0 0 00	

ACCOUNT: Rent Expense   ACCOUNT NO.   521

DATE		ITEM	POST. REF.	DEBIT	CREDIT	BALANCE	
						DEBIT	CREDIT
20--							
Dec.	1	Balance	✔			4 4 0 0 00	
	4		J20	1 2 0 0 00		5 6 0 0 00	

ACCOUNT: Supplies Expense   ACCOUNT NO.   524

DATE	ITEM	POST. REF.	DEBIT	CREDIT	BALANCE	
					DEBIT	CREDIT

ACCOUNT: Utilities Expense   ACCOUNT NO.   533

DATE		ITEM	POST. REF.	DEBIT	CREDIT	BALANCE	
						DEBIT	CREDIT
20--							
Dec.	1	Balance	✔			1 3 0 0 00	
	31		J20	5 7 0 00		1 8 7 0 00	

Problem 9 (Continued)

ACCOUNT: Depreciation Expense—Office Equipment   ACCOUNT NO. 541

DATE	ITEM	POST. REF.	DEBIT	CREDIT	BALANCE DEBIT	BALANCE CREDIT

ACCOUNT: Depreciation Expense—Computer Equipment   ACCOUNT NO. 542

DATE	ITEM	POST. REF.	DEBIT	CREDIT	BALANCE DEBIT	BALANCE CREDIT

ACCOUNT: Miscellaneous Expense   ACCOUNT NO. 549

DATE	ITEM	POST. REF.	DEBIT	CREDIT	BALANCE DEBIT	BALANCE CREDIT
20— Dec. 1	Balance	✔			6 0 0 00	
22		J20	2 0 0 00		8 0 0 00	

Problem 9 (Continued)

1., 2., and 3.

KIM HO EMPLOYMENT

WORK

FOR YEAR ENDED

	ACCOUNT TITLE	TRIAL BALANCE		ADJUSTMENTS	
		DEBIT	CREDIT	DEBIT	CREDIT
1					
2					
3					
4					
5					
6					
7					
8					
9					
10					
11					
12					
13					
14					
15					
16					
17					
18					
19					
20					
21					
22					
23					
24					
25					
26					
27					
28					
29					
30					
31					

Problem 9 (Concluded)

COUNSELING SERVICES

SHEET

DECEMBER 31, 20--

	ADJUSTED TRIAL BALANCE		INCOME STATEMENT		BALANCE SHEET	
	DEBIT	CREDIT	DEBIT	CREDIT	DEBIT	CREDIT
1						
2						
3						
4						
5						
6						
7						
8						
9						
10						
11						
12						
13						
14						
15						
16						
17						
18						
19						
20						
21						
22						
23						
24						
25						
26						
27						
28						
29						
30						
31						

Problem 10 (LO 1/3) PREPARING ADJUSTMENTS AND THE WORK SHEET

The trial balance for Juan's Speedy Delivery Service as of September 30, 20--, is shown on the work sheet that follows.

Data to complete the adjustments are as follows:

(a) Supplies inventory as of September 30, $450.
(b) Insurance expired, $200.
(c) Depreciation on delivery equipment, $350.
(d) Wages earned by employees but not paid as of September 30, $215.

Required:

1. Enter the adjustments in the Adjustments columns on the work sheet.
2. Complete the work sheet.

1. and 2.

JUAN'S SPEEDY
WORK
FOR MONTH ENDED

	ACCOUNT TITLE	TRIAL BALANCE DEBIT	TRIAL BALANCE CREDIT	ADJUSTMENTS DEBIT	ADJUSTMENTS CREDIT
1	Cash	1 5 4 5 00			
2	Accounts Receivable	8 5 0 00			
3	Supplies	7 2 5 00			
4	Prepaid Insurance	1 5 0 0 00			
5	Delivery Equipment	6 3 0 0 00			
6	Accum. Depr.—Delivery Equip.				
7	Accounts Payable		9 8 0 00		
8	Wages Payable				
9	Juan Garcia, Capital		9 0 0 0 00		
10	Juan Garcia, Drawing	1 2 0 0 00			
11	Delivery Fees		5 2 4 0 00		
12	Wages Expense	1 4 7 5 00			
13	Advertising Expense	4 2 0 00			
14	Rent Expense	7 5 0 00			
15	Supplies Expense				
16	Telephone Expense	1 8 0 00			
17	Insurance Expense				
18	Repair Expense	1 9 0 00			
19	Oil and Gas Expense	8 5 00			
20	Depreciation Expense—Del. Equip.				
21		15 2 2 0 00	15 2 2 0 00		
22					
23					

Name _____

Problem 10 (Concluded)

DELIVERY SERVICE

SHEET

SEPTEMBER 30, 20--

ADJUSTED TRIAL BALANCE		INCOME STATEMENT		BALANCE SHEET		
DEBIT	CREDIT	DEBIT	CREDIT	DEBIT	CREDIT	
						1
						2
						3
						4
						5
						6
						7
						8
						9
						10
						11
						12
						13
						14
						15
						16
						17
						18
						19
						20
						21
						22
						23

Problem 11 (LO 4) FINDING AND CORRECTING ERRORS ON A WORK SHEET

A work sheet for George Green's Landscaping Service follows. It should include these adjustments.

(a)   Ending inventory of supplies as of July 31, $350.
(b)   Insurance expired as of July 31, $225.
(c)   Depreciation on tractor, $460.
(d)   Wages earned but not paid as of July 31, $320.

Required:

Errors have been intentionally placed in this work sheet. Review the work sheet for addition mistakes, transpositions, and other errors and make all necessary corrections.

(*Note:* Errors are intentional.)

GREEN'S LANDSCAPING

WORK

FOR MONTH ENDED

	ACCOUNT TITLE	TRIAL BALANCE DEBIT	TRIAL BALANCE CREDIT	ADJUSTMENTS DEBIT	ADJUSTMENTS CREDIT
1	Cash	1 8 2 5 00			
2	Accounts Receivable	7 2 0 00			
3	Supplies	6 0 0 00			(a) 3 5 0 00
4	Prepaid Insurance	8 5 0 00			(b) 2 2 5 00
5	Tractor	6 5 5 0 00			(c) 4 6 0 00
6	Accum. Depr.—Tractor				
7	Accounts Payable		5 2 0 00		
8	Wages Payable				(d) 3 2 0 00
9	George Green, Capital		8 2 5 0 00		
10	George Green, Drawing	1 2 0 0 00			
11	Landscaping Fees		6 1 0 0 00		
12	Wages Expense	1 5 4 0 00		(d) 3 2 0 00	
13	Advertising Expense	2 5 0 00			
14	Rent Expense	7 7 5 00			
15	Supplies Expense			(a) 3 5 0 00	
16	Telephone Expense	1 4 0 00			
17	Utilities Expense	2 2 0 00			
18	Insurance Expense			(b) 2 2 5 00	
19	Depr. Expense—Tractor			(c) 4 6 0 00	
20	Miscellaneous Expense	2 0 0 00			
21		14 8 7 0 00	14 8 7 0 00	1 3 5 5 00	1 3 5 5 00
22	Net Income				
23					

Problem 11 (Concluded)

SERVICE

SHEET

JULY 31, 20--

ADJUSTED TRIAL BALANCE DEBIT	ADJUSTED TRIAL BALANCE CREDIT	INCOME STATEMENT DEBIT	INCOME STATEMENT CREDIT	BALANCE SHEET DEBIT	BALANCE SHEET CREDIT	
1 8 2 5 00				1 8 2 5 00		1
7 2 0 00				7 2 0 00		2
2 5 0 00				2 5 0 00		3
6 5 0 00				6 5 0 00		4
6 0 9 0 00				6 0 9 0 00		5
						6
	5 2 0 00				5 2 0 00	7
	3 2 0 00		3 2 0 00			8
	8 2 5 0 00				8 2 5 0 00	9
						10
1 2 0 0 00		1 2 0 0 00				11
	6 1 0 0 00		6 1 0 0 00		1 8 4 0 00	12
1 5 4 0 00		1 5 4 0 00				13
2 5 0 00		2 5 0 00				14
7 7 5 00		7 7 5 00				15
3 5 0 00		3 5 0 00				16
1 4 0 00		1 4 0 00				17
2 2 0 00		2 2 0 00				18
2 2 5 00		2 2 5 00				19
4 6 0 00		4 6 0 00				20
2 0 0 00		2 0 0 00				
13 3 5 5 00	15 1 9 0 00	2 4 1 7 00	6 4 2 0 00	8 3 4 7 00	8 7 7 0 00	21
		1 7 2 0 00			1 7 2 0 00	22
		4 1 3 7 00	6 4 2 0 00	8 3 4 7 00	10 4 9 0 00	23

Problem 12 (LO 6) CASH, MODIFIED CASH, AND ACCRUAL BASES

Mark Mosley has his own consulting business. Listed below are selected transactions from the month of April.

Apr.	1	Paid office rent, $500.
	2	Purchased office supplies, $250.
	3	Purchased office equipment on account, $1,000.
	4	Earned consulting fees: $400 cash, $150 on account.
	5	Paid telephone bill, $48.
	6	Purchased one-year insurance policy, $200.
	7	Paid $100 on account (for office equipment previously purchased).
	8	Received $150 on account from a customer (previously owed).
	9	Recorded depreciation on office equipment for month, $50.

Required:

Record the transactions in the space provided, using the following bases:

1. The cash basis.

2. The modified cash basis.

3. The accrual basis.

Name _____

Problem 12 (Continued)

1. Cash Basis

GENERAL JOURNAL

PAGE

	DATE		DESCRIPTION	POST. REF.	DEBIT	CREDIT	
1							1
2							2
3							3
4							4
5							5
6							6
7							7
8							8
9							9
10							10
11							11
12							12
13							13
14							14
15							15
16							16
17							17
18							18
19							19
20							20
21							21
22							22
23							23
24							24
25							25
26							26
27							27
28							28
29							29
30							30

Problem 12 (Continued)

2. Modified Cash Basis

GENERAL JOURNAL

	DATE		DESCRIPTION	POST. REF.	DEBIT	CREDIT	
1							1
2							2
3							3
4							4
5							5
6							6
7							7
8							8
9							9
10							10
11							11
12							12
13							13
14							14
15							15
16							16
17							17
18							18
19							19
20							20
21							21
22							22
23							23
24							24
25							25
26							26
27							27
28							28
29							29
30							30

Problem 12 (Concluded)

3. Accrual Basis

GENERAL JOURNAL

	DATE	DESCRIPTION	POST. REF.	DEBIT	CREDIT	
1						1
2						2
3						3
4						4
5						5
6						6
7						7
8						8
9						9
10						10
11						11
12						12
13						13
14						14
15						15
16						16
17						17
18						18
19						19
20						20
21						21
22						22
23						23
24						24
25						25
26						26
27						27
28						28
29						29
30						30

CHAPTER 5 APPENDIX
DEPRECIATION METHODS

APPENDIX LEARNING OBJECTIVES

In Chapter 5, the straight-line method of depreciation was illustrated. In the appendix to Chapter 5, three additional methods are explained. These methods are used when a different schedule of expenses provides a more appropriate matching with the revenues generated.

Objective 1.   **Prepare a depreciation schedule using the straight-line method.**
Objective 2.   **Prepare a depreciation schedule using the sum-of-the-years'-digits method.**
Objective 3.   **Prepare a depreciation schedule using the double-declining-balance method.**
Objective 4.   **Prepare a depreciation schedule for tax purposes using the Modified Accelerated Cost Recovery System.**

Apx. Exercise 1 (LO 1) STRAIGHT-LINE DEPRECIATION

Office equipment was purchased on January 1 at a cost of $48,000. It has an estimated useful life of four years and a salvage value of $6,000. Prepare a depreciation schedule showing the depreciation expense, accumulated depreciation, and book value for each year under the straight-line method.

STRAIGHT-LINE DEPRECIATION

Apx. Exercise 2 (LO 2) SUM-OF-THE-YEARS'-DIGITS DEPRECIATION

Using the information given in Exercise 1, prepare a depreciation schedule showing the depreciation expense, accumulated depreciation, and book value for each year under the sum-of-the-years'-digits method.

SUM-OF-THE-YEARS'-DIGITS DEPRECIATION

Apx. Exercise 3 (LO 3) DOUBLE-DECLINING-BALANCE DEPRECIATION

Using the information given in Exercise 1, prepare a depreciation schedule showing the depreciation expense, accumulated depreciation, and book value for each year under the double-declining-balance method.

DOUBLE-DECLINING-BALANCE DEPRECIATION

Apx. Exercise 4 (LO 4) DEPRECIATION UNDER THE MODIFIED ACCELERATED COST RECOVERY SYSTEM

Using the information given in Exercise 1 and the rates shown in Figure 5A-4 of the text, prepare a depreciation schedule showing the depreciation expense, accumulated depreciation, and book value for each year under the Modified Accelerated Cost Recovery System. For tax purposes, assume that the office equipment has a useful life of five years. (The IRS schedule will spread depreciation over six years.) Round to the nearest dollar.

MODIFIED ACCELERATED COST RECOVERY SYSTEM

CHAPTER 6
FINANCIAL STATEMENTS AND THE CLOSING PROCESS

LEARNING OBJECTIVES

Chapter 5 introduced the work sheet and demonstrated how it is used to prepare year-end adjustments. Chapter 6 completes the discussion of the work sheet by illustrating its role in the preparation of financial statements and closing entries. The purpose of the post-closing trial balance is also explained. It is prepared after closing entries have been posted to the general ledger accounts.

Objective 1.   Prepare financial statements with the aid of a work sheet.

The work sheet contains almost all the information needed to prepare the income statement, the statement of owner's equity, and the balance sheet. Numbers can be taken directly from the Income Statement columns for the income statement. The owner's capital account must be reviewed before completing the statement of owner's equity. If additional investments were made, they must be added to the beginning capital balance to compute the total investment. The net income (or net loss) is added to the total investment, and withdrawals (drawing) are subtracted, giving the ending owner's equity. The balance sheet is prepared using the ending owner's equity balance reported on the statement of owner's equity and the permanent accounts listed in the Balance Sheet columns of the work sheet.

Objective 2.   Journalize and post closing entries.

After the work sheet is completed, the financial statements are prepared. Then the adjusting and closing entries are journalized and posted. All temporary accounts need zero balances to begin the new accounting period. The closing process has four journal entries:

1.   to close revenue account(s) to Income Summary,
2.   to close expense accounts to Income Summary,
3.   to close Income Summary to the owner's capital account, and
4.   to close Drawing to the owner's capital account.

Objective 3.   Prepare a post-closing trial balance.

The **post-closing trial balance** lists all the permanent accounts that have balances to begin the new accounting period. It is prepared to prove the equality of the debit and credit balances in the general ledger accounts following the closing process. Since temporary accounts (drawing, revenues, and expenses) are closed at the end of the period, they do not appear on the post-closing trial balance.

Objective 4.   List and describe the steps in the accounting cycle.

This chapter concludes the accounting cycle that began in Chapter 1. The 10 steps are as follows:

During the Accounting Period
1.   Analyze source documents.
2.   Journalize the transactions.
3.   Post to the general ledger accounts.

End of Accounting Period
4.   Prepare a trial balance.
5.   Determine and prepare the needed adjustments on the work sheet.

6. Complete an end-of-period work sheet.
7. Journalize and post the adjusting entries.
8. Prepare an income statement, a statement of owner's equity, and a balance sheet.
9. Journalize and post the closing entries.
10. Prepare a post-closing trial balance.

REVIEW QUESTIONS

Instructions: Analyze each of the following items carefully before writing your answer in the column at the right.

Question	Answer

LO 1 1. The work sheet provides most of the needed information to prepare which three financial statements? ....

LO 1 2. The income statement contains which two major types of accounts?

LO 1 3. The statement of owner's equity adds _____ to the owner's investment and subtracts _____. ....

LO 1 4. Amounts owed that will be paid within a year are called _____.

LO 1 5. Expenses are listed on the income statement in the order they appear on the chart of accounts or in descending order by _____ amount.

LO 1 6. To find if the owner made any additional investments during the period, we must review the _____ account in the general ledger.

LO 1 7. When net income and additional investments are greater than withdrawals, the difference is called a(n) _____ in capital for the month. ....

LO 1 8. When the balance sheet is shown in _____ form, liabilities and owner's equity sections are placed below the assets section. ....

LO 1 9. When the balance sheet is shown in _____ form, assets are on the left and liabilities and owner's equity are on the right. ....

LO 1 10. A(n) _____ balance sheet groups similar items together such as current assets and current liabilities. ....

LO 1 11. Cash and assets that will be converted to cash or consumed within a year or the normal operating cycle are called _____ assets. ..

LO 1 12. The _____ is the period of time required to purchase supplies and services and convert them back into cash. ....

LO 1 13. Accounts Payable and Wages Payable are classified as _____ liabilities. ....

LO 2 14. Assets, liabilities, and the owner's capital account accumulate information across accounting periods; they are called _____ accounts. ....

LO 2 15. Revenue, expense, and drawing accounts accumulate information for the specific period only, then they go back to _____ balances. _____

LO 2 16. Because revenue, expense, and drawing accounts are closed each accounting period, they are called _____ accounts. .... _____

LO 2 17. The _____ account is used to summarize the effects of revenue and expense accounts; it is then closed to the capital account. .... _____

LO 2 18. When closing entries are posted to the general ledger, the word _____ is written in the Item column of each general ledger account affected. .... _____

LO 3 19. The _____ trial balance only lists permanent accounts. _____

LO 4 20. The _____ begins with analyzing source documents and ends with the post-closing trial balance. .... _____

EXERCISES

Exercise 1 (LO 1) REVIEW: COMPUTE NET INCOME

From the information given below, compute net income. _____

Revenue:	Delivery Fees	$4,826
Expenses:	Wages Expense	2,700
	Rent Expense	350
	Supplies Expense	55
	Insurance Expense	33
	Depreciation Expense	100

Exercise 2 (LO 1) REVIEW: COMPUTE OWNER'S EQUITY

Using the net income from Exercise 1 and the following information, compute the (a) increase to owner's equity and (b) ending owner's equity balance. Assume no additional investments were made by the owner.

(a) _____

(b) _____

Beginning owner's equity:	$5,680
Withdrawals by owner:	1,000

Exercise 3 (LO 2) THE CLOSING PROCESS

Based upon Exercises 1 and 2 above, list the accounts that must be closed at the end of the accounting cycle (in addition to the income summary account).

_____

_____

_____

_____

_____

_____

_____

PROBLEMS

Problems 4–9

To complete Problems 4 through 9, use the completed work sheet for Collins Cycle Service as of April 30, 20--, below and the general ledger on pages 88-92.

COLLINS CYCLE

WORK

FOR MONTH ENDED

	ACCOUNT TITLE	TRIAL BALANCE DEBIT	TRIAL BALANCE CREDIT	ADJUSTMENTS DEBIT	ADJUSTMENTS CREDIT
1	Cash	4 8 0 0 00			
2	Supplies	8 2 6 00			(a) 3 2 6 00
3	Prepaid Insurance	1 3 0 0 00			(b) 2 0 0 00
4	Repair Equipment	2 6 0 0 00			
5	Accum. Depr.—Repair Equip.		4 0 0 00		(c) 4 0 0 00
6	Accounts Payable		1 3 0 0 00		
7	Wages Payable				(d) 1 0 0 00
8	Jean Collins, Capital		6 0 0 0 00		
9	Jean Collins, Drawing	3 0 0 00			
10	Repair Fees		2 8 3 9 00		
11	Wages Expense	2 7 5 00		(d) 1 0 0 00	
12	Rent Expense	4 0 0 00			
13	Supplies Expense			(a) 3 2 6 00	
14	Telephone Expense	3 8 00			
15	Insurance Expense			(b) 2 0 0 00	
16	Depreciation Exp.—Repair Equip.			(c) 4 0 0 00	
17		10 5 3 9 00	10 5 3 9 00	1 0 2 6 00	1 0 2 6 00
18					
19					

Problems 4–9 (Concluded)

SERVICE

SHEET

APRIL 30, 20--

	ADJUSTED TRIAL BALANCE		INCOME STATEMENT		BALANCE SHEET		
	DEBIT	CREDIT	DEBIT	CREDIT	DEBIT	CREDIT	
1	4 8 0 0 00				4 8 0 0 00		1
2	5 0 0 00				5 0 0 00		2
3	1 1 0 0 00				1 1 0 0 00		3
4	2 6 0 0 00				2 6 0 0 00		4
5		8 0 0 00				8 0 0 00	5
6		1 3 0 0 00				1 3 0 0 00	6
7		1 0 0 00				1 0 0 00	7
8		6 0 0 0 00				6 0 0 0 00	8
9	3 0 0 00				3 0 0 00		9
10		2 8 3 9 00		2 8 3 9 00			10
11	3 7 5 00		3 7 5 00				11
12	4 0 0 00		4 0 0 00				12
13	3 2 6 00		3 2 6 00				13
14	3 8 00		3 8 00				14
15	2 0 0 00		2 0 0 00				15
16	4 0 0 00		4 0 0 00				16
17	11 0 3 9 00	11 0 3 9 00	1 7 3 9 00	2 8 3 9 00	9 3 0 0 00	8 2 0 0 00	17
18			1 1 0 0 00			1 1 0 0 00	18
19			2 8 3 9 00	2 8 3 9 00	9 3 0 0 00	9 3 0 0 00	19

Problem 4 REVIEW: PREPARE ADJUSTING ENTRIES

Journalize the adjusting entries and post them to the general ledger accounts. The balances shown in the general ledger accounts are *trial balance* amounts—that is, before adjusting and closing entries are entered.

GENERAL JOURNAL

PAGE 2

	DATE	DESCRIPTION	POST. REF.	DEBIT	CREDIT	
1						1
2						2
3						3
4						4
5						5
6						6
7						7
8						8
9						9
10						10
11						11
12						12
13						13

Use these ledger accounts for Problems 4 and 8.

GENERAL LEDGER

ACCOUNT Cash

ACCOUNT NO. 101

DATE		ITEM	POST. REF.	DEBIT	CREDIT	BALANCE DEBIT	BALANCE CREDIT
20--							
Apr.	30	Balance	✓			4 8 0 0 00	

ACCOUNT Supplies

ACCOUNT NO. 141

DATE		ITEM	POST. REF.	DEBIT	CREDIT	BALANCE DEBIT	BALANCE CREDIT
20--							
Apr.	30	Balance	✓			8 2 6 00	

Problems 4 and 8 (Continued)

ACCOUNT   Prepaid Insurance   ACCOUNT NO.   145

DATE		ITEM	POST. REF.	DEBIT	CREDIT	BALANCE	
						DEBIT	CREDIT
20-- Apr.	30	Balance	✓			1 3 0 0 00	

ACCOUNT   Repair Equipment   ACCOUNT NO.   188

DATE		ITEM	POST. REF.	DEBIT	CREDIT	BALANCE	
						DEBIT	CREDIT
20-- Apr.	30	Balance	✓			2 6 0 0 00	

ACCOUNT   Accumulated Depreciation—Repair Equipment   ACCOUNT NO.   188.1

DATE		ITEM	POST. REF.	DEBIT	CREDIT	BALANCE	
						DEBIT	CREDIT
20-- Apr.	1	Balance	✓				4 0 0 00

ACCOUNT   Accounts Payable   ACCOUNT NO.   202

DATE		ITEM	POST. REF.	DEBIT	CREDIT	BALANCE	
						DEBIT	CREDIT
20-- Apr.	30	Balance	✓				1 3 0 0 00

Problems 4 and 8 (Continued)

ACCOUNT   Wages Payable   ACCOUNT NO.   219

DATE	ITEM	POST. REF.	DEBIT	CREDIT	BALANCE DEBIT	BALANCE CREDIT

ACCOUNT   Jean Collins, Capital   ACCOUNT NO.   311

DATE	ITEM	POST. REF.	DEBIT	CREDIT	BALANCE DEBIT	BALANCE CREDIT
20-- Apr. 1	Balance	✓				5 0 0 0 00
15		J1		1 0 0 0 00		6 0 0 0 00

ACCOUNT   Jean Collins, Drawing   ACCOUNT NO.   312

DATE	ITEM	POST. REF.	DEBIT	CREDIT	BALANCE DEBIT	BALANCE CREDIT
20-- Apr. 30	Balance	✓			3 0 0 00	

ACCOUNT   Income Summary   ACCOUNT NO.   313

DATE	ITEM	POST. REF.	DEBIT	CREDIT	BALANCE DEBIT	BALANCE CREDIT

Problems 4 and 8 (Continued)

ACCOUNT   Repair Fees

ACCOUNT NO.   401

DATE		ITEM	POST. REF.	DEBIT	CREDIT	BALANCE	
						DEBIT	CREDIT
20-- Apr.	30	Balance	✓				2 8 3 9 00

ACCOUNT   Wages Expense

ACCOUNT NO.   511

DATE		ITEM	POST. REF.	DEBIT	CREDIT	BALANCE	
						DEBIT	CREDIT
20-- Apr.	30	Balance	✓			2 7 5 00	

ACCOUNT   Rent Expense

ACCOUNT NO.   521

DATE		ITEM	POST. REF.	DEBIT	CREDIT	BALANCE	
						DEBIT	CREDIT
20-- Apr.	30	Balance	✓			4 0 0 00	

ACCOUNT   Supplies Expense

ACCOUNT NO.   524

DATE		ITEM	POST. REF.	DEBIT	CREDIT	BALANCE	
						DEBIT	CREDIT

Problems 4 and 8 (Continued)

ACCOUNT   Telephone Expense   ACCOUNT NO.   525

DATE		ITEM	POST. REF.	DEBIT	CREDIT	BALANCE	
						DEBIT	CREDIT
20-- Apr.	30	Balance	✓			3 8 00	

ACCOUNT   Insurance Expense   ACCOUNT NO.   535

DATE	ITEM	POST. REF.	DEBIT	CREDIT	BALANCE	
					DEBIT	CREDIT

ACCOUNT   Depreciation Expense—Repair Equipment   ACCOUNT NO.   542

DATE	ITEM	POST. REF.	DEBIT	CREDIT	BALANCE	
					DEBIT	CREDIT

Problem 5 (LO 1) PREPARE AN INCOME STATEMENT

Prepare the income statement.

Problem 6 (LO 2) PREPARE A STATEMENT OF OWNER'S EQUITY

Prepare the statement of owner's equity. Be sure to check the capital account in the general ledger.

Problem 7 (LO 1) PREPARE A BALANCE SHEET

Prepare the balance sheet in report form.

Problem 8 (LO 2) JOURNALIZING AND POSTING CLOSING ENTRIES

Journalize the closing entries and post them to the general ledger accounts. (The general ledger accounts can be found on pages 88-92.)

GENERAL JOURNAL

PAGE 2

DATE	DESCRIPTION	POST. REF.	DEBIT	CREDIT
14				
15				
16				
17				
18				
19				
20				
21				
22				
23				
24				
25				
26				
27				
28				
29				
30				
31				
32				

Problem 9 (LO 3) PREPARE A POST-CLOSING TRIAL BALANCE

Prepare the post-closing trial balance.

ACCOUNT TITLE	ACCT. NO.	DEBIT BALANCE	CREDIT BALANCE

CHAPTER 6 APPENDIX
STATEMENT OF CASH FLOWS

APPENDIX LEARNING OBJECTIVES

In Chapter 6, we reviewed in greater detail the preparation of three financial statements: the income statement, statement of owner's equity, and balance sheet. A fourth important financial statement is the statement of cash flows. The main purpose of this statement is to report the sources and uses of cash. These sources and uses are categorized into three types of business activities: operating, investing, and financing.

Objective 1.   **Classify business transactions as operating, investing, or financing.**

Operating activities include those cash flows that are related to the revenues and expenses reported on the income statement. Examples include cash received for services performed and the payment of cash for expenses.

Investing activities are those transactions associated with buying and selling long-term assets, lending money, and collecting the principal on the related loans.

Financing activities are those cash transactions with owners and creditors. Examples include cash received from the owner to finance the operations and cash paid to the owner as withdrawals. Financing activities also include the receipt of cash from loans and the repayment of the loans.

Objective 2.   **Prepare a statement of cash flows by analyzing and categorizing a series of business transactions.**

The main body of the statement of cash flows consists of three sections: operating, investing, and financing activities.

Name of Business		
Statement of Cash Flows		
For Period Ended Date		
Cash flows from operating activities:		
Cash received from customers		$ x,xxx.xx
List cash paid for various expenses	$ (xxx.xx)	
Total cash paid for operations		(x,xxx.xx)
Net cash provided by (used for) operating activities		$ xxx.xx
Cash flows from investing activities:		
List cash received from the sale of long-term assets and other investing activities	$ x,xxx.xx	
List cash paid for the purchase of long-term assets and other investing activities	(x,xxx.xx)	
Net cash provided by (used for) investing activities		x,xxx.xx
Cash flows from financing activities:		
List cash received from owners and creditors	$ x,xxx.xx	
List cash paid to owners and creditors	(xxx.xx)	
Net cash provided by (used for) financing activities		x,xxx.xx
Net increase (decrease) in cash		$ xxx.xx

Apx. Exercise 1 REVIEW: ENTERING TRANSACTIONS IN T ACCOUNTS

Sung Joon Lee opened an overseas mailing business, "Lee's Quick Sail." The following transactions occurred during August of the current year. Enter the transactions in the cash T account provided on the next page, identifying each with its corresponding letter.

(a)   Lee invested $5,000 in the business.
(b)   Paid office rent, $500.
(c)   Bought supplies for the month, $200.
(d)   Lee made an additional investment in the business, $1,000.
(e)   Bought a new scale for $1,200: $700 cash and $500 on account.
(f)   Received $600 for mailing services.
(g)   Paid $200 on loan [see transaction (e)].
(h)   Paid electricity bill, $64.
(i)   Paid gas bill, $70.
(j)   Received $900 for mailing services.
(k)   Paid part-time employee, $90.
(l)   Lee withdrew cash for personal use, $400.

Apx. Exercise 1 (Concluded)

CASH

Apx. Exercise 2 REVIEW: FOOTING AND BALANCING A T ACCOUNT

Foot and balance the T account in Exercise 1. The cash balance at the end of August is _____ .

Apx. Problem 3 (LO 1) CLASSIFYING BUSINESS TRANSACTIONS AS OPERATING, INVESTING, OR FINANCING

Label each transaction in the cash T account of Exercise 1 as an operating (O), an investing (I), or a financing (F) activity.

Apx. Problem 4 (LO 2) PREPARING A STATEMENT OF CASH FLOWS BY ANALYZING BUSINESS TRANSACTIONS

Prepare a statement of cash flows based on the transactions and cash T account in Exercises 1 and 2, and Problem 3.

CHAPTER 7
ACCOUNTING FOR CASH

LEARNING OBJECTIVES

Managing cash is an essential part of every business's operations. In Chapter 7, we explore the cash account—setting up a bank account, writing checks and making deposits, preparing a bank reconciliation and the journal entries needed, operating a petty cash fund, establishing a change fund and using a cash short and over account.

Objective 1.   Describe how to open and use a checking account.

Most banks have standard procedures for opening and using a **checking account.** They begin with a signature card, whereby the depositor's Social Security number or EIN number and signature are provided. Preparing deposit tickets, endorsing properly, and writing checks are parts of using a checking account wisely.

Objective 2.   Prepare a bank reconciliation and related journal entries.

On a monthly basis, banks send **bank statements** to their checking account customers. The bank statement must be reconciled—compared to the checkbook. Adjustments are made to the ending bank balance and the checkbook balance until they are equal. Once the bank reconciliation is prepared, any changes to the book (checkbook) balance will require journal entries.

Objective 3.   Establish and use a petty cash fund.

A **petty cash fund** is both convenient and cost effective. Rather than writing checks for small amounts, costing time and money, a sum of money is set aside for petty (small) cash payments during the month. Vouchers are issued for all money paid out; the petty cash fund is replenished at the end of the month (brought back up to its original amount). A journal entry is made to record all of the expenses shown in the petty cash record.

Objective 4.   Establish a change fund and use the cash short and over account.

Businesses that receive cash from customers generally need to establish a change fund of currency and coins to use in handling cash sales. When many cash transactions occur, there often will be a difference between what the cash register tape says and the amount of cash actually found in the drawer. An account called Cash Short and Over is used to account for these differences. At the end of the month, if there is more cash short than over, it is an expense to the business. If there is more cash over than short, it is a revenue to the business.

REVIEW QUESTIONS

Instructions: Analyze each of the following items carefully before writing your answer in the column at the right.

Question	**Answer**

LO 1   1. To open a checking account, each person authorized to sign checks must fill out a(n) _____. ....   _____

LO 1   2. A(n) _____ lists items being deposited to a checking account.   _____

LO 1   3. Each check deposited is identified by its _____. ....   _____

LO 1   4. A(n) _____ consists of stamping or writing the depositor's name and other information on the back of a check. ....   _____

LO 1   5. A(n) _____ endorsement consists of a signature on the back of a check. ....   _____

LO 1   6. A(n) _____ endorsement consists of a signature together with words such as "For Deposit."...........   _____

LO 1   7. Depositors using ATMs must first key in their _____.   _____

LO 1   8. A(n) _____ is a document ordering a bank to pay cash from the depositor's account. ....   _____

LO 1   9. The _____ is the bank on which a check is drawn. ....   _____

LO 1 10. The _____ is the person being paid the cash. ....   _____

LO 1 11. The _____ is the depositor who orders the bank to pay the cash.   _____

LO 1 12. Space is contained to record all relevant information about a check on its _____. ....   _____

LO 1 13. A statement issued to the depositor once a month is called a _____. ....   _____

LO 1 14. Checks paid by the bank and returned to the depositor are called _____. ....   _____

LO 2 15. The process of bringing the bank and book balances into agreement is called preparing a(n) _____. ....   _____

LO 2 16. Checks issued during the period but not yet processed by the bank are called _____. ....   _____

LO 2 17. Deposits made but not yet recorded by the bank are called _____.   _____

LO 2 18. Bank charges for services are called _____. ....   _____

LO 2 19. Checks deposited but not paid because the drawer did not have enough money in the account are called _____ checks. ....   _____

LO 2 20. Transactions can be completed by _____ rather than by the manual process of writing checks or using cash...........................   _____

LO 3 21. A fund called the _____ is established to pay for small items with cash. ....   _____

LO 3 22. A receipt called a(n) _____ is prepared for every payment from the petty cash fund. ....

_____

LO 3 23. The _____ is a special multi-column record where petty cash payments are recorded. ....

_____

LO 3 24. At the end of the month, the petty cash fund is _____, or brought up to its original amount. ....

_____

LO 4 25. The cash short and over account is used when actual cash on hand is different from what is on the _____ tape plus the change fund.

_____

LO 4 26. When actual cash on hand exceeds what is on the register tape plus the change fund, this difference is a(n) _____. ....

_____

LO 4 27. When actual cash on hand is less than what is on the register tape plus the change fund, this difference is a(n) _____. ....

_____

EXERCISES

Exercise 1 (LO1) PREPARE DEPOSIT TICKET

Using the deposit ticket shown below, enter the following information:

		Checks:	33-11	$202
Date:	March 28, 20--		123-666	48
Currency:	$318		2-9	211
Coin:	33			

DEPOSIT TICKET

PEOPLE'S BANK
Wilkes-Barre, PA 18704-1456

Date _____ 20 _____

CHECKS AND OTHER ITEMS ARE RECEIVED FOR DEPOSIT SUBJECT TO THE TERMS AND CONDITIONS OF THIS FINANCIAL INSTITUTION'S ACCOUNT AGREEMENT.

_____

SIGN HERE ONLY IF CASH RECEIVED FROM DEPOSIT

⑆063112094⑆ 0001632475⑈

CURRENCY	
COIN	
C H E C K S	
TOTAL FROM OTHER SIDE	
SUBTOTAL	
LESS CASH RECEIVED	
NET DEPOSIT	

Exercise 2 (LO1) PREPARE CHECK AND STUB

During the month of October, you made the following payments by check. Fill in the stubs and write the checks. Use the blank checks provided on page 104. Enter $825.50 as the balance brought forward on Check No. 138, and add a deposit for $85 on October 10.

Oct.   3   Issued Check No. 138 to Emerald Lawn Care, Inc., for work done on the shrubbery around the office building, $125. (Miscellaneous Expense)

8   Issued Check No. 139 to Maxwell Office Supply for stationery, $85.90. (Office Supplies)

10   Issued Check No. 140 to Wesley's Towing for cost of towing company car to repair shop, $50. (Automobile Expense)

Exercise 2 (Concluded)

No. 138

DATE _____ 20 _____
TO _____
FOR _____
_____

ACCT. _____

	DOLLARS	CENTS
BAL BRO'T FOR'D		
AMT. DEPOSITED		
TOTAL		
AMT. THIS CHECK		
BAL CAR'D FOR'D		

No. 138   60-55 / 313

PAY
TO THE
ORDER OF _____ $ _____

_____ Dollars

PEOPLE'S BANK   FOR CLASSROOM USE ONLY
Wilkes-Barre, PA 18704-1456

MEMO _____   BY _____

⑆1300555 16 3247 5⑈

No. 139

DATE _____ 20 _____
TO _____
FOR _____
_____

ACCT. _____

	DOLLARS	CENTS
BAL BRO'T FOR'D		
AMT. DEPOSITED		
TOTAL		
AMT. THIS CHECK		
BAL CAR'D FOR'D		

No. 139   60-55 / 313

_____ 20 _____

PAY
TO THE
ORDER OF _____ $ _____

_____ Dollars

PEOPLE'S BANK   FOR CLASSROOM USE ONLY
Wilkes-Barre, PA 18704-1456

MEMO _____   BY _____

⑆1300555 16 3247 5⑈

No. 140

DATE _____ 20 _____
TO _____
FOR _____
_____

ACCT. _____

	DOLLARS	CENTS
BAL BRO'T FOR'D		
AMT. DEPOSITED		
TOTAL		
AMT. THIS CHECK		
BAL CAR'D FOR'D		

No. 140   60-55 / 313

_____ 20 _____

PAY
TO THE
ORDER OF _____ $ _____

_____ Dollars

PEOPLE'S BANK   FOR CLASSROOM USE ONLY
Wilkes-Barre, PA 18704-1456

MEMO _____   BY _____

⑆1300555 16 3247 5⑈

Name _____

Exercise 3 (LO2) BANK RECONCILIATION PROCEDURES

The bank reconciliation is a process of matching the checkbook balance with the bank statement balance—adding and subtracting items until the two are equal. In the exercise below, indicate which action is taken.

a. Add to checkbook balance.

b. Subtract from checkbook balance.

c. Add to bank statement balance.

d. Subtract from bank statement balance.

_____ 1. Deposits in transit

_____ 2. Error in checkbook whereby a check for $128 was entered into the checkbook as $182

_____ 3. NSF check

_____ 4. Checks outstanding (not yet processed by the bank)

_____ 5. Bank service fees

_____ 6. Credit memo, telling depositor that a note was collected

_____ 7. Error in checkbook whereby a check for $181 was entered into the checkbook as $118

Exercise 4 (LO 2) PREPARE JOURNAL ENTRIES FOR BANK RECONCILIATION

Based on the following bank reconciliation, prepare the necessary journal entries as of January 28, 20--:

Bank statement balance, January 28		$1,896.00
Add: Deposits in transit:		
1/26	$118.00	
1/28	92.00	210.00
		$2,106.00
Deduct: Outstanding checks:		
No. 683	$ 23.00	
No. 685	6.50	
No. 687	102.50	
No. 688	13.00	
No. 689	208.00	353.00
Adjusted bank balance		$1,753.00
Book balance, January 28		$1,994.00
Add: Error on check*	$ 28.00	
Note collected**	142.00	170.00
		$2,164.00
Deduct: Unrecorded ATM withdrawal***	$ 30.00	
Service charge	11.00	
NSF check	370.00	411.00
Adjusted book balance		$1,753.00

*Accounts Payable was debited.
**Credit Notes Receivable.
***Debit Gail Bennett, Drawing.

Exercise 4 (Concluded)

GENERAL JOURNAL

PAGE

	DATE	DESCRIPTION	POST. REF.	DEBIT	CREDIT	
1						1
2						2
3						3
4						4
5						5
6						6
7						7
8						8
9						9
10						10
11						11
12						12
13						13
14						14
15						15
16						16
17						17
18						18
19						19
20						20
21						21
22						22

Exercise 5 (LO3) PETTY CASH JOURNAL ENTRIES

Based on the following petty cash information, prepare journal entries to establish the petty cash fund and to replenish the fund at the end of the month.

1. On March 1, a check is written for $100 to establish a petty cash fund.

2. During the month, the following petty cash payments are made:

Telephone Expense	$ 3.50
Automobile Expense	11.00
Postage Expense	4.50
B. Crenshaw, Drawing	35.00
Charitable Contributions Expense	25.00
Miscellaneous Expense	3.00

Exercise 5 (Concluded)

GENERAL JOURNAL

	DATE	DESCRIPTION	POST. REF.	DEBIT	CREDIT	
1						1
2						2
3						3
4						4
5						5
6						6
7						7
8						8
9						9
10						10
11						11
12						12

Exercise 6 (LO4) CASH SHORT AND OVER JOURNAL ENTRIES

Based on the following information, prepare weekly entries for cash receipts from service fees and cash short and over. A change fund of $100 is maintained.

Aug.		Cash in drawer:		Cash register amount:	
	5		$318.00		$218.00
	12		402.00		300.00
	19		388.00		292.00
	26		411.50		309.50

Exercise 6 (Concluded)

GENERAL JOURNAL

	DATE	DESCRIPTION	POST. REF.	DEBIT	CREDIT	
1						1
2						2
3						3
4						4
5						5
6						6
7						7
8						8
9						9
10						10
11						11
12						12
13						13
14						14
15						15
16						16
17						17
18						18
19						19

PROBLEMS

Problem 7 (LO2) BANK RECONCILIATION AND RELATED JOURNAL ENTRIES

The following information relates to the bank account of the Mini Donut House:

Balance, March 31, per check stub		$2,923
Balance, March 31, per bank statement		3,199
March deposits not shown on bank statement	$ 302	
	_206_	508
Bank service charge shown on bank statement		14
Unrecorded ATM withdrawal*		60
NSF check shown on bank statement		153

Error on Check No. 144, where stub shows $132, but the check was made in the amount of $123. Accounts Payable was originally debited.

Checks outstanding, March 31, are as follows:

No. 148	$201.00
No. 151	300.00
No. 155	501.00

*Funds were withdrawn by the owner, Paolo Goes, for personal use.

Required:

1. Prepare the bank reconciliation.
2. Prepare the required journal entries.

Problem 7 (Continued)

1.

Name _____

Problem 7 (Concluded)

2.

GENERAL JOURNAL

	DATE		DESCRIPTION	POST. REF.	DEBIT	CREDIT	
1							1
2							2
3							3
4							4
5							5
6							6
7							7
8							8
9							9
10							10
11							11
12							12
13							13
14							14
15							15
16							16
17							17
18							18
19							19
20							20
21							21
22							22
23							23
24							24
25							25
26							26
27							27
28							28
29							29

Problem 8 (LO3) PETTY CASH PAYMENTS RECORD AND JOURNAL ENTRIES

On April 1, the Fitzgibbons Furniture Repair Shop established a petty cash fund of $200. The following cash payments were made from the petty cash fund during the first two weeks of April. The fund was replenished to the $200 level on April 16.

Apr.   1   Paid $5.28 for postage due on a package received. Petty Cash Voucher No. 10.

       5   Made a $25 contribution to the Washington Township Baseball League. Petty Cash Voucher No. 11.

       6   Reimbursed $6.25 to an employee for phone calls made from a pay telephone. Petty Cash Voucher No. 12.

       8   Paid $22 for office supplies. Petty Cash Voucher No. 13.

     10   Paid $32 for a newspaper advertisement. Petty Cash Voucher No. 14.

     12   Paid $33 for an oil change for the company truck. Petty Cash Voucher No. 15.

     14   Paid $20 for postage stamps. Petty Cash Voucher No. 16.

     15   Made a $25 contribution to the Girl Scouts. Petty Cash Voucher No. 17.

Required:

1. Prepare the journal entry to establish the petty cash fund.
2. Enter the above payments in the petty cash payments record provided on page 113.
3. Prove the petty cash payments record.
4. Prepare the journal entry to replenish the fund on April 16.

Name _____

**Problem 8 (Continued)
2. and 3.**

PETTY CASH PAYMENTS FOR MONTH OF _____ 20-- PAGE 1

DAY	DESCRIPTION	VOU. NO.	TOTAL AMOUNT	DISTRIBUTION OF PAYMENTS							AMOUNT
				TRUCK EXPENSE	POSTAGE EXPENSE	CHARIT. CONTRIB. EXPENSE	TELE. EXPENSE	OFFICE SUPPLIES	ADVERT. EXPENSE	ACCOUNT	
1											
2											
3											
4											
5											
6											
7											
8											
9											
10											
11											
12											
13											
14											
15											
16											
17											
18											
19											
20											
21											
22											

Problem 8 (Concluded)
1. and 4.

GENERAL JOURNAL   PAGE   1

	DATE		DESCRIPTION	POST. REF.	DEBIT	CREDIT	
1							1
2							2
3							3
4							4
5							5
6							6
7							7
8							8
9							9
10							10
11							11
12							12

Problem 9 (LO4) CASH SHORT AND OVER JOURNAL ENTRIES

Mackie's Salon deposits cash weekly. A record of cash register receipts for the month of April is shown below. A change fund of $100 is maintained.

Apr.		Cash in drawer:		Cash register amount:	
	2	Cash in drawer:	$298.00	Cash register amount:	$196.50
	9		286.50		192.00
	16		293.50		193.50
	23		306.00		204.50
	30		301.50		203.00

Required:

Prepare weekly journal entries for cash receipts from service fees, showing cash short and over when needed.

Name _____

Problem 9 (Concluded)

GENERAL JOURNAL PAGE 1

	DATE	DESCRIPTION	POST. REF.	DEBIT	CREDIT	
1						1
2						2
3						3
4						4
5						5
6						6
7						7
8						8
9						9
10						10
11						11
12						12
13						13
14						14
15						15
16						16
17						17
18						18
19						19
20						20
21						21
22						22
23						23
24						24
25						25
26						26
27						27
28						28
29						29
30						30
31						31
32						32

CHAPTER 8
PAYROLL ACCOUNTING:
EMPLOYEE EARNINGS AND DEDUCTIONS

LEARNING OBJECTIVES

Payroll accounting is an important part of any business, partly because it is such a significant expense and partly because so many laws govern its record keeping. In Chapter 8, we examine the payroll records that employers are required to keep and also those records that help run the business efficiently.

Objective 1.   Distinguish between employees and independent contractors.

An **employee** is one who works under the control and direction of an employer. The employer controls how and when the job is to be done, determines working hours, and in general is responsible for all aspects of the employee's work. An **independent contractor**, on the other hand, performs a service for a fee and does not work under the control and direction of the company paying for his or her service. This is an important distinction because employers are required to maintain payroll records and file many reports for their employees but must file only one form for independent contractors.

Objective 2.   Calculate employee earnings and deductions.

Three steps are required to determine how much to pay an employee for a pay period. (1) Calculate the employee's total earnings for the pay period. (2) Determine the amounts of deductions for the same pay period. (3) Subtract deductions from total earnings. The deductions may be required by law—for example, Social Security and Medicare taxes and federal and state income taxes—or by agreement with the employer—for example, insurance deductions and savings bond deductions.

Objective 3.   Describe and prepare payroll records.

Three types of payroll records are used to accumulate required information for federal and state tax purposes: the payroll register, the payroll check (or record of direct deposit) with earnings statement attached, and the employee earnings record.
The **payroll register** is a multi-column form that accumulates the necessary data to prepare the journal entry. Detailed information on earnings, taxable earnings, deductions, and net pay is provided for each employee and for the employees in total.
The **payroll check** (or record of direct deposit) is prepared from information in the payroll register. The detachable earnings statement attached to the employee's check shows the gross earnings, total deductions, and net pay.
A separate record of each employee's earnings is called an **employee earnings record.** This information is also obtained from the payroll register. The earnings record is designed so that quarterly and annual totals can be accumulated in order for the employer to prepare several reports.

Objective 4.   Account for employee earnings and deductions.

The payroll register provides all the information needed to prepare the journal entry for any pay period. The total gross earnings is debited to a wages and salaries expense account, and each deduction is credited to a current liability account. The difference between gross earnings and total deductions is called **net pay** and is credited to Cash.

Objective 5.   Describe various payroll record-keeping methods.

In addition to a manual system of preparing all the necessary payroll records, payroll processing centers and electronic systems can be used to prepare the same records.

A **payroll processing center** is a business that sells payroll record-keeping services. An **electronic system** is a computer system based on a software package that performs all payroll record keeping and prepares payroll checks or EFTs.

REVIEW QUESTIONS

Instructions: Analyze each of the following items carefully before writing your answer in the column at the right.

Question	Answer
LO 1 1. A(n) _____ is one who works under the control and direction of an employer.	_____
LO 1 2. A(n) _____ performs a service for a fee and does not work under the control and direction of the company paying for the service.	_____
LO 2 3. What three steps are required to determine how much to pay an employee for a pay period?	_____ _____ _____
LO 2 4. Compensation for managerial or administrative services, normally expressed in biweekly, monthly, or annual terms, is called _____.	_____
LO 2 5. Compensation for skilled or unskilled labor, normally expressed in terms of hours, weeks, or units produced, is called _____.	_____
LO 2 6. When compensation is based on time, _____ are helpful for keeping a record of the time worked by each employee.	_____
LO 2 7. An employee's total earnings is also called _____.	_____
LO 2 8. An employee's total earnings less all the deductions is called _____.	_____
LO 2 9. What are the three major categories of deductions from an employee's paycheck?	_____ _____
LO 2 10. David Astin is married with two children, holds only one job, and has a spouse who is not employed. What number of withholding allowances is Astin entitled to claim, assuming that he does not anticipate large itemized deductions?	_____

LO 2 11. Upon employment, each employee is required to furnish the employer a Form _____ that details, among other things, the number of withholding allowances and marital status. .... _____

LO 2 12. Name the four factors that determine the amount to be withheld from an employee's gross pay each pay period. .... _____

_____

_____

_____

LO 3 13. A form used to assemble the data required at the end of each payroll period is called a(n) _____. .... _____

LO 3 14. A method of payment in which the employee's net pay is placed directly in the employee's bank account is called a(n) _____. ..... _____

LO 3 15. A separate, detailed record of each employee's earnings is called a(n) _____. .... _____

LO 5 16. Name two approaches in addition to a manual system used to accumulate and record payroll information. .... _____

_____

EXERCISES

Exercise 1 (LO 2) COMPUTING OVERTIME PAY RATE

Lu-yin Cheng receives a regular salary of $2,500 a month and is entitled to overtime pay at the rate of 1½ times the regular hourly rate for any time worked in excess of 40 hours per week. Compute Cheng's overtime hourly rate.

_____
_____
_____
_____
_____
_____
_____
_____
_____
_____

Exercise 2 (LO 2) COMPUTING GROSS PAY

Roger Watkins earns a regular hourly rate of $12.50 and receives time and a half for any time worked over 8 hours per weekday. Roger earns double time for hours worked on Saturday or Sunday. During the past week, Roger worked 8 hours each day Monday through Wednesday, 5 hours on Thursday, 12 hours on Friday, and 6 hours on Saturday. Compute Watkins's gross pay.

_____

_____

_____

_____

_____

_____

_____

_____

_____

Exercise 3 (LO 2) COMPUTING NET PAY

Bill Burry is married, has three children, and claims five withholding allowances for federal income tax purposes. Burry's gross pay for the week was $683. Using the federal income tax withholding tables provided in Figure 8-4 of the text and the information provided below, compute Burry's net pay for the week.

(a)   Social Security tax rate is 6.2% (Burry's prior earnings equaled $23,455).
(b)   Medicare tax rate is 1.45%.
(c)   State income tax is 2% of gross earnings.
(d)   City income tax is 1% of gross earnings.
(e)   Contribution to pension plan is $25.
(f)   Health insurance deduction is $8.50.

_____

_____

_____

_____

_____

_____

_____

_____

_____

_____

Exercise 4 (LO 4) JOURNALIZING PAYROLL TRANSACTIONS

Using the information provided in Exercise 3, enter the payment of Bill Burry's wages in a general journal. Assume a pay period ending on July 31, 20--.

GENERAL JOURNAL

PAGE 1

	DATE	DESCRIPTION	POST. REF.	DEBIT	CREDIT	
1						1
2						2
3						3
4						4
5						5
6						6
7						7
8						8
9						9
10						10

Exercise 5 (LO 3, 4) PAYROLL JOURNAL ENTRIES

The following data were taken from the payroll register of United Processors as of May 14, 20--.

Regular earnings	$6,516.00
Overtime earnings	710.00
Total earnings	_____
Deductions:	
Federal income tax	_____
Social Security tax	448.01
Medicare tax	104.78
Pension plan	134.00
Health insurance	260.00
United Way	190.00
Net pay	$5,394.21

Required:

1. Determine the missing amounts.
2. Prepare the journal entry for the payroll, crediting Cash for the net pay.

1.

_____

_____

_____

_____

Exercise 5 (Concluded)

2.

GENERAL JOURNAL

	DATE	DESCRIPTION	POST. REF.	DEBIT	CREDIT	
1						1
2						2
3						3
4						4
5						5
6						6
7						7
8						8
9						9
10						10
11						11
12						12

PROBLEMS

Problem 6 (LO 2, 3, 4) PAYROLL REGISTER AND PAYROLL JOURNAL ENTRIES

Earl Wilson operates a business known as Wilson Enterprises. Listed below are the name, number of allowances claimed, marital status, total hours worked, and hourly rate of each employee. All hours worked in excess of 40 a week are paid for at the rate of time and a half.

The employer uses a weekly federal income tax withholding table. A portion of this weekly table is provided in Chapter 8 of your textbook. Social Security tax is withheld at the rate of 6.2%, Medicare tax is withheld at the rate of 1.45%, state income tax is withheld at the rate of 3.5%, and city earnings tax is withheld at the rate of 1%. Kagan, Kennedy, Scalia, and Sotomayor each have $15 withheld this payday for group life insurance. Each employee, except Ginsberg, has $5 withheld for health insurance. All of the employees use payroll deduction to the credit union for varying amounts as listed below. Alito, Kennedy, and Thomas each have $18.25 withheld this payday under a savings bond purchase plan.

Wilson Enterprises follows the practice of drawing a single check for the net amount of the payroll and depositing the check in a special payroll account at the bank. Individual paychecks are then drawn for the amount due each employee. The checks issued this payday were numbered consecutively beginning with Check No. 531.

Wilson Enterprises
Payroll Information for the Week Ended January 15, 20--

Name	Allow-ances	Marital Status	Total Hours Worked	Regular Hourly Rate	Credit Union Deposit	Cumul. Earnings thru 1/8
Alito, Samuel	3	M	45	$12.00	$114.00	$525.00
Breyer, Susan	4	M	50	10.00	110.00	480.00
Ginsberg, Ruth	3	M	43	11.00	97.90	500.00
Kagan, Ellen	2	S	48	11.00	114.40	625.00
Kennedy, Tony	3	M	43	13.00	115.70	730.00
Roberts, John	5	M	40	17.00	136.00	850.00
Scalia, Anton	2	S	38	9.00	68.40	425.00
Sotomayor, Sonja	4	M	47	11.00	111.10	635.00
Thomas, Clarence	1	S	60	10.00	140.00	615.00

Required:

1. Prepare a payroll register for Wilson Enterprises for the pay period ended January 15, 20--. Use the form provided on pages 124–125. (In the Taxable Earnings/Unemployment Compensation column, enter the same amounts as in the Social Security column.)

2. Assuming that the wages for the week ended January 15 were paid on January 17, enter the payment in the general journal provided on page 125.

Problem 6 (Continued)
1.

PAYROLL REGISTER

	NAME	EMP. NO.	NO. ALLOW.	MARIT. STATUS	EARNINGS							TAXABLE EARNINGS			
					REGULAR		OVERTIME		TOTAL		CUMULATIVE TOTAL	UNEMPLOY. COMP.		SOCIAL SECURITY	
1															
2															
3															
4															
5															
6															
7															
8															
9															
10															
11															
12															
13															
14															

Problem 6 (Concluded)

FOR PERIOD ENDED _____ 20--

FEDERAL INC. TAX		SOC. SEC. TAX		MEDICARE TAX		STATE INC. TAX		CITY EARN. TAX		LIFE INS.		HEALTH INS.		CREDIT UNION		OTHER		TOTAL		NET PAY		CK. NO.		
																							1
																							2
																							3
																							4
																							5
																							6
																							7
																							8
																							9
																							10
																							11
																							12
																							13
																							14

(DEDUCTIONS spans FEDERAL INC. TAX through OTHER columns)

2.

GENERAL JOURNAL

PAGE 1

	DATE	DESCRIPTION	POST. REF.	DEBIT	CREDIT	
1						1
2						2
3						3
4						4
5						5
6						6
7						7
8						8
9						9
10						10
11						11
12						12
13						13

Problem 7 (LO 3) EMPLOYEE EARNINGS RECORD

The current employee earnings record for Susan Breyer is provided below and on page 127. Using the information provided in Problem 6, update Breyer's earnings record to reflect the January 15 payroll. Although this information should have been entered earlier, complete the required information at the bottom of the earnings record. The necessary information is provided below.

Name:	Susan Breyer
Address:	422 Long Plain Rd.
	Leverett, MA 01054
Employee No.:	2
Gender:	Female
Department:	Sanitation
Occupation:	Janitor
S.S. No.:	336-56-7534
Marital Status:	Married
Allowances:	4
Pay Rate:	$10 per hour
Birth Date:	7/6/69
Date Employed:	6/22/--

EMPLOYEE EARNINGS RECORD

20 -- PERIOD ENDED	EARNINGS					TAXABLE EARNINGS				DEDUCTIONS				
	REGULAR		OVERTIME	TOTAL		CUMULATIVE TOTAL	UNEMPLOY. COMP.		SOCIAL SECURITY		FEDERAL INCOME TAX		SOCIAL SECURITY TAX	
Jan. 1	200	00		200	00	200	00	200	00	200	00	0	00	12	40
8	280	00		280	00	480	00	280	00	280	00	0	00	17	36

GENDER		DEPARTMENT	OCCUPATION	SOCIAL SECURITY NO.	MARITAL STATUS	ALLOW- ANCES
M	F					

Name _____

Problem 7 (Concluded)

FOR PERIOD ENDED 20--

MEDICARE TAX		STATE INCOME TAX		CITY EARNINGS TAX		LIFE INSUR.		HEALTH INSUR.		CREDIT UNION		OTHER				TOTAL		NET PAY		CK. NO.
2	90	7	00	2	00			5	00	40	00					69	30	130	70	321
4	06	9	80	2	80			5	00	56	00					95	02	184	98	422

PAY RATE	DATE OF BIRTH	DATE HIRED	NAME/ADDRESS	EMP. NO.

CHAPTER 9
PAYROLL ACCOUNTING:
EMPLOYER TAXES AND REPORTS

LEARNING OBJECTIVES

Chapter 8 discussed taxes levied on the employee and withheld by the employer. None of these taxes was an expense of the employer. In Chapter 9, we examine several taxes that represent an additional payroll expense imposed directly on the employer.

Objective 1.   Describe and calculate employer payroll taxes.

Most employers are subject to a matching portion of the Social Security and Medicare taxes and to federal and state unemployment taxes. The employer's **Social Security and Medicare taxes** are levied on employers at the same rates and on the same bases as the employee Social Security and Medicare taxes. The **FUTA** tax is levied only on employers. The purpose of this tax is to raise funds to administer the federal/state unemployment compensation program. The **SUTA** tax is also levied only on employers. The purpose of this tax is to raise funds to pay unemployment benefits.

The Social Security, FUTA, and SUTA taxes are calculated from the accumulated amounts found in the Taxable Earnings columns in the payroll register. The Medicare tax is calculated from the Earnings—Total column.

Objective 2.   Account for employer payroll taxes expense.

To journalize employer payroll taxes, debit the total of the employer Social Security, Medicare, FUTA, and SUTA taxes to a single account entitled Payroll Taxes Expense. The liabilities for the Social Security, Medicare, FUTA, and SUTA taxes payable normally are credited to separate accounts. The general format of this entry appears below.

Payroll Taxes Expense	xx	
Social Security Tax Payable		xx
Medicare Tax Payable		xx
FUTA Tax Payable		xx
SUTA Tax Payable		xx

Objective 3.   Describe employer reporting and payment responsibilities.

Employer payroll reporting and payment responsibilities fall in six areas.

1. Federal income tax withholding and Social Security and Medicare taxes
2. FUTA taxes
3. SUTA taxes
4. Employee Wage and Tax Statement (Form W-2)
5. Summary of employee wages and taxes (Form W-3)
6. Employment eligibility notification (Form I-9)

The due date for federal income tax withholding and Social Security and Medicare taxes varies, depending on the amount of these taxes. Deposits are made using EFTPS. In addition, a Form 941 must be completed each quarter and filed with the IRS.

The federal unemployment taxes must be computed on a quarterly basis. In addition, Form 940 must be filed with the IRS by the beginning of the second week of February.

Deposit rules and forms for state unemployment taxes vary among the states. Deposits usually are required on a quarterly basis.

Employers must furnish each employee with a Wage and Tax Statement (Form W-2) by January 31 of each year. Information needed to complete this form is contained in the employee earnings records. The employer also must file Form W-3 with the Social Security Administration by the last day of February. This form summarizes the employee earnings and tax information from Forms W-2.

The purpose of Form I-9 is to document that each employee is authorized to work in the United States. It must be completed by the employee and employer and retained by the employer.

Objective 4.   Describe and account for workers' compensation insurance.

Workers' compensation insurance provides insurance for employees who suffer a job-related illness or injury. The cost of the insurance depends on the number of employees, the riskiness of the job, and the company's accident history. The employer usually pays the premium at the beginning of the year, based on the estimated annual payroll, and makes an adjustment at the end of the year when the actual annual payroll is known.

REVIEW QUESTIONS

Instructions: Analyze each of the following items carefully before writing your answer in the column at the right.

Question	Answer

LO 1   1. Name the four payroll taxes paid by the employer. .... _____

_____

_____

LO 1   2. The textbook uses a Social Security tax rate of 6.2% applied to maximum employee earnings of _____. .... _____

LO 1   3. The _____ is a key source of information for computing employer payroll taxes. .... _____

LO 1   4. Individuals who own and run their own business are considered ____. _____

LO 1   5. The law requires persons earning net self-employment income of $400 or more to pay a(n) _____. .... _____

LO 1   6. The textbook uses a FUTA tax rate of 0.6% applied to maximum employee earnings of _____. .... _____

LO 2   7. When journalizing the employer's payroll taxes, debit the total of the employer Social Security, Medicare, FUTA, and SUTA taxes to a single account entitled _____. .... _____

LO 3   8. Name the three taxes that are associated with Form 941. .... _____

_____

_____

LO 3   9. In addition to making quarterly deposits, employers are required to file an annual report of federal unemployment tax on Form _____. _____

LO 3 10. By January 31 of each year, employers must furnish each employee with a(n) _____. .... _____

LO 3 11. _____ documents that an employee is authorized to work in the United States. .... _____

LO 4 12. _____ provides insurance for employees who suffer a job-related illness or injury. .... _____

EXERCISES

Exercise 1 (LO 1) CALCULATION OF EMPLOYER PAYROLL TAXES

Sylvania Bookstore pays a SUTA tax of 5.4% and a FUTA tax of 0.6%. The total taxable wages for unemployment compensation on a certain payday amount to $16,800. Compute the unemployment taxes payable to the state and federal government.

_____
_____
_____
_____
_____
_____
_____
_____
_____
_____
_____
_____

Exercise 2 (LO 2) CALCULATION OF PAYROLL TAXES AND PREPARATION OF JOURNAL ENTRIES

The Totals line from Wong Drug Store's payroll register for the week ended December 31, 20--, is shown on pages 132 and 133.

Payroll taxes are imposed as follows:

Social Security tax	6.2%
Medicare tax	1.45%
FUTA tax	0.6%
SUTA tax	5.4%

Required:

1. Prepare the journal entry for payment of this payroll on December 31, 20--.
2. Prepare the journal entry for the employer's payroll taxes for the period ended December 31, 20--.

Exercise 2 (Continued)

PAYROLL REGISTER

	NAME	EMPL. NO.	NO. ALLOW.	MARIT. STATUS	EARNINGS REGULAR		OVERTIME		TOTAL		CUMULATIVE TOTAL		TAXABLE EARNINGS UNEMPLOY. COMP.		SOCIAL SECURITY	
1	Totals				4,200	00	500	00	4,700	00	203,700	00	300	00	3,600	00
2																
3																
4																
5																
6																
7																
8																
9																
10																

1. and 2.

GENERAL JOURNAL   PAGE 1

	DATE	DESCRIPTION	POST. REF.	DEBIT	CREDIT	
1						1
2						2
3						3
4						4
5						5
6						6
7						7
8						8
9						9
10						10
11						11
12						12
13						13
14						14
15						15
16						16

Exercise 2 (Concluded)

FOR PERIOD ENDED

December 31, 20--

			DEDUCTIONS							
FEDERAL INC. TAX	SOC. SEC. TAX	MEDICARE TAX	HEALTH INS.	CREDIT UNION	OTHER		TOTAL	NET PAY	CK. NO.	
420 00	223 20	68 15	80 00	200 00			991 35	3,708 65		1
										2
										3
										4
										5
										6
										7
										8
										9
										10

Exercise 3 (LO1/2) TOTAL COST OF AN EMPLOYEE

Compute the total annual cost to an employer of employing a person whose gross salary is $45,000. (Assume a 5.4% state unemployment tax rate and a FUTA tax rate of 0.6%, both on the first $7,000 of earnings, an employer's Social Security tax rate of 6.2% on the first $110,100 of earnings and a Medicare tax rate of 1.45% on gross earnings.)

_____

_____

_____

_____

_____

_____

_____

_____

Exercise 4 (LO 3) JOURNAL ENTRIES FOR PAYMENT OF PAYROLL TAXES

The general ledger of GNU Co. includes the following accounts and balances related to payroll as of October 15 of the current year:

Social Security Tax Payable	$12,400
Medicare Tax Payable	2,900
FUTA Tax Payable	540
SUTA Tax Payable	4,320
Employee Federal Income Tax Payable	7,780

Required:

Journalize the payment of the employee federal income taxes and Social Security and Medicare taxes on October 15, 20--, and the deposit of the FUTA and SUTA taxes on October 31, 20--.

GENERAL JOURNAL

PAGE

	DATE	DESCRIPTION	POST. REF.	DEBIT	CREDIT	
1						1
2						2
3						3
4						4
5						5
6						6
7						7
8						8
9						9
10						10
11						11
12						12
13						13
14						14

Exercise 5 (LO 4) WORKERS' COMPENSATION INSURANCE AND ADJUSTMENT

Curtis Company paid a premium of $360 for workers' compensation insurance based on the estimated payroll as of the beginning of the year. Based on actual payroll as of the end of the year, the actual premium is $397. Prepare the adjusting entry to reflect the underpayment of the insurance premium.

GENERAL JOURNAL

PAGE   1

	DATE	DESCRIPTION	POST. REF.	DEBIT	CREDIT	
1						1
2						2
3						3
4						4
5						5

PROBLEMS

Problem 6 (LO 1/2) CALCULATING PAYROLL TAXES EXPENSE AND PREPARING JOURNAL ENTRY

A partial payroll register for the pay period ended August 31, 20--, is provided on the following page for the Astroscope Company.

Required:

1. Compute the total earnings subject to federal and state unemployment taxes and the Social Security tax by completing the Taxable Earnings columns of the payroll register.

2. Assume the company is in a state with an unemployment tax rate of 5.4% and a FUTA tax rate of 0.6%, both on the first $7,000 of earnings. The Social Security tax rate is 6.2% on the first $110,100 of earnings, and the Medicare tax rate is 1.45% on gross earnings. Compute the state and federal unemployment taxes and the Social Security and Medicare taxes on the lines provided on page 136.

3. Prepare the entry for the employer's payroll taxes in the general journal provided on page 137.

Problem 6 (Continued)

1.

PAYROLL REGISTER

	NAME	NO. ALLOW.	MARIT. STATUS	EARNINGS						TAXABLE EARNINGS			
				REGULAR	OVERTIME	TOTAL		CUMULATIVE TOTAL		UNEMPLOY. COMP.		SOCIAL SECURITY	
1	Coolie, Betty					350	00	7,150	00				
2	Covar, Mike					200	00	6,800	00				
3	Hagen, Frank					375	00	6,200	00				
4	Gutierrez, Bob					1,540	00	47,300	00				
5	Moten, Alice					1,500	00	50,500	00				
6	Rice, Darlene					3,300	00	113,000	00				
7													

2.

Problem 6 (Concluded)

3.

GENERAL JOURNAL

PAGE   1

	DATE	DESCRIPTION	POST. REF.	DEBIT	CREDIT	
1						1
2						2
3						3
4						4
5						5
6						6
7						7
8						8
9						9

Problem 7 (LO 2/3) JOURNALIZING AND POSTING PAYROLL ENTRIES

Rock Creek Company has five employees. All are paid on a monthly basis. The fiscal year of the business is March 1 to February 28. Payroll taxes are imposed as follows:

Social Security tax to be withheld from employees' wages and imposed on the employer, 6.2% each on the first $110,100 of earnings.

Medicare tax to be withheld from employees' wages and imposed on the employer, 1.45% each on gross earnings.

SUTA tax imposed on the employer, 5.4% on the first $7,000 of earnings.

FUTA tax imposed on the employer, 0.6% on the first $7,000 of earnings.

The accounts kept by Rock Creek Company include the following:

Account Number	Title	Balance on March 1
101	Cash	$62,500.00
211	Employee Federal Income Tax Payable	3,375.00
212	Social Security Tax Payable	4,740.00
213	Medicare Tax Payable	1,110.00
218	Savings Bond Deductions Payable	1,200.00
221	FUTA Tax Payable	320.00
222	SUTA Tax Payable	2,670.00
511	Wages and Salaries Expense	0.00
530	Payroll Taxes Expense	0.00

Problem 7 (Continued)

Following is a narrative of selected transactions relating to payrolls and payroll taxes that occurred during the months of March and April:

Mar. 15   Paid $9,225.00 covering the following February taxes:

	Employee federal income tax withheld	$3,375.00
	Social Security tax	4,740.00
	Medicare tax	1,110.00
	Total	$9,225.00

31   March payroll:

	Total wages and salaries expense		$39,000.00
	Less amounts withheld:		
	Employee federal income tax	$3,690.00	
	Social Security tax	2,418.00	
	Medicare tax	565.50	
	Savings bond deductions payable	1,200.00	7,873.50
	Net amount paid		$31,126.50

31   Purchased savings bonds for employees, $2,400.00

31   Data for completing employer's payroll taxes expense for March:

	Social Security taxable wages	$39,000.00
	Unemployment taxable wages	12,000.00

Apr. 15   Paid $9,657.00 covering the following March taxes:

	Employee federal income tax payable	$ 3,690.00
	Social Security tax	4,836.00
	Medicare tax	1,131.00

30   Paid SUTA tax for the quarter, $3,318.00

30   Paid FUTA tax, $392.00

Required:

1. Using a general journal, journalize the preceding transactions.
2. Open T accounts for the payroll expense and liabilities. Enter the beginning balances and post the transactions recorded in the journal.

Name _____

Problem 7 (Continued)

1.

GENERAL JOURNAL

	DATE		DESCRIPTION	POST. REF.	DEBIT	CREDIT	
1							1
2							2
3							3
4							4
5							5
6							6
7							7
8							8
9							9
10							10
11							11
12							12
13							13
14							14
15							15
16							16
17							17
18							18
19							19
20							20
21							21
22							22
23							23
24							24
25							25
26							26
27							27
28							28
29							29
30							30

Problem 7 (Continued)

GENERAL JOURNAL

PAGE

	DATE		DESCRIPTION	POST. REF.	DEBIT	CREDIT	
1							1
2							2
3							3
4							4
5							5
6							6
7							7
8							8
9							9
10							10
11							11
12							12
13							13
14							14

2.

Cash   101

Employee Federal Income Tax Payable   211

Social Security Tax Payable   212

Medicare Tax Payable   213

Problem 7 (Concluded)

Savings Bond Deductions Payable 218

FUTA Tax Payable 221

SUTA Tax Payable 222

Wages and Salaries Expense 511

Payroll Taxes Expense 530

Problem 8 (LO 4) WORKERS' COMPENSATION INSURANCE AND ADJUSTMENT

Jackson Manufacturing estimated its total payroll for the coming year to be $630,000. The workers' compensation insurance premium rate is 0.35%.

Required:

1. Calculate the estimated workers' compensation insurance premium and prepare the journal entry for the payment as of January 2, 20--.

2. Assume Jackson Manufacturing's actual payroll for the year is $658,000. Calculate the total insurance premium owed. Prepare a journal entry as of December 31, 20--, to record the adjustment for the underpayment. The actual payment of the additional insurance premium will take place in January of the next year.

3. Assume, instead, that Jackson Manufacturing's actual payroll for the year is $607,000. Prepare a journal entry as of December 31, 20--, for the total amount that should be refunded. The refund will not be received until the next year.

1., 2., and 3.

GENERAL JOURNAL

PAGE   1

	DATE		DESCRIPTION	POST. REF.	DEBIT	CREDIT	
1							1
2							2
3							3
4							4
5							5
6							6
7							7
8							8
9							9
10							10
11							11
12							12
13							13
14							14

Name _____

CHAPTER 10
ACCOUNTING FOR SALES AND CASH RECEIPTS

LEARNING OBJECTIVES

Chapter 10 introduces the merchandising business: sales transactions and the related new accounts, a new ledger, and a new schedule. Merchandise sales transactions are shown in general journal format.

Objective 1.   Describe merchandise sales transactions.

Retail businesses make sales on account, as well as cash sales and credit card sales. Sales tickets and cash register receipts are produced for customers and for accounting purposes.

Wholesale businesses also make sales on account, but the process is more complicated and includes purchase orders and sales invoices. Credit approval is required for sales on account.

Both types of businesses have sales returns (merchandise returned for a refund) and allowances (reductions in price because of defects, damage, or other problems with the merchandise).

Objective 2.   Describe and use merchandise sales accounts.

Accounting for sales transactions requires four general ledger accounts: Sales, Sales Tax Payable, Sales Returns and Allowances, and Sales Discounts. Sales is a revenue account; Sales Tax Payable is a liability account; and Sales Returns and Allowances and Sales Discounts are contra-revenue accounts.

When a sale is made and sales tax is added to the sale, the liability account (Sales Tax Payable) is credited for the amount of tax that will be remitted to the government. Therefore, when merchandise is returned for a credit (Sales Returns and Allowances), the customer is also refunded the amount of the sales tax (Sales Tax Payable is debited).

Cash discounts are given to business customers who pay within a discount period such as 10 days. This encourages prompt payment of bills. When a discount is taken, the sales discounts account is debited for the amount of the discount.

Net sales is determined by deducting the contra-revenue accounts (Sales Returns and Allowances and Sales Discounts) from gross sales.

Objective 3.   Describe and use the accounts receivable ledger.

The accounts receivable account in the general ledger provides a record of the total amount owed to a business by its customers. To help run the business, a record also is needed of the amount owed by individual customers. The accounts receivable subsidiary ledger provides this information.

When an accounts receivable subsidiary ledger is used, the accounts receivable account in the general ledger is a "controlling account." The accounts receivable ledger is "subsidiary" to this account. Transactions are posted daily from the general journal to both the general ledger and the accounts receivable ledger.

Objective 4.   Prepare a schedule of accounts receivable.

Once all daily postings are completed to individual accounts, the balance in the accounts receivable general ledger account must agree with the sum of the customer balances in the accounts receivable ledger. The schedule of accounts receivable is prepared at the end of the month to verify that the total of customer balances equals the balance in the controlling account, Accounts Receivable.

REVIEW QUESTIONS

Instructions: Analyze each of the following items carefully before writing your answer in the column at the right.

Question	Answer

LO 1 1. A(n) _____ business purchases merchandise such as clothing, furniture, or computers to sell to its customers. ....

LO 1 2. A(n) _____ is a transfer of merchandise from one individual or business to another in exchange for cash or a promise to pay cash.

LO 1 3. A(n) _____ is a document created as evidence of a sale for a retail business. ....

LO 1 4. A written order to buy merchandise, called a(n) _____, is received from a customer. ....

LO 1 5. A(n) _____ is prepared when merchandise ordered is shipped to a customer. ....

LO 1 6. Merchandise returned by a customer for a refund is called a(n) _____. ....

LO 1 7. Reductions in price of merchandise granted because of defect or damage are called _____. ....

LO 1 8. When credit is given for merchandise returned or for an allowance, a(n) _____ is issued. ....

LO 2 9. The sales account is a _____ account. ....

LO 2 10. When a sale on account is made, _____ is debited. ....

LO 2 11. When a sale is made with sales tax, a liability account, called _____, is credited for the amount of the sales tax. ....

LO 2 12. Sales Returns and Allowances is a contra-_____ account. ....

LO 2 13. A(n) _____ is granted for prompt payment by customers who buy merchandise on account. ....

LO 2 14. Sales Discounts is a contra-_____ account. ....

LO 3 15. A record of each customer's account balance is contained in the _____ ledger. ....

LO 3 16. To indicate that the accounts receivable ledger has been posted, a slash and a _____ are entered in the Posting Reference column of the general journal. ....

LO 3 17. Sales returns and allowances are posted to both the general ledger and the _____ ledger. ....

LO 3 18. When a collection is received on account, _____ is credited.

LO 4 19. The _____ is a listing of the balances of all customers who owe money at the end of the month. ....

LO 4 20. The schedule of accounts receivable is used to verify that the sum of the accounts receivable ledger balances equals the _____ balance. ....

Name _____

EXERCISES

Exercise 1 (LO 1) SALES DOCUMENTS

The following is a copy of a purchase order received from Custom Builders, Inc., by Rogers Building Supplies, Inc. Assuming you are employed by Rogers Building Supplies, Inc., prepare a sales invoice (No. 491) dated July 18 billing Custom Builders, Inc., for the items specified in their Order No. A208. The unit prices are as follows: #6 insulated steel doors, $290.00 each and #28 pine, six-panel doors, $125 each. Indicate terms of 30 days.

	Purchase Order		Order No. **A208**
Date July 15, 20--	**CUSTOM BUILDERS, INC.**		
Terms 30 days	2001 HILLSIDE DR. BLOOMINGTON, IN 47401-2287		

To

Rogers Building Supplies, Inc.
So. Adams
Bloomington, IN 47401-3663

Quantity	Description	Price
10	#6 Insulated steel doors	290.00
15	#28 Pine, six-panel doors	125.00

Deliver no goods without a written order on this form.

By *E. Taylor*

Exercise 1 (Concluded)

Invoice Invoice No. Date Your Order No.		**ROGERS BUILDING SUPPLIES, INC.** So. Adams, Bloomington, IN 47401-3663 Sold to		
Terms				
Quantity	Description		Unit Price	Amount

Exercise 2 (LO 1) SALES DOCUMENTS

On July 28, Custom Builders, Inc., returned one #6 insulated steel door to Rogers Building Supplies, Inc., for credit. Using the blank form on page 147, prepare a credit memorandum (No. 17) covering the cost of the door sold on July 18.

Exercise 2 (Concluded)

	ROGERS BUILDING SUPPLIES, INC.		
Credit Memorandum			So. Adams,
No.			Bloomington, IN 47401-3663

Date   To

We credit your account as follows:

Quantity	Description	Unit Price	Amount

Exercise 3 (LO 2/3) SALES AND SALES RETURNS AND ALLOWANCES TRANSACTIONS

Record the following transactions in a general journal, assuming a 5% sales tax.

(a) Sold $230 of merchandise, plus sales tax, on account. R. B. Jones, Sale No. 28.
(b) R. B. Jones returned $30 worth of merchandise for a credit.
(c) R. B. Jones paid the balance of the account in cash.
(d) Sold $300 of merchandise, plus sales tax, for cash.
(e) Merchandise returned for cash refund, $15.

Exercise 3 (Concluded)

GENERAL JOURNAL

PAGE

	DATE		DESCRIPTION	POST. REF.	DEBIT	CREDIT	
1							1
2							2
3							3
4							4
5							5
6							6
7							7
8							8
9							9
10							10
11							11
12							12
13							13
14							14
15							15
16							16
17							17
18							18
19							19
20							20
21							21
22							22
23							23
24							24

Exercise 4 (LO2) COMPUTING NET SALES

Based on the following information, compute net sales.

Gross sales	$5,010
Sales returns and allowances	565
Sales discounts	97

Name _____

Exercise 5 (LO3) SALES TRANSACTIONS

Diana Brewer operates the Floor and Window Treatment Center and completed the following transactions related to sales of merchandise on account during the month of February. Sales tax of 5% was included in the amount of each sale.

Feb.
2 Sold wallpaper supplies to Dresson Homes, $98.95; terms, n/30. Sale No. 255.
12 Sold paint to Ray Acuff, $105; terms, n/30. Sale No. 256.
23 Sold miniblinds to Clydette Rupert, $114.83; terms, n/30. Sale No. 257.
24 Sold decorator items to Marty Staple, $35.55; terms, n/30. Sale No. 258.
25 Sold paint to Angel Burtin, $25.57; terms, n/30. Sale No. 259.

Required:

Enter the above transactions in a general journal.

GENERAL JOURNAL

PAGE _____

DATE	DESCRIPTION	POST. REF.	DEBIT	CREDIT

Exercise 6 (LO 3) CASH RECEIPTS TRANSACTIONS

Diana Brewer of the Floor and Window Treatment Center received cash during the month of March as described below.

Mar.
2 Received cash from Dresson Homes on account, $98.95.
12 Received cash from Ray Acuff on account, $105.
15 Made cash sale to Jean Granite, $404.76, plus 5% sales tax.
18 Made cash sale to Bill Green, $2,380.95, plus 5% sales tax.
23 Received cash from Clydette Rupert on account, $114.83.
24 Received cash from Marty Staple on account, $35.55.
25 Received cash from Angel Burtin on account, $25.57.
31 Cash sales for the month were $22,000, including 5% sales tax (from cash register tape).
31 Credit card sales for the month were $28,000, including 5% sales tax. Bank credit card expense is $560.

Required:

Enter the above transactions in the general journal below and on the next page.

GENERAL JOURNAL

PAGE

	DATE	DESCRIPTION	POST. REF.	DEBIT	CREDIT	
1						1
2						2
3						3
4						4
5						5
6						6
7						7
8						8
9						9
10						10
11						11
12						12
13						13
14						14
15						15
16						16
17						17
18						18
19						19
20						20

Exercise 6 (Concluded)

GENERAL JOURNAL

PAGE _____

	DATE	DESCRIPTION	POST. REF.	DEBIT	CREDIT	
1						1
2						2
3						3
4						4
5						5
6						6
7						7
8						8
9						9
10						10
11						11
12						12
13						13
14						14
15						15
16						16
17						17
18						18
19						19
20						20
21						21
22						22
23						23
24						24
25						25
26						26
27						27
28						28
29						29
30						30
31						31
32						32
33						33
34						34

PROBLEMS

Problem 7 (LO 2/3) SALES, SALES RETURNS AND ALLOWANCES, AND CASH RECEIPTS TRANSACTIONS

The following information represents transactions for Kwan Chu's Fish Market for the month of July 20--. Sales tax is 6%.

July
1   Sold merchandise on account to B. A. Smith, $137.50, plus sales tax. Sale No. 33.
3   B. A. Smith returned merchandise worth $15, plus sales tax, for a credit. Credit Memo No.11.
5   Sold merchandise on account to L. L. Unis, $218, plus sales tax. Sale No. 34.
7   Cash sales for the week were $325.44, plus sales tax.
10 Sold merchandise on account to W. P. Clark, $208, plus sales tax. Sale No. 35.
11 Received $129.85 from B. A. Smith, on account.
13 W. P. Clark returned merchandise worth $22, plus sales tax, for a credit. Credit Memo No. 12.
14 Cash sales for the week were $411.20, plus sales tax.
16 Sold merchandise on account to B. A. Smith, $282.50, plus sales tax. Sale No. 36.
17 Received $231.08 from L. L. Unis, on account.
21 Cash sales for the week were $292.50, plus sales tax.
24 Sold merchandise on account to L. L. Unis, $224.50, plus sales tax. Sale No. 37.
28 Cash sales for the week were $300.50, plus sales tax.
31 Received $197.16 from W. P. Clark, on account.

Required:

Using the information provided, record the transactions in the general journal below and on pages 153–154.

GENERAL JOURNAL

PAGE

	DATE		DESCRIPTION	POST. REF.	DEBIT	CREDIT	
1							1
2							2
3							3
4							4
5							5
6							6
7							7
8							8
9							9
10							10
11							11
12							12
13							13
14							14
15							15

Problem 7 (Continued)

GENERAL JOURNAL   PAGE _____

	DATE		DESCRIPTION	POST. REF.	DEBIT	CREDIT	
1							1
2							2
3							3
4							4
5							5
6							6
7							7
8							8
9							9
10							10
11							11
12							12
13							13
14							14
15							15
16							16
17							17
18							18
19							19
20							20
21							21
22							22
23							23
24							24
25							25
26							26
27							27
28							28
29							29
30							30

Problem 7 (Concluded)

GENERAL JOURNAL

	DATE		DESCRIPTION	POST. REF.	DEBIT	CREDIT	
1							1
2							2
3							3
4							4
5							5
6							6
7							7
8							8
9							9
10							10
11							11
12							12
13							13
14							14
15							15
16							16
17							17
18							18
19							19
20							20
21							21
22							22
23							23
24							24
25							25
26							26
27							27
28							28
29							29
30							30
31							31

Problem 8 (LO 3/4) SALES, LEDGERS, AND SCHEDULE OF ACCOUNTS RECEIVABLE

H. K. Smythe operates Leather All, a leather shop that sells luggage, handbags, business cases, and other leather goods. During the month of May, the following sales on account were made:

May 3 Sold merchandise on account to T. A. Pigdon, $247.50, plus sales tax of $14.85. Sale No. 51.

4 Sold merchandise on account to J. R. Feyton, $55, plus sales tax of $3.30. Sale No. 52.

6 Sold merchandise on account to P. C. McMurdy, $99, plus sales tax of $5.94. Sale No. 53.

10 Sold merchandise on account to J. T. Messer, $175, plus sales tax of $10.50. Sale No. 54.

12 Sold merchandise on account to A. F. Schlitz, $355, plus sales tax of $21.30. Sale No. 55.

13 Sold merchandise on account to J. R. Feyton, $215, plus sales tax of $12.90. Sale No. 56.

20 Sold merchandise on account to P. C. McMurdy, $400, plus sales tax of $24.00. Sale No. 57.

28 Sold merchandise on account to J. T. Messer, $255, plus sales tax of $15.30. Sale No. 58.

Required:

1. Enter the above transactions in the general journal provided below and on page 156 (start with page 7).
2. Post the entries to the general ledger and accounts receivable ledger on pages 156–158.
3. Prepare a schedule of accounts receivable as of May 31.

1.   **GENERAL JOURNAL**   PAGE _____

	DATE	DESCRIPTION	POST. REF.	DEBIT	CREDIT	
1						1
2						2
3						3
4						4
5						5
6						6
7						7
8						8
9						9
10						10
11						11
12						12
13						13
14						14
15						15
16						16
17						17
18						18
19						19
20						20

Problem 8 (Continued)

GENERAL JOURNAL

PAGE

	DATE	DESCRIPTION	POST. REF.	DEBIT	CREDIT	
1						1
2						2
3						3
4						4
5						5
6						6
7						7
8						8
9						9
10						10
11						11
12						12
13						13
14						14
15						15
16						16
17						17
18						18
19						19

2.

GENERAL LEDGER

ACCOUNT   Accounts Receivable   ACCOUNT NO.   122

DATE		ITEM	POST. REF.	DEBIT	CREDIT	BALANCE DEBIT	BALANCE CREDIT
20-- May	1	Balance	✓			8 3 4 00	

Problem 8 (Continued)

ACCOUNT   Sales Tax Payable   ACCOUNT NO. 231

DATE	ITEM	POST. REF.	DEBIT	CREDIT	BALANCE	
					DEBIT	CREDIT

ACCOUNT   Sales   ACCOUNT NO. 401

DATE	ITEM	POST. REF.	DEBIT	CREDIT	BALANCE	
					DEBIT	CREDIT

ACCOUNTS RECEIVABLE LEDGER

NAME J. R. Feyton

ADDRESS 6022 Columbia, St. Louis, MO 63139-1906

DATE	ITEM	POST. REF.	DEBIT	CREDIT	BALANCE

Problem 8 (Continued)

NAME P. C. McMurdy

ADDRESS 1214 N. 2nd St., E. St. Louis, IL 62201-2679

DATE		ITEM	POST. REF.	DEBIT	CREDIT	BALANCE
20-- May	1	Balance	✓			1 2 5 00

NAME J. T. Messer

ADDRESS P.O. Box 249, Chesterfield, MO 63017-3901

DATE		ITEM	POST. REF.	DEBIT	CREDIT	BALANCE
20-- May	1	Balance	✓			1 7 7 00

NAME T. A. Pigdon

ADDRESS 1070 Purcell, University City, MO 63130-1546

DATE		ITEM	POST. REF.	DEBIT	CREDIT	BALANCE
20-- May	1	Balance	✓			2 8 0 00

NAME A. F. Schlitz

ADDRESS 800 Lindbergh Blvd., St. Louis, MO 63166-1546

DATE		ITEM	POST. REF.	DEBIT	CREDIT	BALANCE
20-- May	1	Balance	✓			2 5 2 00

Problem 8 (Concluded)

3.

Problem 9 (LO 2/3) SALES, SALES RETURNS AND ALLOWANCES, CASH RECEIPTS, AND LEDGERS

Paula Angelillis operates the Hard-to-Find Auto Parts Store. Much of her business is by mail. The following transactions related to sales and cash receipts occurred during June:

June   1   Received $300 from A. K. Wells, including $14.29 of sales tax, for field cash sale. (Field cash sales are not included in cash register tapes.)

       5   Received $125.60 from L. Strous on account.

     10   Received $263.25 from D. Manning on account.

     12   Q. Striker returned merchandise for credit. The sales price was $215, plus sales tax of $10.75.

     18   Received $58.25 from D. Warding on account.

     20   Received $1,000 from B. L. Stryker, including $47.62 tax (field cash sale).

     21   Received $29.99 from L. Clese on account.

     24   R. Popielarz returned merchandise for credit. Sales price was $116.25, plus sales tax of $5.81.

     27   Received $426 from L. LeCount on account.

     30   Cash and bank credit card sales for the month were $8,200, plus sales tax of $410. Bank credit card expense is $80.

Required:

1. Enter each transaction in the general journal provided on pages 160–161 (start with page 8).
2. Post the entries to the general and accounts receivable ledgers (pages 161–164).

Problem 9 (Continued)

1.

GENERAL JOURNAL

PAGE

	DATE	DESCRIPTION	POST. REF.	DEBIT	CREDIT	
1						1
2						2
3						3
4						4
5						5
6						6
7						7
8						8
9						9
10						10
11						11
12						12
13						13
14						14
15						15
16						16
17						17
18						18
19						19
20						20
21						21
22						22
23						23
24						24
25						25
26						26
27						27
28						28
29						29
30						30
31						31
32						32
33						33
34						34
35						35
36						36

Problem 9 (Continued)

GENERAL JOURNAL

	DATE	DESCRIPTION	POST. REF.	DEBIT	CREDIT	
1						1
2						2
3						3
4						4
5						5
6						6
7						7
8						8
9						9
10						10
11						11
12						12
13						13
14						14
15						15
16						16
17						17

GENERAL LEDGER

2.

ACCOUNT Cash

ACCOUNT NO. 101

DATE		ITEM	POST. REF.	DEBIT	CREDIT	BALANCE DEBIT	BALANCE CREDIT
20-- June	1	Balance	✓			13 2 0 0 25	

Problem 9 (Continued)

ACCOUNT Accounts Receivable   ACCOUNT NO. 122

DATE		ITEM	POST. REF.	DEBIT	CREDIT	BALANCE	
						DEBIT	CREDIT
20-- June	1	Balance	✓			1 2 5 0 90	

ACCOUNT Sales Tax Payable   ACCOUNT NO. 231

DATE		ITEM	POST. REF.	DEBIT	CREDIT	BALANCE	
						DEBIT	CREDIT
20-- June	1	Balance	✓				1 2 5 00

ACCOUNT Sales   ACCOUNT NO. 401

DATE	ITEM	POST. REF.	DEBIT	CREDIT	BALANCE	
					DEBIT	CREDIT

ACCOUNT Sales Returns and Allowances   ACCOUNT NO. 401.1

DATE	ITEM	POST. REF.	DEBIT	CREDIT	BALANCE	
					DEBIT	CREDIT

Problem 9 (Continued)

ACCOUNT Bank Credit Card Expense   ACCOUNT NO. 513

DATE	ITEM	POST. REF.	DEBIT	CREDIT	BALANCE DEBIT	BALANCE CREDIT

ACCOUNTS RECEIVABLE LEDGER

NAME L. Clese

ADDRESS 875 Glenway Drive, Glendale, MO 63122-4112

DATE		ITEM	POST. REF.	DEBIT	CREDIT	BALANCE
20-- June	1	Balance	✓			2 9 99

NAME L. LeCount

ADDRESS 1439 East Broad Street, Columbus, OH 43205-9892

DATE		ITEM	POST. REF.	DEBIT	CREDIT	BALANCE
20-- June	1	Balance	✓			4 2 6 00

NAME D. Manning

ADDRESS 2101 Cumberland Road, Noblesville, IN 47870-2435

DATE		ITEM	POST. REF.	DEBIT	CREDIT	BALANCE
20-- June	1	Balance	✓			2 6 3 25

Problem 9 (Concluded)

NAME R. Popielarz

ADDRESS 3001 Hillcrest Drive, Dallas, PA 18612-6854

DATE		ITEM	POST. REF.	DEBIT	CREDIT	BALANCE
20-- June	1	Balance	✓			1 2 2 06

NAME Q. Striker

ADDRESS 4113 Main Street, Beech Grove, IN 46107-9643

DATE		ITEM	POST. REF.	DEBIT	CREDIT	BALANCE
20-- June	1	Balance	✓			2 2 5 75

NAME L. Strous

ADDRESS 2215 N. State Road 135, Greenwood, IN 46142-6432

DATE		ITEM	POST. REF.	DEBIT	CREDIT	BALANCE
20-- June	1	Balance	✓			1 2 5 60

NAME D. Warding

ADDRESS 1100 W. Main Street, Carmel, IN 46032-2364

DATE		ITEM	POST. REF.	DEBIT	CREDIT	BALANCE
20-- June	1	Balance	✓			5 8 25

CHAPTER 11
ACCOUNTING FOR PURCHASES AND CASH PAYMENTS

LEARNING OBJECTIVES

Chapter 11 continues the study of merchandise transactions. In this chapter, purchases and cash payments are emphasized, and another new ledger and new schedule are introduced. As was done in Chapter 10, merchandise purchases transactions are shown in general journal format.

Objective 1.   Define merchandise purchases transactions.

For a merchandising business, **purchases** refers to merchandise acquired for resale. Several important documents are used in the purchasing process of a merchandising business. A **purchase requisition** is a form used to request the purchasing department to purchase merchandise or other property. A **purchase order** is a written order to buy goods from a specific vendor (supplier). A **receiving report** is prepared upon receipt of merchandise and indicates what merchandise has been received. An **invoice** is a document prepared by the seller as a bill for the merchandise shipped. To the seller, this is a sales invoice. To the buyer, it is called a **purchase invoice.**

The accounting department compares the purchase invoice with the purchase requisition, purchase order, and receiving report. If the invoice is for the goods ordered at the correct price, the invoice is paid by the due date.

When credit terms such as 2/10, n/30 are offered by the seller, a **cash discount** is available to the buyer if the bill is paid within the discount period. Another type of discount, called a **trade discount,** is often offered by manufacturers and wholesalers. This discount is a reduction from the list or catalog price. By simply adjusting the trade discount percentages, companies can avoid the cost of reprinting catalogs every time there is a change in price.

Objective 2.   Describe and use merchandise purchases accounts and compute gross profit.

To account for merchandise purchases transactions, four new accounts are used. These are **Purchases, Purchases Returns and Allowances, Purchases Discounts,** and **Freight-In.**

Purchases is an account to which the cost of merchandise (i.e., inventory acquired for resale) is debited.

Purchases Returns and Allowances is a contra-purchases account to which returns of merchandise and price reductions are credited. This account is subtracted from Purchases on the income statement.

Purchases Discounts is a contra-purchases account to which any cash discounts allowed on purchases are credited. This account is subtracted from Purchases on the income statement.

Freight-In is an adjunct-purchases account to which transportation charges on merchandise purchases are debited. This account is added to Purchases on the income statement.

FOB shipping point means that transportation charges are paid by the buyer. **FOB destination** means that transportation charges are paid by the seller.

Gross profit is computed using the following format:

Sales				$xxxx
Less:	Sales returns and allowances	$xxxx		
	Sales discounts	xxxx	xxxx	
Net sales				$xxxx
Cost of goods sold:				
Merchandise inventory, beginning of period			$xxxx	
Purchases		$xxxx		
Less:	Purchases returns and allowances	$xxxx		
	Purchases discounts	xxxx	xxxx	
Net purchases			$xxxx	
Add freight-in			xxxx	
Cost of goods purchased				xxxx
Goods available for sale				$xxxx
Less merchandise inventory, end of period				xxxx
Cost of goods sold				xxxx
Gross profit				$xxxx

Objective 3.   Describe and use the accounts payable ledger.

The accounts payable account in the general ledger provides a record of the total amount owed by a business to its suppliers. To help run the business, a record also is needed of the amount owed to each supplier. The accounts payable subsidiary ledger provides this information.

When an accounts payable subsidiary ledger is used, the accounts payable account in the general ledger is a "controlling account." The accounts payable ledger is "subsidiary" to this account. Transactions are posted daily from the general journal to both the general ledger and the accounts payable ledger.

Objective 4.   Prepare a schedule of accounts payable.

The Accounts Payable balance in the general ledger should equal the sum of the supplier balances in the accounts payable ledger. A listing of supplier accounts and balances is called a **schedule of accounts payable.** This schedule is usually prepared at the end of the month to verify that the sum of the accounts payable ledger balances equals the Accounts Payable balance.

REVIEW QUESTIONS

Instructions: Analyze each of the following items carefully before writing your answer in the column at the right.

		Question	Answer
LO 1	1.	For a merchandising business, _____ refers to merchandise acquired for resale.	_____
LO 1	2.	A(n) _____ is a form used to request the purchasing department to purchase merchandise or other property.	_____
LO 1	3.	A(n) _____ is a written order to buy goods from a specific vendor (supplier).	_____

LO 1   **4.** When the merchandise is received, a(n) _____ indicating what has been received is prepared. .... _____

LO 1   **5.** To the buyer, a document prepared by the seller as a bill for the merchandise shipped is called a(n) _____. .... _____

LO 1   **6.** In the credit terms 2/10, n/30, the 2 represents a(n) _____. .... _____

LO 1   **7.** A(n) _____ is a type of discount offered by manufacturers and wholesalers as a reduction from the list or catalog price offered to different classes of customers. .... _____

LO 2   **8.** List the four accounts used with merchandise purchases transactions. ....

_____

_____

_____

_____

LO 2   **9.** FOB shipping point means that transportation charges are paid by the _____. .... _____

LO 2   **10.** FOB destination means that transportation charges are paid by the _____. .... _____

LO 2   **11.** Cost of merchandise available for sale less the end-of-period merchandise inventory is called _____. .... _____

LO 2   **12.** Net sales minus cost of merchandise sold is called _____. ..... _____

LO 3   **13.** A separate ledger containing an individual account payable for each supplier is called a(n) _____. .... _____

LO 3   **14.** To indicate that the accounts payable ledger has been posted, a slash and a _____ are entered in the Posting Reference column of the general journal. .... _____

LO 3   **15.** If a buyer returns merchandise or is given an allowance for damaged merchandise, the account _____ is credited for the dollar amount. .... _____

LO 3   **16.** Purchases returns and allowances are posted to both the general ledger and the _____ ledger. .... _____

LO 3   **17.** When a payment is made on account, _____ is debited. .... _____

LO 4   **18.** To verify that the sum of the accounts payable ledger balances equals the Accounts Payable balance, a(n) _____ is prepared. _____

EXERCISES

Exercise 1 (LO 1) PURCHASE REQUISITION

You are employed by Eberle Hardware, a retail hardware business, as manager of the lawn and garden department. On October 1, 20--, after completing an inventory, you decide that the following merchandise should be ordered:

15	All steel rubber-tire wheelbarrows	24	Spade shovels
25	Garden hose, 1/2", 50 ft.	6	Long-handle spade shovels
3	Power mower, 21" cut	12	Spade forks
5	Heavy duty rototillers		

You would like delivery within 10 days and should be notified upon receipt of the merchandise. Using the form provided below, prepare the purchase requisition.

Eberle Hardware

110 E. Kirkwood Ave.
Indianapolis, IN 46011-3274

Purchase Requisition

Requisition No. _502_

Required for Department _____

Date Issued _____

Advise _____   On Delivery   Date Required _____

Quantity	Description

Approved By _____   Requisition Placed By _____

DEPARTMENT MANAGER'S MEMORANDUM

Issued To _____

Purchase Order No. _____

Date _____

NOTE: *The department manager's memorandum at the bottom of the form should not be completed until after the purchase order is placed in Exercise 2.*

Exercise 2 (LO 1) PURCHASE ORDER

Assume you are acting as purchasing agent for Eberle Hardware. On October 2, 20--, order the merchandise specified on Requisition No. 502 in Exercise 1 from Wesner's Supply, 1476 S. Spurr Drive, Miami, FL 33161-1516. Use the purchase order form provided below specifying shipment by AAA freight FOB destination; unit prices as follows:

All steel rubber-tire wheelbarrows	$ 20.35
Garden hose, 1/2", 50 ft.	4.65
Power mower, 21" cut	180.75
Heavy duty rototillers	291.50
Spade shovels	7.45
Long-handle spade shovels	9.30
Spade forks	7.70

After preparing the purchase order, fill in the department manager's memorandum at the bottom of Purchase Requisition No. 502 prepared in Exercise 1. Assume the requisition was approved by Scott Roturt.

Eberle Hardware

110 E. Kirkwood Ave.
Indianapolis, IN 46011-3274

Purchase Order

Order No. 361

Date _____

Deliver By _____

Ship via _____

FOB _____

To _____
_____
_____

Quantity	Description	Unit Price	Total

By _____

Exercise 3 (LO 1) PURCHASE INVOICES

The purchase invoice below received from Wesner's Supply has been referred to you for verification. Compare it with Purchase Order No. 361 in Exercise 2 and verify (a) the quantities ordered, (b) the quantities shipped, (c) the unit prices, (d) the extensions, and (e) the total amount of the invoice. For each item that has been verified, report any discrepancies detected.

INVOICE NO	SOLD TO		SHIP TO	
W S **Wesner's** **Supply**	Eberle Hardware 110 E. Kirkwood Ave. Indianapolis, IN 46011-3274		same	
	INVOICE DATE Oct. 7, 20--	YOUR ORDER NO & DATE 361 Oct. 2, 20--	DATE SHIPPED Oct. 7, 20--	
1476 So. Spurr Drive, Miami, FL 33161-1516		REQUISITION NO	OUR ORDER NO	
TERMS 2/10, n/30	FOB Destination	CAR INITIALS & NO	HOW SHIPPED & ROUTE Freight AAA	SHIPPED FROM Miami

QUANTITY SHIPPED	DESCRIPTION	UNIT PRICE	EXTENSION
15	All steel rubber-tire wheelbarrows	$ 20.35	$ 305.25
25	Garden hose, 1/2", 50 ft.	4.65	116.25
4	Power mower, 21" cut	291.50	1,166.00
5	Heavy duty rototillers	180.75	903.75
24	Spade shovels	7.95	178.80
6	Long-handle spade shovels	9.30	57.00
12	Spade forks	7.70	92.40
			$2,819.45

_____

_____

_____

_____

_____

_____

_____

_____

Exercise 4 (LO 1) TRADE DISCOUNT

Skirvin Enterprises purchased merchandise with a list price of $800, less a trade discount of 10%. Compute the amount to be paid.

_____

_____

_____

Exercise 5 (LO1) CASH DISCOUNT

Geisel's Boating Supplies purchased life preservers and other boating equipment for resale costing $1,200, terms 3/10, n/60.

1. If Geisel makes payment within the discount period, how much will be paid?

_____

_____

2. If the invoice terms were 2/10, n/30, compute the cash discount available to Geisel's if payment is made within the discount period.

_____

_____

Exercise 6 (LO2) GROSS PROFIT

The following information was taken from the records of Hi-Fi Specialists for the month of August 20--:

Sales	$257,800
Sales returns and allowances	1,900
Sales discounts	400
Merchandise inventory, August 1	38,000
Merchandise inventory, August 31	32,000
Purchases	200,000
Purchases returns and allowances	10,200
Purchases discounts	4,000
Freight-In	2,000

Required:

Using the form on page 172, show the computation of gross profit on the income statement for the month of August.

Exercise 6 (Concluded)

Exercise 7 (LO 3) JOURNALIZING PURCHASES AND CASH PAYMENTS

The following transactions occurred during the month of November at O'Henesy Office Equipment and Supply:

Nov. 5   Purchased the following merchandise on account; unit prices are given:

20	Mini-shredders	$ 63.95
10	Hi-speed printer-scanners	900.00
5	Laptop computers	1,995.00

The purchase has a trade discount of 15% and credit terms of 2/10, n/30.

15   Issued a check for the amount due on the November 5 purchase.

Required:

1. Journalize the above transactions in the general journal below.
2. Give the appropriate general journal entry if the payment is not made until December 5.

1. and 2.

GENERAL JOURNAL   PAGE _____

	DATE	DESCRIPTION	POST. REF.	DEBIT	CREDIT	
1						1
2						2
3						3
4						4
5						5
6						6
7						7
8						8
9						9
10						10
11						11

Supporting calculations:

_____

_____

_____

_____

_____

_____

PROBLEMS

Problem 8 (LO3) JOURNALIZING AND POSTING PURCHASES TRANSACTIONS

J. R. Lang, owner of Lang's Galleria, made the following purchases of merchandise on account during the month of November 20--:

Nov. 2 Purchase Invoice No. 611, $4,145, from Ford Distributors.

 5 Purchase Invoice No. 216, $2,165, from Mueller Wholesaler.

15 Purchase Invoice No. 399, $2,895, from Grant White & Co.

19 Purchase Invoice No. 106, $1,845, from Bailey & Hinds, Inc.

22 Purchase Invoice No. 914, $3,225, from Ford Distributors.

28 Purchase Invoice No. 661, $2,175, from Jackson Company.

30 Purchase Invoice No. 716, $3,500, from Mueller Wholesaler.

Required:

1. Record the transactions in the general journal (page 9) on page 175.
2. Post from the journal to the general ledger accounts and the accounts payable ledger accounts (pages 176–177).

Problem 8 (Continued)

1.

GENERAL JOURNAL

PAGE

	DATE	DESCRIPTION	POST. REF.	DEBIT	CREDIT	
1						1
2						2
3						3
4						4
5						5
6						6
7						7
8						8
9						9
10						10
11						11
12						12
13						13
14						14
15						15
16						16
17						17
18						18
19						19
20						20
21						21
22						22
23						23
24						24
25						25
26						26
27						27
28						28
29						29
30						30

Problem 8 (Continued)

2.

GENERAL LEDGER

ACCOUNT Accounts Payable

ACCOUNT NO. 202

DATE	ITEM	POST. REF.	DEBIT	CREDIT	BALANCE	
					DEBIT	CREDIT

ACCOUNT Purchases

ACCOUNT NO. 501

DATE	ITEM	POST. REF.	DEBIT	CREDIT	BALANCE	
					DEBIT	CREDIT

ACCOUNTS PAYABLE LEDGER

NAME Bailey & Hinds, Inc.

ADDRESS

DATE	ITEM	POST. REF.	DEBIT	CREDIT	BALANCE

Problem 8 (Concluded)

NAME Ford Distributors

ADDRESS

DATE	ITEM	POST. REF.	DEBIT	CREDIT	BALANCE

NAME Grant White & Co.

ADDRESS

DATE	ITEM	POST. REF.	DEBIT	CREDIT	BALANCE

NAME Jackson Company

ADDRESS

DATE	ITEM	POST. REF.	DEBIT	CREDIT	BALANCE

NAME Mueller Wholesaler

ADDRESS

DATE	ITEM	POST. REF.	DEBIT	CREDIT	BALANCE

Problem 9 (LO 3/4) PURCHASES TRANSACTIONS AND SCHEDULE OF ACCOUNTS PAYABLE

Tom Bowers operates a business under the name of Tom's Sporting Goods. The books include a general journal and an accounts payable ledger. The following transactions are related to purchases for the month of February:

Feb.	3	Purchased merchandise from Ringer's on account, $498.64. Invoice No. 611; terms 2/10, n/30.
	4	Purchased merchandise on account from Klein Brothers, $780.11. Invoice No. 112; terms 30 days.
	11	Purchased merchandise from Corleon's on account, $2,300.00. Invoice No. 432; terms 30 days.
	15	Received a credit memorandum from Ringer's for $30.00 for merchandise returned that had been purchased on account.

Required:

1. Enter the above transactions in the general journal provided below (page 5).
2. Post from the journal to the general ledger and accounts payable ledger on pages 179–180.
3. Prepare a schedule of accounts payable as of February 28.

1.

GENERAL JOURNAL

PAGE

	DATE	DESCRIPTION	POST. REF.	DEBIT	CREDIT	
1						1
2						2
3						3
4						4
5						5
6						6
7						7
8						8
9						9
10						10
11						11
12						12
13						13
14						14
15						15

Name _____

Problem 9 (Continued)

2.

GENERAL LEDGER

ACCOUNT Accounts Payable   ACCOUNT NO. 202

DATE		ITEM	POST. REF.	DEBIT	CREDIT	BALANCE DEBIT	BALANCE CREDIT
20-- Feb.	1	Balance	✓				3 1 2 5 50

ACCOUNT Purchases   ACCOUNT NO. 501

DATE		ITEM	POST. REF.	DEBIT	CREDIT	BALANCE DEBIT	BALANCE CREDIT
20-- Feb.	1	Balance	✓			2 5 0 0 00	

ACCOUNT Purchases Returns and Allowances   ACCOUNT NO. 501.1

DATE		ITEM	POST. REF.	DEBIT	CREDIT	BALANCE DEBIT	BALANCE CREDIT
20-- Feb.	1	Balance	✓				2 0 0 00

Problem 9 (Concluded)

ACCOUNTS PAYABLE LEDGER

NAME Corleon's

ADDRESS 1894 Winthrop Ave., White Plains, NY 10606-6915

DATE		ITEM	POST. REF.	DEBIT	CREDIT	BALANCE
20-- Feb.	1	Balance	✓			1 6 2 5 50

NAME Klein Brothers

ADDRESS 1728 Camino Real, San Antonio, TX 78238-4420

DATE		ITEM	POST. REF.	DEBIT	CREDIT	BALANCE
20-- Feb.	1	Balance	✓			6 2 5 00

NAME Ringer's

ADDRESS 1500 North Street, Bakersfield, CA 93301-4747

DATE		ITEM	POST. REF.	DEBIT	CREDIT	BALANCE
20-- Feb.	1	Balance	✓			8 7 5 00

3.

Problem 10 (LO 3/4) CASH PAYMENTS TRANSACTIONS AND SCHEDULE OF ACCOUNTS PAYABLE

Chris Bultman operates a retail shoe store called Bultman Shoes. The books include a general journal and an accounts payable ledger. The following transactions are related to cash payments for the month of August:

Aug.   1   Issued Check No. 47 for $900.00 in payment of rent (Rent Expense) for August.

3   Issued Check No. 48 to Blue Suede Shoes Company in payment on account, $640.00, less 2% discount.

9   Issued Check No. 49 to Style-Rite in payment on account, $800.00, less 3% discount.

14   Issued Check No. 50 for $125.28 in payment of utility bill (Utilities Expense).

20   Issued Check No. 51 to Baldo Company in payment for cash purchase, $525.00.

22   Issued Check No. 52 to West Coast Shoes in payment on account, $625.00. A discount of 2% was lost because Bultman neglected to pay the invoice within the discount period.

27   Issued Check No. 53 for $2,000.00 to Bultman for a cash withdrawal for personal use.

Required:

1. Enter the above transactions in the general journal (page 4) on page 182.
2. Post from the journal to the general ledger and accounts payable ledger accounts provided on pages 183–185.
3. Prepare a schedule of accounts payable for Bultman Shoes on August 31, 20--, using the form on page 185.

Problem 10 (Continued)
1.

GENERAL JOURNAL

	DATE		DESCRIPTION	POST. REF.	DEBIT	CREDIT	
1							1
2							2
3							3
4							4
5							5
6							6
7							7
8							8
9							9
10							10
11							11
12							12
13							13
14							14
15							15
16							16
17							17
18							18
19							19
20							20
21							21
22							22
23							23
24							24
25							25
26							26
27							27
28							28
29							29
30							30

Problem 10 (Continued)

2.

GENERAL LEDGER

ACCOUNT   Cash   ACCOUNT NO.   101

DATE		ITEM	POST. REF.	DEBIT	CREDIT	BALANCE	
						DEBIT	CREDIT
20-- Aug.	1	Balance	✓			25 0 0 0 00	

ACCOUNT   Accounts Payable   ACCOUNT NO.   202

DATE		ITEM	POST. REF.	DEBIT	CREDIT	BALANCE	
						DEBIT	CREDIT
20-- Aug.	1	Balance	✓				3 3 6 6 00

ACCOUNT   C. Bultman, Drawing   ACCOUNT NO.   312

DATE		ITEM	POST. REF.	DEBIT	CREDIT	BALANCE	
						DEBIT	CREDIT
20-- Aug.	1	Balance	✓			14 0 0 0 00	

ACCOUNT   Purchases   ACCOUNT NO.   501

DATE		ITEM	POST. REF.	DEBIT	CREDIT	BALANCE	
						DEBIT	CREDIT
20-- Aug.	1	Balance	✓			54 2 6 5 43	

Problem 10 (Continued)

ACCOUNT   Purchases Discounts   ACCOUNT NO.   501.2

DATE		ITEM	POST. REF.	DEBIT	CREDIT	BALANCE	
						DEBIT	CREDIT
20-- Aug.	1	Balance	✓				3 2 5 20

ACCOUNT   Rent Expense   ACCOUNT NO.   521

DATE		ITEM	POST. REF.	DEBIT	CREDIT	BALANCE	
						DEBIT	CREDIT
20-- Aug.	1	Balance	✓			7 2 0 0 00	
			,				

ACCOUNT   Utilities Expense   ACCOUNT NO.   533

DATE		ITEM	POST. REF.	DEBIT	CREDIT	BALANCE	
						DEBIT	CREDIT
20-- Aug.	1	Balance	✓			8 2 2 87	

ACCOUNTS PAYABLE LEDGER

NAME Blue Suede Shoes Company

ADDRESS 2805 South Meridian, Indianapolis, IN 46225-3460

DATE		ITEM	POST. REF.	DEBIT	CREDIT	BALANCE
20-- Aug.	1	Balance	✓			6 4 0 00

Problem 10 (Concluded)

NAME Style-Rite

ADDRESS 6500 9th Street, New Orleans, LA 70115-1122

DATE		ITEM	POST. REF.	DEBIT	CREDIT	BALANCE
20-- Aug.	1	Balance	✓			1 2 0 0 00

NAME West Coast Shoes

ADDRESS 705 Rialto Avenue, Fresno, CA 93705-7845

DATE		ITEM	POST. REF.	DEBIT	CREDIT	BALANCE
20-- Aug.	1	Balance	✓			1 5 2 6 00

3.

Problem 11 (LO 3) CASH PAYMENTS TRANSACTIONS

The following cash payments were made by Demis Music Company during the month of July:

July 5 Paid $600 for rent. Issued Check No. 222.

     12 Purchased $3,250 in merchandise from Hamilton Music Company. Issued Check No. 223.

     18 Made a payment on account to Martinez Guitar Company for $4,500, less a 2% discount for paying within the discount period. Issued Check No. 224.

     25 Paid $2,000 to First National Bank to pay off a note. Issued Check No. 225.

     31 Anna Demis withdrew $5,500 from the business for personal use. Issued Check No. 226.

Required:

Enter the above transactions in a general journal.

GENERAL JOURNAL   PAGE

	DATE	DESCRIPTION	POST. REF.	DEBIT	CREDIT	
1						1
2						2
3						3
4						4
5						5
6						6
7						7
8						8
9						9
10						10
11						11
12						12
13						13
14						14
15						15
16						16
17						17
18						18
19						19
20						20

CHAPTER 11 APPENDIX
THE NET-PRICE METHOD OF RECORDING PURCHASES

LEARNING OBJECTIVES

Objective 1. **Describe the net-price method of recording purchases.**

Under the net-price method, purchases are recorded at the net amount, assuming that all cash discounts will be taken.

Objective 2. **Record purchases and cash payments using the net-price method.**

At the time of purchase, Purchases is debited and Accounts Payable is credited for the gross price less the cash discount. If payment is made within the discount period, Accounts Payable is debited and Cash is credited for the net price. If payment is not made until after the discount period, Accounts Payable is debited for the net price, Purchases Discounts Lost is debited for the discount lost, and Cash is credited for the gross price.

Apx. Exercise (LO 1/2) PURCHASES AND CASH PAYMENTS TRANSACTIONS

Jiang's Accessory Shop had the following transactions during April:

Apr.	2	Purchased merchandise on account from Sag's Apparel for $2,000, terms 2/10, n/30.
	5	Purchased merchandise on account from Lee's Wholesale for $1,800, terms 1/10, n/30.
	11	Paid the amount due to Sag's Apparel for the purchase on April 2.
	25	Paid the amount due to Lee's Wholesale for the purchase on April 5.

Required:
1. Prepare general journal entries for these transactions using the gross-price method.
2. Prepare general journal entries for these transactions using the net-price method.

1.

GENERAL JOURNAL

PAGE

	DATE		DESCRIPTION	POST. REF.	DEBIT	CREDIT	
1							1
2							2
3							3
4							4
5							5
6							6
7							7
8							8
9							9
10							10
11							11
12							12
13							13

Apx. Exercise (Concluded)

2.

GENERAL JOURNAL

PAGE

	DATE	DESCRIPTION	POST. REF.	DEBIT	CREDIT	
1						1
2						2
3						3
4						4
5						5
6						6
7						7
8						8
9						9
10						10
11						11
12						12
13						13
14						14
15						15
16						16
17						17
18						18
19						19
20						20
21						21
22						22
23						23
24						24
25						25
26						26
27						27
28						28
29						29
30						30

CHAPTER 12
SPECIAL JOURNALS

LEARNING OBJECTIVES

Chapter 12 continues the study of sales, cash receipts, purchases, and cash payments transactions in a merchandising business. The focus is on how to account for these transactions more efficiently. Four special journals that speed up and simplify the recording process are introduced.

Objective 1.   Describe, explain the purpose of, and identify transactions recorded in special journals.

A **special journal** is a journal designed for recording only certain kinds of transactions. The types of special journals used by a business should depend on the types of transactions that occur frequently for the business. Four special journals commonly used by businesses are the sales journal, cash receipts journal, purchases journal, and cash payments journal.

Objective 2.   Describe and use the sales journal.

The **sales journal** saves time and energy by simplifying the recording and posting of transactions. It is a "special journal" used to record only credit sales of merchandise.

Credit sales affect Accounts Receivable (debit), Sales (credit), and, if there is a sales tax, Sales Tax Payable (credit). The sales journal provides separate columns for Accounts Receivable Debit, Sales Credit, and Sales Tax Payable Credit. The column totals are posted monthly to the general ledger accounts. Individual customer accounts in the accounts receivable ledger are posted daily.

Objective 3.   Describe and use the cash receipts journal.

Like the sales journal, a **cash receipts journal** saves time and energy in recording and posting transactions. Any time cash is received, the cash receipts journal is the book of original entry, and Cash is always debited. Column headings are established for Cash and other accounts that are frequently used, such as Sales (credit), Accounts Receivable (credit), Bank Credit Card Expense (debit), and Sales Tax Payable (credit). There usually also is a General Credit column for accounts that do not have a special column.

As with other special journals, column totals are posted at the end of the month. Daily postings are made for items in the General Credit column, as well as to the accounts receivable ledger.

Objective 4.   Describe and use the purchases journal.

A **purchases journal** is a special journal used to record only purchases of merchandise on account. This journal may have only a single column for Purchases Debit/Accounts Payable Credit Alternatively, there may be three columns for Purchases Debit, Freight-In Debit, and Accounts Payable Credit.

Each general ledger account used in the purchases journal requires only one posting each period. Individual supplier accounts in the accounts payable ledger are posted daily.

Objective 5.   Describe and use the cash payments journal.

A **cash payments journal** is a special journal used to record only cash payments transactions. The column headings of the cash payments journal will be those accounts that are most frequently affected by the company's cash payments transactions. Column totals are posted to the general ledger accounts at the end of the month. Items in the General Debit column are posted daily. Individual supplier accounts in the accounts payable ledger also are posted daily.

REVIEW QUESTIONS

Instructions: Analyze each of the following items carefully before writing your answer in the column at the right.

	Question	**Answer**
LO 1	1. A journal designed for recording only certain kinds of transactions is called a _____.	_____
LO 1	2. Transactions that occur infrequently, and adjusting and closing entries usually are recorded in the _____.	_____
LO 2	3. A sale is recorded in a sales journal by entering what four pieces of information?	_____ _____ _____ _____
LO 2	4. A(n) _____ journal is a special journal used to record only sales of merchandise on account.	_____
LO 2	5. Sales returns and allowances are generally recorded in the _____ journal.	_____
LO 2	6. Each sales journal entry is posted to the accounts receivable ledger _____.	_____
LO 3	7. Any time the cash receipts journal is used, a debit is made to _____.	_____
LO 3	8. The cash receipts journal is a special journal used to record only _____ transactions.	_____
LO 3	9. Each amount in the General Credit column of the cash receipts journal is posted _____.	_____
LO 4	10. A(n) _____ is a special journal used to record only purchases of merchandise on account.	_____
LO 4	11. Purchases returns and allowances are recorded in the _____.	_____
LO 4	12. The purchases journal for a company like Northern Micro, whose suppliers generally pay the freight charges, would have only a single column labeled Purchases Debit/_____.	_____
LO 4	13. A separate ledger containing an individual account payable for each supplier is called a(n) _____.	_____
LO 4	14. Each purchases journal entry is posted to the accounts payable ledger _____.	_____
LO 5	15. A(n) _____ is a special journal used to record only cash payments transactions.	_____

LO 5 16. Any time the cash payments journal is used, a credit is made to the account called _____. ....   _____

LO 5 17. A cash payment is recorded in the cash payments journal by entering what four pieces of information? ....   _____

_____

_____

_____

LO 5 18. Each amount in the General Debit column of the cash payments journal is posted _____. ....   _____

EXERCISES

Exercise 1 (LO 1) RECORDING TRANSACTIONS IN THE PROPER JOURNAL

Indicate the proper journal in which to record each transaction below by placing an "X" in the appropriate box.

	Journal				
Transaction	**Sales**	**Cash Receipts**	**Purchases**	**Cash Payments**	**General**
a. Made payment to supplier on account.					
b. Sold old delivery equipment for cash.					
c. Sold merchandise on account.					
d. Purchased merchandise for cash.					
e. Returned merchandise to supplier for credit.					
f. Invested additional funds in the business.					
g. Purchased merchandise on account.					

Exercise 2 (LO 2) SALES JOURNAL

Diana Brewer operates the Floor and Window Treatment Center and completed the following transactions related to sales of merchandise on account during the month of February. Sales tax of 5% was included in the amount of each sale.

Feb.   2   Sold wallpaper supplies to Dresson Homes, $98.95, terms n/30. Sale No. 255.
       12   Sold paint to Ray Acuff, $105, terms n/30. Sale No. 256.
       23   Sold miniblinds to Clydette Rupert, $114.83, terms n/30. Sale No. 257.
       24   Sold decorator items to Marty Staple, $35.55, terms n/30. Sale No. 258.
       25   Sold paint to Angel Burtin, $25.57, terms n/30. Sale No. 259.

Exercise 2 (Concluded)

Required:

1. Enter the transactions from the previous page in the sales journal.
2. Total and rule the journal.

1. and 2.

SALES JOURNAL
PAGE

	DATE	SALE NO.	TO WHOM SOLD	POST. REF.	ACCOUNTS RECEIVABLE DEBIT	SALES CREDIT	SALES TAX PAYABLE CREDIT	
1								1
2								2
3								3
4								4
5								5
6								6
7								7

Exercise 3 (LO 3) CASH RECEIPTS JOURNAL

Diana Brewer of the Floor and Window Treatment Center received cash during the month of March as described below.

Mar.		
	2	Received cash from Dresson Homes on account, $98.95.
	12	Received cash from Ray Acuff on account, $105.
	15	Made cash sale to Jean Granite, $404.76, plus 5% sales tax.
	18	Made cash sale to Bill Green, $2,380.95, plus 5% sales tax.
	23	Received cash from Clydette Rupert on account, $114.83.
	24	Received cash from Marty Staple on account, $35.55.
	25	Received cash from Angel Burtin on account, $25.57.
	31	Made cash sales for the month of $22,000, including 5% sales tax (from cash register tape).
	31	Made credit card sales for the month of $28,000, including 5% sales tax.

Required:

1. Enter the above transactions in the cash receipts journal on page 193.
2. Total and rule the journal.

Exercise 3 (Concluded)
1. and 2.

CASH RECEIPTS JOURNAL   PAGE

	DATE	ACCOUNT CREDITED	POST. REF.	GENERAL CREDIT	ACCOUNTS RECEIVABLE CREDIT	SALES CREDIT	SALES TAX PAYABLE CREDIT	CASH DEBIT	
1									1
2									2
3									3
4									4
5									5
6									6
7									7
8									8
9									9
10									10
11									11

Exercise 4 (LO 4) PURCHASES JOURNAL

Tom Bowers operates a business under the name of Tom's Sporting Goods. The books of original entry include a purchases journal and a general journal, in which entries such as Purchase Returns and Allowances are recorded. An accounts payable ledger is used to maintain a record of the amount owed to suppliers. The following transactions are related to purchases for the month of February:

Feb. 3 Purchased merchandise from Ringer's on account, $498.64, Invoice No. 611, terms 2/10, n/30.

4 Purchased merchandise on account from Klein Brothers, $780.11, Invoice No. 112, terms 30 days.

11 Purchased merchandise from Corleon's on account, $2,300, Invoice No. 432, terms 30 days.

15 Received a credit memo from Ringer's for $30 for merchandise returned that had been purchased on account.

Required:

Enter the above transactions in the following purchases journal and general journal:

PURCHASES JOURNAL   PAGE

	DATE	INVOICE NO.	FROM WHOM PURCHASED	POST. REF.	PURCHASES DEBIT ACCTS. PAY. CREDIT	
1						1
2						2
3						3
4						4
5						5

Exercise 4 (Concluded)

GENERAL JOURNAL

PAGE

	DATE	DESCRIPTION	POST. REF.	DEBIT	CREDIT	
1						1
2						2
3						3

Exercise 5 (LO 5) CASH PAYMENTS JOURNAL

The following cash payments were made by Demis Music Company during the month of July:

July   5   Paid $600 for rent. Issued Check No. 222.

      12   Purchased $3,250 in merchandise from Hamilton Music Company. Issued Check No. 223.

      18   Made a payment on account to Martinez Guitar Company for $4,500, less a 2% discount for paying within the discount period. Issued Check No. 224.

      25   Paid $2,000 to First National Bank to pay off a note. Issued Check No. 225.

      31   Anna Demis withdrew $5,500 from the business for personal use. Issued Check No. 226.

Required:

1. Enter the above transactions in the cash payments journal.
2. Total, rule, and prove the journal.

1. and 2.

CASH PAYMENTS JOURNAL

PAGE

	DATE	CK. NO.	ACCOUNT DEBITED	POST. REF.	GENERAL DEBIT	ACCOUNTS PAYABLE DEBIT	PURCHASES DEBIT	PURCHASES DISCOUNTS CREDIT	CASH CREDIT	
1										1
2										2
3										3
4										4
5										5
6										6
7										7

PROBLEMS

Problem 6 (LO 2/3) SALES JOURNAL AND CASH RECEIPTS JOURNAL

The following information represents transactions for Kwan Chu's Fish Market for the month of July 20--. Sales tax is 6%.

July 1 Sold merchandise on account to B. A. Smith, $137.50, plus sales tax. Sale No. 33.

3 B. A. Smith returned merchandise, $15, plus sales tax, for a credit. Credit Memo No. 11.

5 Sold merchandise on account to L. L. Unis, $218, plus sales tax. Sale No. 34.

7 Made cash sales for the week, $325.44, plus sales tax.

10 Sold merchandise on account to W. P. Clark, $208, plus sales tax. Sale No. 35.

11 Received $129.85 from B. A. Smith, on account.

13 W. P. Clark returned merchandise, $22, plus sales tax, for a credit. Credit Memo No. 12.

14 Made cash sales for the week, $411.20, plus sales tax.

16 Sold merchandise on account to B. A. Smith, $282.50, plus sales tax. Sale No. 36.

17 Received $231.08 from L. L. Unis, on account.

21 Made cash sales for the week, $292.50, plus sales tax.

24 Sold merchandise on account to L. L. Unis, $224.50, plus sales tax. Sale No. 37.

28 Made cash sales for the week, $300.50, plus sales tax.

31 Received $197.16 from W. P. Clark, on account.

Required:

1. Using the information provided, record the transactions in the sales journal, cash receipts journal, or general journal as required.

2. Total and rule the column totals.

1. and 2.

GENERAL JOURNAL   PAGE

	DATE		DESCRIPTION	POST. REF.	DEBIT	CREDIT	
1							1
2							2
3							3
4							4
5							5
6							6
7							7
8							8
9							9
10							10

Problem 6 (Concluded)

SALES JOURNAL

PAGE

	DATE	SALE NO.	TO WHOM SOLD	POST. REF.	ACCOUNTS RECEIVABLE DEBIT	SALES CREDIT	SALES TAX PAYABLE CREDIT	
1								1
2								2
3								3
4								4
5								5
6								6
7								7
8								8

CASH RECEIPTS JOURNAL

PAGE

	DATE	ACCOUNT CREDITED	POST. REF.	GENERAL CREDIT	ACCOUNTS RECEIVABLE CREDIT	SALES CREDIT	SALES TAX PAYABLE CREDIT	CASH DEBIT	
1									1
2									2
3									3
4									4
5									5
6									6
7									7
8									8
9									9
10									10

Problem 7 (LO 2) SALES JOURNAL, GENERAL LEDGER, AND ACCOUNTS RECEIVABLE LEDGER

H. K. Smythe operates Leather All, a leather shop that sells luggage, handbags, business cases, and other leather goods. During the month of May, the following sales on account were made:

May
3 Sold merchandise on account to T. A. Pigdon, $247.50, plus sales tax of $14.85. Sale No. 51.
4 Sold merchandise on account to J. R. Feyton, $55, plus sales tax of $3.30. Sale No. 52.
6 Sold merchandise on account to P. C. McMurdy, $99, plus sales tax of $5.94. Sale No. 53.
10 Sold merchandise on account to J. T. Messer, $175, plus sales tax of $10.50. Sale No. 54.
12 Sold merchandise on account to A. F. Schlitz, $355, plus sales tax of $21.30. Sale No. 55.
13 Sold merchandise on account to J. R. Feyton, $215, plus sales tax of $12.90. Sale No. 56.
20 Sold merchandise on account to P. C. McMurdy, $400, plus sales tax of $24. Sale No. 57.
28 Sold merchandise on account to J. T. Messer, $255, plus sales tax of $15.30. Sale No. 58.

Required:

1. Enter the above transactions in the sales journal (page 1) provided below.
2. Post the entries in the sales journal to the accounts receivable ledger on pages 198–199.
3. Total and verify the column totals and rule the sales journal. Complete the summary postings to the general ledger on page 198.

1. and 3.

SALES JOURNAL

PAGE 1

	DATE	SALE NO.	TO WHOM SOLD	POST. REF.	ACCOUNTS RECEIVABLE DEBIT	SALES CREDIT	SALES TAX PAYABLE CREDIT	
1								1
2								2
3								3
4								4
5								5
6								6
7								7
8								8
9								9
10								10

Problem 7 (Continued)

3.

GENERAL LEDGER

ACCOUNT Accounts Receivable   ACCOUNT NO. 122

DATE		ITEM	POST. REF.	DEBIT	CREDIT	BALANCE	
						DEBIT	CREDIT
20-- May	1	Balance	✓			8 3 4 00	

ACCOUNT Sales Tax Payable   ACCOUNT NO. 231

DATE		ITEM	POST. REF.	DEBIT	CREDIT	BALANCE	
						DEBIT	CREDIT

ACCOUNT Sales   ACCOUNT NO. 401

DATE		ITEM	POST. REF.	DEBIT	CREDIT	BALANCE	
						DEBIT	CREDIT

2.

ACCOUNTS RECEIVABLE LEDGER

NAME J. R. Feyton

ADDRESS 6022 Columbia, St. Louis, MO 63139-1906

DATE		ITEM	POST. REF.	DEBIT	CREDIT	BALANCE

Problem 7 (Concluded)

NAME P. C. McMurdy

ADDRESS 1214 N. 2nd St., E. St. Louis, IL 62201-2679

DATE		ITEM	POST. REF.	DEBIT	CREDIT	BALANCE
20-- May	1	Balance	✓			1 2 5 00

NAME J. T. Messer

ADDRESS P.O. Box 249, Chesterfield, MO 63017-3901

DATE		ITEM	POST. REF.	DEBIT	CREDIT	BALANCE
20-- May	1	Balance	✓			1 7 7 00

NAME T. A. Pigdon

ADDRESS 1070 Purcell, University City, MO 63130-1546

DATE		ITEM	POST. REF.	DEBIT	CREDIT	BALANCE
20-- May	1	Balance	✓			2 8 0 00

NAME A. F. Schlitz

ADDRESS 800 Lindbergh Blvd., St. Louis, MO 63166-1546

DATE		ITEM	POST. REF.	DEBIT	CREDIT	BALANCE
20-- May	1	Balance	✓			2 5 2 00

Problem 8 (LO 3) CASH RECEIPTS JOURNAL, GENERAL JOURNAL, GENERAL LEDGER, AND ACCOUNTS RECEIVABLE LEDGER

Paula Angelillis operates Hard-to-Find Auto Parts Store. Much of her business is by mail. The books of original entry include a cash receipts journal and a general journal. The following transactions related to sales and cash receipts occurred during June:

June	1	Received $300 from A. K. Wells, including $14.29 of sales tax, for field cash sale. (Field cash sales are not included in cash register tapes.)
	5	Received $125.60 from L. Strous on account.
	10	Received $263.25 from D. Manning on account.
	12	Q. Striker returned merchandise for credit. The sales price was $215, plus sales tax of $10.75.
	18	Received $58.25 from D. Warding on account.
	20	Received $1,000 from B. L. Stryker, including $47.62 tax (field cash sale).
	21	Received $29.99 from L. Clese on account.
	24	R. Popielarz returned merchandise for credit. The sales price was $116.25, plus sales tax of $5.81.
	27	Received $426 from L. LeCount on account.
	30	Made cash and bank credit card sales for the month of $8,200, plus sales tax of $410. Bank credit card expense is $80.

Required:

1. Enter each transaction in either the cash receipts journal (page 18) or the general journal (page 5) provided. Total, verify the totals, and rule the cash receipts journal.
2. Make the individual postings required from the cash receipts journal and the general journal to the general and accounts receivable ledgers.
3. Make the summary postings from the cash receipts journal to the general ledger.

1.

GENERAL JOURNAL

PAGE 5

	DATE		DESCRIPTION	POST. REF.	DEBIT	CREDIT	
1							1
2							2
3							3
4							4
5							5
6							6
7							7
8							8
9							9
10							10

Problem 8 (Continued)

CASH RECEIPTS JOURNAL

PAGE 18

	DATE	ACCOUNT CREDITED	POST. REF.	GENERAL CREDIT	ACCOUNTS REC. CREDIT	SALES CREDIT	SALES TAX PAYABLE CREDIT	BANK CR. CARD EXP. DEBIT	CASH DEBIT	
1										1
2										2
3										3
4										4
5										5
6										6
7										7
8										8
9										9
10										10
11										11
12										12

2. and 3.

GENERAL LEDGER

ACCOUNT Cash   ACCOUNT NO. 101

DATE		ITEM	POST. REF.	DEBIT	CREDIT	BALANCE DEBIT	BALANCE CREDIT
20-- June	1	Balance	✓			13 2 0 0 25	

ACCOUNT Accounts Receivable   ACCOUNT NO. 122

DATE		ITEM	POST. REF.	DEBIT	CREDIT	BALANCE DEBIT	BALANCE CREDIT
20-- June	1	Balance	✓			1 2 5 0 90	

Problem 8 (Continued)

ACCOUNT   Sales Tax Payable   ACCOUNT NO. 231

DATE		ITEM	POST. REF.	DEBIT	CREDIT	BALANCE	
						DEBIT	CREDIT
20-- June	1	Balance	✓				1 2 5 00

ACCOUNT   Sales   ACCOUNT NO. 401

DATE	ITEM	POST. REF.	DEBIT	CREDIT	BALANCE	
					DEBIT	CREDIT

ACCOUNT   Sales Returns and Allowances   ACCOUNT NO. 401.1

DATE	ITEM	POST. REF.	DEBIT	CREDIT	BALANCE	
					DEBIT	CREDIT

ACCOUNT   Bank Credit Card Expense   ACCOUNT NO. 513

DATE	ITEM	POST. REF.	DEBIT	CREDIT	BALANCE	
					DEBIT	CREDIT

Problem 8 (Continued)

ACCOUNTS RECEIVABLE LEDGER

NAME L. Clese

ADDRESS 875 Glenway Drive, Glendale, MO 63122-4112

DATE		ITEM	POST. REF.	DEBIT	CREDIT	BALANCE
20-- June	1	Balance	✓			2 9 99

NAME L. LeCount

ADDRESS 1439 East Broad Street, Columbus, OH 43205-9892

DATE		ITEM	POST. REF.	DEBIT	CREDIT	BALANCE
20-- June	1	Balance	✓			4 2 6 00

NAME D. Manning

ADDRESS 2101 Cumberland Road, Noblesville, IN 47870-2435

DATE		ITEM	POST. REF.	DEBIT	CREDIT	BALANCE
20-- June	1	Balance	✓			2 6 3 25

Problem 8 (Concluded)

NAME R. Popielarz

ADDRESS 3001 Hillcrest Drive, Dallas, PA 18612-6854

DATE		ITEM	POST. REF.	DEBIT	CREDIT	BALANCE
20-- June	1	Balance	✓			1 2 2 06

NAME Q. Striker

ADDRESS 4113 Main Street, Beech Grove, IN 46107-9643

DATE		ITEM	POST. REF.	DEBIT	CREDIT	BALANCE
20-- June	1	Balance	✓			2 2 5 75

NAME L. Strous

ADDRESS 2215 N. State Road 135, Greenwood, IN 46142-6432

DATE		ITEM	POST. REF.	DEBIT	CREDIT	BALANCE
20-- June	1	Balance	✓			1 2 5 60

NAME D. Warding

ADDRESS 1100 W. Main Street, Carmel, IN 46032-2364

DATE		ITEM	POST. REF.	DEBIT	CREDIT	BALANCE
20-- June	1	Balance	✓			5 8 25

Problem 9 (LO 4) PURCHASES JOURNAL, GENERAL LEDGER, AND ACCOUNTS PAYABLE LEDGER

J. R. Lang, owner of Lang's Galleria, made the following purchases of merchandise on account during the month of November 20--.

Nov. 2 Purchase Invoice No. 611, $4,145, from Ford Distributors.
5 Purchase Invoice No. 216, $2,165, from Mueller Wholesaler.
15 Purchase Invoice No. 399, $2,895, from Grant White & Co.
19 Purchase Invoice No. 106, $1,845, from Bailey & Hinds, Inc.
22 Purchase Invoice No. 914, $3,225, from Ford Distributors.
28 Purchase Invoice No. 661, $2,175, from Jackson Company.
30 Purchase Invoice No. 716, $3,500, from Mueller Wholesaler.

Required:

1. Record the transactions in the purchases journal (page 9). Total and rule the journal.
2. Post from the purchases journal to the general ledger accounts and to the accounts payable ledger accounts.

1.

PURCHASES JOURNAL PAGE 9

	DATE	INVOICE NO.	FROM WHOM PURCHASED	POST. REF.	PURCHASES DEBIT ACCTS. PAY. CREDIT	
1						1
2						2
3						3
4						4
5						5
6						6
7						7
8						8
9						9
10						10

2.

GENERAL LEDGER

ACCOUNT Accounts Payable   ACCOUNT NO. 202

DATE	ITEM	POST. REF.	DEBIT	CREDIT	BALANCE DEBIT	CREDIT

Problem 9 (Continued)

ACCOUNT   Purchases

ACCOUNT NO.   501

DATE	ITEM	POST. REF.	DEBIT	CREDIT	BALANCE	
					DEBIT	CREDIT

ACCOUNTS PAYABLE LEDGER

NAME   Bailey & Hinds, Inc.

ADDRESS

DATE	ITEM	POST. REF.	DEBIT	CREDIT	BALANCE

NAME   Ford Distributors

ADDRESS

DATE	ITEM	POST. REF.	DEBIT	CREDIT	BALANCE

NAME   Grant White & Co.

ADDRESS

DATE	ITEM	POST. REF.	DEBIT	CREDIT	BALANCE

Problem 9 (Concluded)

NAME Jackson Company

ADDRESS

DATE	ITEM	POST. REF.	DEBIT	CREDIT	BALANCE

NAME Mueller Wholesaler

ADDRESS

DATE	ITEM	POST. REF.	DEBIT	CREDIT	BALANCE

Problem 10 (LO 5) CASH PAYMENTS JOURNAL, GENERAL LEDGER, AND ACCOUNTS PAYABLE LEDGER

Chris Bultman operates a retail shoe store. The following transactions are related to cash payments for the month of August:

Aug. 1   Issued Check No. 47 for $900 in payment of rent (Rent Expense) for August.
3   Issued Check No. 48 to Blue Suede Shoes Company in payment on account, $640, less 2% discount.
9   Issued Check No. 49 to Style-Rite in payment on account, $800, less 3% discount.
14   Issued Check No. 50 for $125.28 in payment of utility bill (Utilities Expense).
20   Issued Check No. 51 to Baldo Company in payment for cash purchase, $525.
22   Issued Check No. 52 to West Coast Shoes in payment on account, $625. A discount of 2% was lost because Bultman neglected to pay the invoice within the discount period.
27   Issued Check No. 53 for $2,000 to Bultman for a cash withdrawal for personal use.

Required:

1. Enter the above transactions in the cash payments journal (page 9).
2. Enter the totals, rule, and prove the journal.
3. Complete individual postings to the general ledger and accounts payable ledger and summary postings to the general ledger. The relevant accounts are provided on pages 208–210.

Problem 10 (Continued)

1. and 2.

CASH PAYMENTS JOURNAL

	DATE		CK. NO.	ACCOUNT DEBITED	POST. REF.	GENERAL DEBIT	ACCOUNTS PAYABLE DEBIT	PURCHASES DEBIT	PURCHASES DISCOUNTS CREDIT	CASH CREDIT	
1											1
2											2
3											3
4											4
5											5
6											6
7											7
8											8
9											9
10											10

3.

GENERAL LEDGER

ACCOUNT   Cash

ACCOUNT NO.   101

DATE		ITEM	POST. REF.	DEBIT	CREDIT	BALANCE DEBIT	BALANCE CREDIT
20-- Aug.	1	Balance	✓			25 0 0 0 00	

ACCOUNT   Accounts Payable

ACCOUNT NO.   202

DATE		ITEM	POST. REF.	DEBIT	CREDIT	BALANCE DEBIT	BALANCE CREDIT
20-- Aug.	1	Balance	✓				3 3 6 6 00

Problem 10 (Continued)

ACCOUNT C. Bultman, Drawing   ACCOUNT NO. 312

DATE		ITEM	POST. REF.	DEBIT	CREDIT	BALANCE DEBIT	BALANCE CREDIT
20-- Aug.	1	Balance	✓			14 0 0 0 00	

ACCOUNT Purchases   ACCOUNT NO. 501

DATE		ITEM	POST. REF.	DEBIT	CREDIT	BALANCE DEBIT	BALANCE CREDIT
20-- Aug.	1	Balance	✓			54 2 6 5 43	

ACCOUNT Purchases Discounts   ACCOUNT NO. 501.2

DATE		ITEM	POST. REF.	DEBIT	CREDIT	BALANCE DEBIT	BALANCE CREDIT
20-- Aug.	1	Balance	✓				3 2 5 20

ACCOUNT Rent Expense   ACCOUNT NO. 521

DATE		ITEM	POST. REF.	DEBIT	CREDIT	BALANCE DEBIT	BALANCE CREDIT
20-- Aug.	1	Balance	✓			7 2 0 0 00	

ACCOUNT Utilities Expense   ACCOUNT NO. 533

DATE		ITEM	POST. REF.	DEBIT	CREDIT	BALANCE DEBIT	BALANCE CREDIT
20-- Aug.	1	Balance	✓			8 2 2 87	

Problem 10 (Concluded)

ACCOUNTS PAYABLE LEDGER

NAME Blue Suede Shoes Company

ADDRESS

DATE		ITEM	POST. REF.	DEBIT	CREDIT	BALANCE
20-- Aug.	1	Balance	✓			6 4 0 00

NAME Style-Rite

ADDRESS

DATE		ITEM	POST. REF.	DEBIT	CREDIT	BALANCE
20-- Aug.	1	Balance	✓			1 2 0 0 00

NAME West Coast Shoes

ADDRESS

DATE		ITEM	POST. REF.	DEBIT	CREDIT	BALANCE
20-- Aug.	1	Balance	✓			1 5 2 6 00

CHAPTER 13
ACCOUNTING FOR MERCHANDISE INVENTORY

LEARNING OBJECTIVES

Merchandise inventory plays an important role in determining the amount of net income on the income statement. For a merchandising business, the cost of goods sold is the largest individual expense on the income statement. In this chapter, you will learn how to determine the dollar amounts assigned to the cost of goods sold and ending merchandise inventory.

Objective 1.   Explain the impact of merchandise inventory on the financial statements.

It is important to report accurately the dollar amount of merchandise inventory on the income statement. An error in counting the physical ending merchandise inventory will not only affect the current year's net income but will also affect the following year's net income. This is because the ending merchandise inventory for the current year becomes the beginning merchandise inventory for the following year. In the year that the error in counting the merchandise inventory is made, the statement of owner's equity and balance sheet will also be in error. However, at the end of the second year, the income statement will be in error, but the statement of owner's equity and balance sheet will be correctly stated. This is because an ending inventory error in the first year "washes out" over the two-year period.

Objective 2.   Describe the two principal systems of accounting for merchandise inventory—the periodic system and the perpetual system.

There are two principal systems of accounting for inventory: (1) the periodic system and (2) the perpetual system.

Under the **periodic system**, the current merchandise inventory and the cost of goods sold are not determined until the end of the accounting period when a **physical inventory** is taken. The purchases account is debited for the cost of all goods purchased. The balance in the merchandise inventory account is merely a record of the most recent physical inventory.

Under the **perpetual system**, the merchandise inventory account is debited for the cost of all goods bought, including freight charges, and credited for the cost of all goods sold. In addition, this account is debited when customers return merchandise and credited when returns, allowances, and discounts are granted by suppliers. The balance of the merchandise inventory account represents the cost of goods on hand at all times.

Objective 3.   Compute the costs allocated to the ending inventory and cost of goods sold using different inventory methods.

A **physical inventory** is a count of all the goods that have not been sold. This is normally done when the inventory is at its lowest level, which corresponds with the end of the company's **natural business year**. Only goods that are the property of the firm should be included in a physical inventory. Goods held on **consignment** and goods shipped **FOB shipping point** as of the balance sheet date should be excluded. Goods shipped **FOB destination** and in transit as of the balance sheet date should be included in the inventory count. Because prices are constantly changing, there are four acceptable methods to assigning costs to the ending inventory.

When each unit of inventory can be specifically identified, the **specific identification method** can be used. To use this method, inventory items must be physically different from each other or must have serial numbers.

The **first-in, first-out (FIFO)** method assumes that the first goods bought are the first goods sold. Therefore, the latest goods bought remain in inventory.

Another method of allocating merchandise cost is called the **weighted-average method, or average cost method**. This costing method is based on the average cost of identical units. The weighted average is calculated

by dividing the total cost of merchandise available for sale by the total number of units available for sale. To compute the cost of goods sold, simply multiply the number of units sold by the weighted-average cost per unit.

A fourth method of allocating merchandise cost is called the **last-in, first-out (LIFO) method**. It assumes that the sales in the period were made from the most recently purchased goods. Therefore, the earliest goods bought remain in inventory. It is important to emphasize that this method is used to allocate costs to inventory. In most cases, it does not correspond to the physical flow of merchandise. When prices are rising, net income calculated by using the LIFO method will be less than net income calculated by using either the FIFO or the weighted-average method.

When a firm uses a **perpetual inventory system**, a continuous record is maintained for the quantities and costs of goods on hand at all times. Perpetual inventories do not eliminate the need for taking periodic physical inventories. If a difference is found between the physical count and the amount in the perpetual inventory records, the adjustment to merchandise inventory is required. This adjustment is illustrated in Chapter 14.

The **lower-of-cost-or-market method** is used whenever the replacement cost of the ending inventory is less than its actual cost. When this happens, the following entry is made:

Loss on Write-Down of Inventory	xxx	
Merchandise Inventory		xxx

This practice is consistent with the practice of conservatism.

Objective 4.   Estimate the ending inventory and cost of goods sold by using the gross profit and retail inventory methods.

Businesses using the periodic inventory method must estimate their ending inventory and cost of goods sold in order to provide interim financial statements. Two generally accepted methods are the gross profit method and the retail inventory method.

Under the **gross profit method**, the firm's normal gross profit percentage [(net sales – cost of goods sold)/net sales] can be used to estimate the cost of goods sold and ending inventory. Cost of goods sold can be estimated by multiplying the gross profit percentage by the net sales and subtracting this amount from net sales.

The **retail inventory method** requires keeping records of both the cost and selling (retail) prices of all goods purchased. The percentage of total goods available for sale at cost divided by the total goods available for sale at retail is used to estimate cost of goods sold and ending inventory.

REVIEW QUESTIONS

Instructions: Analyze each of the following items carefully before writing your answer in the column at the right.

	Question	**Answer**
LO 1	**1.** Understating the ending inventory for the year 20-1 will cause net income for the year 20-1 to be _____.	_____
LO 1	**2.** Overstating the ending inventory for the year 20-1 will cause net income for the year 20-2 to be _____.	_____
LO 2	**3.** The two principal systems of accounting for inventory are the _____ and _____.	_____ _____

LO 2   **4.** Under the _____ system, the merchandise inventory account is debited for the cost of all goods purchased. ....   _____

LO 3   **5.** The process of counting all the goods on hand at the end of the period is called taking a(n) _____. ....   _____

LO 3   **6.** A fiscal year that starts and ends at the time the stock of goods is normally at its lowest level is known as a(n) _____. ....   _____

LO 3   **7.** A special form used to record information when taking a physical inventory is called a(n) _____. ....   _____

LO 3   **8.** In the term "FOB shipping point," FOB stands for _____. ....   _____

LO 3   **9.** If goods are shipped "FOB _____," the seller pays for shipping and the goods are the property of the selling company until received by the buying company. ....   _____

LO 3   **10.** Name the four methods of assigning cost to the ending inventory and cost of goods sold. . ...   _____

_____

_____

_____

LO 3   **11.** A costing method that assumes the first goods bought were the first goods sold and, therefore, the latest goods bought remain in inventory is called _____. ....   _____

LO 3   **12.** A costing method that assumes the sales in the period were made from the most recently purchased goods and, therefore, the earliest goods bought remain in inventory is called _____. ....   _____

LO 3   **13.** When prices are rising, the cost method that will result in the highest net income is _____. ....   _____

LO 3   **14.** When prices are rising, the cost method that will result in the lowest ending inventory is _____. ....   _____

LO 3   **15.** In the application of "lower-of-cost-or-market," the term "market" refers to _____. ....   _____

LO 3   **16.** The practice of conservatism states we should never anticipate _____ but always anticipate _____. ....   _____

_____

LO 3   **17.** The difference between the cost and market value is considered a loss due to holding _____. ....   _____

LO 3   **18.** The dollar amount of the loss due to holding inventory is normally charged to an account entitled _____. ....   _____

LO 4   **19.** Under the _____ method, the firm's normal gross profit can be used to estimate the cost of goods sold and ending inventory. ....   _____

LO 4   **20.** The _____ method of estimating inventory requires keeping records of both the cost and selling (retail) prices of all goods purchased. .....   _____

EXERCISES

Exercise 1 (LO 2) JOURNAL ENTRIES FOR PERIODIC AND PERPETUAL INVENTORY METHODS

The following inventory transactions occurred for Riegler Company during the month of April:

Apr.   2   Purchased merchandise on account, $2,500.
          5   Purchased merchandise for cash, $3,000.
          10   Sold merchandise on account for $500. The cost of the merchandise sold was $300.
          15   Sold merchandise that cost $250 for $400 cash.

Required:

1.   Prepare general journal entries for the above transactions. Assume the periodic inventory system is used.
2.   Prepare general journal entries for the above transactions. Assume the perpetual inventory system is used.

Exercise 1 (Continued)
1. Periodic Inventory System

GENERAL JOURNAL   PAGE _____

	DATE	DESCRIPTION	POST. REF.	DEBIT	CREDIT	
1						1
2						2
3						3
4						4
5						5
6						6
7						7
8						8
9						9
10						10
11						11
12						12
13						13
14						14
15						15
16						16
17						17
18						18
19						19
20						20
21						21
22						22
23						23
24						24
25						25
26						26
27						27
28						28
29						29
30						30
31						31
32						32
33						33

Exercise 1 (Concluded)
2. Perpetual Inventory System

GENERAL JOURNAL

PAGE

	DATE	DESCRIPTION	POST. REF.	DEBIT	CREDIT	
1						1
2						2
3						3
4						4
5						5
6						6
7						7
8						8
9						9
10						10
11						11
12						12
13						13
14						14
15						15
16						16
17						17
18						18
19						19
20						20
21						21
22						22
23						23
24						24
25						25
26						26
27						27
28						28
29						29
30						30
31						31
32						32
33						33

Exercise 2 (LO 3) COMPUTING COST OF GOODS SOLD, ENDING INVENTORY, AND GROSS PROFIT

Sally Holvey operates Sally's Used Cars. Sally uses the specific identification costing method for determining ending inventory and cost of goods sold. Provided below is a list of the cars that were available for sale during the past month with the cost and selling price if sold. Based on this information, compute the cost of goods sold, cost of the ending inventory, and gross profit.

Year	Model	Cost	Selling Price
2009	Mercury Grand Marquis	$12,000	$13,450
2008	Ford Explorer	21,500	
2008	Ford Focus	12,400	13,992
2006	Ford Mustang	13,200	14,450
2005	Honda Accord	10,200	12,900
2005	Jeep Wrangler	11,400	
2005	Porsche 911	42,500	49,900
2007	Porsche Boxster	32,500	34,200
2004	Honda CR-V	10,500	
2006	BMW M5	39,500	
1990	BMW 325i	4,200	

Exercise 3 (LO 3) LOWER-OF-COST-OR-MARKET

Keast Enterprises has four items of inventory with costs and market values at year-end as follows:

Item	Cost	Market Value
1	$20,000	$18,000
2	45,000	48,000
3	18,000	16,000
4	88,000	90,000

Compute the amount of Keast's inventory at year-end using the lower-of-cost-or-market method applied to:

a. The total inventory.

b. Each item in the inventory.

Exercise 4 (LO 4) RETAIL INVENTORY METHOD

Tyrone Sales Company started in the retail business on July 1. Net purchases to December 31 amounted to $140,000, and the goods were marked to sell at retail for $200,000. Net sales amounted to $160,000. Using the retail method, compute the approximate cost of the inventory on December 31.

_____

_____

_____

_____

_____

_____

_____

_____

_____

_____

_____

_____

_____

_____

_____

_____

_____

_____

_____

_____

_____

_____

_____

_____

PROBLEMS

Problem 5 (LO 3) FIFO, LIFO, AND WEIGHTED-AVERAGE

Hickman Equipment Co. sells stereo equipment and is interested in the effect that the inventory method has on the information provided in the financial statements. You have been asked to demonstrate the impact of various inventory methods for one item of merchandise handled by Hickman. Use the information provided below for your analysis.

	Units	Unit Price	Total Cost
Beginning inventory	50	$120	$ 6,000
Purchases during period:			
1st purchase	80	130	10,400
2nd purchase	100	150	15,000
3rd purchase	70	160	11,200
Total	300		$42,600

Number of units sold: 280
Net sales revenue for the period: $54,000

Required:

Compute cost of goods sold, ending inventory, and gross profit using the FIFO, LIFO, and weighted-average cost methods.

FIFO Inventory Method

Date 20-1/ 20-2		Cost of Goods Sold			Cost of Ending Inventory		
		Units	Unit Price	Total	Units	Unit Price	Total

Problem 5 (Concluded)

LIFO Inventory Method

Date 20-1/ 20-2		Cost of Goods Sold			Cost of Ending Inventory		
		Units	Unit Price	Total	Units	Unit Price	Total

_____
_____
_____
_____

Weighted-Average Method

_____
_____
_____
_____
_____
_____
_____
_____
_____
_____
_____
_____

Problem 6 (LO 4) GROSS PROFIT METHOD OF ESTIMATING INVENTORY

The normal gross profit of Zello Company is 30%. The store was destroyed by fire the night of May 27, but the records were saved. The accounts show that the inventory at the start of the year cost $120,000, net purchases to May 27 were $140,000, and net sales to date were $230,000.

Required:

Calculate the estimated cost of the goods destroyed by the fire.

Problem 7 (LO 4) RETAIL INVENTORY METHOD

Assume the following information for Vargo Company:

	Cost	Retail
Inventory, June 1	$200,000	$300,000
Net purchases for June	400,000	700,000
Net sales for June		780,000

Required:

Estimate the June 30 inventory using the retail inventory method.

CHAPTER 13 APPENDIX
PERPETUAL INVENTORY METHOD:
LIFO AND MOVING-AVERAGE METHODS

APPENDIX LEARNING OBJECTIVES

In Chapter 13, you learned how to apply the LIFO and weighted-average inventory methods under the **periodic inventory system**. In the appendix to Chapter 13, the **perpetual inventory system** is illustrated. Recall that all calculations under the periodic system are done at the end of the accounting period. Under the perpetual system, costs are computed every time merchandise is purchased and sold. These costs are used to maintain a running record of the cost of goods sold to date and the balance of inventory on hand.

Objective 1.   Compute the costs allocated to the ending inventory and cost of goods sold using the perpetual LIFO inventory method.

LIFO has layers. Under perpetual LIFO, each time inventory is purchased, a new layer of inventory is formed. Each time inventory is sold, it is assumed that the units came from the most recently purchased layer, followed by the next most recently purchased layer.

Objective 2.   Compute the costs allocated to the ending inventory and cost of goods sold using the perpetual moving-average inventory method.

When using the perpetual moving-average inventory method, each time inventory is purchased, a new average cost per unit is calculated. When inventory is sold, the most recent average cost is used to measure cost of goods sold and the remaining inventory on hand.

APPENDIX EXERCISES

Apx. Exercise 1 (LO 1) PERPETUAL LIFO INVENTORY METHOD

The beginning inventory, purchases, and sales for Smaltz Sailing Company for the month of September are provided below.

Date	Beginning Inventory and Purchases		Sales
	Units	Cost/Unit	Units
Sept. 1 (BI)	100	$6.00	
	100	6.20	
	200	6.30	
Sept. 10			250
Sept. 15	600	6.50	
Sept. 30			300
BI: Beginning Inventory			

Required:

Calculate the total amount assigned to cost of goods sold during September and the ending inventory on September 30 using the perpetual LIFO inventory method.

Apx. Exercise 1 (Concluded)

Date	Purchases			Cost of Goods Sold				Inventory on Hand				
	Units	Cost/ Unit	Total	Units	Cost/ Unit	CGS	Cum. CGS	Layer	Units	Cost/ Unit	Layer Cost	Total
9/1 (BI)												
9/10												
9/15												
9/30												
Cost of Goods Sold during September												

BI: Beginning Inventory

Apx. Exercise 2 (LO 2) PERPETUAL MOVING-AVERAGE INVENTORY METHOD

Required:

Using the inventory data provided in Apx. Exercise 1, calculate the total amount assigned to cost of goods sold during September and the ending inventory on September 30 using the perpetual moving-average inventory method.

Date	Purchases			Cost of Goods Sold			Inventory on Hand and Average Cost per Unit		
	Units	Cost/ Unit	Total	Units	Cost/ Unit	CGS	Cum. CGS	Cost of Purchase or (Sale)	Cost of Inventory on Hand	Units on Hand	Average Cost/ Unit
9/1 (BI)											
9/10											
9/15											
9/30											
Cost of Goods Sold during September											

BI: Beginning Inventory

Apx. Exercise 3 (LO 1) PERPETUAL LIFO INVENTORY METHOD

The beginning inventory, purchases, and sales for McGuire Flag Company for the month of October are provided below.

Date	Beginning Inventory and Purchases		Sales
	Units	Cost/Unit	Units
Oct. 1 (BI)	100	$3.00	
	150	3.20	
	250	3.50	
Oct. 8			450
Oct. 20	300	3.80	
Oct. 31			200
BI: Beginning Inventory			

Required:

Calculate the total amount to be assigned to cost of goods sold during October and the ending inventory on October 31 using the perpetual LIFO inventory method.

Apx. Exercise 3 (Concluded)

Date	Purchases				Cost of Goods Sold					Inventory on Hand				
	Units	Cost/ Unit	Total		Units	Cost/ Unit	CGS	Cum. CGS		Layer	Units	Cost/ Unit	Layer Cost	Total
10/1 (BI)														
10/8														
10/20														
10/31														
Cost of Goods Sold during October														

BI: Beginning Inventory

Apx. Exercise 4 (LO 2) PERPETUAL MOVING-AVERAGE INVENTORY METHOD

Required:

Using the inventory data provided in Apx. Exercise 3, calculate the total amount assigned to cost of goods sold during October and the ending inventory on October 31 using the perpetual moving-average inventory method.

Date	Purchases			Cost of Goods Sold				Inventory on Hand and Average Cost per Unit		
	Units	Cost/ Unit	Total	Units	Cost/ Unit	CGS	Cum. CGS	Cost of Purchase or (Sale)	Cost of Inventory on Hand	Units on Hand	Average Cost/ Unit
10/1 (BI)										
10/8										
10/20										
10/31										
Cost of Goods Sold during October										

BI: Beginning Inventory

APPENDIX PROBLEMS

Apx. Problem 5 (LO 1) PERPETUAL LIFO INVENTORY METHOD

The beginning inventory, purchases, and sales for Snyder Ball Company for the month of February are provided below.

Date	Beginning Inventory and Purchases		Sales
	Units	**Cost/ Unit**	**Units**
Feb. 1 (BI)	30	$6.70	
	70	6.90	
Feb. 3	400	7.10	
Feb. 5			250
Feb. 11	700	7.20	
Feb. 13			500
Feb. 16	300	7.50	
Feb. 18	500	7.70	
Feb. 24			600
Feb. 25			50
Feb. 28	300	8.00	
BI: Beginning Inventory			

Required:

Calculate the total amount to be assigned to cost of goods sold during February and the ending inventory on February 28 using the perpetual LIFO inventory method.

SG-231

Name _____

Date	Purchases				Cost of Goods Sold						Inventory on Hand				
	Units	Cost/Unit	Total		Units	Cost/Unit	CGS	Cum. CGS			Layer	Units	Cost/Unit	Layer Cost	Total
2/1 (BI)															
2/3															
2/5															
2/11															
2/13															
2/16															

© 2014 Cengage Learning. All Rights Reserved. May not be scanned, copied or duplicated, or posted to a publicly accessible website, in whole or in part.

Apx. Problem 5 (Concluded)

Date	Purchases			Cost of Goods Sold				Inventory on Hand				
	Units	Cost/ Unit	Total	Units	Cost/ Unit	CGS	Cum. CGS	Layer	Units	Cost/ Unit	Layer Cost	Total
2/18												
2/24												
2/25												
2/28												

Cost of Goods Sold during February

BI: Beginning Inventory

Apx. Problem 6 (LO 2) PERPETUAL MOVING-AVERAGE INVENTORY METHOD

Required:

Using the inventory data provided in Apx. Problem 5, calculate the total amount assigned to cost of goods sold during February and the ending inventory on February 28 using the perpetual moving-average inventory method.

Date	Purchases			Cost of Goods Sold				Inventory on Hand and Average Cost per Unit			
	Units	Cost/ Unit	Total	Units	Cost/ Unit	CGS	Cum. CGS	Cost of Purchase or (Sale)	Cost of Inventory on Hand	Units on Hand	Average Cost/ Unit
2/1 (BI)											
2/3											
2/5											
2/11											
2/13											
2/16											
2/18											
2/24											
2/25											
2/28											
Cost of Goods Sold during February											

BI: Beginning Inventory

Apx. Problem 7 (LO 1)   PERPETUAL LIFO INVENTORY METHOD

The beginning inventory, purchases, and sales for Rafalko Candy Company for the month of July are provided below.

| Date | Beginning Inventory and Purchases | | Sales |
	Units	Cost/ Unit	Units
July 1 (BI)	50	$5.90	
	50	6.10	
July 5	400	6.20	
July 7			300
July 12	300	6.40	
July 15			200
July 18	100	6.50	
July 20	600	6.80	
July 24			800
July 27			100
July 31	100	6.90	
BI: Beginning Inventory			

Required:

Calculate the total amount to be assigned to cost of goods sold during July and the ending inventory on July 31 using the perpetual LIFO inventory method.

Apx. Problem 7 (Continued)

Date	Purchases Units	Purchases Cost/ Unit	Purchases Total	Cost of Goods Sold Units	Cost of Goods Sold Cost/ Unit	Cost of Goods Sold CGS	Cum. CGS	Inventory on Hand Layer	Inventory on Hand Units	Inventory on Hand Cost/ Unit	Inventory on Hand Layer Cost	Total
7/1 (BI)												
7/5												
7/7												
7/12												
7/15												
7/18												

Apx. Problem 7 (Concluded)

Date	Purchases			Cost of Goods Sold					Inventory on Hand				
	Units	Cost/ Unit	Total	Units	Cost/ Unit	CGS	Cum. CGS		Layer	Units	Cost/ Unit	Layer Cost	Total
7/20													
7/24													
7/27													
7/31													
Cost of Goods Sold during July													

BI: Beginning Inventory

Apx. Problem 8 (LO 2) PERPETUAL MOVING-AVERAGE INVENTORY METHOD

Required:

Using the inventory data provided in Apx. Problem 7, calculate the total amount assigned to cost of goods sold during July and the ending inventory on July 31 using the perpetual moving-average inventory method.

Date	Purchases			Cost of Goods Sold				Inventory on Hand and Average Cost per Unit			
	Units	Cost/ Unit	Total	Units	Cost/ Unit	CGS	Cum. CGS	Cost of Purchase or (Sale)	Cost of Inventory on Hand	Units on Hand	Average Cost/ Unit
7/1 (BI)											
7/5											
7/7											
7/12											
7/15											
7/18											
7/20											
7/24											
7/27											
7/31											

Cost of Goods Sold during July

BI: Beginning Inventory

CHAPTER 14
ADJUSTMENTS AND THE WORK SHEET
FOR A MERCHANDISING BUSINESS

LEARNING OBJECTIVES

Chapter 14 covers the end-of-period adjustments and the preparation of a work sheet for a merchandising business. Adjustments for merchandise inventory and unearned revenue are emphasized.

Objective 1.   Prepare an adjustment for merchandise inventory using the periodic inventory system.

During the year, the purchase and sale of merchandise is not entered in the merchandise inventory account. Thus, at the end of the year, it is necessary to adjust the merchandise inventory account to properly reflect the amount of inventory on hand. This is accomplished by removing the beginning inventory from the books (the current balance), and entering the ending inventory, based on a physical count. This adjustment is made on the work sheet in a two-step process as shown below. This technique is used so that all of the information required to compute cost of goods sold is available in the Income Statement columns of the work sheet.

Account Title	Trial Balance		Adjustments			Adjusted Trial Balance		Income Statement		Balance Sheet	
	Debit	Credit		Debit	Credit	Debit	Credit	Debit	Credit	Debit	Credit
Merchandise Inventory	20		(Step 2)	30	20 (Step 1)	30		BI	EI	30	
Income Summary			(Step 1)	20	30 (Step 2)	20	30	-- 20	30		
								80	Purchases		
Purchases	80										

Step 1: Remove beginning inventory

| Income Summary | 20 | |
| Merchandise Inventory | | 20 |

Step 2: Insert ending inventory

| **Merchandise Inventory** | **30** | |
| **Income Summary** | | **30** |

BI: Beginning Inventory ($20); EI: Ending Inventory ($30)

Cost of goods sold:
Merchandise inventory, January 1 .... $ 20
Purchases 80
Goods available for sale $100
Less merchandise inventory, December 31 30
Cost of goods sold .... $ 70

Objective 2.   Prepare an adjustment for unearned revenue.

A liability account is created when cash is received before the product or service is provided. This liability is called **unearned revenue**. If all, or part, of the revenue has been earned by the end of the period, an adjustment is made in order to reduce the liability, Unearned Revenue, and increase the related revenue account.

The entry to record receipt of cash for revenue to be earned later is as follows:

| Cash | xxx | |
| Unearned Revenue | | xxx |

The entry when all, or part, of revenue has been earned is as follows:

Unearned Revenue	xxx	
Sales		xxx

Objective 3.   Prepare a work sheet for a merchandising business.

At the end of the accounting period, a work sheet is prepared to make the remaining steps of the accounting cycle easier. The work sheet is similar to the one you learned about in Chapter 5 for a service business, except for the new accounts introduced for a merchandising business and the unearned revenue account that was introduced in this chapter.

Adjusting entries are entered on the work sheet, including adjustments for supplies used, insurance expired, depreciation, and wages earned but not paid. From the Adjusted Trial Balance columns, all amounts are extended to either the Income Statement columns or the Balance Sheet columns of the work sheet.

Of particular importance is the method of extending the amounts for Merchandise Inventory and Income Summary on the work sheet. Merchandise Inventory is extended in the usual manner. The adjusted balance is extended to the Adjusted Trial Balance columns and then to the Balance Sheet columns. However, both the debit *and* credit adjustments to Income Summary are extended to the Adjusted Trial Balance columns and then to the Income Statement columns (see table below). The debit to Income Summary represents the beginning balance of Merchandise Inventory. The credit to Income Summary represents the ending balance of Merchandise Inventory. Both amounts are used on the income statement. Thus, both amounts are extended to the Income Statement columns.

The other accounts identified with merchandise accounting will be extended into the Income Statement columns of the work sheet. Also, any unearned revenue that has been earned as of the balance sheet date will be adjusted into revenue (see table below).

WORK SHEET

	Trial Balance		Adjustments		Adj. Trial Balance		Income Statement		Balance Sheet	
	Dr.	Cr.	Dr.	Cr.	Dr.	Cr.	Dr.	Cr.	Dr.	Cr.
Merchandise Inv.	BI		EI	BI	EI				EI	
Unearned Rev.		xx	xx			xx				xx
Income Summary			BI	EI	BI	EI	BI	EI		
Revenue		xx		xx		xx		xx		
Sales		xx				xx		xx		
Sales Ret. & Allow.	xx				xx		xx			
Sales Discounts	xx				xx		xx			
Purchases	xx				xx		xx			
Purch. Ret. & Allow.		xx				xx		xx		
Purch. Discounts		xx				xx		xx		
Freight-In	xx				xx		xx			

All of the accounts needed to arrive at net income for a merchandising business are in the Income Statement columns of the work sheet. The difference between the debits and credits in the Income Statement columns and between the debits and credits in the Balance Sheet columns will equal either net income or net loss.

Objective 4.   Journalize adjusting entries for a merchandising business.

Just because adjusting entries were analyzed and placed on the work sheet does not mean that they have been entered into the accounts in the general ledger. Adjusting entries need to be entered in the general journal and posted to the general ledger. This information can be taken from the Adjustments columns of the work sheet.

Objective 5.   Prepare adjusting journal entries under the perpetual inventory system.

Under the perpetual inventory system, the merchandise inventory and cost of goods sold accounts are continually updated throughout the year to reflect purchases and sales of inventory. Comparative entries under the periodic and perpetual inventory systems are shown below.

Transaction	Periodic System		Perpetual System	

1. Purchased merchandise on account, $100.	Purchases 100
	    Accounts Payable
		100	Merchandise Inventory 100
			    Accounts Payable
				100

2. Sold merchandise on account, $60. The cost of the merchandise sold was $50.	Accounts Receivable 60
	    Sales
		60	Accounts Receivable 60
			    Sales
			
			Cost of Goods Sold 50
			    Merchandise Inventory
				60
				
				50

3. Periodic system: Beginning inventory, $40. Ending inventory, $90.	Income Summary 40
	    Merchandise Inventory
	Merchandise Inventory 90
	    Income Summary
		40
		
		90		

4. Perpetual system: Ending balance of merchandise inventory, $100. Ending inventory based on physical count, $90.			Inventory Short and Over 10 Merchandise Inventory	10

REVIEW QUESTIONS

Instructions: Analyze each of the following items carefully before writing your answer in the column at the right.

	Question	Answer
LO 1	1. At the end of an accounting period, a(n) _____ is used to analyze and prepare adjustments and to determine the amount of net income or net loss for the time period.	_____
LO 1	2. The amount of inventory on hand at the end of the accounting period is determined by taking a(n) _____ of the goods on hand.	_____
LO 1	3. Under the periodic system of adjusting for the ending inventory, the beginning inventory is removed from the merchandise inventory account with a(n) _____ , and a debit is entered into the _____ account.	_____ _____
LO 1	4. Under the periodic system of accounting for the ending inventory, the ending inventory is entered by debiting Merchandise Inventory and crediting the _____ account.	_____

LO 1   **5.** Purchases less purchases returns and allowances and purchases discounts equals _____. ....

_____

LO 1   **6.** Beginning inventory plus net purchases and freight-in equals _____. ....

_____

LO 1   **7.** Merchandise available for sale less ending inventory is equal to _____. ....

_____

LO 1   **8.** On the work sheet, both the debit and credit amounts of the income summary account are extended to the _____ and the _____ columns of the work sheet. ....

_____

_____

LO 1   **9.** Purchases Returns and Allowances and Purchases Discounts are deducted from the _____ account on the income statement. ......

_____

LO 2   **10.** The cash received in advance of delivering a product or performing a service is called _____. ....

_____

LO 2   **11.** Unearned revenue is reported as a(n) _____ on the balance sheet.

_____

LO 2   **12.** At the end of an accounting period, unearned revenue is adjusted into a(n) _____ account for the amount of revenue that has been earned. ....

_____

LO 2   **13.** Purchases Returns and Allowances and Purchases Discounts are classified as _____ accounts. ....

_____

LO 3   **14.** The first step in preparing a work sheet is to prepare the _____.

_____

LO 3   **15.** On the work sheet, amounts are extended from the Adjusted Trial Balance columns to the _____ and _____ columns. ....

_____

_____

LO 3   **16.** If credits exceed debits on the Income Statement columns of the work sheet, this represents a net _____. ....

_____

LO 3   **17.** The most helpful aid in entering adjustments into the general journal is the _____. ....

_____

LO 5   **18.** Under the perpetual inventory system, _____ is debited when inventory is purchased. ....

_____

LO 5   **19.** Under the perpetual inventory system, _____ is (are) debited when inventory is sold. ....

_____

EXERCISES

Exercise 1 (LO 1) ADJUSTING ENTRIES FOR MERCHANDISE INVENTORY

Kendall's TV and Appliances had merchandise inventory of $60,300 at the beginning of the year and $54,800 at the end of the year. Prepare the necessary adjusting entries in a general journal.

GENERAL JOURNAL
PAGE _____

	DATE	DESCRIPTION	POST. REF.	DEBIT	CREDIT	
1						1
2						2
3						3
4						4
5						5
6						6
7						7

Exercise 2 (LO 1) CALCULATION OF COST OF GOODS SOLD

The following amounts are known for Casey's Card and Gift Shop:

Beginning merchandise inventory	$33,000
Ending merchandise inventory	41,000
Purchases	86,000
Purchases returns and allowances	4,500
Purchases discounts	2,500
Freight-in	1,000

Prepare the cost of goods sold section of the income statement for Casey's Card and Gift Shop.

Exercise 3 (LO 2) ADJUSTMENT FOR UNEARNED REVENUE

The following transactions took place for Hamilton Theaters. Journalize these transactions in a general journal.

Feb.   22   Sold 2,000 season tickets at $25 each, receiving cash of $50,000. Received cash before the services were provided.

Dec.   31   An end-of-period adjustment is needed to recognize that $45,000 in ticket revenue has been earned.

GENERAL JOURNAL   PAGE

	DATE	DESCRIPTION	POST. REF.	DEBIT	CREDIT	
1						1
2						2
3						3
4						4
5						5
6						6
7						7

Exercise 4 (LO 4) JOURNALIZING ADJUSTING ENTRIES

The partial work sheet below is taken from the books of Long Auto Repair for the year ended December 31, 20--.

Long Auto Repair

Work Sheet (Partial)

For Year Ended December 31, 20--

	ACCOUNT TITLE	TRIAL BALANCE DEBIT	TRIAL BALANCE CREDIT	ADJUSTMENTS DEBIT	ADJUSTMENTS CREDIT	
1	Merchandise Inventory	60 0 0 0 00		(b) 57 0 0 0 00	(a) 60 0 0 0 00	1
2	Supplies	6 0 0 0 00			(d) 3 2 0 0 00	2
3	Building	150 0 0 0 00				3
4	Accum. Depr.—Building		45 0 0 0 00		(e) 8 0 0 0 00	4
5	Wages Payable				(f) 2 4 0 0 00	5
6	Unearned Repair Revenue		6 0 0 0 00	(c) 5 0 0 0 00		6
7	Income Summary			(a) 60 0 0 0 00	(b) 57 0 0 0 00	7
8	Repair Revenue		30 0 0 0 00		(c) 5 0 0 0 00	8
9	Wages Expense	39 0 0 0 00		(f) 2 4 0 0 00		9
10	Supplies Expense			(d) 3 2 0 0 00		10
11	Depr. Exp.—Building			(e) 8 0 0 0 00		11
12						12
13						13
14						14
15						15

Journalize the above adjustments in a general journal.

Exercise 4 (Concluded)

GENERAL JOURNAL

PAGE

	DATE		DESCRIPTION	POST. REF.	DEBIT	CREDIT	
1							1
2							2
3							3
4							4
5							5
6							6
7							7
8							8
9							9
10							10
11							11
12							12
13							13
14							14
15							15
16							16
17							17
18							18
19							19
20							20

Exercise 5 (LO 5) JOURNAL ENTRIES UNDER THE PERPETUAL INVENTORY SYSTEM

Bahita Business Supplies entered into the following transactions. Prepare journal entries under the perpetual inventory system.

Aug. 1   Purchased merchandise on account from Gul Paper, $10,000.
      5   Purchased merchandise for cash, $5,000.
      10 Sold merchandise on account to Padam Medical Services for $2,000. The merchandise cost $1,500.

GENERAL JOURNAL   PAGE

	DATE	DESCRIPTION	POST. REF.	DEBIT	CREDIT	
1						1
2						2
3						3
4						4
5						5
6						6
7						7
8						8
9						9
10						10
11						11
12						12
13						13

Exercise 6 (LO 5) PREPARE ADJUSTING ENTRY FOR A MERCHANDISING BUSINESS: PERPETUAL INVENTORY SYSTEM

On December 31, Ranjit Enterprises completed a physical count of its inventory. Although the merchandise inventory account shows a balance of $8,000, the physical count comes to $7,800. Prepare the appropriate adjusting entry under the perpetual inventory system.

GENERAL JOURNAL

PAGE

	DATE	DESCRIPTION	POST. REF.	DEBIT	CREDIT	
1						1
2						2
3						3
4						4
5						5
6						6
7						7
8						8

PROBLEMS

Problem 7 (LO 1/2/3) PREPARE A WORK SHEET

The work sheet provided on pages 248–249 is taken from the books of Ocean Beach Sail Shop, a business owned by Nicole Smith. Adjustment information is provided below. Smith uses the periodic inventory system.

(a and b) Based on a physical count, merchandise inventory on hand as of December 31, 20--, $36,000.
(c) Supplies remaining at end of the year, $2,350.
(d) Unexpired insurance on December 31, $1,875.
(e) Depreciation expense on the building for 20--, $7,000.
(f) Depreciation expense on the store equipment for 20--, $2,800.
(g) Unearned tour revenue as of December 31, $2,700.
(h) Wages earned but not paid as of December 31, $1,100.

Required:

1. Complete the Adjustments columns. Identify each adjustment with its corresponding letter.
2. Complete the work sheet.

Problem 7 (Continued)
1. and 2.

Ocean Beach

Work

For Year Ended

	ACCOUNT TITLE	TRIAL BALANCE												ADJUSTMENTS									
		DEBIT					CREDIT					DEBIT					CREDIT				
1	Cash	27	0	0	0	00															
2	Accounts Receivable	9	0	0	0	00															
3	Merchandise Inventory	31	0	0	0	00															
4	Supplies	7	5	0	0	00															
5	Prepaid Insurance	4	9	0	0	00															
6	Land	40	0	0	0	00															
7	Building	60	0	0	0	00															
8	Accum. Depr.—Building						25	0	0	0	00										
9	Store Equipment	29	0	0	0	00															
10	Accum. Depr.—Store Equipment						9	0	0	0	00										
11	Accounts Payable						7	6	0	0	00										
12	Wages Payable																				
13	Sales Tax Payable						6	1	0	0	00										
14	Unearned Tour Revenue						6	8	0	0	00										
15	Mortgage Payable						43	0	0	0	00										
16	N. Smith, Capital						124	5	9	0	00										
17	N. Smith, Drawing	33	0	0	0	00															
18	Income Summary																				
19	Sales						122	0	0	0	00										
20	Sales Returns and Allowances	4	2	0	0	00															
21	Tour Revenue																				
22	Purchases	38	0	0	0	00															
23	Purchases Returns and Allowances						2	6	0	0	00										
24	Purchases Discounts						1	4	0	0	00										
25	Freight-In	2	5	0	0	00															
26	Wages Expense	47	0	0	0	00															
27	Advertising Expense	4	8	0	0	00															
28	Supplies Expense																				
29	Telephone Expense	1	8	0	0	00															
30	Utilities Expense	7	6	0	0	00															
31	Insurance Expense																				
32	Depr. Expense—Building																				
33	Depr. Expense—Store Equipment																				
34	Miscellaneous Expense		7	9	0	00															
35		348	0	9	0	00	348	0	9	0	00										
36																					
37																					
38																					

Problem 7 (Concluded)

Sail Shop

Sheet

December 31, 20--

ADJUSTED TRIAL BALANCE		INCOME STATEMENT		BALANCE SHEET		
DEBIT	CREDIT	DEBIT	CREDIT	DEBIT	CREDIT	

Problem 8 (LO 4) JOURNALIZING ADJUSTING ENTRIES

From the work sheet prepared for Ocean Beach Sail Shop (Problem 7), record the adjusting entries in a general journal.

GENERAL JOURNAL   PAGE

	DATE	DESCRIPTION	POST. REF.	DEBIT	CREDIT	
1						1
2						2
3						3
4						4
5						5
6						6
7						7
8						8
9						9
10						10
11						11
12						12
13						13
14						14
15						15
16						16
17						17
18						18
19						19
20						20
21						21
22						22
23						23
24						24
25						25
26						26
27						27
28						28
29						29
30						30

CHAPTER 14 APPENDIX
EXPENSE METHOD OF ACCOUNTING FOR PREPAID EXPENSES

LEARNING OBJECTIVES

The appendix to Chapter 14 covers the expense method of accounting for prepaid expenses.

Objective 1. Use the expense method of accounting for prepaid expenses.

Under the **expense method** of accounting for prepaid expenses, supplies and other prepaid items are entered as **expenses** when purchased. Under this method, we must adjust the accounts at the end of each accounting period to record the **unused** portions as assets.

Objective 2. Make the appropriate adjusting entries when the expense method is used for prepaid expenses.

To illustrate the appropriate entries, let's assume that the following entry was made on November 1, 20--, when six months' office rent was paid in advance:

```
20--
Nov. 1    Office Rent Expense          6,000
              Cash                              6,000
                  Paid six months' office
                  rent in advance
```

At the end of December, adjusting entries must be made to prepare year-end financial statements. The office has been used for two months. Thus, the office expense for the year should be $2,000 ($1,000 per month × 2). This leaves $4,000 that should be recorded as an asset, Prepaid Office Rent. The following adjusting entry is made for office rent:

```
20--              Adjusting Entry
Dec. 31   Prepaid Office Rent          4,000
              Office Rent Expense               4,000
```

As shown in the T accounts below, after this entry is posted, the office rent expense account has a debit balance of $2,000 ($6,000 – $4,000). This amount is reported on the income statement as an operating expense. The prepaid office rent account has a debit balance of $4,000. It is reported on the balance sheet as a current asset.

Prepaid Office Rent		Office Rent Expense	
Adj. Dec. 31 4,000		Nov. 1 6,000	Adj. Dec. 31 4,000
		Bal. Dec. 31 2,000	

Apx. Exercise 1 (LO 2) EXPENSE METHOD OF ACCOUNTING FOR PREPAID EXPENSES

Dalton's Fishery paid $2,400 for a one-year insurance premium on its delivery van on October 1. The following entry was made:

20--

Oct. 1   Insurance Expense   2,400
                Cash   2,400
                    Paid insurance premium

Insurance coverage started on October 1. Prepare the adjusting entry on December 31.

GENERAL JOURNAL

PAGE

	DATE		DESCRIPTION	POST. REF.	DEBIT	CREDIT	
1							1
2							2
3							3
4							4
5							5

Apx. Exercise 2 (LO 1/2) EXPENSE METHOD OF ACCOUNTING FOR PREPAID EXPENSES

On August 21, Georgio's Dry Goods purchased supplies costing $6,000 for cash. This amount was debited to the supplies expense account. At the end of the year, an inventory shows that supplies costing $1,000 still remain. Prepare the entries for the purchase and year-end adjustment.

GENERAL JOURNAL

PAGE

	DATE		DESCRIPTION	POST. REF.	DEBIT	CREDIT	
1							1
2							2
3							3
4							4
5							5
6							6
7							7
8							8
9							9
10							10

CHAPTER 15
FINANCIAL STATEMENTS AND YEAR-END
ACCOUNTING FOR A MERCHANDISING BUSINESS

LEARNING OBJECTIVES

Chapter 15 covers the year-end accounting process as it applies to a merchandising business—the work sheet, closing and reversing entries, and the financial statements. In addition, financial ratios are introduced for the merchandising business.

Objective 1.   Prepare a single-step and multiple-step income statement for a merchandising business.

The **single-step** form of income statement lists all revenue items and their total first, followed by all expense items and their total. The difference, which is either net income or net loss, is then calculated.

The **multiple-step income statement** contains the computation of net sales and cost of goods sold. It also reports gross profit, income from operations, and net income. The multiple-step income statement begins with gross sales less deductions to arrive at *net sales*. Then, cost of goods sold is calculated—beginning inventory plus net purchases and freight-in, less ending inventory. Net sales minus cost of goods sold results in *gross profit*. Then, operating expenses are subtracted, resulting in income from operations. Finally, other revenue and expenses not from operations (such as interest) are included to compute *net income.*

Objective 2.   Prepare a statement of owner's equity.

The statement of owner's equity summarizes all changes in the owner's equity, including net income or loss and any additional investments or withdrawals by the owner.

Objective 3.   Prepare a classified balance sheet.

The **classified balance sheet** distinguishes between *current* and long-term assets and liabilities. Current assets include cash and assets that will be converted to cash or consumed within the year or operating cycle (whichever is longer). Property, plant, and equipment are assets with long useful lives and much less liquidity. Current liabilities are generally due within a year and require the use of current assets. Long-term liabilities extend longer than one year.

Objective 4.   Compute standard financial ratios.

Financial ratios help evaluate the current financial condition and profitability of a company. **Working capital** is current assets minus current liabilities; it tells whether a business has enough current assets to meet current operating debts.

The **current** and **quick ratios** measure a firm's ability to pay its current liabilities. The current ratio is calculated by dividing current assets by current liabilities. The desirable ratio is 2:1 ($2 of current assets for every $1 of current liabilities). **Quick assets** include cash and other very liquid assets—such as accounts receivable. The quick ratio is calculated by dividing quick assets by current liabilities. The desirable ratio is 1:1.

Return on owner's equity is calculated by dividing net income by average owner's equity (beginning equity plus ending equity, divided by 2). This rate of return can be compared with other years' rates and with other businesses' rates.

The **accounts receivable turnover** is determined by dividing net credit sales by average accounts receivable. This number is then divided into 365 days to determine the average number of days credit customers are taking to pay for their purchases.

Inventory turnover reveals how many times merchandise inventory "turned over" or was sold during the period. It is calculated by dividing cost of goods sold by the average inventory (beginning inventory plus ending inventory, divided by 2). This number is then divided into 365 days to determine the average number of days merchandise is held before it is sold.

Objective 5.   Prepare closing entries for a merchandising business.

As with a service business, closing entries for a merchandising business are facilitated by the work sheet. All temporary accounts are closed—sales, contra-sales accounts, purchases, contra-purchases accounts, and expenses. The income summary account already contains two entries for merchandise inventory adjustments (debited to remove the old balance; credited to enter the new balance). First, all income statement accounts with credit balances are debited, crediting the income summary account. Then, all income statement accounts with debit balances are credited, debiting the income summary account. The balance in the income summary account is then transferred to the owner's equity account; a credit balance (indicating net income) is debited to close the income summary account. Finally, the drawing account is closed to the owner's capital account.

After the closing entries are posted, the post-closing trial balance is prepared. It reflects balances after the adjusting and closing entries are posted; only permanent accounts still have balances.

Objective 6.   Prepare reversing entries.

Year-end adjusting entries may be reversed in the next accounting period if it helps to simplify entries to be made in the new year. Except for the first year of operation, **reversing entries** are helpful whenever an adjusting entry has increased an asset or liability account from a zero balance. The reversing entries are made on the first day of the new accounting period.

REVIEW QUESTIONS

Instructions: Analyze each of the following items carefully before writing your answer in the column at the right.

		Question	Answer
LO 1	1.	The primary purpose of the _____ is to serve as an aid in preparing the financial statements.	_____
LO 1	2.	The _____ form of income statement lists all revenue items first, followed by all expense items and their totals.	_____
LO 1	3.	Gross sales less sales returns and allowances is called _____.	_____
LO 1	4.	_____ is the result of net sales less cost of goods sold.	_____
LO 1	5.	When operating expenses are subtracted from gross profit, the result is called _____.	_____
LO 1	6.	After other revenues are added and other expenses are subtracted, the final result is called _____.	_____

LO 2 7. The statement of owner's equity shows the net _____ or _____ in owner's equity for the period. ....   _____

_____

LO 3 8. The report form of a(n) _____ balance sheet distinguishes between current and long-term assets and between current and long-term liabilities. ....   _____

LO 3 9. The speed with which assets can be converted to cash is called _____. ....   _____

LO 3 10. The difference between the cost of a long-term asset and the amount of accumulated depreciation is called _____ or book value. ......   _____

LO 3 11. _____ are obligations that are due within one year or during the normal operating cycle of the business, whichever is longer. ....   _____

LO 3 12. A(n) _____ is an example of a long-term liability based on a written agreement evidencing a debt secured by property. ....   _____

LO 4 13. The difference between current assets and current liabilities is called _____. ....   _____

LO 4 14. The _____ ratio is current assets divided by current liabilities.   _____

LO 4 15. _____ assets include cash and all other current assets that can be quickly converted to cash. ....   _____

LO 4 16. The _____ ratio is calculated by dividing net income by average owner's equity. ....   _____

LO 4 17. The _____ measures the number of times the accounts receivable were collected during the accounting period. ....   _____

LO 4 18. The _____ measures the number of times merchandise is sold during the accounting period. ....   _____

LO 5 19. All _____ owner's equity accounts are closed at the end of the accounting period. ....   _____

LO 5 20. The purpose of the _____ is to prove that the general ledger is in balance at the beginning of the new accounting period and that all temporary accounts have zero balances. ....   _____

LO 6 21. A reversing entry is the opposite of a(n) _____ entry. ....   _____

LO 6 22. Adjusting entries that increase an asset or liability account from a(n) _____ balance may be reversed. ....   _____

EXERCISES

Exercise 1 (LO 1) MULTIPLE-STEP INCOME STATEMENT

From the information below, prepare a multiple-step income statement for Morse Motor Company for the year ended December 31, 20-1.

Merchandise Inventory, January 1, 20-1	$ 28,900
Merchandise Inventory, December 31, 20-1	29,600
Sales	118,300
Sales Returns and Allowances	1,000
Sales Discounts	280
Interest Revenue	1,900
Purchases	68,000
Purchases Returns and Allowances	2,140
Purchases Discounts	1,360
Freight-In	540
Wages Expense	23,200
Rent Expense	8,000
Supplies Expense	900
Telephone Expense	2,600
Utilities Expense	3,800
Insurance Expense	1,000
Depreciation Expense—Equipment	2,000
Miscellaneous Expense	300
Interest Expense	700

Exercise 1 (Concluded)

Exercise 2 (LO 2/3)   PREPARE A STATEMENT OF OWNER'S EQUITY AND CLASSIFIED BALANCE SHEET

From the information below and the income statement prepared for Exercise 1, prepare a statement of owner's equity and a report form of a classified balance sheet for Morse Motor Company as of December 31, 20-1.

Cash	$19,200
Accounts Receivable	28,500
Merchandise Inventory	29,600
Supplies	1,800
Prepaid Insurance	1,100
Equipment	32,000
Accumulated Depreciation—Equipment	4,000
Accounts Payable	18,620
Wages Payable	280
Sales Tax Payable	480
Mortgage Payable—current portion	1,200
Mortgage Payable	8,000
K. T. Morse, Capital, January 1, 20-1	66,740
K. T. Morse, Drawing (during year)	8,000
Additional investment by K. T. Morse, May 1, 20-1	10,000

Exercise 2 (Concluded)

Exercise 3 (LO 4) FINANCIAL RATIOS

From the Morse Motor Company financial statements prepared in Exercises 1 and 2, compute the following ratios: (Net credit sales for the year were $88,000; accounts receivable on January 1 was $24,200.)

1. Working capital

2. Current ratio

3. Quick ratio

4. Return on owner's equity

5. Accounts receivable turnover

6. Inventory turnover

Exercise 4 (LO 5/6) CLOSING AND REVERSING ENTRIES

Based on the foregoing information provided for Morse Motor Company in Exercises 1-3, prepare closing and reversing entries in the general journal on page 262. Adjusting entries are shown below.

Income Summary	28,900	
Merchandise Inventory		28,900
Merchandise Inventory	29,600	
Income Summary		29,600
Insurance Expense	1,000	
Prepaid Insurance		1,000
Depreciation Expense	2,000	
Accumulated Depreciation—Equipment		2,000
Supplies Expense	900	
Supplies		900
Wages Expense	280	
Wages Payable		280

Exercise 4 (Concluded)

GENERAL JOURNAL

	DATE		DESCRIPTION	POST. REF.	DEBIT	CREDIT	
1							1
2							2
3							3
4							4
5							5
6							6
7							7
8							8
9							9
10							10
11							11
12							12
13							13
14							14
15							15
16							16
17							17
18							18
19							19
20							20
21							21
22							22
23							23
24							24
25							25
26							26
27							27
28							28
29							29
30							30
31							31

PROBLEMS

Problem 5 (REVIEW) COMPLETE A WORK SHEET

Complete the work sheet for Clark's Clothing Store on pages 264–265 by using the adjustment information provided below.

(a and b)   Merchandise Inventory, December 31, 20-1, $12,400.

(c)   Unused supplies on December 31, 20-1, $2,100.

(d)   Expired insurance on December 31, 20-1, $500.

(e)   Depreciation expense on building for the year, $10,000.

(f)   Depreciation expense on fixtures for the year, $2,000.

(g)   Wages accrued (earned but not yet paid), $380.

(h)   Unearned revenues on December 31, 20-1, $3,000.

Problem 5 (Continued)

	ACCOUNT TITLE	TRIAL BALANCE DEBIT					TRIAL BALANCE CREDIT					ADJUSTMENTS DEBIT					ADJUSTMENTS CREDIT				
1	Cash	16	4	0	0	00															
2	Accounts Receivable	7	1	0	0	00															
3	Merchandise Inventory	28	0	0	0	00															
4	Supplies	3	0	0	0	00															
5	Prepaid Insurance	2	0	0	0	00															
6	Land	10	0	0	0	00															
7	Building	100	0	0	0	00															
8	Accum. Depr.—Building						10	0	0	0	00										
9	Fixtures	33	0	0	0	00															
10	Accum. Depr.—Fixtures						6	0	0	0	00										
11	Accounts Payable						9	0	0	0	00										
12	Wages Payable																				
13	Sales Tax Payable						1	2	0	0	00										
14	Unearned Revenue						10	0	0	0	00										
15	Mortgage Payable						58	0	0	0	00										
16	Alex Clark, Capital						73	3	0	0	00										
17	Alex Clark, Drawing	12	5	0	0	00															
18	Income Summary																				
19	Sales						225	5	0	0	00										
20	Sales Returns and Allowances	2	0	0	0	00															
21	Sales Discounts		5	0	0	00															
22	Purchases	68	5	0	0	00															
23	Purchases Returns and Allowances						1	2	0	0	00										
24	Purchases Discounts						1	3	0	0	00										
25	Freight-In		4	4	0	00															
26	Wages Expense	19	8	0	0	00															
27	Advertising Expense		7	0	0	00															
28	Rent Expense	82	6	6	0	00															
29	Supplies Expense																				
30	Telephone Expense	2	1	0	0	00															
31	Utilities Expense	1	8	0	0	00															
32	Insurance Expense																				
33	Depr. Expense—Building																				
34	Depr. Expense—Fixtures																				
35	Miscellaneous Expense		6	0	0	00															
36	Interest Expense	4	4	0	0	00															
37		395	5	0	0	00	395	5	0	0	00										
38	Net Income																				
39																					

Name _____

Problem 5 (Concluded)

Store _____

Sheet _____

December 31, 20-1

	ADJUSTED TRIAL BALANCE		INCOME STATEMENT		BALANCE SHEET		
	DEBIT	CREDIT	DEBIT	CREDIT	DEBIT	CREDIT	
							1
							2
							3
							4
							5
							6
							7
							8
							9
							10
							11
							12
							13
							14
							15
							16
							17
							18
							19
							20
							21
							22
							23
							24
							25
							26
							27
							28
							29
							30
							31
							32
							33
							34
							35
							36
							37
							38
							39

Problem 6 (LO 1/2/3) PREPARATION OF AN INCOME STATEMENT, STATEMENT OF OWNER'S EQUITY, AND BALANCE SHEET

Based on the work sheet for Clark's Clothing Store, prepare the following financial statements:

1. Multiple-step income statement.
2. Statement of owner's equity. (Alex made no additional investments during the year.)
3. Classified balance sheet. (Mortgage Payable—current portion is $1,000.)

1. (See page 267)

2.

Problem 6 (Continued)

1. _____

Problem 6 (Concluded)

3.

Problem 7 (LO 4) FINANCIAL RATIOS

For Clark's Clothing Store, calculate the following financial statement ratios. (*Note*: Net credit sales for the year were $115,000, and accounts receivable on January 1 was $8,400.)

1. Working capital

_____

_____

_____

2. Current ratio

_____

_____

_____

3. Quick ratio

_____

_____

_____

4. Return on owner's equity

_____

_____

_____

5. Accounts receivable turnover

_____

_____

_____

6. Inventory turnover

_____

_____

_____

_____

Problem 8 (LO 5/6) ADJUSTING, CLOSING, AND REVERSING ENTRIES

From the work sheet prepared for Clark's Clothing Store (Problem 5), record the adjusting, closing, and reversing entries on the general journal page below and on the next page.

GENERAL JOURNAL

PAGE

DATE		DESCRIPTION	POST. REF.	DEBIT	CREDIT
1					
2					
3					
4					
5					
6					
7					
8					
9					
10					
11					
12					
13					
14					
15					
16					
17					
18					
19					
20					
21					
22					
23					
24					
25					
26					
27					
28					
29					

Problem 8 (Concluded)

GENERAL JOURNAL   PAGE _____

	DATE		DESCRIPTION	POST. REF.	DEBIT	CREDIT	
1							1
2							2
3							3
4							4
5							5
6							6
7							7
8							8
9							9
10							10
11							11
12							12
13							13
14							14
15							15
16							16
17							17
18							18
19							19
20							20
21							21
22							22
23							23
24							24
25							25
26							26
27							27
28							28
29							29
30							30
31							31

NOTES

NOTES

NOTES

NOTES

NOTES

NOTES

NOTES

NOTES

NOTES

NOTES

NOTES

END PAGE OF
STUDY GUIDE

END PAGE OF

WORKING PAPERS

NOTES

NOTES

NOTES

Exercise 2-5A

Account	Classification	Financial Statement
Cash	_____	_____
Rent Expense	_____	_____
Accounts Payable	_____	_____
Service Fees	_____	_____
Supplies	_____	_____
Wages Expense	_____	_____
Ramon Martinez, Drawing	_____	_____
Ramon Martinez, Capital	_____	_____
Prepaid Insurance	_____	_____
Accounts Receivable	_____	_____

Exercise 2-6A

Exercise 2-7A

Problem 2-8A

	Assets	=	Liabilities	+	Owner's Equity
1.					
2.					
3.					

Problem 2-9A: See page WP-7

Problem 2-10A

Problem 2-9A

Assets				=	Liabilities	+	Owner's Equity					
(Items Owned)					(Amts. Owed)		(Owner's Investment)		(Earnings)			
Cash	Accounts Receivable	Office Supplies	Prepaid Insurance	=	Accounts Payable	+	J. Pembroke, Capital	J. Pembroke, Drawing	Revenues	Expenses	Description
+	+	+		=		+	−	+	−		
(a)											
(b)											
(c)											
(d)											
(e)											
(f)											
(g)											
Bal.											

Problem 2-11A

Problem 2-12A

Exercise 2-1B

Account	Classification
Cash	_____
Accounts Payable	_____
Supplies	_____
Bill Jones, Drawing	_____
Prepaid Insurance	_____
Accounts Receivable	_____
Bill Jones, Capital	_____

Exercise 2-2B

Assets	=	Liabilities	+	Owner's Equity
_____	=	$20,000	+	$ 5,000
$30,000	=	$15,000	+	_____
$20,000	=	_____	+	$10,000

Exercise 2-3B

	Assets	=	Liabilities	+	Owner's Equity
(a)	_____		_____		_____
Bal.	_____		_____		_____
(b)	_____		_____		_____
Bal.	_____		_____		_____
(c)	_____		_____		_____
	_____		_____		_____
Bal.	_____		_____		_____
(d)	_____		_____		_____
Bal.	_____		_____		_____

Exercise 2-4B

Assets	=	Liabilities	+	Capital	−	Drawing	+	Revenues	−	Expenses	Description

Owner's Equity

Bal. from E 2-3B
(d)

(e)

(f)

(g)

(h)

(i)

(j)

(k)

Bal.

Exercise 2-5B

Account	Classification	Financial Statement
Cash	_____	_____
Rent Expense	_____	_____
Accounts Payable	_____	_____
Service Fees	_____	_____
Supplies	_____	_____
Wages Expense	_____	_____
Amanda Wong, Drawing	_____	_____
Amanda Wong, Capital	_____	_____
Prepaid Insurance	_____	_____
Accounts Receivable	_____	_____

Exercise 2-6B

Exercise 2-7B

Problem 2-8B

	Assets	=	Liabilities	+	Owner's Equity
1.	_____		_____		_____
2.	_____		_____		_____
3.	_____		_____		_____

Problem 2-9B: See page WP-13

Problem 2-10B

Problem 2-9B

Assets				=	Liabilities	+	Owner's Equity				
	(Items Owned)				(Amts. Owed)		(Owner's Investment)		(Earnings)		
Cash	+ Accounts Receivable	+ Office Supplies	+ Prepaid Insurance	=	Accounts Payable	+	D. Segal, Capital	– D. Segal, Drawing	+ Revenues	– Expenses	Description
(a)											
(b)											
(c)											
(d)											
(e)											
(f)											
(g)											
Bal.											

Problem 2-11B

Problem 2-12B

Mastery Problem

1.

	Assets					=	Liabilities	+	Owner's Equity				
	(Items Owned)						(Amts. Owed)		(Owner's Investment)			(Earnings)	
Cash	Accts. Rec.	Sup-plies	Prepaid Ins.	Tools	Van	=	Accts. Payable	+	L. Vozniak, Capital	L. Vozniak, Drawing	+ Rev.	− Exp.	Description
+	+	+	+	+				+	−				
(a)													
(b)													
(c)													
(d)													
(e)													
(f)													
(g)													
(h)													
(i)													
(j)													
(k)													
(l)													
(m)													
(n)													
(o)													
(p)													
2. Bal.													

Mastery Problem (Continued)

3.

4.

Mastery Problem (Concluded)

5.

Challenge Problem

Cash from customers		
Cash paid for wages		
Cash paid for rent		
Cash paid for utilities		
Cash paid for insurance		
Cash paid for supplies		
Cash paid for telephone		
Total cash paid for operating items		
Difference between cash received from customers and		
cash paid for goods and services		

Exercise 3-1A

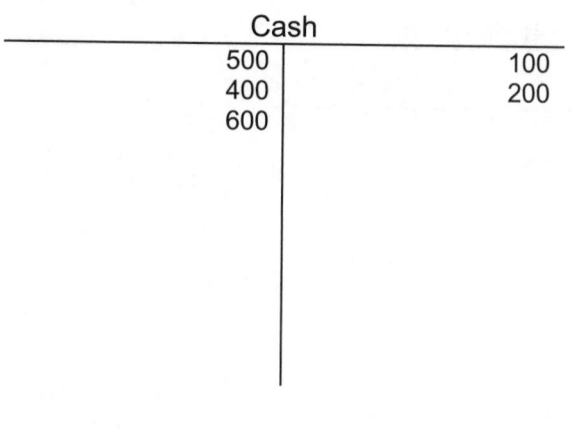

Cash

500	100
400	200
600	

Exercise 3-2A

a.   The cash account is increased with a ....   _____

b.   The owner's capital account is increased with a ....   _____

c.   The delivery equipment account is increased with a ....   _____

d.   The cash account is decreased with a ....   _____

e.   The liability account Accounts Payable is increased with a ....   _____

f.   The revenue account Delivery Fees is increased with a ....   _____

g.   The asset account Accounts Receivable is increased with a ....   _____

h.   The rent expense account is increased with a ....   _____

i.   The owner's drawing account is increased with a ....   _____

Exercise 3-3A

1. and 2.

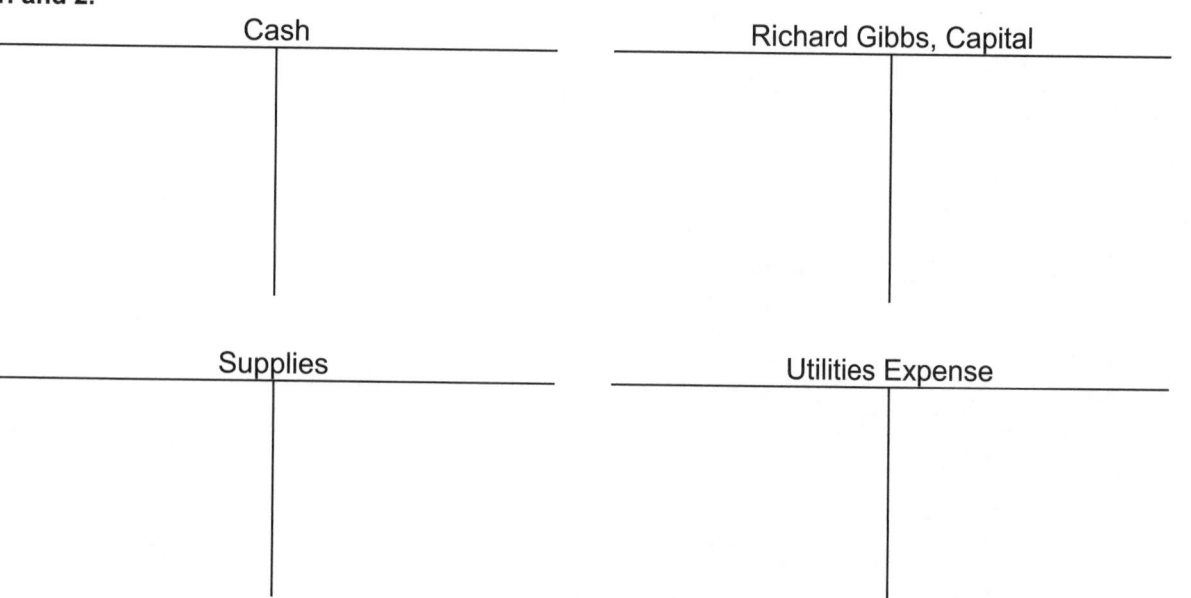

Cash	Richard Gibbs, Capital

Supplies	Utilities Expense

Exercise 3-4A

<u>Account</u>	<u>Debit or Credit</u>
1. Cash	_____
2. Wages Expense	_____
3. Accounts Payable	_____
4. Owner's Drawing	_____
5. Supplies	_____
6. Owner's Capital	_____
7. Equipment	_____

Exercises 3-5A and 3-6A: See page WP-21

Exercises 3-5A and 3-6A

Assets			=	Liabilities			+	Owner's Equity		
Dr. +		Cr. −		Dr. −		Cr. +		Dr. −		Cr. +

Drawing	**Expenses**
Dr. + Cr. −	Dr. + Cr. −

Revenues	
Dr. − Cr. +	

Exercise 3-7A

Assets		=	Liabilities		+	Owner's Equity	
Dr. +	Cr. −		Dr. −	Cr. +		Dr. −	Cr. +

Drawing
Dr. +	Cr. −

Expenses
Dr. +	Cr. −

Revenues
Dr. −	Cr. +

Exercise 3-8A

ACCOUNT	DEBIT BALANCE	CREDIT BALANCE

Exercise 3-9A

ACCOUNT	DEBIT BALANCE	CREDIT BALANCE

Exercise 3-10A

Exercise 3-11A

Exercise 3-12A

Problem 3-13A

1. and 2.

Assets			=	Liabilities			+	Owner's Equity		
Dr. +		Cr. −		Dr. −		Cr. +		Dr. −		Cr. +

Drawing			Expenses			Revenues		
Dr. +		Cr. −	Dr. +		Cr. −	Dr. −		Cr. +

Problem 3-13A (Concluded)

3.

_____

_____

_____

ACCOUNT	DEBIT BALANCE	CREDIT BALANCE

Problem 3-14A

1.

a. Total revenue for the month.. _____

b. Total expenses for the month .... _____

c. Net income for the month... _____

2.

a. Wilhelm Kohl's original investment in the business .... _____

   + Net income for the month.. _____

   – Owner's drawing .... _____

   Increase in capital... _____

   = Ending owner's equity.. _____

b. End-of-month accounting equation:

Assets	=	Liabilities	+	Owner's Equity
_____		_____		_____

Problem 3-15A

1.

Problem 3-15A (Concluded)

2.

3.

Exercise 3-1B

Accounts Payable	
300	450
250	350
	150

Exercise 3-2B

a. The asset account Prepaid Insurance is increased with a.................................. _____

b. The owner's drawing account is increased with a .... _____

c. The asset account Accounts Receivable is decreased with a .... _____

d. The liability account Accounts Payable is decreased with a.............................. _____

e. The owner's capital account is increased with a .... _____

f. The revenue account Professional Fees is increased with a........................... _____

g. The expense account Repair Expense is increased with a .... _____

h. The asset account Cash is decreased with a.. _____

i. The asset account Delivery Equipment is decreased with a............................ _____

Exercise 3-3B

1. and 2.

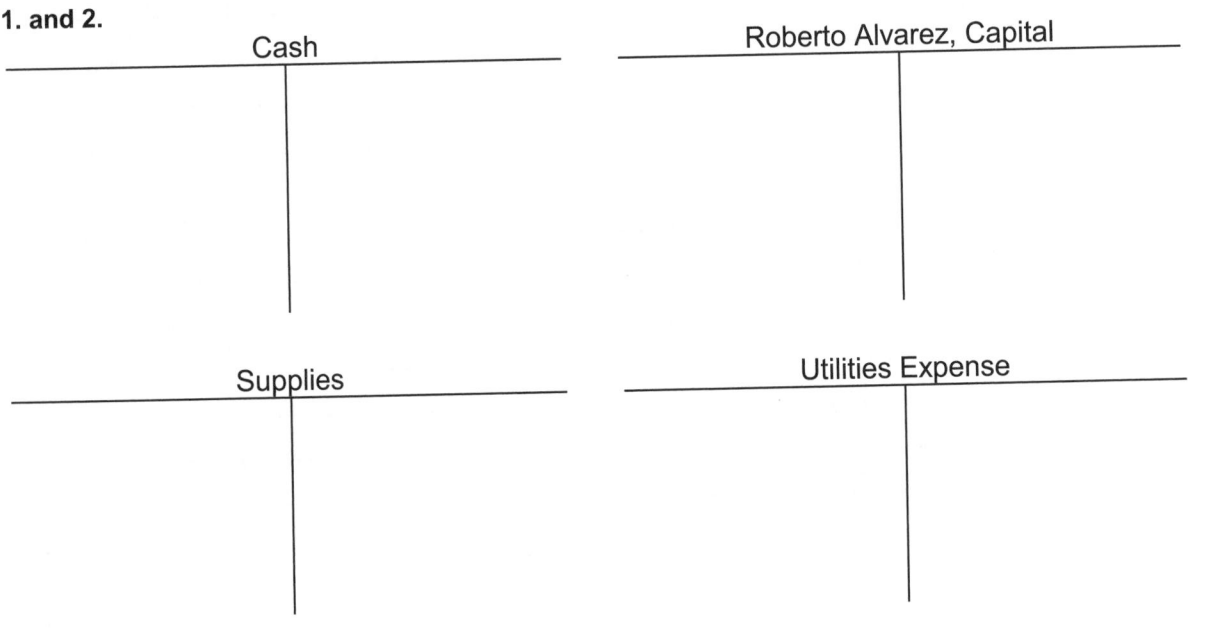

Cash

Roberto Alvarez, Capital

Supplies

Utilities Expense

Name _____

Exercise 3-4B

	Account	**Debit or Credit**
1.	Cash	_____
2.	Rent Expense	_____
3.	Notes Payable	_____
4.	Owner's Drawing	_____
5.	Accounts Receivable	_____
6.	Owner's Capital	_____
7.	Tools	_____

Exercises 3-5B and 3-6B: See page WP-32

Exercises 3-5B and 3-6B

Assets			=	Liabilities			+	Owner's Equity		
Dr.		Cr.		Dr.		Cr.		Dr.		Cr.
+		–		–		+		–		+

Drawing			Expenses			Revenues		
Dr.		Cr.	Dr.		Cr.	Dr.		Cr.
+		–	+		–	–		+

Exercise 3-7B

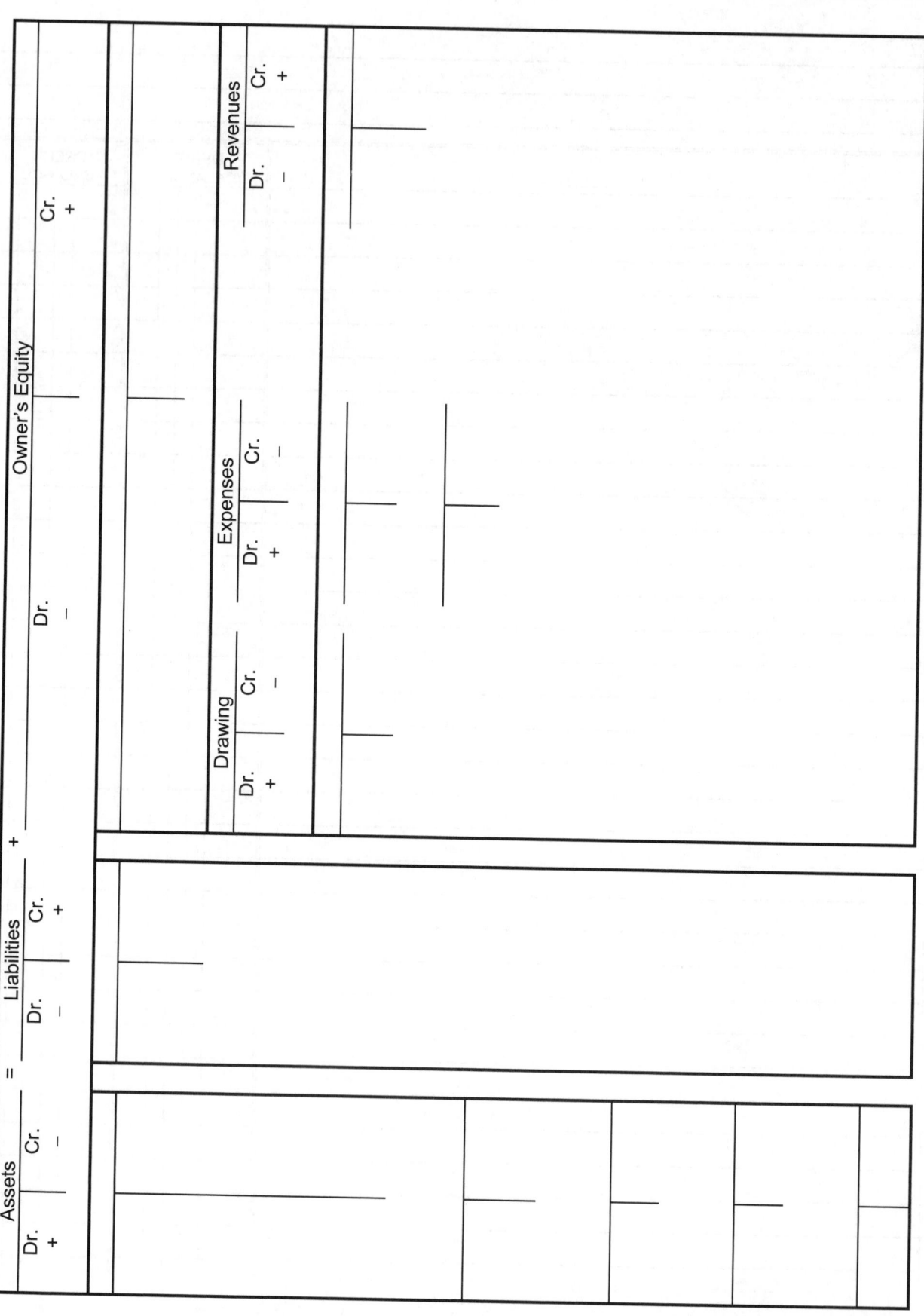

Exercise 3-8B

ACCOUNT	DEBIT BALANCE	CREDIT BALANCE

Exercise 3-9B

ACCOUNT	DEBIT BALANCE	CREDIT BALANCE

Exercise 3-10B

Exercise 3-11B

Exercise 3-12B

Problem 3-13B
1. and 2.

Assets		=	Liabilities		+	Owner's Equity		
Dr. +	Cr. −		Dr. −	Cr. +		Dr. −	Cr. +	

Drawing

Dr. +	Cr. −

Expenses

Dr. +	Cr. −

Revenues

Dr. −	Cr. +

Problem 3-13B (Concluded)

3.

ACCOUNT	DEBIT BALANCE	CREDIT BALANCE

Problem 3-14B

1.

a. Total revenue for the month... _____

b. Total expenses for the month .... _____

c. Net income for the month .... _____

2.

a. Sue Jantz's original investment in the business......... _____

+ Net income for the month .... _____

– Owner's drawing... _____

Increase in capital... _____

= Ending owner's equity... _____

b. End-of-month accounting equation:

Assets	=	Liabilities	+	Owner's Equity
_____		_____		_____

Problem 3-15B

1.

Problem 3-15B (Concluded)

2.

3.

Mastery Problem

1. and 2.

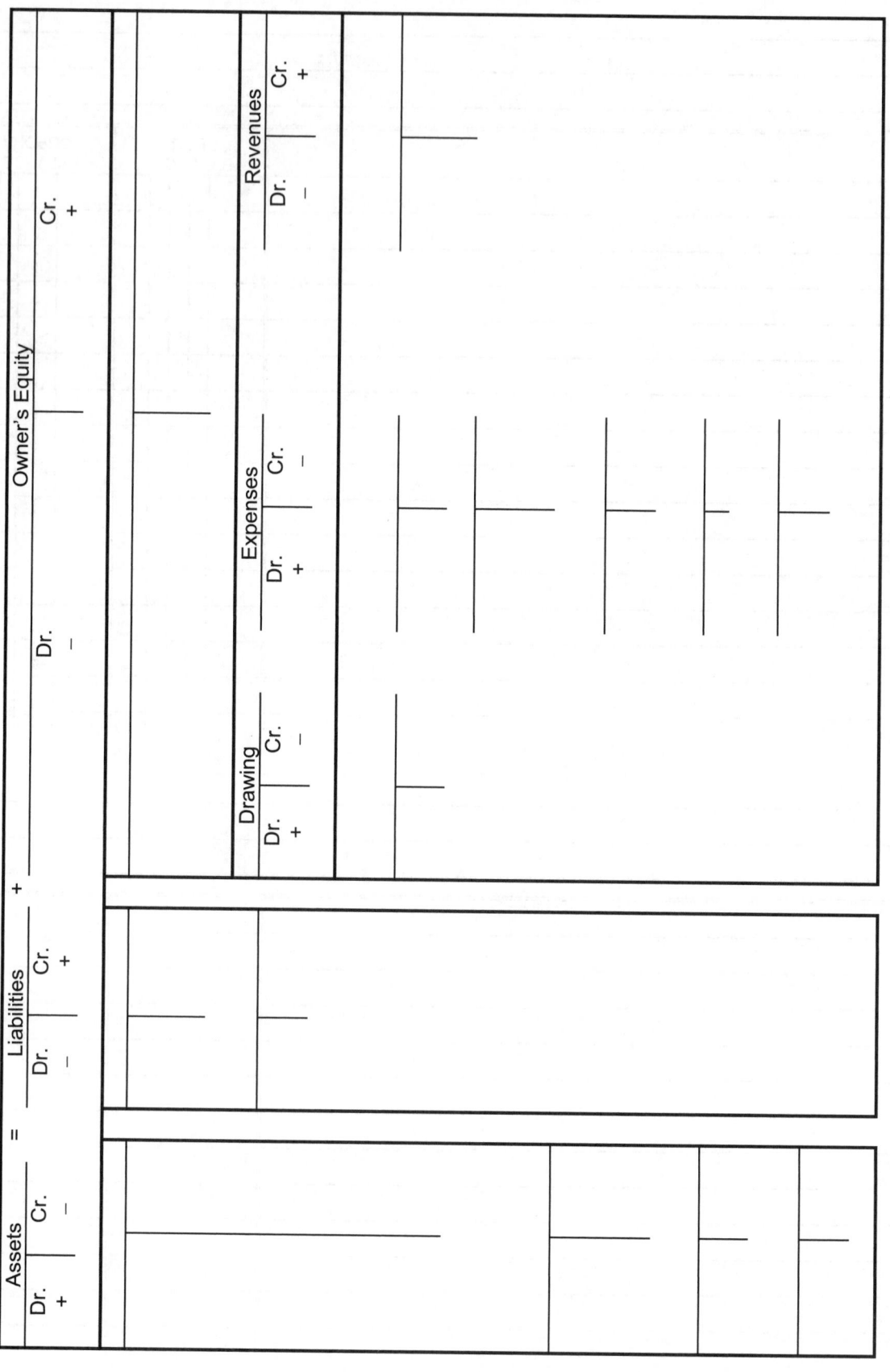

Mastery Problem (Continued)

3.

ACCOUNT	DEBIT BALANCE	CREDIT BALANCE

4.

Mastery Problem (Concluded)

5.

6.

Challenge Problem

1.

2.

Exercise 4-1A

1. _____ Check stubs or check register   a. A good or service has been sold.

2. _____ Purchase invoice from suppliers (vendors)   b. Cash has been received by the business.

3. _____ Sales tickets or invoices to customers   c. Cash has been paid by the business.

4. _____ Receipts or cash register tapes   d. Goods or services have been purchased by the business.

Exercise 4-2A

Transaction	Debit	Credit
1. Invested cash in the business, $5,000.	_____	_____
2. Paid office rent, $500.	_____	_____
3. Purchased office supplies on account, $300.	_____	_____
4. Received cash for services rendered (fees), $400.	_____	_____
5. Paid cash on account, $50.	_____	_____
6. Rendered services on account, $300.	_____	_____
7. Received cash for an amount owed by a customer, $100.	_____	_____

Exercise 4-3A

Exercise 4-3A (Concluded)

	Total Debits:	**Total Credits:**

Exercise 4-4A

GENERAL JOURNAL

	DATE	DESCRIPTION	POST. REF.	DEBIT	CREDIT	
1						1
2						2
3						3
4						4
5						5
6						6
7						7
8						8
9						9
10						10
11						11
12						12
13						13
14						14
15						15
16						16
17						17
18						18
19						19
20						20
21						21
22						22
23						23
24						24

Exercise 4-4A (Concluded)

GENERAL JOURNAL

	DATE		DESCRIPTION	POST. REF.	DEBIT	CREDIT	
1							1
2							2
3							3
4							4
5							5
6							6
7							7
8							8
9							9
10							10
11							11
12							12
13							13
14							14
15							15
16							16
17							17
18							18
19							19
20							20
21							21
22							22
23							23
24							24
25							25
26							26
27							27
28							28
29							29
30							30
31							31
32							32
33							33
34							34
35							35
36							36

Exercise 4-5A

GENERAL LEDGER

ACCOUNT _____   ACCOUNT NO. _____

DATE	ITEM	POST. REF.	DEBIT	CREDIT	BALANCE DEBIT	BALANCE CREDIT

ACCOUNT _____   ACCOUNT NO. _____

DATE	ITEM	POST. REF.	DEBIT	CREDIT	BALANCE DEBIT	BALANCE CREDIT

ACCOUNT _____   ACCOUNT NO. _____

DATE	ITEM	POST. REF.	DEBIT	CREDIT	BALANCE DEBIT	BALANCE CREDIT

Name _____

Exercise 4-5A (Continued)

ACCOUNT _____ ACCOUNT NO. _____

DATE	ITEM	POST. REF.	DEBIT	CREDIT	BALANCE DEBIT	BALANCE CREDIT

(four identical blank account ledger forms)

Exercise 4-5A (Continued)

ACCOUNT _____   ACCOUNT NO. _____

DATE	ITEM	POST. REF.	DEBIT	CREDIT	BALANCE	
					DEBIT	CREDIT

ACCOUNT _____   ACCOUNT NO. _____

DATE	ITEM	POST. REF.	DEBIT	CREDIT	BALANCE	
					DEBIT	CREDIT

ACCOUNT _____   ACCOUNT NO. _____

DATE	ITEM	POST. REF.	DEBIT	CREDIT	BALANCE	
					DEBIT	CREDIT

ACCOUNT _____   ACCOUNT NO. _____

DATE	ITEM	POST. REF.	DEBIT	CREDIT	BALANCE	
					DEBIT	CREDIT

ACCOUNT _____   ACCOUNT NO. _____

DATE	ITEM	POST. REF.	DEBIT	CREDIT	BALANCE	
					DEBIT	CREDIT

Exercise 4-5A (Concluded)

ACCOUNT TITLE	ACCT. NO.	DEBIT BALANCE	CREDIT BALANCE

Exercise 4-6A

Exercise 4-6A (Concluded)

Exercise 4-7A

Exercise 4-7A (Concluded)

Exercise 4-8A

GENERAL JOURNAL   PAGE

	DATE		DESCRIPTION	POST. REF.	DEBIT	CREDIT	
15	May	17	Office Equipment		4 0 0 00		15
16			Cash			4 0 0 00	16
17			Purchased copy paper				17
18							18
23		23	Cash	101	1 0 0 0 00		23
24			Service Fees	401		1 0 0 0 00	24
25			Received cash for services previously earned				25
26							26
27							27
28							28
29							29
30							30
31							31
32							32
33							33

Problem 4-9A
2. (For 1. and 3., see page WP-58.)

GENERAL JOURNAL

PAGE   1

	DATE		DESCRIPTION	POST. REF.	DEBIT	CREDIT	
1							1
2							2
3							3
4							4
5							5
6							6
7							7
8							8
9							9
10							10
11							11
12							12
13							13
14							14
15							15
16							16
17							17
18							18
19							19
20							20
21							21
22							22
23							23
24							24
25							25
26							26
27							27
28							28
29							29
30							30
31							31
32							32
33							33
34							34
35							35
36							36

Problem 4-9A (Continued)

GENERAL JOURNAL

DATE	DESCRIPTION	POST. REF.	DEBIT	CREDIT	
					1
					2
					3
					4
					5
					6
					7
					8
					9
					10
					11
					12
					13
					14
					15
					16
					17
					18
					19
					20
					21
					22
					23
					24
					25
					26
					27
					28
					29
					30
					31
					32
					33
					34
					35
					36

Problem 4-9A (Continued)

GENERAL JOURNAL

	DATE		DESCRIPTION	POST. REF.	DEBIT	CREDIT	
1							1
2							2
3							3
4							4
5							5
6							6
7							7
8							8
9							9
10							10
11							11
12							12
13							13
14							14
15							15
16							16
17							17
18							18
19							19
20							20
21							21
22							22
23							23
24							24
25							25
26							26
27							27
28							28
29							29
30							30
31							31
32							32
33							33
34							34
35							35
36							36

Problm 4-9A (Continued)

1. and 3.

GENERAL LEDGER

ACCOUNT Cash
ACCOUNT NO. 101

DATE	ITEM	POST. REF.	DEBIT	CREDIT	BALANCE DEBIT	BALANCE CREDIT

ACCOUNT Office Supplies
ACCOUNT NO. 142

DATE	ITEM	POST. REF.	DEBIT	CREDIT	BALANCE DEBIT	BALANCE CREDIT

Problem 4-9A (Continued)

ACCOUNT **Office Equipment**   ACCOUNT NO. 181

DATE	ITEM	POST. REF.	DEBIT	CREDIT	BALANCE DEBIT	CREDIT

ACCOUNT **Accounts Payable**   ACCOUNT NO. 202

DATE	ITEM	POST. REF.	DEBIT	CREDIT	BALANCE DEBIT	CREDIT

ACCOUNT **Annette Creighton, Capital**   ACCOUNT NO. 311

DATE	ITEM	POST. REF.	DEBIT	CREDIT	BALANCE DEBIT	CREDIT

ACCOUNT **Annette Creighton, Drawing**   ACCOUNT NO. 312

DATE	ITEM	POST. REF.	DEBIT	CREDIT	BALANCE DEBIT	CREDIT

Problem 4-9A (Continued)

ACCOUNT Consulting Fees   ACCOUNT NO. 401

DATE	ITEM	POST. REF.	DEBIT	CREDIT	BALANCE	
					DEBIT	CREDIT

ACCOUNT Wages Expense   ACCOUNT NO. 511

DATE	ITEM	POST. REF.	DEBIT	CREDIT	BALANCE	
					DEBIT	CREDIT

ACCOUNT Advertising Expense   ACCOUNT NO. 512

DATE	ITEM	POST. REF.	DEBIT	CREDIT	BALANCE	
					DEBIT	CREDIT

ACCOUNT Rent Expense   ACCOUNT NO. 521

DATE	ITEM	POST. REF.	DEBIT	CREDIT	BALANCE	
					DEBIT	CREDIT

Problem 4-9A (Continued)

ACCOUNT Telephone Expense   ACCOUNT NO. 525

DATE	ITEM	POST. REF.	DEBIT	CREDIT	BALANCE DEBIT	CREDIT

ACCOUNT Transportation Expense   ACCOUNT NO. 526

DATE	ITEM	POST. REF.	DEBIT	CREDIT	BALANCE DEBIT	CREDIT

ACCOUNT Utilities Expense   ACCOUNT NO. 533

DATE	ITEM	POST. REF.	DEBIT	CREDIT	BALANCE DEBIT	CREDIT

ACCOUNT Miscellaneous Expense   ACCOUNT NO. 549

DATE	ITEM	POST. REF.	DEBIT	CREDIT	BALANCE DEBIT	CREDIT

Problem 4-9A (Continued)

4.

ACCOUNT TITLE	ACCT. NO.	DEBIT BALANCE	CREDIT BALANCE

Problem 4-9A (Continued)

5.

Problem 4-9A (Concluded)

Problem 4-10A

2. (For 1. and 3., see page WP-68.)

GENERAL JOURNAL

PAGE 7

DATE	DESCRIPTION	POST. REF.	DEBIT	CREDIT
1				
2				
3				
4				
5				
6				
7				
8				
9				
10				
11				
12				
13				
14				
15				
16				
17				
18				
19				
20				
21				
22				
23				
24				
25				
26				
27				
28				
29				
30				
31				
32				
33				
34				

Problem 4-10A (Continued)

GENERAL JOURNAL

	DATE		DESCRIPTION	POST. REF.	DEBIT	CREDIT	
1							1
2							2
3							3
4							4
5							5
6							6
7							7
8							8
9							9
10							10
11							11
12							12
13							13
14							14
15							15
16							16
17							17
18							18
19							19
20							20
21							21
22							22
23							23
24							24
25							25
26							26
27							27
28							28
29							29
30							30
31							31
32							32
33							33
34							34
35							35
36							36

Problem 4-10A (Continued)

GENERAL JOURNAL

PAGE 9

	DATE	DESCRIPTION	POST. REF.	DEBIT	CREDIT	
1						1
2						2
3						3
4						4
5						5
6						6
7						7
8						8
9						9
10						10
11						11
12						12
13						13
14						14
15						15
16						16
17						17
18						18
19						19
20						20
21						21
22						22
23						23
24						24
25						25
26						26
27						27
28						28
29						29
30						30
31						31
32						32
33						33
34						34
35						35
36						36

Problem 4-10A (Continued)

1. and 3.

ACCOUNT Cash

GENERAL LEDGER

ACCOUNT NO. 101

DATE	ITEM	POST. REF.	DEBIT	CREDIT	BALANCE	
					DEBIT	CREDIT

Problem 4-10A (Continued)

ACCOUNT Accounts Receivable   ACCOUNT NO. 122

DATE	ITEM	POST. REF.	DEBIT	CREDIT	BALANCE	
					DEBIT	CREDIT

ACCOUNT Office Supplies   ACCOUNT NO. 142

DATE	ITEM	POST. REF.	DEBIT	CREDIT	BALANCE	
					DEBIT	CREDIT

ACCOUNT Office Equipment   ACCOUNT NO. 181

DATE	ITEM	POST. REF.	DEBIT	CREDIT	BALANCE	
					DEBIT	CREDIT

ACCOUNT Delivery Truck   ACCOUNT NO. 185

DATE	ITEM	POST. REF.	DEBIT	CREDIT	BALANCE	
					DEBIT	CREDIT

Problem 4-10A (Continued)

ACCOUNT Accounts Payable   ACCOUNT NO. 202

DATE	ITEM	POST. REF.	DEBIT	CREDIT	BALANCE DEBIT	BALANCE CREDIT

ACCOUNT Jim Andrews, Capital   ACCOUNT NO. 311

DATE	ITEM	POST. REF.	DEBIT	CREDIT	BALANCE DEBIT	BALANCE CREDIT

ACCOUNT Jim Andrews, Drawing   ACCOUNT NO. 312

DATE	ITEM	POST. REF.	DEBIT	CREDIT	BALANCE DEBIT	BALANCE CREDIT

ACCOUNT Delivery Fees   ACCOUNT NO. 401

DATE	ITEM	POST. REF.	DEBIT	CREDIT	BALANCE DEBIT	BALANCE CREDIT

Problem 4-10A (Continued)

ACCOUNT Wages Expense   ACCOUNT NO. 511

DATE	ITEM	POST. REF.	DEBIT	CREDIT	BALANCE DEBIT	BALANCE CREDIT

ACCOUNT Advertising Expense   ACCOUNT NO. 512

DATE	ITEM	POST. REF.	DEBIT	CREDIT	BALANCE DEBIT	BALANCE CREDIT

ACCOUNT Rent Expense   ACCOUNT NO. 521

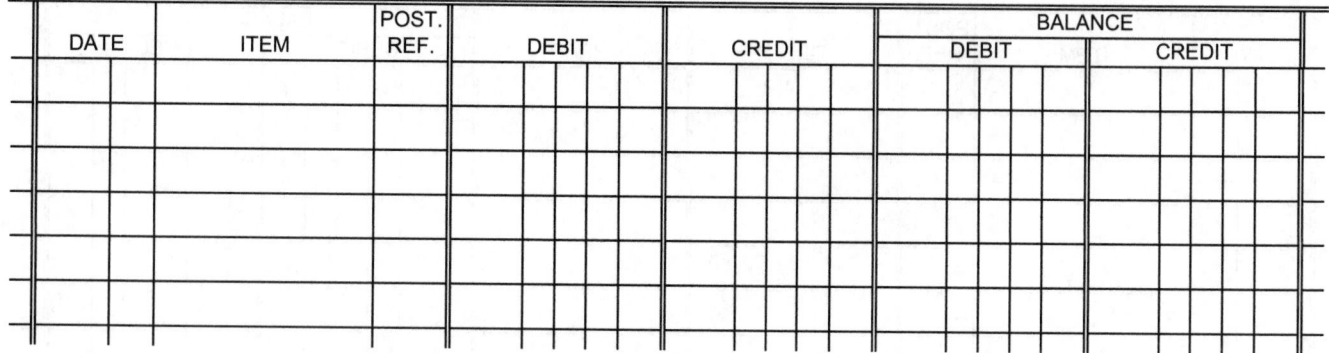

DATE	ITEM	POST. REF.	DEBIT	CREDIT	BALANCE DEBIT	BALANCE CREDIT

ACCOUNT Telephone Expense   ACCOUNT NO. 525

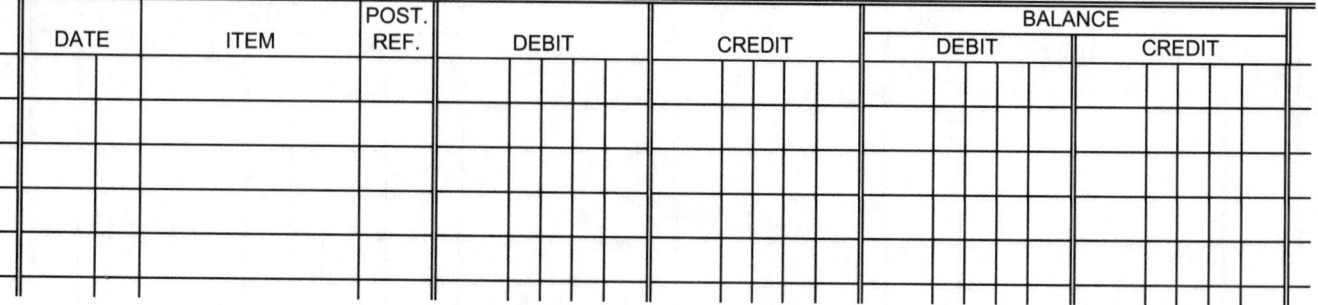

DATE	ITEM	POST. REF.	DEBIT	CREDIT	BALANCE DEBIT	BALANCE CREDIT

Problem 4-10A (Continued)

ACCOUNT Electricity Expense   ACCOUNT NO. 533

DATE	ITEM	POST. REF.	DEBIT	CREDIT	BALANCE DEBIT	BALANCE CREDIT

ACCOUNT Charitable Contributions Expense   ACCOUNT NO. 534

DATE	ITEM	POST. REF.	DEBIT	CREDIT	BALANCE DEBIT	BALANCE CREDIT

ACCOUNT Gas and Oil Expense   ACCOUNT NO. 538

DATE	ITEM	POST. REF.	DEBIT	CREDIT	BALANCE DEBIT	BALANCE CREDIT

ACCOUNT Miscellaneous Expense   ACCOUNT NO. 549

DATE	ITEM	POST. REF.	DEBIT	CREDIT	BALANCE DEBIT	BALANCE CREDIT

Problem 4-10A (Concluded)

4.

ACCOUNT TITLE	ACCT. NO.	DEBIT BALANCE	CREDIT BALANCE

Problem 4-11A

	GENERAL JOURNAL			PAGE	
DATE	DESCRIPTION	POST. REF.	DEBIT	CREDIT	

(blank journal rows numbered 1 through 20)

Exercise 4-1B

1. Cash register tape

_____

_____

_____

2. Sales ticket (issued to customer)

_____

_____

_____

3. Purchase invoice (received from supplier or vendor)

_____

_____

4. Check stub

_____

_____

_____

Exercise 4-2B

Transaction	Debit	Credit
1. Invested cash in the business, $1,000.	_____	_____
2. Performed services on account, $200.	_____	_____
3. Purchased office equipment on account, $500.	_____	_____
4. Received cash on account for services previously rendered, $200.	_____	_____
5. Made a payment on account, $100.	_____	_____

Exercise 4-3B

Total Debits: **Total Credits:**

_____   _____
_____   _____
_____   _____
_____   _____

Exercise 4-4B

GENERAL JOURNAL

	DATE	DESCRIPTION	POST. REF.	DEBIT	CREDIT	
1						1
2						2
3						3
4						4
5						5
6						6
7						7
8						8
9						9
10						10
11						11
12						12
13						13
14						14
15						15
16						16
17						17
18						18
19						19
20						20
21						21
22						22
23						23
24						24
25						25
26						26
27						27
28						28
29						29
30						30
31						31
32						32
33						33
34						34
35						35
36						36

Exercise 4-4B (Concluded)

GENERAL JOURNAL

	DATE		DESCRIPTION	POST. REF.	DEBIT	CREDIT	
1							1
2							2
3							3
4							4
5							5
6							6
7							7
8							8
9							9
10							10
11							11
12							12
13							13
14							14
15							15
16							16
17							17
18							18
19							19
20							20
21							21
22							22
23							23
24							24
25							25
26							26
27							27
28							28
29							29
30							30
31							31
32							32
33							33
34							34
35							35
36							36

Exercise 4-5B

GENERAL LEDGER

ACCOUNT _____ ACCOUNT NO. _____

DATE	ITEM	POST. REF.	DEBIT	CREDIT	BALANCE	
					DEBIT	CREDIT

ACCOUNT _____ ACCOUNT NO. _____

DATE	ITEM	POST. REF.	DEBIT	CREDIT	BALANCE	
					DEBIT	CREDIT

ACCOUNT _____ ACCOUNT NO. _____

DATE	ITEM	POST. REF.	DEBIT	CREDIT	BALANCE	
					DEBIT	CREDIT

Exercise 4-5B (Continued)

ACCOUNT _____   ACCOUNT NO. _____

DATE	ITEM	POST. REF.	DEBIT	CREDIT	BALANCE DEBIT	BALANCE CREDIT

ACCOUNT _____   ACCOUNT NO. _____

DATE	ITEM	POST. REF.	DEBIT	CREDIT	BALANCE DEBIT	BALANCE CREDIT

ACCOUNT _____   ACCOUNT NO. _____

DATE	ITEM	POST. REF.	DEBIT	CREDIT	BALANCE DEBIT	BALANCE CREDIT

ACCOUNT _____   ACCOUNT NO. _____

DATE	ITEM	POST. REF.	DEBIT	CREDIT	BALANCE DEBIT	BALANCE CREDIT

Exercise 4-5B (Continued)

ACCOUNT _____ ACCOUNT NO. _____

DATE	ITEM	POST. REF.	DEBIT	CREDIT	BALANCE	
					DEBIT	CREDIT

ACCOUNT _____ ACCOUNT NO. _____

DATE	ITEM	POST. REF.	DEBIT	CREDIT	BALANCE	
					DEBIT	CREDIT

ACCOUNT _____ ACCOUNT NO. _____

DATE	ITEM	POST. REF.	DEBIT	CREDIT	BALANCE	
					DEBIT	CREDIT

ACCOUNT _____ ACCOUNT NO. _____

DATE	ITEM	POST. REF.	DEBIT	CREDIT	BALANCE	
					DEBIT	CREDIT

ACCOUNT _____ ACCOUNT NO. _____

DATE	ITEM	POST. REF.	DEBIT	CREDIT	BALANCE	
					DEBIT	CREDIT

Exercise 4-5B (Concluded)

ACCOUNT TITLE	ACCT. NO.	DEBIT BALANCE	CREDIT BALANCE

Exercise 4-6B

Exercise 4-6B (Concluded)

Exercise 4-7B

Exercise 4-7B (Concluded)

Exercise 4-8B

GENERAL JOURNAL

PAGE

	DATE		DESCRIPTION	POST. REF.	DEBIT	CREDIT	
15	Apr.	6	Office Supplies		530 00		15
16			Cash			530 00	16
17			Purchased office equipment				17
18							18
23		21	Cash	101	300 00		23
24			Service Fees	401		300 00	24
25			Revenue earned from services				25
26			previously rendered				26
27							27
28							28
29							29
30							30
31							31
32							32
33							33

Problem 4-9B
2. (For 1. and 3., see page WP-88.)

GENERAL JOURNAL

	DATE		DESCRIPTION	POST. REF.	DEBIT	CREDIT	
1							1
2							2
3							3
4							4
5							5
6							6
7							7
8							8
9							9
10							10
11							11
12							12
13							13
14							14
15							15
16							16
17							17
18							18
19							19
20							20
21							21
22							22
23							23
24							24
25							25
26							26
27							27
28							28
29							29
30							30
31							31
32							32
33							33
34							34
35							35
36							36

Problem 4-9B (Continued)

GENERAL JOURNAL

PAGE 2

DATE	DESCRIPTION	POST. REF.	DEBIT	CREDIT	
					1
					2
					3
					4
					5
					6
					7
					8
					9
					10
					11
					12
					13
					14
					15
					16
					17
					18
					19
					20
					21
					22
					23
					24
					25
					26
					27
					28
					29
					30
					31
					32
					33
					34
					35
					36

Problem 4-9B (Continued)

GENERAL JOURNAL

	DATE	DESCRIPTION	POST. REF.	DEBIT	CREDIT	
1						1
2						2
3						3
4						4
5						5
6						6
7						7
8						8
9						9
10						10
11						11
12						12
13						13
14						14
15						15
16						16
17						17
18						18
19						19
20						20
21						21
22						22
23						23
24						24
25						25
26						26
27						27
28						28
29						29
30						30
31						31
32						32
33						33
34						34
35						35
36						36

Problem 4-9B (Continued)

1, and 3.

GENERAL LEDGER

ACCOUNT Cash   ACCOUNT NO. 101

DATE	ITEM	POST. REF.	DEBIT	CREDIT	BALANCE	
					DEBIT	CREDIT

ACCOUNT Accounts Receivable   ACCOUNT NO. 122

DATE	ITEM	POST. REF.	DEBIT	CREDIT	BALANCE	
					DEBIT	CREDIT

Problem 4-9B (Continued)

ACCOUNT Office Supplies   ACCOUNT NO. 142

DATE	ITEM	POST. REF.	DEBIT	CREDIT	BALANCE DEBIT	BALANCE CREDIT

ACCOUNT Office Equipment   ACCOUNT NO. 181

DATE	ITEM	POST. REF.	DEBIT	CREDIT	BALANCE DEBIT	BALANCE CREDIT

ACCOUNT Accounts Payable   ACCOUNT NO. 202

DATE	ITEM	POST. REF.	DEBIT	CREDIT	BALANCE DEBIT	BALANCE CREDIT

ACCOUNT Benito Mendez, Capital   ACCOUNT NO. 311

DATE	ITEM	POST. REF.	DEBIT	CREDIT	BALANCE DEBIT	BALANCE CREDIT

Problem 4-9B (Continued)

ACCOUNT Benito Mendez, Drawing   ACCOUNT NO. 312

DATE	ITEM	POST. REF.	DEBIT	CREDIT	BALANCE DEBIT	BALANCE CREDIT

ACCOUNT Appraisal Fees   ACCOUNT NO. 401

DATE	ITEM	POST. REF.	DEBIT	CREDIT	BALANCE DEBIT	BALANCE CREDIT

ACCOUNT Wages Expense   ACCOUNT NO. 511

DATE	ITEM	POST. REF.	DEBIT	CREDIT	BALANCE DEBIT	BALANCE CREDIT

ACCOUNT Advertising Expense   ACCOUNT NO. 512

DATE	ITEM	POST. REF.	DEBIT	CREDIT	BALANCE DEBIT	BALANCE CREDIT

Problem 4-9B (Continued)

ACCOUNT Rent Expense   ACCOUNT NO. 521

DATE	ITEM	POST. REF.	DEBIT	CREDIT	BALANCE	
					DEBIT	CREDIT

ACCOUNT Telephone Expense   ACCOUNT NO. 525

DATE	ITEM	POST. REF.	DEBIT	CREDIT	BALANCE	
					DEBIT	CREDIT

ACCOUNT Transportation Expense   ACCOUNT NO 526

DATE	ITEM	POST. REF.	DEBIT	CREDIT	BALANCE	
					DEBIT	CREDIT

ACCOUNT Electricity Expense   ACCOUNT NO. 533

DATE	ITEM	POST. REF.	DEBIT	CREDIT	BALANCE	
					DEBIT	CREDIT

ACCOUNT Miscellaneous Expense   ACCOUNT NO. 549

DATE	ITEM	POST. REF.	DEBIT	CREDIT	BALANCE	
					DEBIT	CREDIT

Problem 4-9B (Continued)

4.

ACCOUNT TITLE	ACCT. NO.	DEBIT BALANCE	CREDIT BALANCE

Problem 4-9B (Continued)

5.

Problem 4-9B (Concluded)

Problem 4-10B

2. (For 1. and 3., see page WP-98.)

GENERAL JOURNAL

	DATE		DESCRIPTION	POST. REF.	DEBIT	CREDIT	
1							1
2							2
3							3
4							4
5							5
6							6
7							7
8							8
9							9
10							10
11							11
12							12
13							13
14							14
15							15
16							16
17							17
18							18
19							19
20							20
21							21
22							22
23							23
24							24
25							25
26							26
27							27
28							28
29							29
30							30
31							31
32							32
33							33
34							34

Problem 4-10B (Continued)

GENERAL JOURNAL

	DATE		DESCRIPTION	POST. REF.	DEBIT	CREDIT	
1							1
2							2
3							3
4							4
5							5
6							6
7							7
8							8
9							9
10							10
11							11
12							12
13							13
14							14
15							15
16							16
17							17
18							18
19							19
20							20
21							21
22							22
23							23
24							24
25							25
26							26
27							27
28							28
29							29
30							30
31							31
32							32
33							33
34							34
35							35
36							36

Problem 4-10B (Continued)

GENERAL JOURNAL

	DATE	DESCRIPTION	POST. REF.	DEBIT	CREDIT	
1						1
2						2
3						3
4						4
5						5
6						6
7						7
8						8
9						9
10						10
11						11
12						12
13						13
14						14
15						15
16						16
17						17
18						18
19						19
20						20
21						21
22						22
23						23
24						24
25						25
26						26
27						27
28						28
29						29
30						30
31						31
32						32
33						33
34						34
35						35
36						36

Problem 4-10B (Continued)

1. and 3.

GENERAL LEDGER

ACCOUNT Cash   ACCOUNT NO. 101

DATE	ITEM	POST. REF.	DEBIT	CREDIT	BALANCE DEBIT	BALANCE CREDIT

ACCOUNT Accounts Receivable   ACCOUNT NO. 122

DATE	ITEM	POST. REF.	DEBIT	CREDIT	BALANCE DEBIT	BALANCE CREDIT

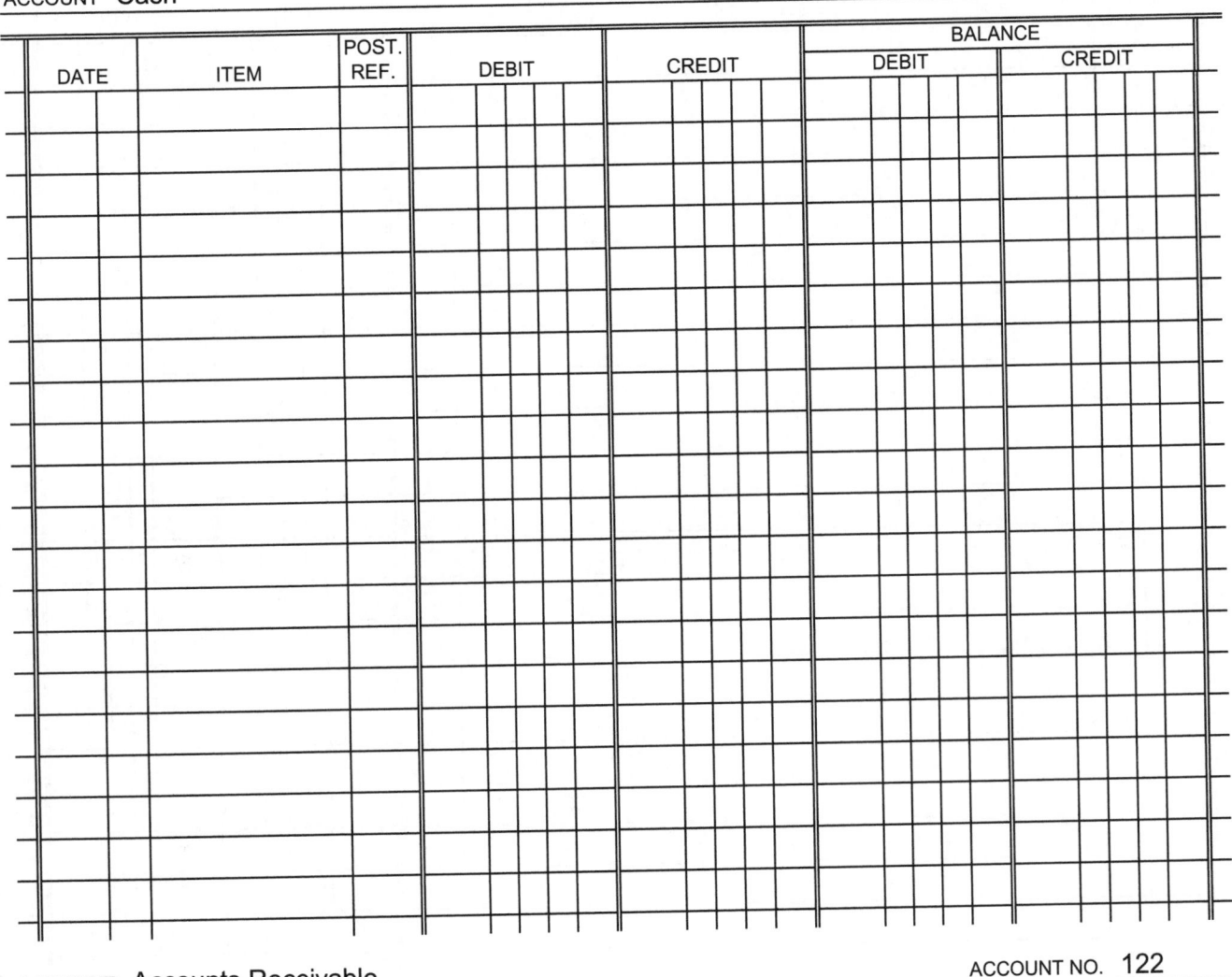

Problem 4-10B (Continued)

ACCOUNT Tailoring Supplies   ACCOUNT NO. 141

DATE	ITEM	POST. REF.	DEBIT	CREDIT	BALANCE DEBIT	BALANCE CREDIT

ACCOUNT Tailoring Equipment   ACCOUNT NO. 183

DATE	ITEM	POST. REF.	DEBIT	CREDIT	BALANCE DEBIT	BALANCE CREDIT

ACCOUNT Accounts Payable   ACCOUNT NO. 202

DATE	ITEM	POST. REF.	DEBIT	CREDIT	BALANCE DEBIT	BALANCE CREDIT

ACCOUNT Ann Taylor, Capital   ACCOUNT NO. 311

DATE	ITEM	POST. REF.	DEBIT	CREDIT	BALANCE DEBIT	BALANCE CREDIT

Problem 4-10B (Continued)

ACCOUNT Ann Taylor, Drawing   ACCOUNT NO. 312

DATE	ITEM	POST. REF.	DEBIT	CREDIT	BALANCE DEBIT	BALANCE CREDIT

ACCOUNT Tailoring Fees   ACCOUNT NO. 401

DATE	ITEM	POST. REF.	DEBIT	CREDIT	BALANCE DEBIT	BALANCE CREDIT

ACCOUNT Wages Expense   ACCOUNT NO. 511

DATE	ITEM	POST. REF.	DEBIT	CREDIT	BALANCE DEBIT	BALANCE CREDIT

ACCOUNT Advertising Expense   ACCOUNT NO. 512

DATE	ITEM	POST. REF.	DEBIT	CREDIT	BALANCE DEBIT	BALANCE CREDIT

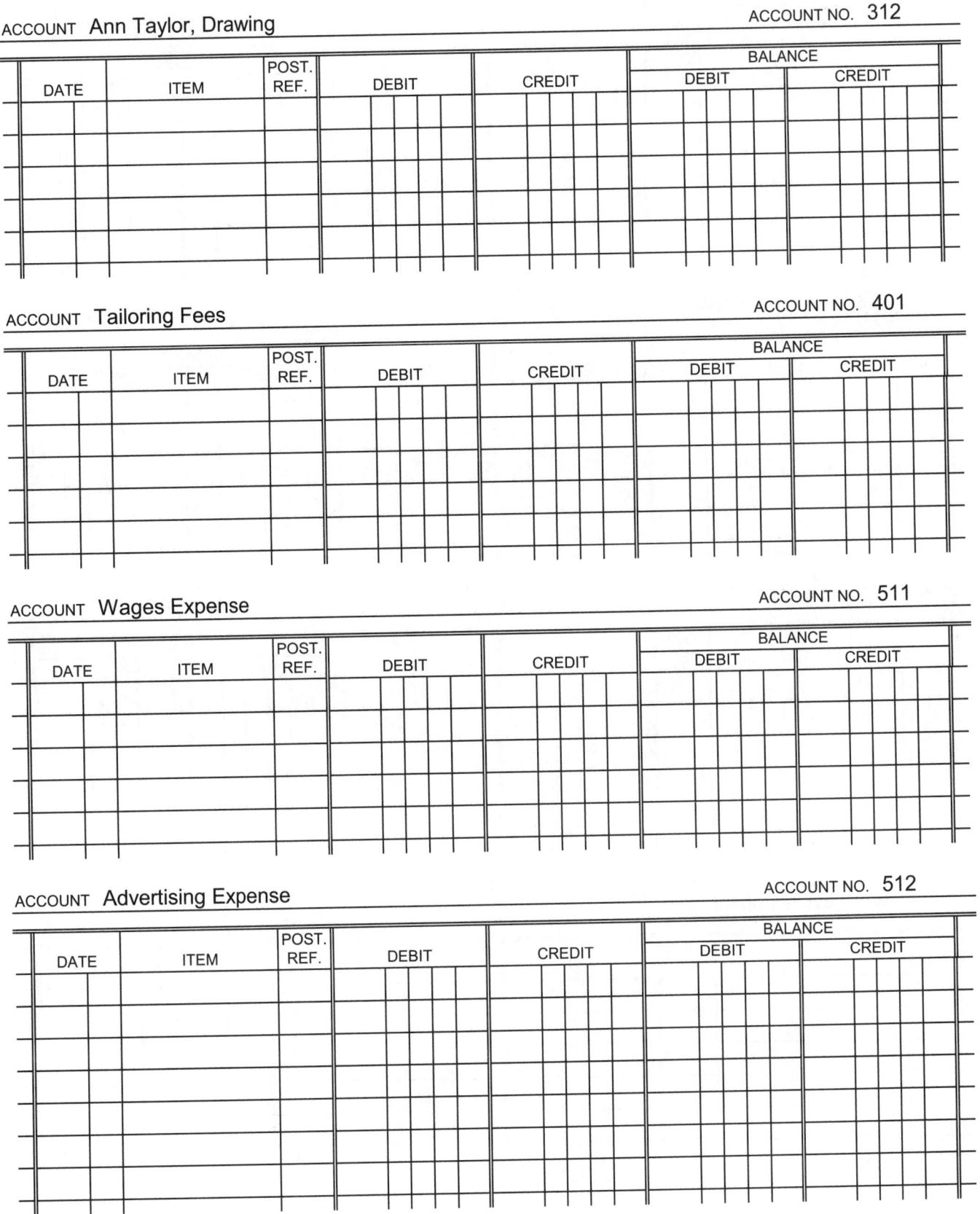

Problem 4-10B (Continued)

ACCOUNT Rent Expense   ACCOUNT NO. 521

DATE	ITEM	POST. REF.	DEBIT	CREDIT	BALANCE	
					DEBIT	CREDIT

ACCOUNT Telephone Expense   ACCOUNT NO. 525

DATE	ITEM	POST. REF.	DEBIT	CREDIT	BALANCE	
					DEBIT	CREDIT

ACCOUNT Electricity Expense   ACCOUNT NO. 533

DATE	ITEM	POST. REF.	DEBIT	CREDIT	BALANCE	
					DEBIT	CREDIT

ACCOUNT Miscellaneous Expense   ACCOUNT NO. 549

DATE	ITEM	POST. REF.	DEBIT	CREDIT	BALANCE	
					DEBIT	CREDIT

Problem 4-10B (Concluded)

4.

ACCOUNT TITLE	ACCT. NO.	DEBIT BALANCE	CREDIT BALANCE

Problem 4-11B

GENERAL JOURNAL

PAGE _____

	DATE		DESCRIPTION	POST. REF.	DEBIT	CREDIT	
1							1
2							2
3							3
4							4
5							5
6							6
7							7
8							8
9							9
10							10
11							11
12							12
13							13
14							14
15							15
16							16
17							17
18							18
19							19
20							20
21							21
22							22
23							23

Mastery Problem

1.

GENERAL JOURNAL

DATE	DESCRIPTION	POST. REF.	DEBIT	CREDIT	
					1
					2
					3
					4
					5
					6
					7
					8
					9
					10
					11
					12
					13
					14
					15
					16
					17
					18
					19
					20
					21
					22
					23
					24
					25
					26
					27
					28
					29
					30
					31
					32
					33
					34
					35

Mastery Problem (Continued)

GENERAL JOURNAL

	DATE	DESCRIPTION	POST. REF.	DEBIT	CREDIT	
1						1
2						2
3						3
4						4
5						5
6						6
7						7
8						8
9						9
10						10
11						11
12						12
13						13
14						14
15						15
16						16
17						17
18						18
19						19
20						20
21						21
22						22
23						23
24						24
25						25
26						26
27						27
28						28
29						29
30						30
31						31
32						32
33						33
34						34
35						35

Mastery Problem (Continued)

GENERAL JOURNAL

PAGE 3

	DATE	DESCRIPTION	POST. REF.	DEBIT	CREDIT	
1						1
2						2
3						3
4						4
5						5
6						6
7						7
8						8
9						9
10						10
11						11
12						12
13						13
14						14
15						15
16						16
17						17
18						18
19						19
20						20
21						21
22						22
23						23
24						24
25						25
26						26
27						27
28						28
29						29
30						30
31						31
32						32
33						33
34						34
35						35

Mastery Problem (Continued)

2.

ACCOUNT Cash   **GENERAL LEDGER**   ACCOUNT NO. 101

DATE	ITEM	POST. REF.	DEBIT	CREDIT	BALANCE	
					DEBIT	CREDIT

ACCOUNT Office Supplies   ACCOUNT NO. 142

DATE	ITEM	POST. REF.	DEBIT	CREDIT	BALANCE	
					DEBIT	CREDIT

ACCOUNT Athletic Equipment   ACCOUNT NO. 183

DATE	ITEM	POST. REF.	DEBIT	CREDIT	BALANCE	
					DEBIT	CREDIT

Mastery Problem (Continued)

ACCOUNT **Basketball Facilities**   ACCOUNT NO. **184**

DATE	ITEM	POST. REF.	DEBIT	CREDIT	BALANCE DEBIT	BALANCE CREDIT

ACCOUNT **Accounts Payable**   ACCOUNT NO. **202**

DATE	ITEM	POST. REF.	DEBIT	CREDIT	BALANCE DEBIT	BALANCE CREDIT

ACCOUNT **Barry Bird, Capital**   ACCOUNT NO. **311**

DATE	ITEM	POST. REF.	DEBIT	CREDIT	BALANCE DEBIT	BALANCE CREDIT

ACCOUNT **Barry Bird, Drawing**   ACCOUNT NO. **312**

DATE	ITEM	POST. REF.	DEBIT	CREDIT	BALANCE DEBIT	BALANCE CREDIT

Mastery Problem (Continued)

ACCOUNT **Registration Fees**   ACCOUNT NO. **401**

DATE	ITEM	POST. REF.	DEBIT	CREDIT	BALANCE	
					DEBIT	CREDIT

ACCOUNT **Wages Expense**   ACCOUNT NO. **511**

DATE	ITEM	POST. REF.	DEBIT	CREDIT	BALANCE	
					DEBIT	CREDIT

ACCOUNT **Advertising Expense**   ACCOUNT NO. **512**

DATE	ITEM	POST. REF.	DEBIT	CREDIT	BALANCE	
					DEBIT	CREDIT

Mastery Problem (Continued)

ACCOUNT Food Expense   ACCOUNT NO. 524

DATE	ITEM	POST. REF.	DEBIT	CREDIT	BALANCE DEBIT	CREDIT

ACCOUNT Telephone Expense   ACCOUNT NO. 525

DATE	ITEM	POST. REF.	DEBIT	CREDIT	BALANCE DEBIT	CREDIT

ACCOUNT Utilities Expense   ACCOUNT NO. 533

DATE	ITEM	POST. REF.	DEBIT	CREDIT	BALANCE DEBIT	CREDIT

ACCOUNT Postage Expense   ACCOUNT NO. 536

DATE	ITEM	POST. REF.	DEBIT	CREDIT	BALANCE DEBIT	CREDIT

Mastery Problem (Concluded)

3.

_____

_____

ACCOUNT TITLE	ACCT. NO.	DEBIT BALANCE	CREDIT BALANCE

Challenge Problem

1. and 2.

_____

_____

_____

_____

_____

_____

_____

_____

_____

_____

_____

_____

_____

_____

3.

Fred Phaler Consulting

Trial Balance

June 30, 20--

ACCOUNT TITLE	ACCT. NO.	DEBIT BALANCE	CREDIT BALANCE
Cash	101		
Accounts Receivable	122		
Office Supplies	142		
Accounts Payable	202		
Fred Phaler, Capital	311		
Fred Phaler, Drawing	312		
Professional Fees	401		
Wages Expense	511		
Rent Expense	521		
Telephone Expense	525		
Automobile Expense	526		
Utilities Expense	533		

Exercise 5-1A

	(Balance Sheet) Supplies			(Income Statement) Supplies Expense

GENERAL JOURNAL

PAGE ____

	DATE	DESCRIPTION	POST. REF.	DEBIT	CREDIT	
1						1
2						2
3						3
4						4
5						5
6						6

Exercise 5-2A

	(Balance Sheet) Prepaid Insurance			(Income Statement) Insurance Expense

GENERAL JOURNAL

PAGE ____

	DATE	DESCRIPTION	POST. REF.	DEBIT	CREDIT	
1						1
2						2
3						3
4						4
5						5
6						6

Exercise 5-3A

(Income Statement) Wages Expense	(Balance Sheet) Wages Payable

GENERAL JOURNAL

PAGE

	DATE	DESCRIPTION	POST. REF.	DEBIT	CREDIT	
1						1
2						2
3						3
4						4

Exercise 5-4A

(Income Statement) Depr. Expense—Delivery Equipment	(Balance Sheet) Accum. Depr.—Delivery Equipment

GENERAL JOURNAL

PAGE

	DATE	DESCRIPTION	POST. REF.	DEBIT	CREDIT	
1						1
2						2
3						3
4						4

Exercise 5-5A

Exercise 5-6A

1.

	(Balance Sheet) Supplies		(Income Statement) Supplies Expense
TB	580		
Bal.	_____		

2.

	(Balance Sheet) Supplies		(Income Statement) Supplies Expense
TB	435		
Bal.	_____		

Exercise 5-7A

1.

	(Balance Sheet) Prepaid Insurance		(Income Statement) Insurance Expense
TB	1,450		
Bal.	_____		

2.

	(Balance Sheet) Prepaid Insurance		(Income Statement) Insurance Expense
TB	1,350		
Bal.	_____		

Exercise 5-8A

GENERAL JOURNAL

	DATE		DESCRIPTION	POST. REF.	DEBIT	CREDIT	
1			Adjusting Entries				1
2	20-- Dec.	31	Supplies Expense		8 5 00		2
3			Supplies			8 5 00	3
4							4
5		31	Wages Expense		2 2 0 00		5
6			Wages Payable			2 2 0 00	6
7							7
8							8
9							9
10							10
11							11
12							12
13							13
14							14
15							15
16							16
17							17
18							18

Exercise 5-8A (Concluded)

GENERAL LEDGER

ACCOUNT Supplies   ACCOUNT NO. 141

DATE		ITEM	POST. REF.	DEBIT			CREDIT			BALANCE				
										DEBIT			CREDIT	
20-- Dec.	1	Balance	✓							1 5 0	00			
	15		J8		5 0	00				2 0 0	00			

ACCOUNT Wages Payable   ACCOUNT NO. 219

DATE		ITEM	POST. REF.	DEBIT			CREDIT			BALANCE				
										DEBIT			CREDIT	

ACCOUNT Wages Expense   ACCOUNT NO. 511

DATE		ITEM	POST. REF.	DEBIT				CREDIT			BALANCE				
												DEBIT			CREDIT
20-- Dec.	1	Balance	✓									9 0 0	00		
	15		J8	3 0 0	00							1 2 0 0	00		

ACCOUNT Supplies Expense   ACCOUNT NO. 523

DATE		ITEM	POST. REF.	DEBIT				CREDIT			BALANCE				
												DEBIT			CREDIT

Exercise 5-9A

Jim Jacobs' Furniture Repair
Work Sheet (Partial)
For Year Ended December 31, 20--

	ACCOUNT TITLE	TRIAL BALANCE DEBIT	TRIAL BALANCE CREDIT	ADJUSTMENTS DEBIT	ADJUSTMENTS CREDIT	ADJUSTED TRIAL BALANCE DEBIT	ADJUSTED TRIAL BALANCE CREDIT	
1	Cash	1 0 0 0 00				1 0 0 0 00		1
2	Supplies	8 5 0 00				2 0 0 00		2
3	Prepaid Insurance	9 0 0 00				3 0 0 00		3
4	Delivery Equipment	3 6 0 0 00				3 6 0 0 00		4
5	Accum. Depr.—Delivery Equip.		6 0 0 00				8 0 0 00	5
6	Wages Payable						1 0 0 00	6
7	Jim Jacobs, Capital		4 0 0 0 00				4 0 0 0 00	7
8	Repair Fees		1 6 5 0 00				1 6 5 0 00	8
9	Wages Expense	6 0 0 00				7 0 0 00		9
10	Advertising Expense	2 0 0 00				2 0 0 00		10
11	Supplies Expense					6 5 0 00		11
12	Insurance Expense					6 0 0 00		12
13	Depr. Exp.—Delivery Equip.	6 2 5 0 00	6 2 5 0 00			2 0 0 00		13
14						6 5 5 0 00	6 5 5 0 00	14
15								15
16								16
17								17
18								18
19								19
20								20
21								21
22								22
23								23
24								24
25								25

Exercise 5-10A

GENERAL JOURNAL

	DATE		DESCRIPTION	POST. REF.	DEBIT	CREDIT	
1							1
2							2
3							3
4							4
5							5
6							6
7							7
8							8
9							9
10							10
11							11
12							12
13							13
14							14
15							15

Exercise 5-11A

	Income Statement		Balance Sheet	
	Debit	Credit	Debit	Credit
Cash	_____	_____	_____	_____
Accounts Receivable	_____	_____	_____	_____
Supplies	_____	_____	_____	_____
Prepaid Insurance	_____	_____	_____	_____
Delivery Equipment	_____	_____	_____	_____
Accum. Depr.—Delivery Equip.	_____	_____	_____	_____
Accounts Payable	_____	_____	_____	_____
Wages Payable	_____	_____	_____	_____
Owner, Capital	_____	_____	_____	_____
Owner, Drawing	_____	_____	_____	_____
Delivery Fees	_____	_____	_____	_____
Wages Expense	_____	_____	_____	_____
Rent Expense	_____	_____	_____	_____
Supplies Expense	_____	_____	_____	_____
Insurance Expense	_____	_____	_____	_____
Depr. Exp.—Delivery Equip.	_____	_____	_____	_____

Exercise 5-12A

	Income Statement		Balance Sheet	
	Debit	Credit	Debit	Credit
Net Income	_____	_____	_____	_____
Net Loss	_____	_____	_____	_____

Exercise 5-13A

	Cash Basis	Modified Cash Basis	Accrual Basis
1. Purchase supplies on account.			
2. Make payment on asset previously purchased.			
3. Purchase supplies for cash.			
4. Purchase insurance for cash.			
5. Pay cash for wages.			
6. Pay cash for telephone expense.			
7. Pay cash for new equipment.			
8. Wages earned but not paid.			
9. Prepaid item purchased, partly used.			
10. Depreciation on long-term assets.			

Problem 5-14A

	ACCOUNT TITLE	TRIAL BALANCE			ADJUSTMENTS			
		DEBIT	CREDIT		DEBIT		CREDIT	
1	Cash	1 6 0 0 00						
2	Accounts Receivable	9 4 0 00						
3	Supplies	6 3 5 00						
4	Prepaid Insurance	1 2 0 0 00						
5	Delivery Equipment	6 4 0 0 00						
6	Accum. Depr.—Delivery Equip.							
7	Accounts Payable		1 2 2 0 00					
8	Wages Payable							
9	Jill Mason, Capital		8 0 0 0 00					
10	Jill Mason, Drawing	1 4 0 0 00						
11	Delivery Fees		6 2 0 0 00					
12	Wages Expense	1 5 0 0 00						
13	Advertising Expense	4 6 0 00						
14	Rent Expense	8 0 0 00						
15	Supplies Expense							
16	Telephone Expense	1 6 5 00						
17	Insurance Expense							
18	Repair Expense	2 3 0 00						
19	Oil and Gas Expense	9 0 00						
20	Depr. Exp.—Delivery Equip.							
21		15 4 2 0 00	15 4 2 0 00					
22								
23								
24								
25								
26								
27								
28								
29								
30								
31								
32								
33								

Problem 5-14A (Concluded)

Service _____

Sheet _____

September 30, 20-- _____

	ADJUSTED TRIAL BALANCE		INCOME STATEMENT		BALANCE SHEET	
	DEBIT	CREDIT	DEBIT	CREDIT	DEBIT	CREDIT
1						
2						
3						
4						
5						
6						
7						
8						
9						
10						
11						
12						
13						
14						
15						
16						
17						
18						
19						
20						
21						
22						
23						
24						
25						
26						
27						
28						
29						
30						
31						
32						
33						

Problem 5-15A

Campus Delivery

Work

For Month Ended

	ACCOUNT TITLE	TRIAL BALANCE									ADJUSTMENTS								
		DEBIT					CREDIT					DEBIT				CREDIT			
1	Cash		9	8	0	00													
2	Accounts Receivable		5	9	0	00													
3	Supplies		5	7	5	00													
4	Prepaid Insurance	1	3	0	0	00													
5	Van	5	8	0	0	00													
6	Accumulated Depreciation—Van																		
7	Accounts Payable							9	6	0	00								
8	Wages Payable																		
9	Jason Armstrong, Capital						10	0	0	0	00								
10	Jason Armstrong, Drawing		6	0	0	00													
11	Delivery Fees						2	6	0	0	00								
12	Wages Expense	1	8	0	0	00													
13	Advertising Expense		3	8	0	00													
14	Rent Expense		9	0	0	00													
15	Supplies Expense																		
16	Telephone Expense		2	2	0	00													
17	Insurance Expense																		
18	Repair Expense		3	1	5	00													
19	Oil and Gas Expense		1	0	0	00													
20	Depreciation Expense—Van																		
21		13	5	6	0	00	13	5	6	0	00								
22																			
23																			
24																			
25																			
26																			
27																			
28																			
29																			
30																			
31																			
32																			
33																			

Problem 5-15A (Concluded)

Service

Sheet

November 30, 20--

ADJUSTED TRIAL BALANCE		INCOME STATEMENT		BALANCE SHEET	
DEBIT	CREDIT	DEBIT	CREDIT	DEBIT	CREDIT

(rows numbered 1 through 33)

Problem 5-16A

GENERAL JOURNAL

1.

DATE	DESCRIPTION	POST. REF.	DEBIT	CREDIT
1				
2				
3				
4				
5				
6				
7				
8				
9				
10				
11				
12				
13				
14				
15				
16				
17				
18				
19				
20				
21				
22				
23				
24				
25				
26				
27				
28				
29				
30				
31				
32				
33				
34				
35				
36				

Problem 5-16A (Continued)

2.

GENERAL LEDGER

ACCOUNT   Supplies   ACCOUNT NO.   141

DATE		ITEM	POST. REF.	DEBIT	CREDIT	BALANCE DEBIT	BALANCE CREDIT
20-- Nov.	1		J1	4 7 5 00		4 7 5 00	
	15		J4	1 0 0 00		5 7 5 00	

ACCOUNT   Prepaid Insurance   ACCOUNT NO.   145

DATE		ITEM	POST. REF.	DEBIT	CREDIT	BALANCE DEBIT	BALANCE CREDIT
20-- Nov.	1		J1	1 3 0 0 00		1 3 0 0 00	

ACCOUNT   Accumulated Depreciation—Van   ACCOUNT NO.   185.1

DATE	ITEM	POST. REF.	DEBIT	CREDIT	BALANCE DEBIT	BALANCE CREDIT

ACCOUNT   Wages Payable   ACCOUNT NO.   219

DATE	ITEM	POST. REF.	DEBIT	CREDIT	BALANCE DEBIT	BALANCE CREDIT

Problem 5-16A (Concluded)

GENERAL LEDGER

ACCOUNT Wages Expense   ACCOUNT NO. 511

DATE		ITEM	POST. REF.	DEBIT	CREDIT	BALANCE	
						DEBIT	CREDIT
20-- Nov.	15		J3	9 0 0 00		9 0 0 00	
	26		J4	9 0 0 00		1 8 0 0 00	

ACCOUNT Supplies Expense   ACCOUNT NO. 523

DATE	ITEM	POST. REF.	DEBIT	CREDIT	BALANCE	
					DEBIT	CREDIT

ACCOUNT Insurance Expense   ACCOUNT NO. 535

DATE	ITEM	POST. REF.	DEBIT	CREDIT	BALANCE	
					DEBIT	CREDIT

ACCOUNT Depreciation Expense—Van   ACCOUNT NO. 541

DATE	ITEM	POST. REF.	DEBIT	CREDIT	BALANCE	
					DEBIT	CREDIT

Name _____

Problem 5-17A: See pages 130 and 131

Exercise 5-1B

(Balance Sheet)	(Income Statement)
Supplies	Supplies Expense

GENERAL JOURNAL

PAGE

	DATE	DESCRIPTION	POST. REF.	DEBIT	CREDIT	
1						1
2						2
3						3
4						4
5						5
6						6

Exercise 5-2B

(Balance Sheet)	(Income Statement)
Prepaid Insurance	Insurance Expense

GENERAL JOURNAL

PAGE

	DATE	DESCRIPTION	POST. REF.	DEBIT	CREDIT	
1						1
2						2
3						3
4						4
5						5
6						6

Problem 5-17A

	ACCOUNT TITLE	TRIAL BALANCE										ADJUSTMENTS									
		DEBIT					CREDIT					DEBIT					CREDIT				
1	Cash	1	7	2	5	00															
2	Accounts Receivable		9	6	0	00															
3	Supplies		5	2	5	00															
4	Prepaid Insurance		9	3	0	00															
5	Office Equipment	5	4	5	0	00															
6	Accum. Depr.—Office Equipment																				
7	Accounts Payable							4	8	0	00										
8	Wages Payable																				
9	Joyce Lee, Capital							7	5	0	0	00									
10	Joyce Lee, Drawing	1	1	2	5	00															
11	Professional Fees							5	7	0	0	00									
12	Wages Expense	1	4	2	0	00															
13	Advertising Expense		3	5	0	00															
14	Rent Expense		7	0	0	00															
15	Supplies Expense																				
16	Telephone Expense		1	3	0	00															
17	Utilities Expense		1	9	0	00															
18	Insurance Expense																				
19	Depr. Expense—Office Equipment																				
20	Miscellaneous Expense		1	7	5	00															
21		13	6	8	0	00	13	6	8	0	00										
22																					
23																					
24																					
25																					
26																					
27																					
28																					
29																					
30																					
31																					

Problem 5-17A (Concluded)

Tax Service

Sheet

March 31, 20--

ADJUSTED TRIAL BALANCE		INCOME STATEMENT		BALANCE SHEET		
DEBIT	CREDIT	DEBIT	CREDIT	DEBIT	CREDIT	
						1
						2
						3
						4
						5
						6
						7
						8
						9
						10
						11
						12
						13
						14
						15
						16
						17
						18
						19
						20
						21
						22
						23
						24
						25
						26
						27
						28
						29
						30
						31

Exercise 5-3B

	(Income Statement) Wages Expense		(Balance Sheet) Wages Payable

GENERAL JOURNAL   PAGE

	DATE		DESCRIPTION	POST. REF.	DEBIT	CREDIT	
1							1
2							2
3							3
4							4

Exercise 5-4B

	(Income Statement) Depr. Expense—Delivery Equipment		(Balance Sheet) Accum. Depr.—Delivery Equipment

GENERAL JOURNAL   PAGE

	DATE		DESCRIPTION	POST. REF.	DEBIT	CREDIT	
1							1
2							2
3							3
4							4

Exercise 5-5B

Exercise 5-6B

1.

(Balance Sheet) Supplies		(Income Statement) Supplies Expense
TB	540	
Bal.	_____	

2.

(Balance Sheet) Supplies		(Income Statement) Supplies Expense
TB	330	
Bal.	_____	

Exercise 5-7B

1.

(Balance Sheet) Prepaid Insurance		(Income Statement) Insurance Expense
TB	960	
Bal.	_____	

2.

(Balance Sheet) Prepaid Insurance		(Income Statement) Insurance Expense
TB	1,135	
Bal.	_____	

Exercise 5-8B

GENERAL JOURNAL

	DATE		DESCRIPTION	POST. REF.	DEBIT	CREDIT	
1			Adjusting Entries				1
2	20-- July	31	Insurance Expense		3 2 0 00		2
3			Prepaid Insurance			3 2 0 00	3
4							4
5		31	Depreciation Expense—Cleaning Equipment		1 4 5 00		5
6			Accumulated Depreciation—Cleaning Equipment			1 4 5 00	6
7							7
8							8
9							9
10							10
11							11
12							12
13							13
14							14
15							15
16							16

Exercise 5-8B (Concluded)

GENERAL LEDGER

ACCOUNT   Prepaid Insurance   ACCOUNT NO.   145

DATE		ITEM	POST. REF.	DEBIT	CREDIT	BALANCE DEBIT	BALANCE CREDIT
20-- July	1	Balance	✓			3 2 0 00	
	15		J6	6 4 0 00		9 6 0 00	

ACCOUNT   Accumulated Depreciation—Cleaning Equipment   ACCOUNT NO.   183.1

DATE		ITEM	POST. REF.	DEBIT	CREDIT	BALANCE DEBIT	BALANCE CREDIT
20-- July	1	Balance	✓				8 7 0 00

ACCOUNT   Insurance Expense   ACCOUNT NO.   535

DATE	ITEM	POST. REF.	DEBIT	CREDIT	BALANCE DEBIT	BALANCE CREDIT

ACCOUNT   Depreciation Expense—Cleaning Equipment   ACCOUNT NO.   541

DATE	ITEM	POST. REF.	DEBIT	CREDIT	BALANCE DEBIT	BALANCE CREDIT

Jasmine Kah's Auto Detailing

Work Sheet (Partial)

For Month Ended June 30, 20--

ACCOUNT TITLE	TRIAL BALANCE DEBIT	TRIAL BALANCE CREDIT	ADJUSTMENTS DEBIT	ADJUSTMENTS CREDIT	ADJUSTED TRIAL BALANCE DEBIT	ADJUSTED TRIAL BALANCE CREDIT
1 Cash	1 5 0 0 00				1 5 0 0 00	
2 Supplies	5 2 0 0 00				2 9 0 0 00	
3 Prepaid Insurance	7 5 0 00				2 0 0 00	
4 Cleaning Equipment	5 4 0 0 00				5 4 0 0 00	
5 Accum. Depr.—Cleaning Equip.		8 5 0 00				1 1 5 0 00
6 Wages Payable						2 5 0 00
7 Jasmine Kah, Capital		4 6 0 0 00				4 6 0 0 00
8 Detailing Fees		2 2 2 0 00				2 2 2 0 00
9 Wages Expense	7 0 0 00				9 5 0 00	
10 Advertising Expense	1 5 0 00				1 5 0 00	
11 Supplies Expense					4 3 0 00	
12 Insurance Expense					5 5 0 00	
13 Depr. Exp.—Cleaning Equip.					3 0 0 00	
14	7 6 7 0 00	7 6 7 0 00			8 2 2 0 00	8 2 2 0 00
15						
16						
17						
18						
19						
20						
21						
22						
23						
24						
25						

Exercise 5-10B

GENERAL JOURNAL

	DATE	DESCRIPTION	POST. REF.	DEBIT	CREDIT	
1						1
2						2
3						3
4						4
5						5
6						6
7						7
8						8
9						9
10						10
11						11
12						12
13						13
14						14
15						15

Exercise 5-11B

	Income Statement		Balance Sheet	
	Debit	**Credit**	**Debit**	**Credit**
Cash				
Accounts Receivable				
Supplies				
Prepaid Insurance				
Automobile				
Accum. Depr.—Automobile				
Accounts Payable				
Wages Payable				
Owner, Capital				
Owner, Drawing				
Service Fees				
Wages Expense				
Supplies Expense				
Utilities Expense				
Insurance Expense				
Depr. Exp.—Automobile				

Exercise 5-12B

	Income Statement		Balance Sheet	
	Debit	**Credit**	**Debit**	**Credit**
Net Income				
Net Loss				

Exercise 5-13B

	Cash Basis	Modified Cash Basis	Accrual Basis

1. Office Equipment
    Cash
       Purchased equipment for cash			

2. Office Equipment
    Accounts Payable
       Purchased equipment on account			

3. Cash
    Revenue
       Cash receipts for week			

4. Accounts Receivable
    Revenue
       Services performed on account			

5. Prepaid Insurance
    Cash
       Purchased prepaid asset			

6. Supplies
    Accounts Payable
       Purchased prepaid asset			

7. Telephone Expense
    Cash
       Paid telephone bill			

8. Wages Expense
    Cash
       Paid wages for month			

9. Accounts Payable
    Cash
       Made payment on account			

10. Supplies Expense Supplies			

Exercise 5-13B (Concluded)

	Cash Basis	Modified Cash Basis	Accrual Basis
11. Wages Expense Wages Payable			
12. Depreciation Expense—Office Equipment Accum. Depr.—Office Equipment			

This page intentionally left blank.

Problem 5-14B

	ACCOUNT TITLE	TRIAL BALANCE		ADJUSTMENTS	
		DEBIT	CREDIT	DEBIT	CREDIT
1	Cash	1 3 7 5 00			
2	Accounts Receivable	8 8 0 00			
3	Supplies	4 9 0 00			
4	Prepaid Insurance	8 0 0 00			
5	Lawn Equipment	5 7 0 0 00			
6	Accum. Depr.—Lawn Equipment				
7	Accounts Payable		7 8 0 00		
8	Wages Payable				
9	Louie Long, Capital		6 5 0 0 00		
10	Louie Long, Drawing	1 2 5 0 00			
11	Lawn Service Fees		6 1 0 0 00		
12	Wages Expense	1 1 4 5 00			
13	Advertising Expense	5 4 0 00			
14	Rent Expense	7 2 5 00			
15	Supplies Expense				
16	Telephone Expense	1 6 0 00			
17	Insurance Expense				
18	Repair Expense	2 5 0 00			
19	Depr. Expense—Lawn Equipment				
20	Miscellaneous Expense	6 5 00			
21		13 3 8 0 00	13 3 8 0 00		
22					
23					
24					
25					
26					
27					
28					
29					
30					
31					
32					
33					

Problem 5-14B (Concluded)

Service

Sheet

March 31, 20--

ADJUSTED TRIAL BALANCE		INCOME STATEMENT		BALANCE SHEET		
DEBIT	CREDIT	DEBIT	CREDIT	DEBIT	CREDIT	
						1
						2
						3
						4
						5
						6
						7
						8
						9
						10
						11
						12
						13
						14
						15
						16
						17
						18
						19
						20
						21
						22
						23
						24
						25
						26
						27
						28
						29
						30
						31
						32
						33

Problem 5-15B

	ACCOUNT TITLE	TRIAL BALANCE DEBIT	TRIAL BALANCE CREDIT	ADJUSTMENTS DEBIT	ADJUSTMENTS CREDIT
1	Cash	8 3 0 00			
2	Accounts Receivable	7 6 0 00			
3	Supplies	6 2 5 00			
4	Prepaid Insurance	9 5 0 00			
5	Automobile	6 5 0 0 00			
6	Accum. Depr.—Automobile				
7	Accounts Payable		1 5 0 0 00		
8	Wages Payable				
9	Val Nolan, Capital		9 9 0 0 00		
10	Val Nolan, Drawing	1 1 0 0 00			
11	Appraisal Fees		3 0 0 0 00		
12	Wages Expense	1 5 6 0 00			
13	Advertising Expense	4 2 0 00			
14	Rent Expense	1 0 5 0 00			
15	Supplies Expense				
16	Telephone Expense	2 5 5 00			
17	Insurance Expense				
18	Repair Expense	2 7 0 00			
19	Oil and Gas Expense	8 0 00			
20	Depr. Expense—Automobile				
21		14 4 0 0 00	14 4 0 0 00		

Problem 5-15B (Concluded)

Appraisals

Sheet _____

October 31, 20--

	ADJUSTED TRIAL BALANCE		INCOME STATEMENT		BALANCE SHEET	
	DEBIT	CREDIT	DEBIT	CREDIT	DEBIT	CREDIT
1						
2						
3						
4						
5						
6						
7						
8						
9						
10						
11						
12						
13						
14						
15						
16						
17						
18						
19						
20						
21						
22						
23						
24						
25						
26						
27						
28						
29						
30						
31						
32						
33						

Problem 5-16B

1.

		GENERAL JOURNAL			PAGE 3

	DATE	DESCRIPTION	POST. REF.	DEBIT	CREDIT	
1						1
2						2
3						3
4						4
5						5
6						6
7						7
8						8
9						9
10						10
11						11
12						12
13						13
14						14
15						15
16						16
17						17
18						18
19						19
20						20
21						21
22						22
23						23
24						24
25						25
26						26
27						27
28						28
29						29
30						30
31						31
32						32
33						33
34						34
35						35
36						36

Problem 5-16B (Continued)

2.

GENERAL LEDGER

ACCOUNT   Supplies   ACCOUNT NO.   141

DATE		ITEM	POST. REF.	DEBIT	CREDIT	BALANCE DEBIT	BALANCE CREDIT
20-- Oct.	2		J1	6 2 5 00		6 2 5 00	

ACCOUNT   Prepaid Insurance   ACCOUNT NO.   145

DATE		ITEM	POST. REF.	DEBIT	CREDIT	BALANCE DEBIT	BALANCE CREDIT
20-- Oct.	3		J1	9 5 0 00		9 5 0 00	

ACCOUNT   Accumulated Depreciation—Automobile   ACCOUNT NO.   185.1

DATE	ITEM	POST. REF.	DEBIT	CREDIT	BALANCE DEBIT	BALANCE CREDIT

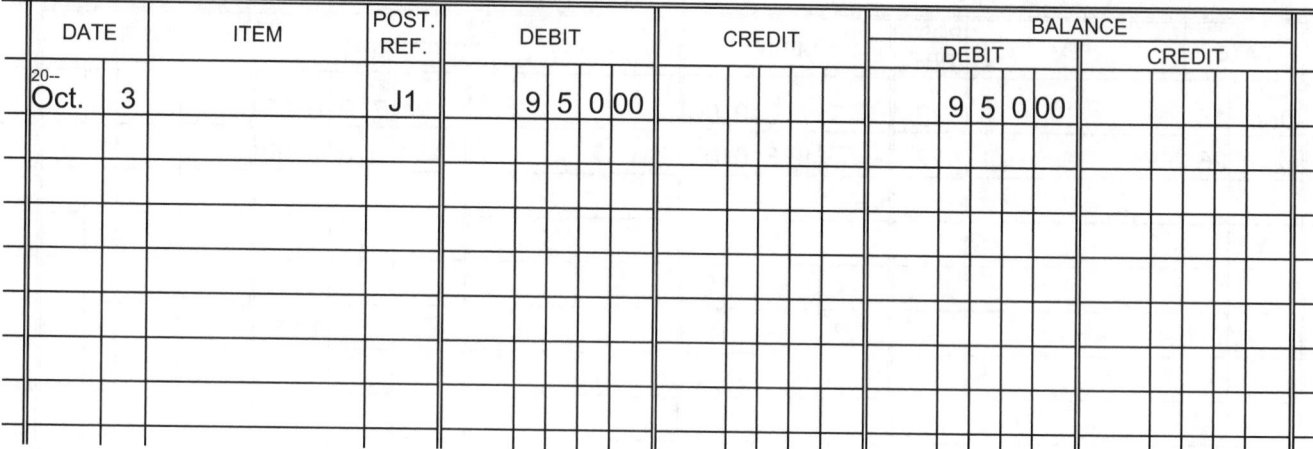

Problem 5-16B (Continued)

ACCOUNT Wages Payable

ACCOUNT NO. 219

DATE	ITEM	POST. REF.	DEBIT	CREDIT	BALANCE DEBIT	BALANCE CREDIT

ACCOUNT Wages Expense

ACCOUNT NO. 511

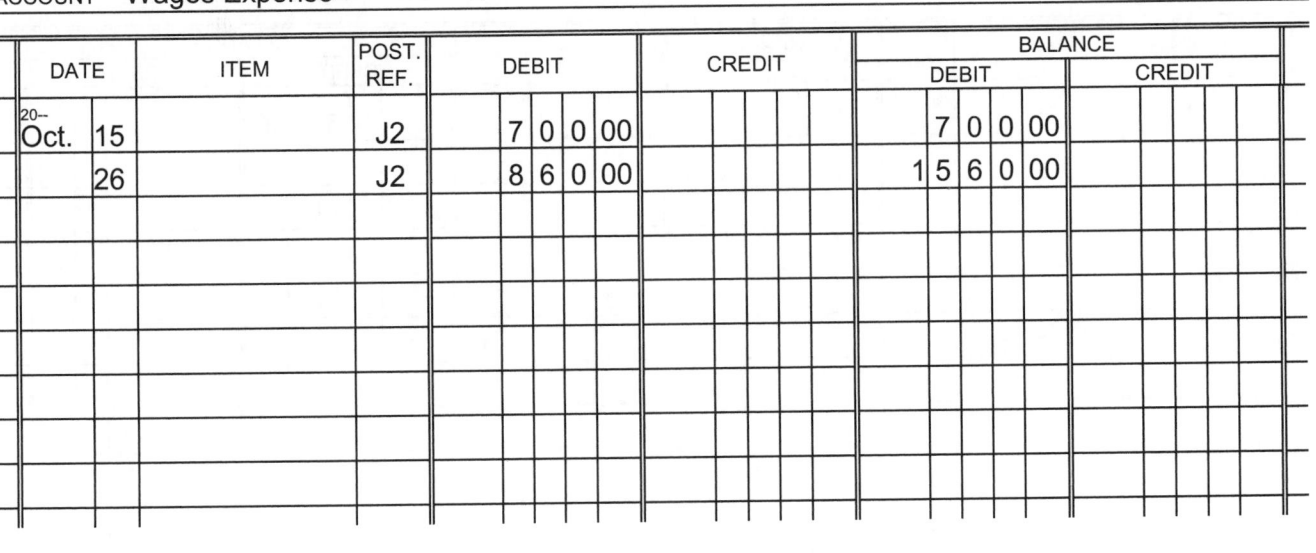

DATE	ITEM	POST. REF.	DEBIT	CREDIT	BALANCE DEBIT	BALANCE CREDIT
20-- Oct. 15		J2	7 0 0 00		7 0 0 00	
26		J2	8 6 0 00		1 5 6 0 00	

ACCOUNT Supplies Expense

ACCOUNT NO. 523

DATE	ITEM	POST. REF.	DEBIT	CREDIT	BALANCE DEBIT	BALANCE CREDIT

Problem 5-16B (Concluded)

ACCOUNT Insurance Expense

ACCOUNT NO. 535

DATE	ITEM	POST. REF.	DEBIT	CREDIT	BALANCE	
					DEBIT	CREDIT

ACCOUNT Depreciation Expense—Automobile

ACCOUNT NO. 541

DATE	ITEM	POST. REF.	DEBIT	CREDIT	BALANCE	
					DEBIT	CREDIT

Problem 5-17B

Dick Ady's

Work

For Month Ended

	ACCOUNT TITLE	TRIAL BALANCE									ADJUSTMENTS								
		DEBIT					CREDIT					DEBIT				CREDIT				
1	Cash	1	3	6	5	00														
2	Accounts Receivable		8	4	5	00														
3	Supplies		6	2	0	00														
4	Prepaid Insurance	1	1	5	0	00														
5	Office Equipment	6	4	0	0	00														
6	Accum. Depr.—Office Equipment																			
7	Accounts Payable							7	3	5	00									
8	Wages Payable																			
9	Dick Ady, Capital							7	8	0	0	00								
10	Dick Ady, Drawing	1	2	0	0	00														
11	Professional Fees							6	3	5	0	00								
12	Wages Expense	1	4	9	5	00														
13	Advertising Expense		3	8	0	00														
14	Rent Expense		8	5	0	00														
15	Supplies Expense																			
16	Telephone Expense		2	0	5	00														
17	Utilities Expense		2	8	5	00														
18	Insurance Expense																			
19	Depr. Expense—Office Equipment																			
20	Miscellaneous Expense			9	0	00														
21		14	8	8	5	00	14	8	8	5	00									
22																				
23																				
24																				
25																				
26																				
27																				
28																				
29																				
30																				
31																				
32																				

Problem 5-17B (Concluded)

Bookkeeping Service

Sheet _____

July 31, 20--

	ADJUSTED TRIAL BALANCE		INCOME STATEMENT		BALANCE SHEET	
	DEBIT	CREDIT	DEBIT	CREDIT	DEBIT	CREDIT
1						
2						
3						
4						
5						
6						
7						
8						
9						
10						
11						
12						
13						
14						
15						
16						
17						
18						
19						
20						
21						
22						
23						
24						
25						
26						
27						
28						
29						
30						
31						
32						

Mastery Problem

1.

Kristi Williams Family

Work

For Year Ended

	ACCOUNT TITLE	TRIAL BALANCE		ADJUSTMENTS	
		DEBIT	CREDIT	DEBIT	CREDIT
1	Cash	8 7 3 0 00			
2	Office Supplies	7 0 0 00			
3	Prepaid Insurance	6 0 0 00			
4	Office Equipment	18 0 0 0 00			
5					
6	Computer Equipment	6 0 0 0 00			
7					
8	Notes Payable		8 0 0 0 00		
9	Accounts Payable		5 0 0 00		
10	Kristi Williams, Capital		11 4 0 0 00		
11	Kristi Williams, Drawing	3 0 0 0 00			
12	Client Fees		35 8 0 0 00		
13	Wages Expense	9 5 0 0 00			
14	Rent Expense	6 0 0 0 00			
15					
16	Utilities Expense	2 1 7 0 00			
17					
18					
19					
20	Miscellaneous Expense	1 0 0 0 00			
21		55 7 0 0 00	55 7 0 0 00		
22					
23					
24					
25					
26					
27					
28					
29					
30					
31					
32					

Mastery Problem (Continued)

Counseling Services

Sheet

December 31, 20--

	ADJUSTED TRIAL BALANCE		INCOME STATEMENT		BALANCE SHEET	
	DEBIT	CREDIT	DEBIT	CREDIT	DEBIT	CREDIT
1						
2						
3						
4						
5						
6						
7						
8						
9						
10						
11						
12						
13						
14						
15						
16						
17						
18						
19						
20						
21						
22						
23						
24						
25						
26						
27						
28						
29						
30						
31						
32						

Mastery Problem (Concluded)

2.

GENERAL JOURNAL

	DATE		DESCRIPTION	POST. REF.	DEBIT	CREDIT	
1							1
2							2
3							3
4							4
5							5
6							6
7							7
8							8
9							9
10							10
11							11
12							12
13							13
14							14
15							15
16							16
17							17
18							18
19							19
20							20
21							21
22							22
23							23
24							24
25							25
26							26
27							27
28							28
29							29
30							30
31							31
32							32
33							33
34							34
35							35

Challenge Problem

See pages 156–157 for work sheet for Challenge Problem.

Challenge Problem

1.

Diane Kiefner's Wilderness

Work

For Summer

	ACCOUNT TITLE	TRIAL BALANCE				ADJUSTMENTS			
		DEBIT		CREDIT		DEBIT		CREDIT	
1	Cash	11 5 0 0 00							
2									
3									
4									
5	Diane Kiefner, Capital			15 0 0 0 00					
6	Tour Revenue			10 0 0 0 00					
7	Advertising Supplies Expense	1 0 0 0 00							
8	Food Expense	2 0 0 0 00							
9	Equipment Rental Expense	3 0 0 0 00							
10	Travel Expense	4 0 0 0 00							
11	Kayak Expense	3 5 0 0 00							
12									
13		25 0 0 0 00		25 0 0 0 00					
14									
15									
16									
17									
18									
19									

Challenge Problem (Concluded)

Kayaking Tours
_____

Sheet
_____

Ended 20--
_____

ADJUSTED TRIAL BALANCE		INCOME STATEMENT		BALANCE SHEET		
DEBIT	CREDIT	DEBIT	CREDIT	DEBIT	CREDIT	
						1
						2
						3
						4
						5
						6
						7
						8
						9
						10
						11
						12
						13
						14
						15
						16
						17
						18
						19

2.
_____
_____
_____
_____
_____
_____
_____
_____
_____
_____
_____
_____
_____

APPENDIX: DEPRECIATION METHODS

Exercise 5Apx-1A

Straight-Line Depreciation

Year	Depreciable Cost	×	Rate	=	Depreciation Expense	Accumulated Depreciation End of Year	Book Value End of Year

Exercise 5Apx-2A

Sum-of-the-Years'-Digits

Year	Depreciable Cost	×	Rate	=	Depreciation Expense	Accumulated Depreciation End of Year	Book Value End of Year

Exercise 5Apx-3A

Double-Declining-Balance Method

Year	Book Value Beginning of Year	×	Rate	=	Depreciation Expense	Accumulated Depreciation End of Year	Book Value End of Year

Exercise 5Apx-4A

Modified Accelerated Cost Recovery System

Year	Cost	×	Rate	=	Depreciation Expense	Accumulated Depreciation End of Year	Book Value End of Year
_____	_____		_____		_____	_____	_____
_____	_____		_____		_____	_____	_____
_____	_____		_____		_____	_____	_____
_____	_____		_____		_____	_____	_____
_____	_____		_____		_____	_____	_____
_____	_____		_____		_____	_____	_____

Exercise 5Apx-1B

Straight-Line Depreciation

Year	Depreciable Cost	×	Rate	=	Depreciation Expense	Accumulated Depreciation End of Year	Book Value End of Year
_____	_____		_____		_____	_____	_____
_____	_____		_____		_____	_____	_____
_____	_____		_____		_____	_____	_____
_____	_____		_____		_____	_____	_____

Exercise 5Apx-2B

Sum-of-the-Years'-Digits

Year	Depreciable Cost	×	Rate	=	Depreciation Expense	Accumulated Depreciation End of Year	Book Value End of Year
_____	_____		_____		_____	_____	_____
_____	_____		_____		_____	_____	_____
_____	_____		_____		_____	_____	_____
_____	_____		_____		_____	_____	_____
_____	_____		_____		_____	_____	_____

Exercise 5Apx-3B

Double-Declining-Balance Method

Year	Book Value Beginning of Year	×	Rate	=	Depreciation Expense	Accumulated Depreciation End of Year	Book Value End of Year

Exercise 5Apx-4B

Modified Accelerated Cost Recovery System

Year	Cost	×	Rate	=	Depreciation Expense	Accumulated Depreciation End of Year	Book Value End of Year

Exercise 6-1A

Exercise 6-2A

Exercise 6-3A

Exercise 6-4A

GENERAL JOURNAL   PAGE 1

DATE	DESCRIPTION	POST. REF.	DEBIT	CREDIT	
					1
					2
					3
					4
					5
					6
					7
					8
					9
					10
					11
					12
					13
					14
					15
					16
					17
					18
					19
					20
					21
					22
					23

Exercise 6-4A (Concluded)

Exercise 6-5A

GENERAL JOURNAL

	DATE		DESCRIPTION	POST. REF.	DEBIT	CREDIT	
1							1
2							2
3							3
4							4
5							5
6							6
7							7
8							8
9							9
10							10
11							11
12							12
13							13
14							14
15							15
16							16
17							17
18							18
19							19
20							20
21							21
22							22
23							23
24							24
25							25
26							26
27							27
28							28
29							29
30							30
31							31
32							32
33							33
34							34
35							35
36							36

Exercise 6-5A (Concluded)

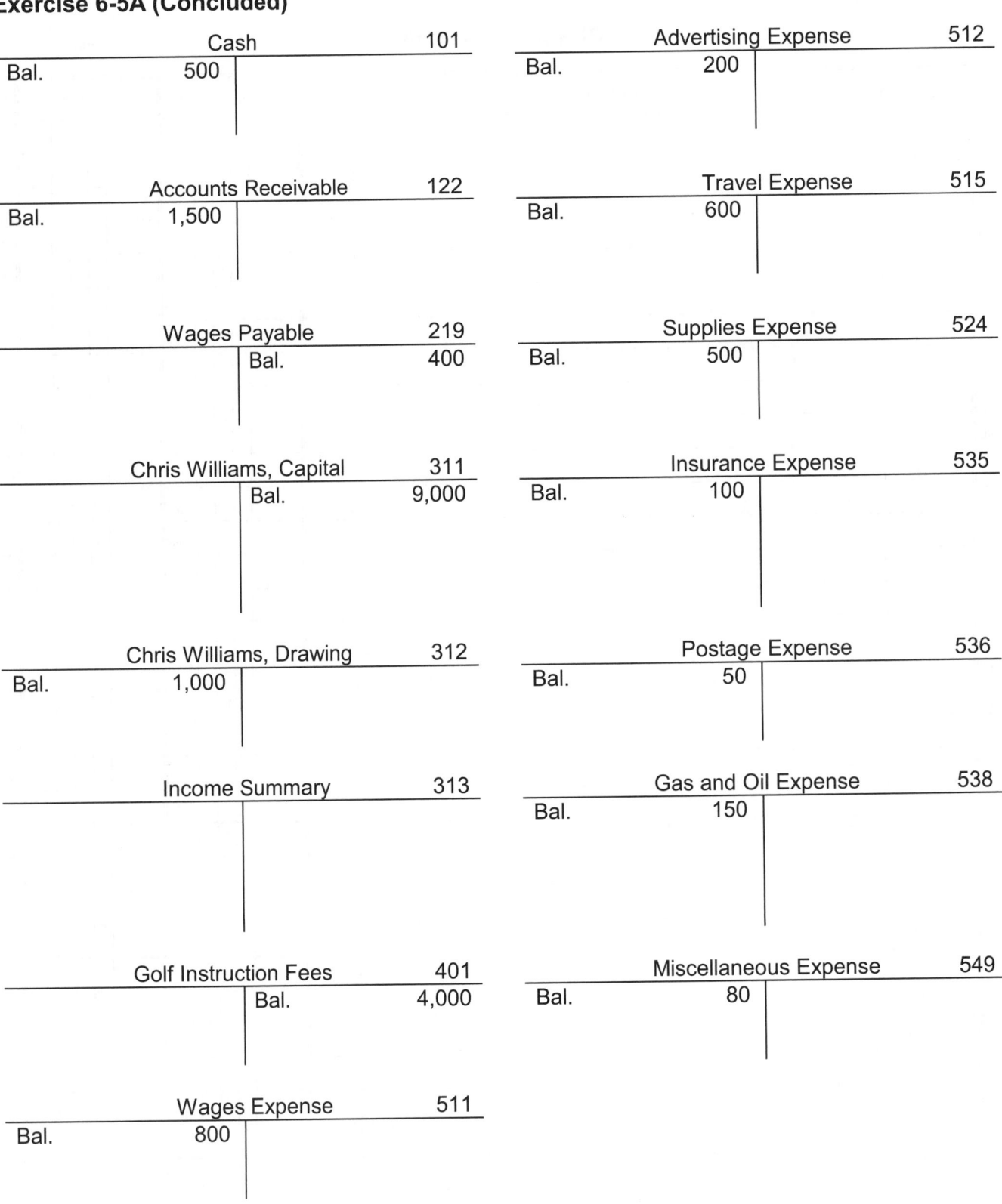

Cash		101
Bal.	500	

Accounts Receivable		122
Bal.	1,500	

Wages Payable		219
	Bal.	400

Chris Williams, Capital		311
	Bal.	9,000

Chris Williams, Drawing		312
Bal.	1,000	

Income Summary		313

Golf Instruction Fees		401
	Bal.	4,000

Wages Expense		511
Bal.	800	

Advertising Expense		512
Bal.	200	

Travel Expense		515
Bal.	600	

Supplies Expense		524
Bal.	500	

Insurance Expense		535
Bal.	100	

Postage Expense		536
Bal.	50	

Gas and Oil Expense		538
Bal.	150	

Miscellaneous Expense		549
Bal.	80	

Exercise 6-6A

GENERAL JOURNAL

	DATE		DESCRIPTION	POST. REF.	DEBIT	CREDIT	
1							1
2							2
3							3
4							4
5							5
6							6
7							7
8							8
9							9
10							10
11							11
12							12
13							13
14							14
15							15
16							16
17							17
18							18
19							19
20							20
21							21
22							22
23							23
24							24
25							25
26							26
27							27
28							28
29							29
30							30
31							31
32							32
33							33
34							34
35							35
36							36

Exercise 6-6A (Concluded)

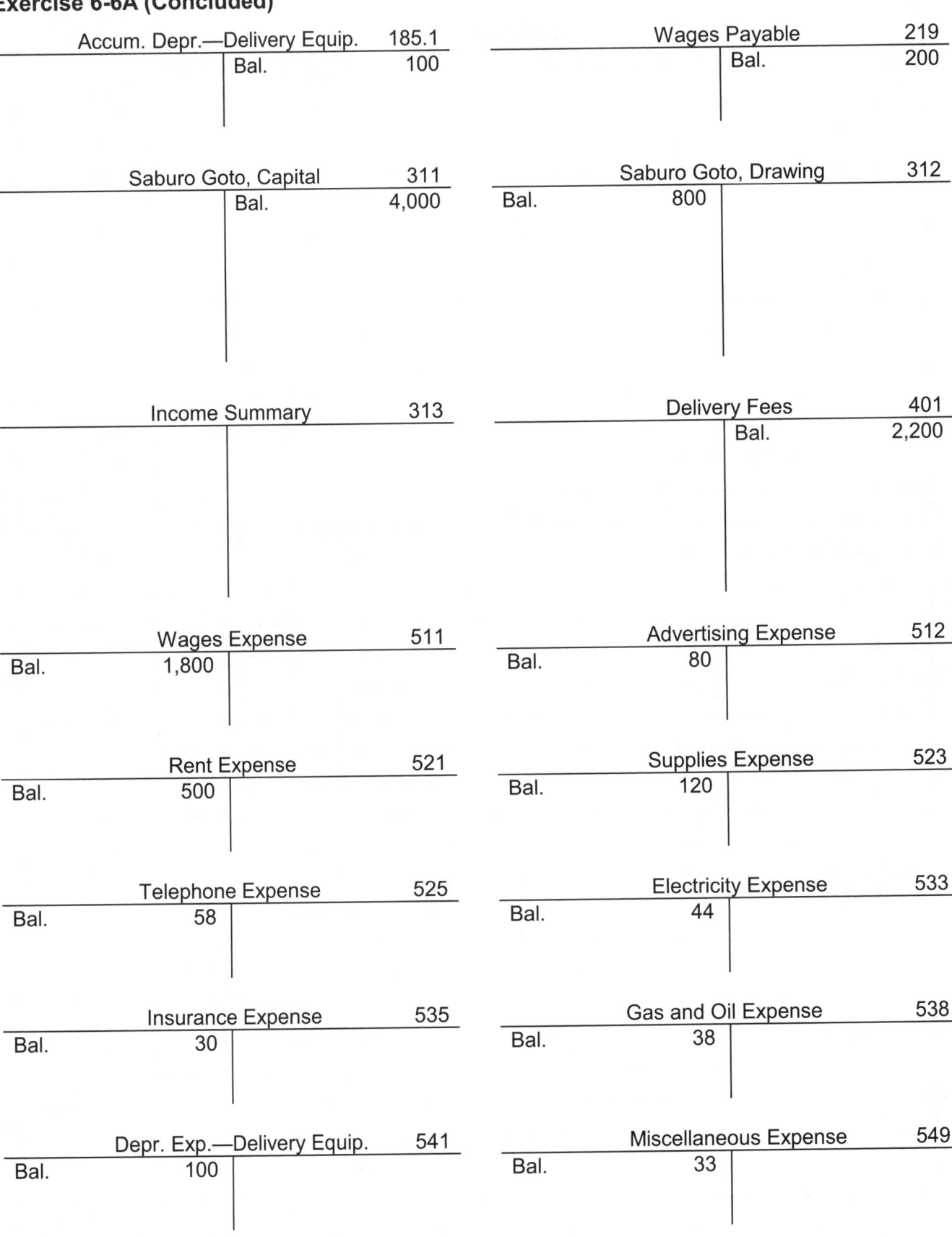

Accum. Depr.—Delivery Equip.	185.1		Wages Payable	219
	Bal. 100			Bal. 200

Saburo Goto, Capital	311		Saburo Goto, Drawing	312
	Bal. 4,000		Bal. 800	

Income Summary	313		Delivery Fees	401
				Bal. 2,200

Wages Expense	511		Advertising Expense	512
Bal. 1,800			Bal. 80	

Rent Expense	521		Supplies Expense	523
Bal. 500			Bal. 120	

Telephone Expense	525		Electricity Expense	533
Bal. 58			Bal. 44	

Insurance Expense	535		Gas and Oil Expense	538
Bal. 30			Bal. 38	

Depr. Exp.—Delivery Equip.	541		Miscellaneous Expense	549
Bal. 100			Bal. 33	

Problem 6-7A

1.

2.

Problem 6-7A (Concluded)

3.

Problem 6-8A

1.

GENERAL JOURNAL

	DATE		DESCRIPTION	POST. REF.	DEBIT	CREDIT	
1							1
2							2
3							3
4							4
5							5
6							6
7							7
8							8
9							9
10							10
11							11
12							12
13							13
14							14
15							15
16							16
17							17
18							18

Problem 6-8A (Continued)

2.

GENERAL JOURNAL

DATE		DESCRIPTION	POST. REF.	DEBIT	CREDIT	
						1
						2
						3
						4
						5
						6
						7
						8
						9
						10
						11
						12
						13
						14
						15
						16
						17
						18
						19
						20
						21
						22
						23

1. and 2.

GENERAL LEDGER

ACCOUNT Cash

ACCOUNT NO. 101

DATE		ITEM	POST. REF.	DEBIT	CREDIT	BALANCE DEBIT	BALANCE CREDIT
20-- Jan.	31	Balance	✓			3 6 7 3 00	

Problem 6-8A (Continued)

ACCOUNT Accounts Receivable   ACCOUNT NO. 122

DATE		ITEM	POST. REF.	DEBIT	CREDIT	BALANCE	
						DEBIT	CREDIT
20-- Jan.	31	Balance	✓			1 4 5 0 00	

ACCOUNT Supplies   ACCOUNT NO. 141

DATE		ITEM	POST. REF.	DEBIT	CREDIT	BALANCE	
						DEBIT	CREDIT
20-- Jan.	31	Balance	✓			7 0 0 00	

ACCOUNT Prepaid Insurance   ACCOUNT NO. 145

DATE		ITEM	POST. REF.	DEBIT	CREDIT	BALANCE	
						DEBIT	CREDIT
20-- Jan.	31	Balance	✓			9 0 0 00	

ACCOUNT Delivery Equipment   ACCOUNT NO. 185

DATE		ITEM	POST. REF.	DEBIT	CREDIT	BALANCE	
						DEBIT	CREDIT
20-- Jan.	31	Balance	✓			3 2 0 0 00	

ACCOUNT Accumulated Depreciation—Delivery Equipment   ACCOUNT NO. 185.1

DATE	ITEM	POST. REF.	DEBIT	CREDIT	BALANCE	
					DEBIT	CREDIT

Problem 6-8A (Continued)

ACCOUNT **Accounts Payable**   ACCOUNT NO. **202**

DATE		ITEM	POST. REF.	DEBIT	CREDIT	BALANCE DEBIT	BALANCE CREDIT
20-- Jan.	31	Balance	✓				1 2 0 0 00

ACCOUNT **Wages Payable**   ACCOUNT NO. **219**

DATE		ITEM	POST. REF.	DEBIT	CREDIT	BALANCE DEBIT	BALANCE CREDIT

ACCOUNT **Don Megaffin, Capital**   ACCOUNT NO. **311**

DATE		ITEM	POST. REF.	DEBIT	CREDIT	BALANCE DEBIT	BALANCE CREDIT
20-- Jan.	31	Balance	✓				8 0 0 0 00

ACCOUNT **Don Megaffin, Drawing**   ACCOUNT NO. **312**

DATE		ITEM	POST. REF.	DEBIT	CREDIT	BALANCE DEBIT	BALANCE CREDIT
20-- Jan.	31	Balance	✓			1 1 0 0 00	

ACCOUNT **Income Summary**   ACCOUNT NO. **313**

DATE		ITEM	POST. REF.	DEBIT	CREDIT	BALANCE DEBIT	BALANCE CREDIT

Problem 6-8A (Continued)

ACCOUNT   Repair Fees

ACCOUNT NO.   401

DATE		ITEM	POST. REF.	DEBIT	CREDIT	BALANCE	
						DEBIT	CREDIT
20-- Jan.	31	Balance	✓				4 7 0 0 00

ACCOUNT   Wages Expense

ACCOUNT NO.   511

DATE		ITEM	POST. REF.	DEBIT	CREDIT	BALANCE	
						DEBIT	CREDIT
20-- Jan.	31	Balance	✓			1 7 5 0 00	

ACCOUNT   Advertising Expense

ACCOUNT NO.   512

DATE		ITEM	POST. REF.	DEBIT	CREDIT	BALANCE	
						DEBIT	CREDIT
20-- Jan.	31	Balance	✓			2 0 0 00	

ACCOUNT   Rent Expense

ACCOUNT NO.   521

DATE		ITEM	POST. REF.	DEBIT	CREDIT	BALANCE	
						DEBIT	CREDIT
20-- Jan.	31	Balance	✓			6 4 0 00	

ACCOUNT   Supplies Expense

ACCOUNT NO.   523

DATE		ITEM	POST. REF.	DEBIT	CREDIT	BALANCE	
						DEBIT	CREDIT

Problem 6-8A (Continued)

ACCOUNT Telephone Expense   ACCOUNT NO. 525

DATE		ITEM	POST. REF.	DEBIT	CREDIT	BALANCE	
						DEBIT	CREDIT
20-- Jan.	31	Balance	✓			5 0 00	

ACCOUNT Insurance Expense   ACCOUNT NO. 535

DATE		ITEM	POST. REF.	DEBIT	CREDIT	BALANCE	
						DEBIT	CREDIT

ACCOUNT Gas and Oil Expense   ACCOUNT NO. 538

DATE		ITEM	POST. REF.	DEBIT	CREDIT	BALANCE	
						DEBIT	CREDIT
20-- Jan.	31	Balance	✓			2 0 0 00	

ACCOUNT Depreciation Expense—Delivery Equipment   ACCOUNT NO. 541

DATE		ITEM	POST. REF.	DEBIT	CREDIT	BALANCE	
						DEBIT	CREDIT

ACCOUNT Miscellaneous Expense   ACCOUNT NO. 549

DATE		ITEM	POST. REF.	DEBIT	CREDIT	BALANCE	
						DEBIT	CREDIT
20-- Jan.	31	Balance	✓			3 7 00	

Problem 6-8A (Concluded)

3.

ACCOUNT TITLE	ACCT. NO.	DEBIT BALANCE	CREDIT BALANCE

Problem 6-9A

Exercise 6-1B

Exercise 6-2B

Exercise 6-3B

Exercise 6-4B

GENERAL JOURNAL

	DATE		DESCRIPTION	POST. REF.	DEBIT	CREDIT	
1							1
2							2
3							3
4							4
5							5
6							6
7							7
8							8
9							9
10							10
11							11
12							12
13							13
14							14
15							15
16							16
17							17
18							18
19							19
20							20
21							21
22							22
23							23

Exercise 6-4B (Concluded)

Exercise 6-5B

GENERAL JOURNAL

PAGE

DATE	DESCRIPTION	POST. REF.	DEBIT	CREDIT	
					1
					2
					3
					4
					5
					6
					7
					8
					9
					10
					11
					12
					13
					14
					15
					16
					17
					18
					19
					20
					21
					22
					23
					24
					25
					26
					27
					28
					29
					30
					31
					32
					33
					34
					35
					36

Exercise 6-5B (Concluded)

Cash		101
Bal.	600	

Advertising Expense		512
Bal.	600	

Accounts Receivable		122
Bal.	1,800	

Travel Expense		515
Bal.	100	

Wages Payable		219
	Bal.	500

Supplies Expense		524
Bal.	900	

Mark Thrasher, Capital		311
	Bal.	8,000

Insurance Expense		535
Bal.	300	

Mark Thrasher, Drawing		312
Bal.	800	

Postage Expense		536
Bal.	40	

Income Summary		313

Gas and Oil Expense		538
Bal.	700	

Lawn Service Fees		401
	Bal.	5,000

Miscellaneous Expense		549
Bal.	200	

Wages Expense		511
Bal.	400	

Exercise 6-6B

GENERAL JOURNAL

PAGE

	DATE	DESCRIPTION	POST. REF.	DEBIT	CREDIT	
1						1
2						2
3						3
4						4
5						5
6						6
7						7
8						8
9						9
10						10
11						11
12						12
13						13
14						14
15						15
16						16
17						17
18						18
19						19
20						20
21						21
22						22
23						23
24						24
25						25
26						26
27						27
28						28
29						29
30						30
31						31
32						32
33						33
34						34
35						35
36						36

Exercise 6-6B (Concluded)

Accum. Depr.—Office Equip.	181.1
	Bal. 110

Wages Payable	219
	Bal. 260

Raquel Zapata, Capital	311
	Bal. 6,000

Raquel Zapata, Drawing	312
Bal. 2,000	

Income Summary	313

Referral Fees	401
	Bal. 2,813

Wages Expense	511
Bal. 1,080	

Advertising Expense	512
Bal. 34	

Rent Expense	521
Bal. 900	

Supplies Expense	523
Bal. 322	

Telephone Expense	525
Bal. 133	

Utilities Expense	533
Bal. 102	

Insurance Expense	535
Bal. 120	

Gas and Oil Expense	538
Bal. 88	

Depr. Exp.—Office Equip.	541
Bal. 110	

Miscellaneous Expense	549
Bal. 98	

Problem 6-7B

1.

2.

Problem 6-7B (Concluded)

3.

Problem 6-8B

1.

	DATE	DESCRIPTION	POST. REF.	DEBIT	CREDIT	
1						1
2						2
3						3
4						4
5						5
6						6
7						7
8						8
9						9
10						10
11						11
12						12
13						13
14						14
15						15
16						16
17						17
18						18

Problem 6-8B (Continued)

2.

GENERAL JOURNAL

PAGE 11

	DATE		DESCRIPTION	POST. REF.	DEBIT	CREDIT	
1							1
2							2
3							3
4							4
5							5
6							6
7							7
8							8
9							9
10							10
11							11
12							12
13							13
14							14
15							15
16							16
17							17
18							18
19							19
20							20
21							21
22							22
23							23

1. and 2.

GENERAL LEDGER

ACCOUNT   Cash

ACCOUNT NO.   101

DATE		ITEM	POST. REF.	DEBIT	CREDIT	BALANCE DEBIT	BALANCE CREDIT
20-- June	30	Balance	✓			5 2 8 5 00	

Problem 6-8B (Continued)

ACCOUNT Accounts Receivable   ACCOUNT NO. 122

DATE		ITEM	POST. REF.	DEBIT	CREDIT	BALANCE DEBIT	BALANCE CREDIT
20-- June	30	Balance	✓			1 0 7 5 00	

ACCOUNT Supplies   ACCOUNT NO. 141

DATE		ITEM	POST. REF.	DEBIT	CREDIT	BALANCE DEBIT	BALANCE CREDIT
20-- June	30	Balance	✓			7 5 0 00	

ACCOUNT Prepaid Insurance   ACCOUNT NO. 145

DATE		ITEM	POST. REF.	DEBIT	CREDIT	BALANCE DEBIT	BALANCE CREDIT
20-- June	30	Balance	✓			5 0 0 00	

ACCOUNT Office Equipment   ACCOUNT NO. 181

DATE		ITEM	POST. REF.	DEBIT	CREDIT	BALANCE DEBIT	BALANCE CREDIT
20-- June	30	Balance	✓			2 2 0 0 00	

ACCOUNT Accumulated Depreciation—Office Equipment   ACCOUNT NO. 181.1

DATE	ITEM	POST. REF.	DEBIT	CREDIT	BALANCE DEBIT	BALANCE CREDIT

Problem 6-8B (Continued)

ACCOUNT Accounts Payable   ACCOUNT NO. 202

DATE	ITEM	POST. REF.	DEBIT	CREDIT	BALANCE DEBIT	BALANCE CREDIT
20-- June 30	Balance	✓				1 5 0 0 00

ACCOUNT Wages Payable   ACCOUNT NO. 219

DATE	ITEM	POST. REF.	DEBIT	CREDIT	BALANCE DEBIT	BALANCE CREDIT

ACCOUNT Juanita Alvarez, Capital   ACCOUNT NO. 311

DATE	ITEM	POST. REF.	DEBIT	CREDIT	BALANCE DEBIT	BALANCE CREDIT
20-- June 30	Balance	✓				7 0 0 0 00

ACCOUNT Juanita Alvarez, Drawing   ACCOUNT NO. 312

DATE	ITEM	POST. REF.	DEBIT	CREDIT	BALANCE DEBIT	BALANCE CREDIT
20-- June 30	Balance	✓			8 0 0 00	

ACCOUNT Income Summary   ACCOUNT NO. 313

DATE	ITEM	POST. REF.	DEBIT	CREDIT	BALANCE DEBIT	BALANCE CREDIT

Problem 6-8B (Continued)

ACCOUNT Consulting Fees   ACCOUNT NO. 401

DATE	ITEM	POST. REF.	DEBIT	CREDIT	BALANCE DEBIT	BALANCE CREDIT
20-- June 30	Balance	✓				4 2 0 4 00

ACCOUNT Wages Expense   ACCOUNT NO. 511

DATE	ITEM	POST. REF.	DEBIT	CREDIT	BALANCE DEBIT	BALANCE CREDIT
20-- June 30	Balance	✓			1 4 0 0 00	

ACCOUNT Advertising Expense   ACCOUNT NO. 512

DATE	ITEM	POST. REF.	DEBIT	CREDIT	BALANCE DEBIT	BALANCE CREDIT
20-- June 30	Balance	✓			6 0 00	

ACCOUNT Rent Expense   ACCOUNT NO. 521

DATE	ITEM	POST. REF.	DEBIT	CREDIT	BALANCE DEBIT	BALANCE CREDIT
20-- June 30	Balance	✓			5 0 0 00	

ACCOUNT Supplies Expense   ACCOUNT NO. 523

DATE	ITEM	POST. REF.	DEBIT	CREDIT	BALANCE DEBIT	BALANCE CREDIT

Problem 6-8B (Continued)

ACCOUNT   Telephone Expense   ACCOUNT NO.   525

DATE		ITEM	POST. REF.	DEBIT	CREDIT	BALANCE	
						DEBIT	CREDIT
20-- June	30	Balance	✓			4 6 00	

ACCOUNT   Electricity Expense   ACCOUNT NO.   533

DATE		ITEM	POST. REF.	DEBIT	CREDIT	BALANCE	
						DEBIT	CREDIT
20-- June	30	Balance	✓			3 9 00	

ACCOUNT   Insurance Expense   ACCOUNT NO.   535

DATE		ITEM	POST. REF.	DEBIT	CREDIT	BALANCE	
						DEBIT	CREDIT

ACCOUNT   Gas and Oil Expense   ACCOUNT NO.   538

DATE		ITEM	POST. REF.	DEBIT	CREDIT	BALANCE	
						DEBIT	CREDIT
20-- June	30	Balance	✓			2 8 00	

ACCOUNT   Depreciation Expense—Office Equipment   ACCOUNT NO.   541

DATE		ITEM	POST. REF.	DEBIT	CREDIT	BALANCE	
						DEBIT	CREDIT

Problem 6-8B (Concluded)

ACCOUNT   Miscellaneous Expense   ACCOUNT NO.   549

DATE		ITEM	POST. REF.	DEBIT	CREDIT	BALANCE	
						DEBIT	CREDIT
20-- June	30	Balance	✓			2 1 00	

3.

ACCOUNT TITLE	ACCT. NO.	DEBIT BALANCE	CREDIT BALANCE

Problem 6-9B

Mastery Problem

GENERAL JOURNAL

PAGE 4

DATE	DESCRIPTION	POST. REF.	DEBIT	CREDIT

Mastery Problem (Continued)

Mastery Problem (Concluded)

Challenge Problem

Exercise 6Apx-1A

a. _____ g. _____

b. _____ h. _____

c. _____ i. _____

d. _____ j. _____

e. _____ k. _____

f. _____

Problem 6Apx-2A

Exercise 6APx-1B

a. _____
b. _____
c. _____
d. _____
e. _____
f. _____

g. _____
h. _____
i. _____
j. _____
k. _____

Problem 6APx-2B

Comprehensive Problem 1: The Accounting Cycle

1.

GENERAL JOURNAL

PAGE 1

	DATE	DESCRIPTION	POST. REF.	DEBIT	CREDIT	
1						1
2						2
3						3
4						4
5						5
6						6
7						7
8						8
9						9
10						10
11						11
12						12
13						13
14						14
15						15
16						16
17						17
18						18
19						19
20						20
21						21
22						22
23						23
24						24
25						25
26						26
27						27
28						28
29						29
30						30
31						31
32						32
33						33
34						34

Comprehensive Problem 1 (Continued)

GENERAL JOURNAL

PAGE 2

	DATE		DESCRIPTION	POST. REF.	DEBIT	CREDIT	
1							1
2							2
3							3
4							4
5							5
6							6
7							7
8							8
9							9
10							10
11							11
12							12
13							13
14							14
15							15
16							16
17							17
18							18
19							19
20							20
21							21
22							22
23							23
24							24
25							25
26							26
27							27
28							28
29							29
30							30
31							31
32							32
33							33
34							34
35							35

Comprehensive Problem 1 (Continued)

GENERAL JOURNAL

	DATE		DESCRIPTION	POST. REF.	DEBIT	CREDIT	
1							1
2							2
3							3
4							4
5							5
6							6
7							7
8							8
9							9
10							10
11							11
12							12
13							13
14							14
15							15
16							16
17							17
18							18
19							19
20							20
21							21
22							22
23							23
24							24
25							25
26							26
27							27
28							28
29							29
30							30
31							31
32							32
33							33
34							34
35							35

Comprehensive Problem 1 (Continued)

GENERAL JOURNAL

PAGE 4

	DATE		DESCRIPTION	POST. REF.	DEBIT	CREDIT	
1							1
2							2
3							3
4							4
5							5
6							6
7							7
8							8
9							9
10							10
11							11

2., 6., and 11.

GENERAL LEDGER

ACCOUNT   Cash   ACCOUNT NO.   101

DATE	ITEM	POST. REF.	DEBIT	CREDIT	BALANCE DEBIT	BALANCE CREDIT

Comprehensive Problem 1 (Continued)

ACCOUNT Office Supplies   ACCOUNT NO. 142

DATE	ITEM	POST. REF.	DEBIT	CREDIT	BALANCE	
					DEBIT	CREDIT

ACCOUNT Food Supplies   ACCOUNT NO. 144

DATE	ITEM	POST. REF.	DEBIT	CREDIT	BALANCE	
					DEBIT	CREDIT

ACCOUNT Prepaid Insurance   ACCOUNT NO. 145

DATE	ITEM	POST. REF.	DEBIT	CREDIT	BALANCE	
					DEBIT	CREDIT

ACCOUNT Fishing Boats   ACCOUNT NO. 181

DATE	ITEM	POST. REF.	DEBIT	CREDIT	BALANCE	
					DEBIT	CREDIT

Comprehensive Problem 1 (Continued)

ACCOUNT Accumulated Depreciation—Fishing Boats   ACCOUNT NO. 181.1

DATE	ITEM	POST. REF.	DEBIT	CREDIT	BALANCE DEBIT	BALANCE CREDIT

ACCOUNT Accounts Payable   ACCOUNT NO. 202

DATE	ITEM	POST. REF.	DEBIT	CREDIT	BALANCE DEBIT	BALANCE CREDIT

ACCOUNT Wages Payable   ACCOUNT NO. 219

DATE	ITEM	POST. REF.	DEBIT	CREDIT	BALANCE DEBIT	BALANCE CREDIT

ACCOUNT Bob Night, Capital   ACCOUNT NO. 311

DATE	ITEM	POST. REF.	DEBIT	CREDIT	BALANCE DEBIT	BALANCE CREDIT

Comprehensive Problem 1 (Continued)

ACCOUNT Bob Night, Drawing   ACCOUNT NO. 312

DATE	ITEM	POST. REF.	DEBIT	CREDIT	BALANCE DEBIT	CREDIT

ACCOUNT Income Summary   ACCOUNT NO. 313

DATE	ITEM	POST. REF.	DEBIT	CREDIT	BALANCE DEBIT	CREDIT

ACCOUNT Registration Fees   ACCOUNT NO. 401

DATE	ITEM	POST. REF.	DEBIT	CREDIT	BALANCE DEBIT	CREDIT

Comprehensive Problem 1 (Continued)

ACCOUNT **Wages Expense**   ACCOUNT NO.   511

DATE	ITEM	POST. REF.	DEBIT	CREDIT	BALANCE	
					DEBIT	CREDIT

ACCOUNT **Rent Expense**   ACCOUNT NO.   521

DATE	ITEM	POST. REF.	DEBIT	CREDIT	BALANCE	
					DEBIT	CREDIT

ACCOUNT **Office Supplies Expense**   ACCOUNT NO.   523

DATE	ITEM	POST. REF.	DEBIT	CREDIT	BALANCE	
					DEBIT	CREDIT

ACCOUNT **Food Supplies Expense**   ACCOUNT NO.   524

DATE	ITEM	POST. REF.	DEBIT	CREDIT	BALANCE	
					DEBIT	CREDIT

Comprehensive Problem 1 (Continued)

ACCOUNT Telephone Expense   ACCOUNT NO. 525

DATE	ITEM	POST. REF.	DEBIT	CREDIT	BALANCE DEBIT	CREDIT

ACCOUNT Utilities Expense   ACCOUNT NO. 533

DATE	ITEM	POST. REF.	DEBIT	CREDIT	BALANCE DEBIT	CREDIT

ACCOUNT Insurance Expense   ACCOUNT NO. 535

DATE	ITEM	POST. REF.	DEBIT	CREDIT	BALANCE DEBIT	CREDIT

ACCOUNT Postage Expense   ACCOUNT NO. 536

DATE	ITEM	POST. REF.	DEBIT	CREDIT	BALANCE DEBIT	CREDIT

ACCOUNT Depreciation Expense—Fishing Boats   ACCOUNT NO. 542

DATE	ITEM	POST. REF.	DEBIT	CREDIT	BALANCE DEBIT	CREDIT

Comprehensive Problem 1 (Continued)

3. and 4.

ACCOUNT TITLE	TRIAL BALANCE		ADJUSTMENTS		
	DEBIT	CREDIT	DEBIT	CREDIT	
					1
					2
					3
					4
					5
					6
					7
					8
					9
					10
					11
					12
					13
					14
					15
					16
					17
					18
					19
					20
					21
					22
					23
					24
					25
					26
					27
					28
					29
					30
					31

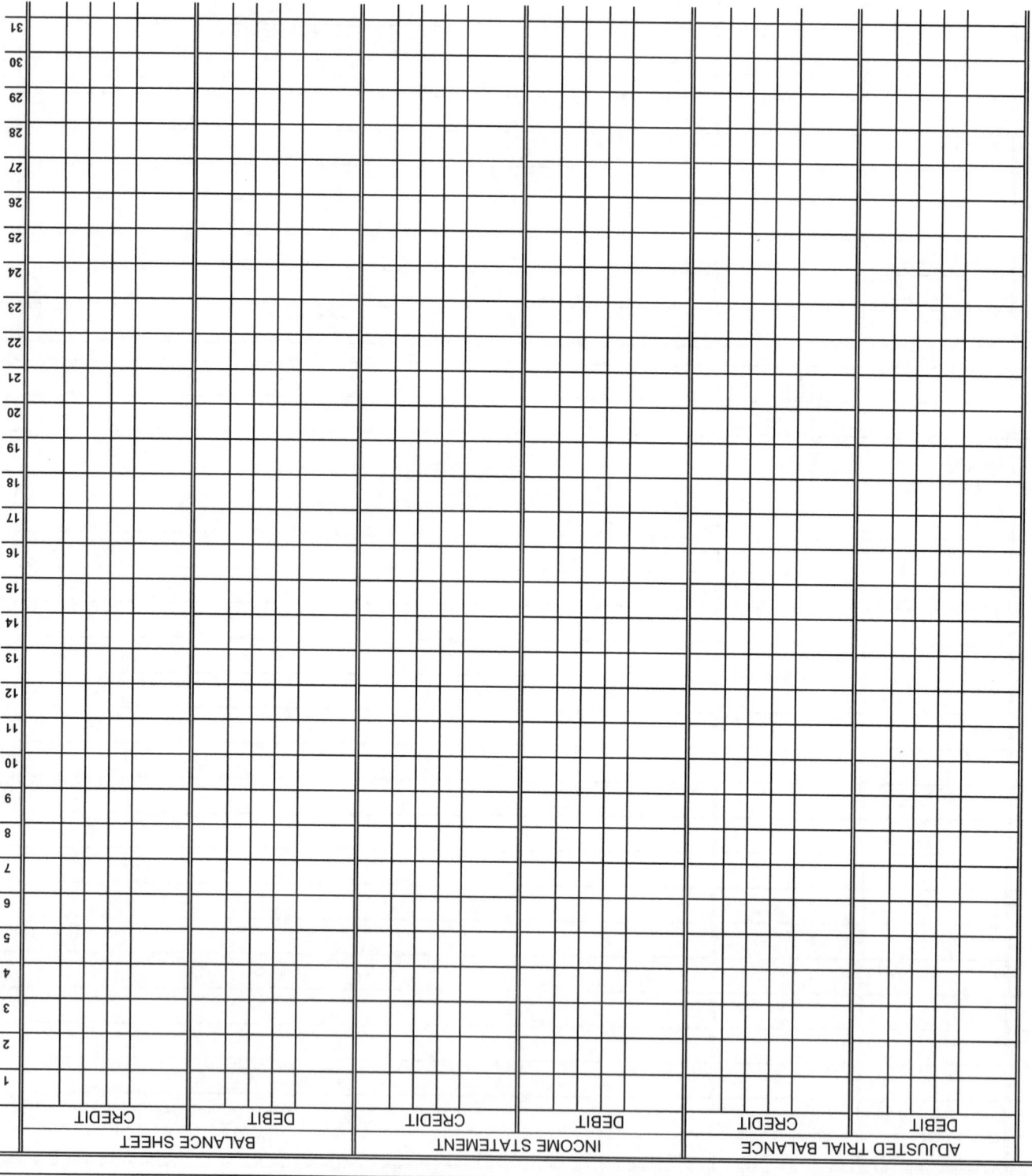

	ADJUSTED TRIAL BALANCE		INCOME STATEMENT		BALANCE SHEET	
	DEBIT	CREDIT	DEBIT	CREDIT	DEBIT	CREDIT

Comprehensive Problem 1 (Continued)

Comprehensive Problem 1 (Continued)

7.

8.

Comprehensive Problem 1 (Continued)

9.

COMPREHENSIVE PROBLEM

Comprehensive Problem 1 (Continued)

5. and 10.

GENERAL JOURNAL   PAGE 5

DATE	DESCRIPTION	POST. REF.	DEBIT	CREDIT	
					1
					2
					3
					4
					5
					6
					7
					8
					9
					10
					11
					12
					13
					14
					15
					16
					17
					18
					19
					20
					21
					22
					23
					24
					25
					26
					27
					28
					29
					30
					31
					32
					33
					34
					35

Comprehensive Problem 1 (Concluded)

GENERAL JOURNAL

	DATE		DESCRIPTION	POST. REF.	DEBIT	CREDIT	
1							1
2							2
3							3
4							4
5							5
6							6
7							7
8							8
9							9

12.

_____

_____

_____

	ACCOUNT	ACCT. NO.	DEBIT BALANCE	CREDIT BALANCE	

Comprehensive Problem 1, Period 2: The Accounting Cycle

1.

GENERAL JOURNAL

	DATE		DESCRIPTION	POST. REF.	DEBIT	CREDIT	
1							1
2							2
3							3
4							4
5							5
6							6
7							7
8							8
9							9
10							10
11							11
12							12
13							13
14							14
15							15
16							16
17							17
18							18
19							19
20							20
21							21
22							22
23							23
24							24
25							25
26							26
27							27
28							28
29							29
30							30
31							31
32							32
33							33
34							34
35							35

Comprehensive Problem 1, Period 2 (Continued)

GENERAL JOURNAL

PAGE 6

	DATE		DESCRIPTION	POST. REF.	DEBIT	CREDIT	
1							1
2							2
3							3
4							4
5							5
6							6
7							7
8							8
9							9
10							10
11							11
12							12
13							13
14							14
15							15
16							16
17							17
18							18
19							19
20							20
21							21
22							22
23							23
24							24
25							25
26							26
27							27
28							28
29							29
30							30
31							31
32							32
33							33
34							34
35							35
36							36
37							37
38							38
39							39
40							40
41							41
42							42

Comprehensive Problem 1, Period 2 (Continued)

GENERAL JOURNAL

PAGE 7

	DATE		DESCRIPTION	POST. REF.	DEBIT	CREDIT	
1							1
2							2
3							3
4							4
5							5
6							6
7							7
8							8
9							9
10							10
11							11
12							12
13							13
14							14
15							15
16							16
17							17
18							18
19							19
20							20
21							21
22							22
23							23
24							24
25							25
26							26
27							27
28							28
29							29
30							30
31							31
32							32
33							33
34							34

Comprehensive Problem 1, Period 2 (Continued)

2., 6., and 11.

GENERAL LEDGER

ACCOUNT Cash   ACCOUNT NO. 101

DATE		ITEM	POST. REF.	DEBIT	CREDIT	BALANCE DEBIT	BALANCE CREDIT
20-- Apr.	30	Balance	✔			130 6 5 0 00	

ACCOUNT Accounts Receivable   ACCOUNT NO. 122

DATE	ITEM	POST. REF.	DEBIT	CREDIT	BALANCE DEBIT	BALANCE CREDIT

Comprehensive Problem 1, Period 2 (Continued)

ACCOUNT **Office Supplies**   ACCOUNT NO.   142

DATE		ITEM	POST. REF.	DEBIT	CREDIT	BALANCE DEBIT	BALANCE CREDIT
20-- Apr.	30	Balance	✔			1 0 0 00	

ACCOUNT **Food Supplies**   ACCOUNT NO.   144

DATE		ITEM	POST. REF.	DEBIT	CREDIT	BALANCE DEBIT	BALANCE CREDIT
20-- Apr.	30	Balance	✔			8 0 0 0 00	

ACCOUNT **Prepaid Insurance**   ACCOUNT NO.   145

DATE		ITEM	POST. REF.	DEBIT	CREDIT	BALANCE DEBIT	BALANCE CREDIT
20-- Apr.	30	Balance	✔			7 5 0 0 00	

ACCOUNT **Prepaid Subscriptions**   ACCOUNT NO.   146

DATE		ITEM	POST. REF.	DEBIT	CREDIT	BALANCE DEBIT	BALANCE CREDIT

Comprehensive Problem 1, Period 2 (Continued)

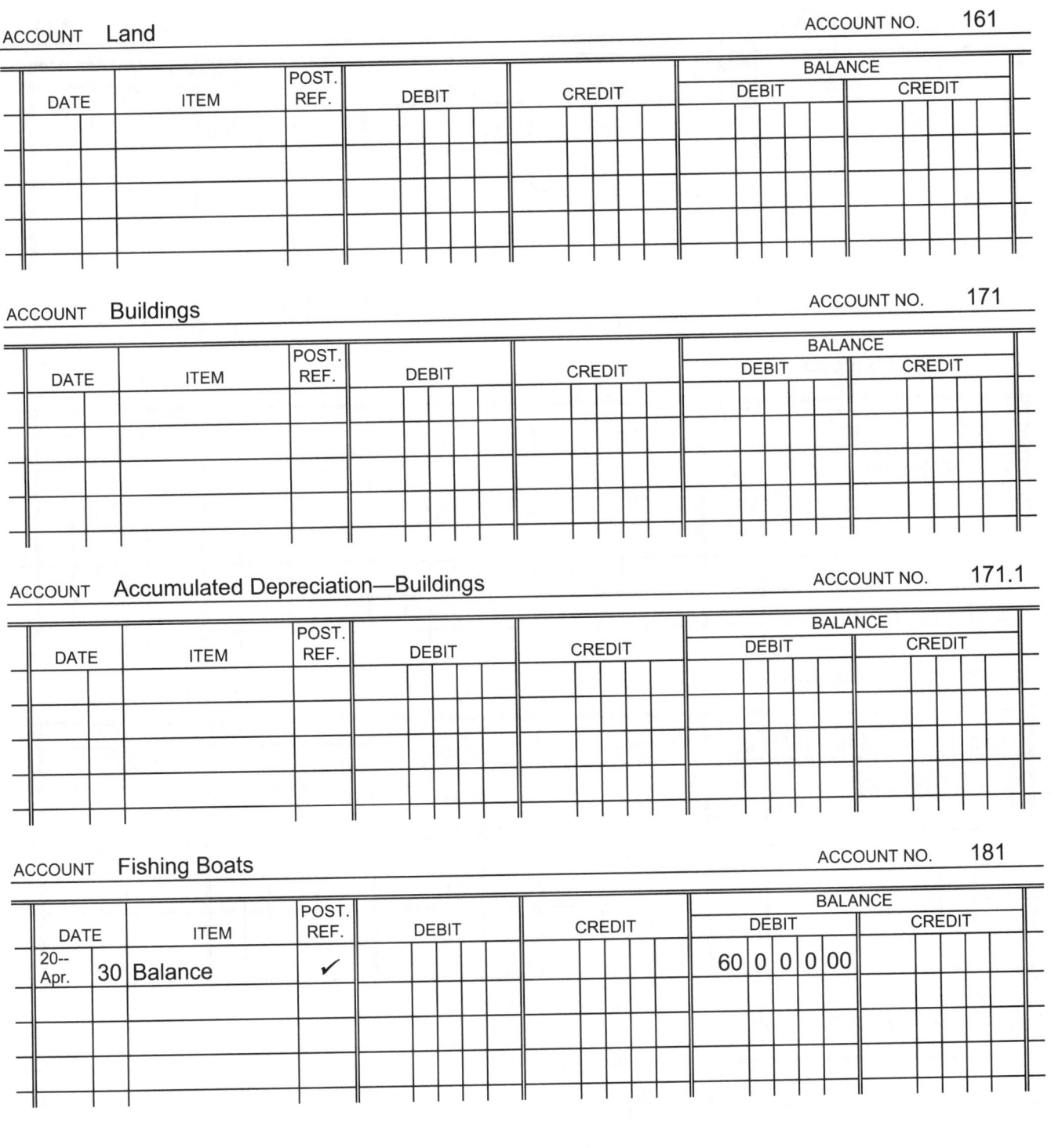

ACCOUNT Land   ACCOUNT NO. 161

DATE	ITEM	POST. REF.	DEBIT	CREDIT	BALANCE DEBIT	BALANCE CREDIT

ACCOUNT Buildings   ACCOUNT NO. 171

DATE	ITEM	POST. REF.	DEBIT	CREDIT	BALANCE DEBIT	BALANCE CREDIT

ACCOUNT Accumulated Depreciation—Buildings   ACCOUNT NO. 171.1

DATE	ITEM	POST. REF.	DEBIT	CREDIT	BALANCE DEBIT	BALANCE CREDIT

ACCOUNT Fishing Boats   ACCOUNT NO. 181

DATE	ITEM	POST. REF.	DEBIT	CREDIT	BALANCE DEBIT	BALANCE CREDIT
20-- Apr. 30	Balance	✔			60 0 0 0 00	

Comprehensive Problem 1, Period 2 (Continued)

ACCOUNT   Accumulated Depreciation—Fishing Boats   ACCOUNT NO.   181.1

DATE		ITEM	POST. REF.	DEBIT	CREDIT	BALANCE DEBIT	BALANCE CREDIT
20-- Apr.	30	Balance	✓				1 0 0 0 00

ACCOUNT   Surround Sound System   ACCOUNT NO.   182

DATE	ITEM	POST. REF.	DEBIT	CREDIT	BALANCE DEBIT	BALANCE CREDIT

ACCOUNT   Accumulated Depreciation—Surround Sound System   ACCOUNT NO.   182.1

DATE	ITEM	POST. REF.	DEBIT	CREDIT	BALANCE DEBIT	BALANCE CREDIT

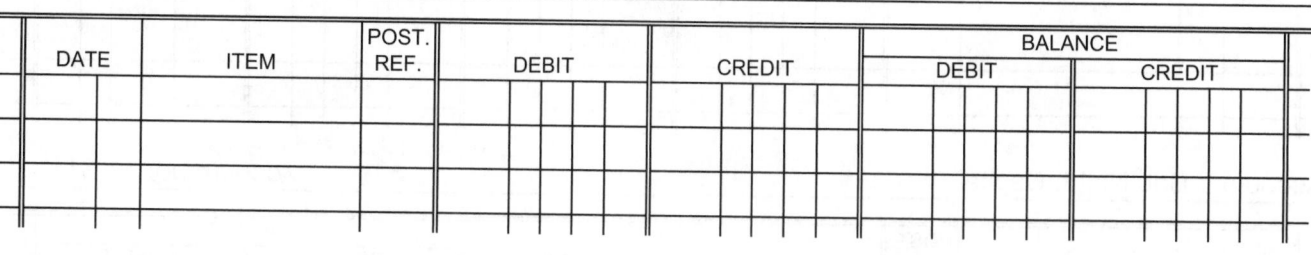

ACCOUNT   Big Screen TV   ACCOUNT NO.   183

DATE	ITEM	POST. REF.	DEBIT	CREDIT	BALANCE DEBIT	BALANCE CREDIT

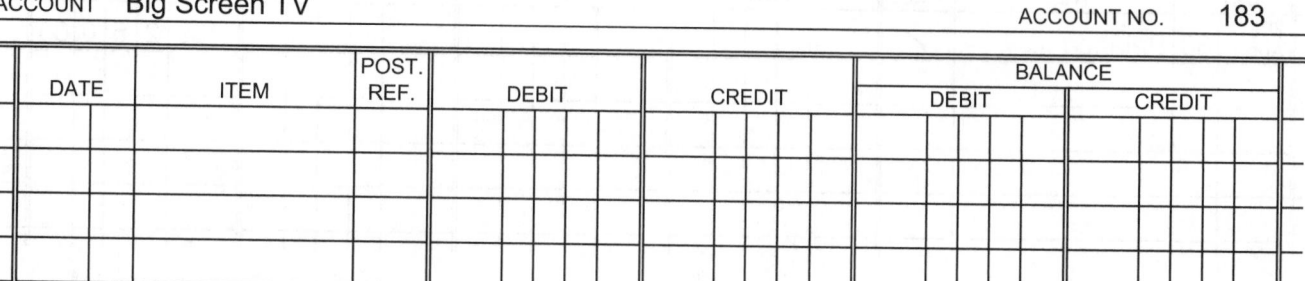

ACCOUNT   Accumulated Depreciation—Big Screen TV   ACCOUNT NO.   183.1

DATE	ITEM	POST. REF.	DEBIT	CREDIT	BALANCE DEBIT	BALANCE CREDIT

Comprehensive Problem 1, Period 2 (Continued)

ACCOUNT   Accounts Payable   ACCOUNT NO.   202

DATE		ITEM	POST. REF.	DEBIT	CREDIT	BALANCE DEBIT	BALANCE CREDIT
20-- Apr.	30	Balance	✓				66 5 0 0 00

ACCOUNT   Wages Payable   ACCOUNT NO.   219

DATE		ITEM	POST. REF.	DEBIT	CREDIT	BALANCE DEBIT	BALANCE CREDIT
20-- Apr.	30	Balance	✓				5 0 0 00

ACCOUNT   Bob Night, Capital   ACCOUNT NO.   311

DATE		ITEM	POST. REF.	DEBIT	CREDIT	BALANCE DEBIT	BALANCE CREDIT
20-- Apr.	30	Balance	✓				138 2 5 0 00

ACCOUNT   Bob Night, Drawing   ACCOUNT NO.   312

DATE		ITEM	POST. REF.	DEBIT	CREDIT	BALANCE DEBIT	BALANCE CREDIT

Comprehensive Problem 1, Period 2 (Continued)

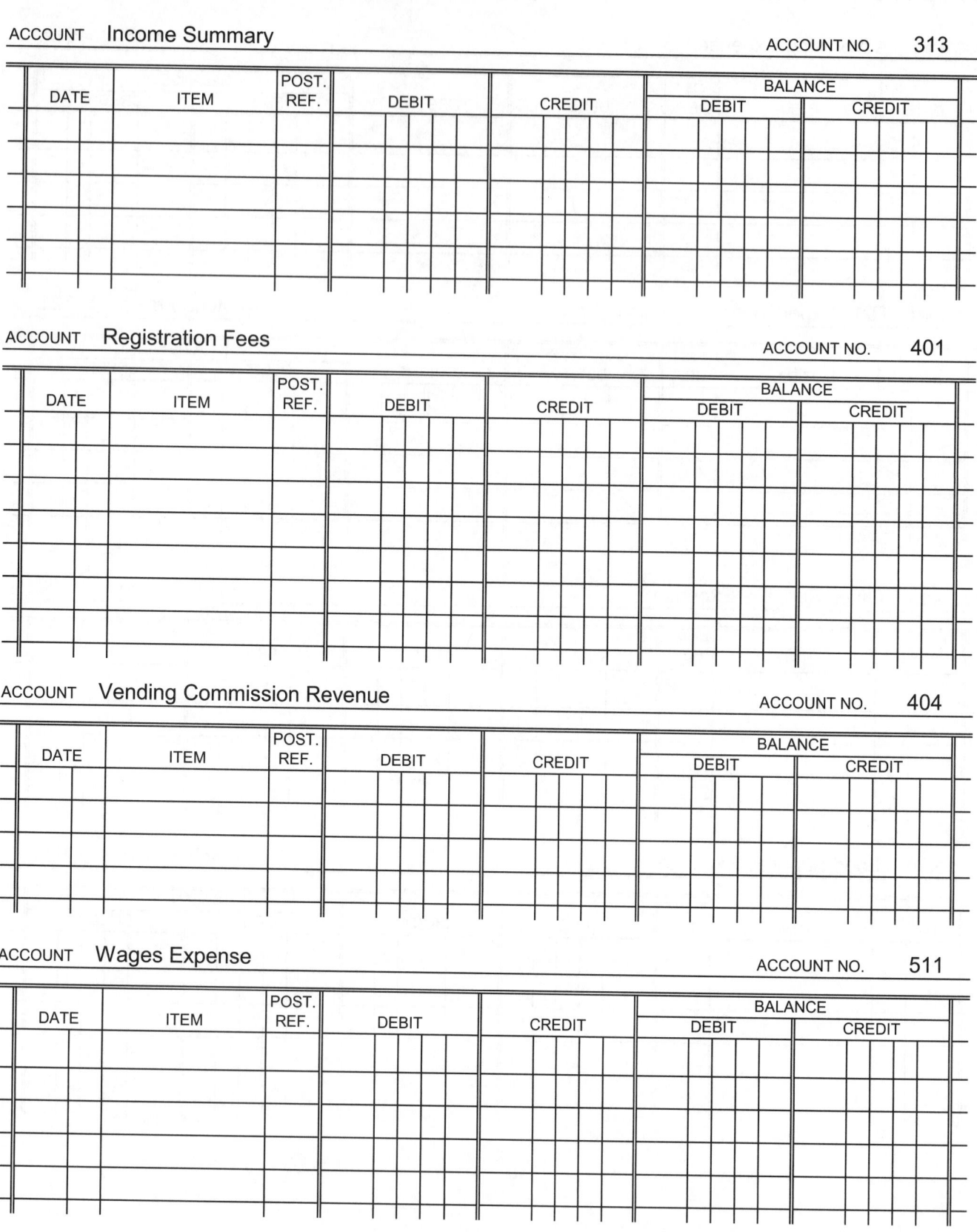

ACCOUNT Income Summary   ACCOUNT NO. 313

DATE	ITEM	POST. REF.	DEBIT	CREDIT	BALANCE DEBIT	BALANCE CREDIT

ACCOUNT Registration Fees   ACCOUNT NO. 401

DATE	ITEM	POST. REF.	DEBIT	CREDIT	BALANCE DEBIT	BALANCE CREDIT

ACCOUNT Vending Commission Revenue   ACCOUNT NO. 404

DATE	ITEM	POST. REF.	DEBIT	CREDIT	BALANCE DEBIT	BALANCE CREDIT

ACCOUNT Wages Expense   ACCOUNT NO. 511

DATE	ITEM	POST. REF.	DEBIT	CREDIT	BALANCE DEBIT	BALANCE CREDIT

Comprehensive Problem 1, Period 2 (Continued)

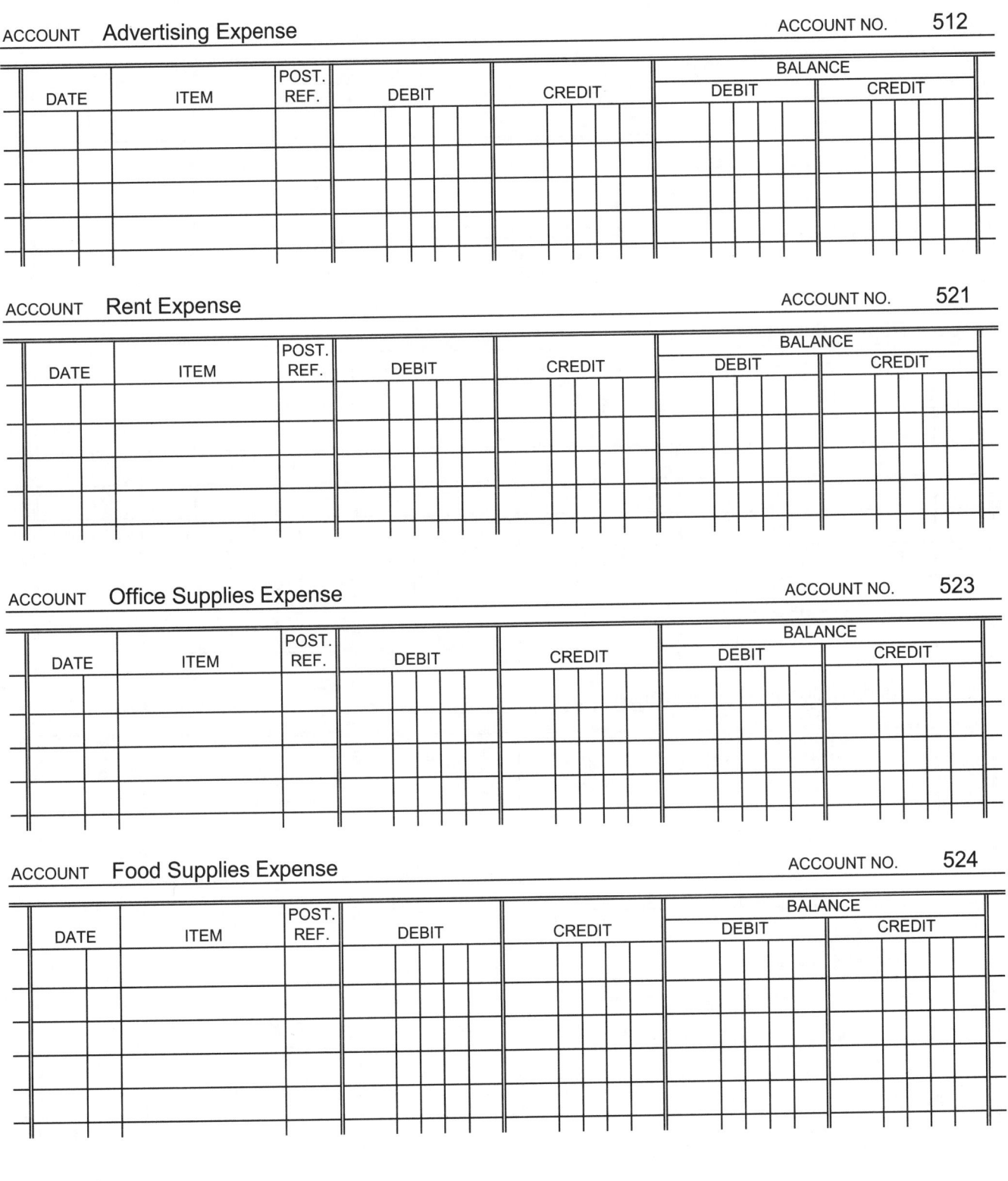

ACCOUNT Advertising Expense   ACCOUNT NO. 512

DATE	ITEM	POST. REF.	DEBIT	CREDIT	BALANCE DEBIT	BALANCE CREDIT

ACCOUNT Rent Expense   ACCOUNT NO. 521

DATE	ITEM	POST. REF.	DEBIT	CREDIT	BALANCE DEBIT	BALANCE CREDIT

ACCOUNT Office Supplies Expense   ACCOUNT NO. 523

DATE	ITEM	POST. REF.	DEBIT	CREDIT	BALANCE DEBIT	BALANCE CREDIT

ACCOUNT Food Supplies Expense   ACCOUNT NO. 524

DATE	ITEM	POST. REF.	DEBIT	CREDIT	BALANCE DEBIT	BALANCE CREDIT

Comprehensive Problem 1, Period 2 (Continued)

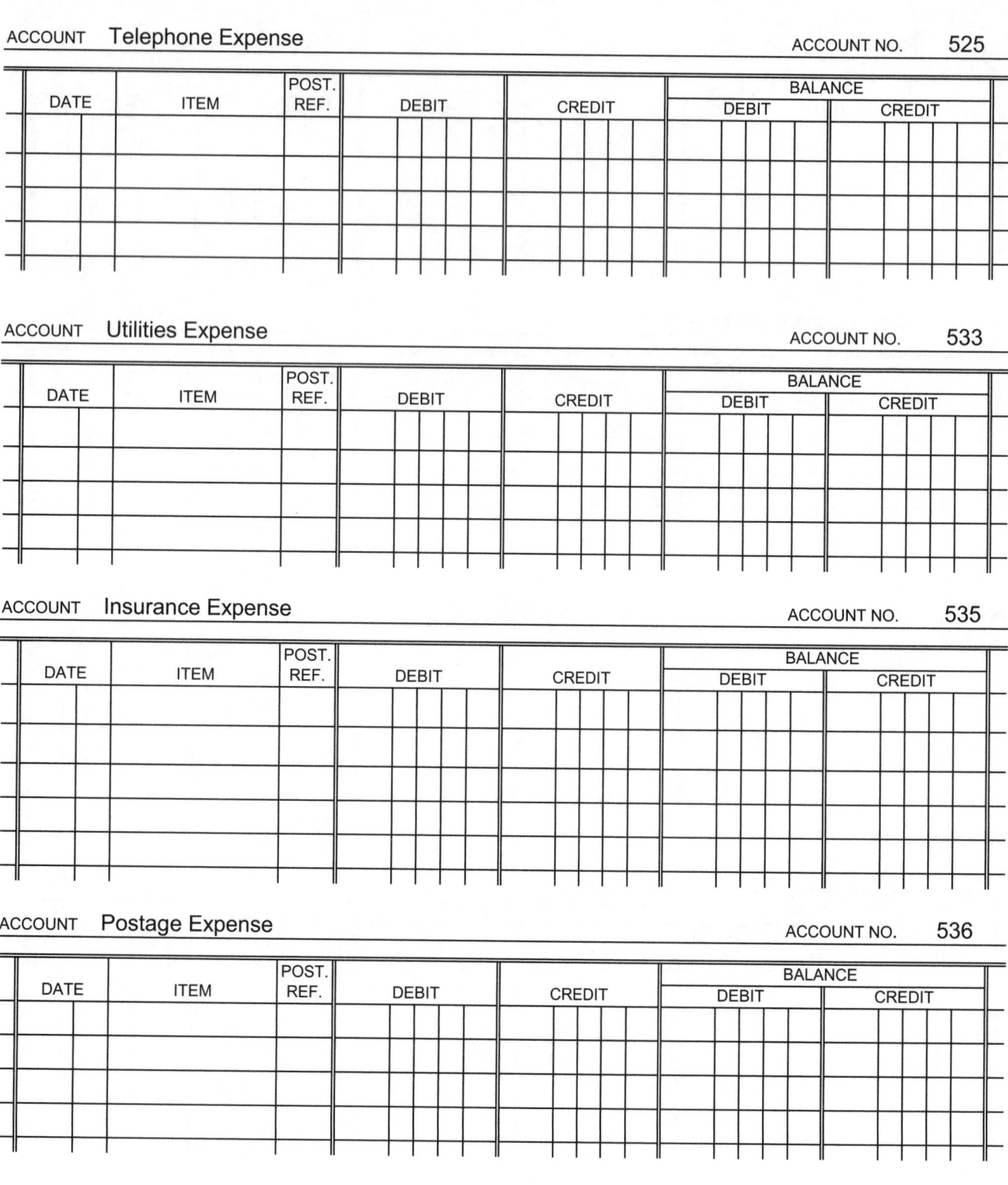

ACCOUNT Telephone Expense   ACCOUNT NO. 525

DATE	ITEM	POST. REF.	DEBIT	CREDIT	BALANCE	
					DEBIT	CREDIT

ACCOUNT Utilities Expense   ACCOUNT NO. 533

DATE	ITEM	POST. REF.	DEBIT	CREDIT	BALANCE	
					DEBIT	CREDIT

ACCOUNT Insurance Expense   ACCOUNT NO. 535

DATE	ITEM	POST. REF.	DEBIT	CREDIT	BALANCE	
					DEBIT	CREDIT

ACCOUNT Postage Expense   ACCOUNT NO. 536

DATE	ITEM	POST. REF.	DEBIT	CREDIT	BALANCE	
					DEBIT	CREDIT

Comprehensive Problem 1, Period 2 (Continued)

ACCOUNT Repair Expense   ACCOUNT NO. 537

DATE	ITEM	POST. REF.	DEBIT	CREDIT	BALANCE DEBIT	BALANCE CREDIT

ACCOUNT Depreciation Expense—Buildings   ACCOUNT NO. 540

DATE	ITEM	POST. REF.	DEBIT	CREDIT	BALANCE DEBIT	BALANCE CREDIT

ACCOUNT Depreciation Expense—Surround Sound System   ACCOUNT NO. 541

DATE	ITEM	POST. REF.	DEBIT	CREDIT	BALANCE DEBIT	BALANCE CREDIT

ACCOUNT Depreciation Expense—Fishing Boats   ACCOUNT NO. 542

DATE	ITEM	POST. REF.	DEBIT	CREDIT	BALANCE DEBIT	BALANCE CREDIT

Comprehensive Problem 1, Period 2 (Continued)

ACCOUNT Depreciation Expense—Big Screen TV

ACCOUNT NO. 543

DATE	ITEM	POST. REF.	DEBIT	CREDIT	BALANCE	
					DEBIT	CREDIT

ACCOUNT Satellite Programming Expense

ACCOUNT NO. 546

DATE	ITEM	POST. REF.	DEBIT	CREDIT	BALANCE	
					DEBIT	CREDIT

ACCOUNT Subscriptions Expense

ACCOUNT NO. 548

DATE	ITEM	POST. REF.	DEBIT	CREDIT	BALANCE	
					DEBIT	CREDIT

Comprehensive Problem 1, Period 2 (Continued)

3. and 4.

ACCOUNT TITLE	TRIAL BALANCE		ADJUSTMENTS	
	DEBIT	CREDIT	DEBIT	CREDIT
1				
2				
3				
4				
5				
6				
7				
8				
9				
10				
11				
12				
13				
14				
15				
16				
17				
18				
19				
20				
21				
22				
23				
24				
25				
26				
27				
28				
29				
30				
31				
32				
33				
34				
35				
36				
37				
38				
39				
40				

Comprehensive Problem 1, Period 2 (Continued)

	ADJUSTED TRIAL BALANCE		INCOME STATEMENT		BALANCE SHEET	
	DEBIT	CREDIT	DEBIT	CREDIT	DEBIT	CREDIT
1						
2						
3						
4						
5						
6						
7						
8						
9						
10						
11						
12						
13						
14						
15						
16						
17						
18						
19						
20						
21						
22						
23						
24						
25						
26						
27						
28						
29						
30						
31						
32						
33						
34						
35						
36						
37						
38						
39						
40						

Comprehensive Problem 1, Period 2 (Continued)

5.

GENERAL JOURNAL   PAGE 8

	DATE		DESCRIPTION	POST. REF.	DEBIT	CREDIT	
1							1
2							2
3							3
4							4
5							5
6							6
7							7
8							8
9							9
10							10
11							11
12							12
13							13
14							14
15							15
16							16
17							17
18							18
19							19
20							20
21							21
22							22
23							23
24							24
25							25
26							26
27							27
28							28
29							29
30							30
31							31
32							32
33							33
34							34
35							35

Comprehensive Problem 1, Period 2 (Continued)

7.

8.

9.

Comprehensive Problem 1, Period 2 (Continued)

Comprehensive Problem 1, Period 2 (Continued)
10.

GENERAL JOURNAL   PAGE 9

	DATE		DESCRIPTION	POST. REF.	DEBIT	CREDIT	
1							1
2							2
3							3
4							4
5							5
6							6
7							7
8							8
9							9
10							10
11							11
12							12
13							13
14							14
15							15
16							16
17							17
18							18
19							19
20							20
21							21
22							22
23							23
24							24
25							25
26							26
27							27
28							28
29							29
30							30
31							31
32							32
33							33
34							34
35							35

Comprehensive Problem 1, Period 2 (Concluded)

12.

ACCOUNT TITLE	ACCT. NO.	DEBIT BALANCE	CREDIT BALANCE

Exercise 7-1A

1. _____
2. _____
3. _____
4. _____

5. _____
6. _____
7. _____

Exercise 7-2A

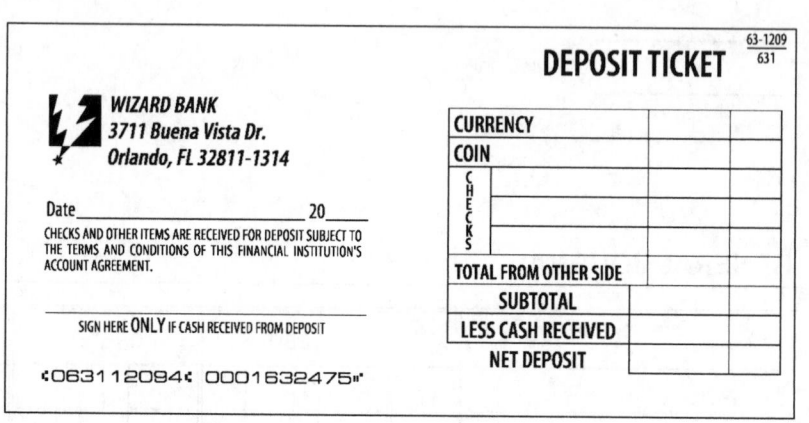

DEPOSIT TICKET 63-1209 / 631

WIZARD BANK
3711 Buena Vista Dr.
Orlando, FL 32811-1314

Date_____ 20_____

CHECKS AND OTHER ITEMS ARE RECEIVED FOR DEPOSIT SUBJECT TO
THE TERMS AND CONDITIONS OF THIS FINANCIAL INSTITUTION'S
ACCOUNT AGREEMENT.

SIGN HERE ONLY IF CASH RECEIVED FROM DEPOSIT

⑆063112094⑆ 0001632475⑈

CURRENCY		
COIN		
C H E C K S		
TOTAL FROM OTHER SIDE		
SUBTOTAL		
LESS CASH RECEIVED		
NET DEPOSIT		

Exercise 7-3A

No. **1**

DATE _____ 20_____
TO _____
FOR _____

ACCT. _____

	DOLLARS	CENTS
BAL BRO'T FOR'D		
AMT. DEPOSITED		
TOTAL		
AMT. THIS CHECK		
BAL CAR'D FOR'D		

No. **1**   63-1209 / 631

_____ 20 _____

PAY
TO THE
ORDER OF_____ $ _____

_____ Dollars

WIZARD BANK   FOR CLASSROOM USE ONLY
3711 Buena Vista Dr.
Orlando, FL 32811-1314

MEMO_____   BY _____

⑆063112094⑆ 0001632475⑈

Exercise 7-4A

	Ending Bank Balance	Ending Check-book Balance
1.	_____	_____
2.	_____	_____
3.	_____	_____
4.	_____	_____
5.	_____	_____
6.	_____	_____
7.	_____	_____

Exercise 7-5A

GENERAL JOURNAL   PAGE

	DATE	DESCRIPTION	POST. REF.	DEBIT	CREDIT	
1						1
2						2
3						3
4						4
5						5
6						6
7						7
8						8
9						9
10						10
11						11
12						12
13						13
14						14
15						15
16						16
17						17
18						18
19						19
20						20
21						21

Exercise 7-6A

GENERAL JOURNAL

PAGE

	DATE	DESCRIPTION	POST. REF.	DEBIT	CREDIT	
1						1
2						2
3						3
4						4
5						5
6						6
7						7
8						8
9						9
10						10
11						11
12						12
13						13
14						14
15						15
16						16
17						17
18						18
19						19
20						20
21						21
22						22
23						23
24						24
25						25
26						26
27						27
28						28
29						29
30						30
31						31
32						32
33						33
34						34
35						35
36						36

Exercise 7-7A

GENERAL JOURNAL   PAGE

	DATE		DESCRIPTION	POST. REF.	DEBIT	CREDIT	
1							1
2							2
3							3
4							4
5							5
6							6
7							7
8							8
9							9
10							10
11							11
12							12
13							13
14							14
15							15
16							16
17							17
18							18
19							19
20							20
21							21
22							22
23							23
24							24
25							25
26							26
27							27
28							28
29							29
30							30
31							31
32							32
33							33
34							34
35							35
36							36

Problem 7-8A

1.

Problem 7-8A (Concluded)
2.

GENERAL JOURNAL

PAGE

	DATE	DESCRIPTION	POST. REF.	DEBIT	CREDIT	
1						1
2						2
3						3
4						4
5						5
6						6
7						7
8						8
9						9
10						10
11						11
12						12
13						13
14						14
15						15

Problem 7-9A

1.

Problem 7-9A (Concluded)

2.

GENERAL JOURNAL

PAGE

	DATE	DESCRIPTION	POST. REF.	DEBIT	CREDIT	
1						1
2						2
3						3
4						4
5						5
6						6
7						7
8						8
9						9
10						10
11						11
12						12
13						13
14						14
15						15
16						16
17						17
18						18
19						19

Problem 7-10A

1. and 3.

GENERAL JOURNAL

	DATE		DESCRIPTION	POST. REF.	DEBIT	CREDIT	
1							1
2							2
3							3
4							4
5							5
6							6
7							7
8							8
9							9
10							10
11							11
12							12
13							13

Problem 7-10A (Concluded)
2. and 3.

PETTY CASH PAYMENTS FOR MONTH OF _____ 20-- ____ PAGE

DAY	DESCRIPTION	VOU. NO.	TOTAL AMOUNT	OFFICE SUPPLIES	POSTAGE EXPENSE	CHARIT. CONTRIB. EXPENSE	TELEPHONE EXPENSE	TRAVEL & ENTER. EXPENSE	MISC. EXPENSE	ACCOUNT	AMOUNT
1											
2											
3											
4											
5											
6											
7											
8											
9											
10											
11											
12											
13											
14											
15											
16											
17											
18											
19											
20											
21											
22											

DISTRIBUTION OF PAYMENTS

Problem 7-11A

1.

GENERAL JOURNAL

DATE	DESCRIPTION	POST. REF.	DEBIT	CREDIT	
					1
					2
					3
					4
					5
					6
					7
					8
					9
					10
					11
					12
					13
					14
					15
					16
					17
					18
					19
					20
					21
					22
					23

2.

ACCOUNT _____ ACCOUNT NO. _____

DATE	ITEM	POST. REF.	DEBIT	CREDIT	BALANCE	
					DEBIT	CREDIT

3. The balance represents:

Exercise 7-1B

1. _____   5. _____

2. _____   6. _____

3. _____   7. _____

4. _____

Exercise 7-2B

	63-1209
DEPOSIT TICKET	631

WIZARD BANK
3711 Buena Vista Dr.
Orlando, FL 32811-1314

Date_____ 20____

CHECKS AND OTHER ITEMS ARE RECEIVED FOR DEPOSIT SUBJECT TO
THE TERMS AND CONDITIONS OF THIS FINANCIAL INSTITUTION'S
ACCOUNT AGREEMENT.

SIGN HERE ONLY IF CASH RECEIVED FROM DEPOSIT

⑆063112094⑈ 0001632475⑈

CURRENCY		
COIN		
C H E C K S		
TOTAL FROM OTHER SIDE		
SUBTOTAL		
LESS CASH RECEIVED		
NET DEPOSIT		

Exercise 7-3B

No. 1

DATE _____ 20____
TO _____
FOR _____

ACCT. _____

	DOLLARS	CENTS
BAL BRO'T FOR'D		
AMT. DEPOSITED		
TOTAL		
AMT. THIS CHECK		
BAL CAR'D FOR'D		

No. 1   63-1209 / 631

_____ 20_____

PAY
TO THE
ORDER OF _____ $ _____

_____ Dollars

WIZARD BANK   FOR CLASSROOM USE ONLY
3711 Buena Vista Dr.
Orlando, FL 32811-1314

MEMO_____   BY _____

⑆063112094⑈ 0001632475⑈

Exercise 7-4B

	Ending Bank Balance	Ending Check-book Balance
1.	_____	_____
2.	_____	_____
3.	_____	_____
4.	_____	_____
5.	_____	_____
6.	_____	_____
7.	_____	_____

Exercise 7-5B

GENERAL JOURNAL

PAGE _____

	DATE	DESCRIPTION	POST. REF.	DEBIT	CREDIT	
1						1
2						2
3						3
4						4
5						5
6						6
7						7
8						8
9						9
10						10
11						11
12						12
13						13
14						14
15						15
16						16
17						17
18						18
19						19
20						20
21						21

Exercise 7-6B

GENERAL JOURNAL

PAGE

	DATE	DESCRIPTION	POST. REF.	DEBIT	CREDIT	
1						1
2						2
3						3
4						4
5						5
6						6
7						7
8						8
9						9
10						10
11						11
12						12
13						13
14						14
15						15
16						16
17						17
18						18
19						19
20						20
21						21
22						22
23						23
24						24
25						25
26						26
27						27
28						28
29						29
30						30
31						31
32						32
33						33
34						34
35						35
36						36

Exercise 7-7B

GENERAL JOURNAL

PAGE _____

DATE	DESCRIPTION	POST. REF.	DEBIT	CREDIT	
					1
					2
					3
					4
					5
					6
					7
					8
					9
					10
					11
					12
					13
					14
					15
					16
					17
					18
					19
					20
					21
					22
					23
					24
					25
					26
					27
					28
					29
					30
					31
					32
					33
					34
					35
					36

Problem 7-8B

1.

Problem 7-8B (Concluded)
2.

GENERAL JOURNAL

	DATE		DESCRIPTION	POST. REF.	DEBIT	CREDIT	
1							1
2							2
3							3
4							4
5							5
6							6
7							7
8							8
9							9
10							10
11							11
12							12
13							13
14							14
15							15

Problem 7-9B

1.

Problem 7-9B (Concluded)

2.

GENERAL JOURNAL

	DATE		DESCRIPTION	POST. REF.	DEBIT	CREDIT	
1							1
2							2
3							3
4							4
5							5
6							6
7							7
8							8
9							9
10							10
11							11
12							12
13							13
14							14
15							15
16							16
17							17
18							18
19							19

Problem 7-10B

1. and 3.

GENERAL JOURNAL

PAGE

	DATE	DESCRIPTION	POST. REF.	DEBIT	CREDIT	
1						1
2						2
3						3
4						4
5						5
6						6
7						7
8						8
9						9
10						10
11						11
12						12
13						13

Problem 7-10B (Concluded)

2. and 3.

PETTY CASH PAYMENTS FOR MONTH OF _____ **20--** **PAGE** _____

DAY	DESCRIPTION	VOU. NO.	TOTAL AMOUNT	DISTRIBUTION OF PAYMENTS							
				OFFICE SUPPLIES	POSTAGE EXPENSE	CHARIT. CONTRIB. EXPENSE	TELEPHONE EXPENSE	TRAVEL & ENTER. EXPENSE	MISC. EXPENSE	ACCOUNT	AMOUNT
1											
2											
3											
4											
5											
6											
7											
8											
9											
10											
11											
12											
13											
14											
15											
16											
17											
18											
19											
20											
21											
22											

Problem 7-11B

1.

| | GENERAL JOURNAL | | | PAGE 8 |

DATE	DESCRIPTION	POST. REF.	DEBIT	CREDIT	
1					1
2					2
3					3
4					4
5					5
6					6
7					7
8					8
9					9
10					10
11					11
12					12
13					13
14					14
15					15
16					16
17					17
18					18
19					19
20					20
21					21
22					22
23					23

2.

ACCOUNT   ACCOUNT NO.

DATE	ITEM	POST. REF.	DEBIT	CREDIT	BALANCE DEBIT	BALANCE CREDIT

3. The balance represents:

Mastery Problem

1.

PETTY CASH PAYMENTS FOR MONTH OF 20--

PAGE

DAY	DESCRIPTION	VOU. NO.	TOTAL AMOUNT	TRUCK EXPENSE	POSTAGE EXPENSE	CHARIT. CONTRIB. EXPENSE	TELEPHONE EXPENSE	ADVERT. EXPENSE.	MISC. EXPENSE	ACCOUNT	AMOUNT
							DISTRIBUTION OF PAYMENTS				
1											
2											
3											
4											
5											
6											
7											
8											
9											
10											
11											
12											
13											
14											
15											
16											
17											
18											
19											
20											
21											
22											

Mastery Problem (Continued)

2. and 3.

GENERAL JOURNAL PAGE 1

DATE	DESCRIPTION	POST. REF.	DEBIT	CREDIT	
					1
					2
					3
					4
					5
					6
					7
					8
					9
					10
					11
					12
					13
					14
					15
					16
					17
					18
					19
					20
					21
					22
					23
					24
					25
					26
					27
					28
					29
					30
					31
					32
					33
					34
					35

Mastery Problem (Concluded)

GENERAL JOURNAL

PAGE 2

	DATE	DESCRIPTION	POST. REF.	DEBIT	CREDIT	
1						1
2						2
3						3
4						4
5						5
6						6
7						7
8						8
9						9
10						10
11						11
12						12
13						13
14						14

3.

Challenge Problem

1. Panera Bakery

GENERAL JOURNAL

PAGE

DATE	DESCRIPTION	POST. REF.	DEBIT	CREDIT	
					1
					2
					3
					4
					5
					6
					7
					8
					9
					10
					11
					12
					13
					14
					15
					16
					17
					18
					19
					20
					21
					22
					23
					24
					25
					26
					27
					28
					29

Challenge Problem (Concluded)

2. Lawrence Bank

GENERAL JOURNAL   PAGE _____

	DATE		DESCRIPTION	POST. REF.	DEBIT	CREDIT	
1							1
2							2
3							3
4							4
5							5
6							6
7							7
8							8
9							9
10							10
11							11
12							12
13							13
14							14
15							15
16							16
17							17
18							18
19							19
20							20
21							21
22							22
23							23
24							24
25							25
26							26
27							27
28							28
29							29

APPENDIX: Internal Controls

Exercise 7Apx-1A

1. _____

   _____

2. _____

   _____

3. _____

   _____

4. _____

   _____

5. _____

   _____

Exercise 7Apx-2A

1. _____

2. _____

3. _____

4. _____

5. _____

Exercise 7Apx-3A

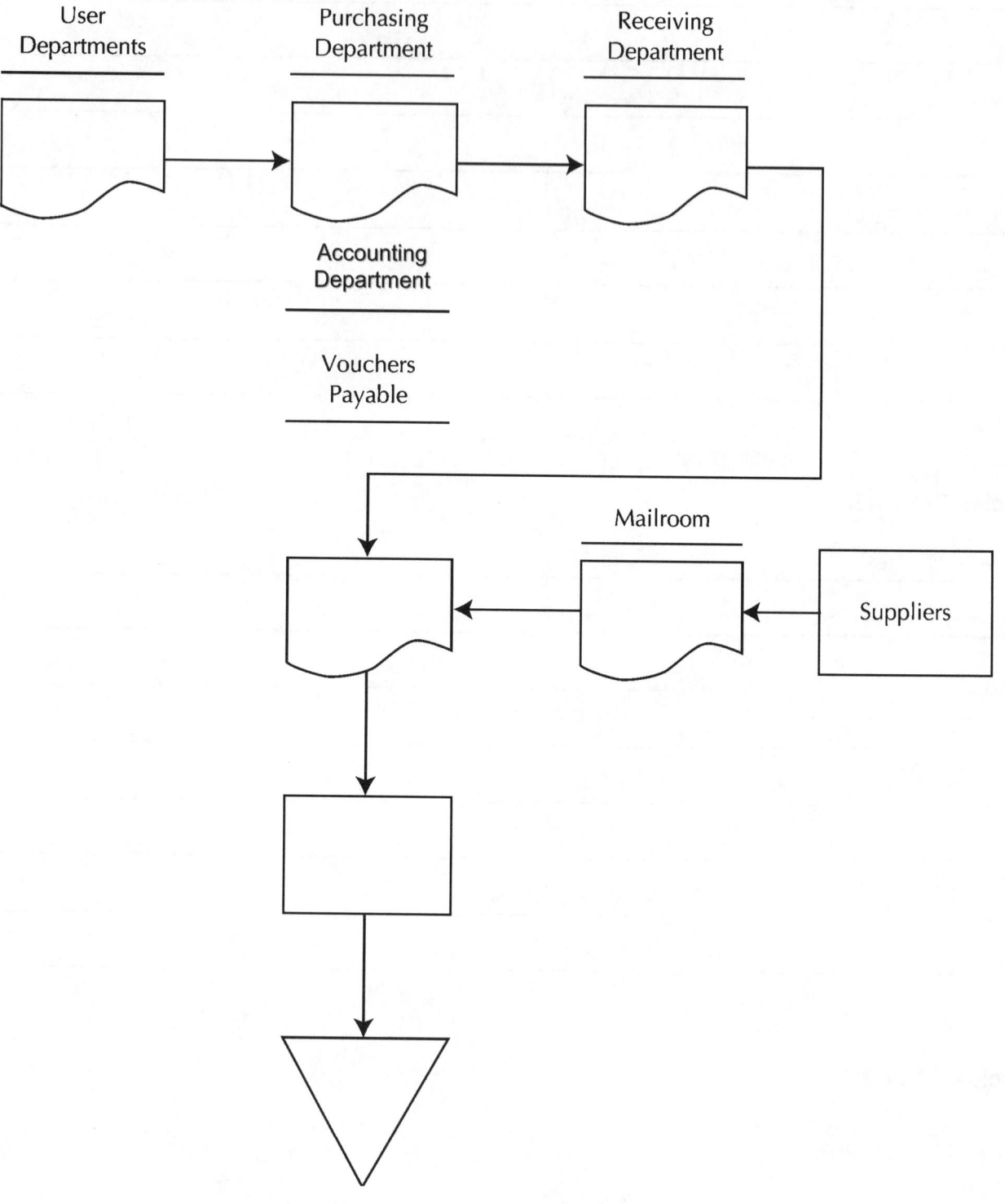

Problem 7Apx-4A

1. _____

_____

2. _____

_____

3. _____

_____

4. _____

_____

Exercise 7Apx-1B

1. _____

_____

2. _____

_____

3. _____

_____

4. _____

_____

Exercise 7Apx-2B

1. _____

2. _____

3. _____

4. _____

Exercise 7Apx-3B

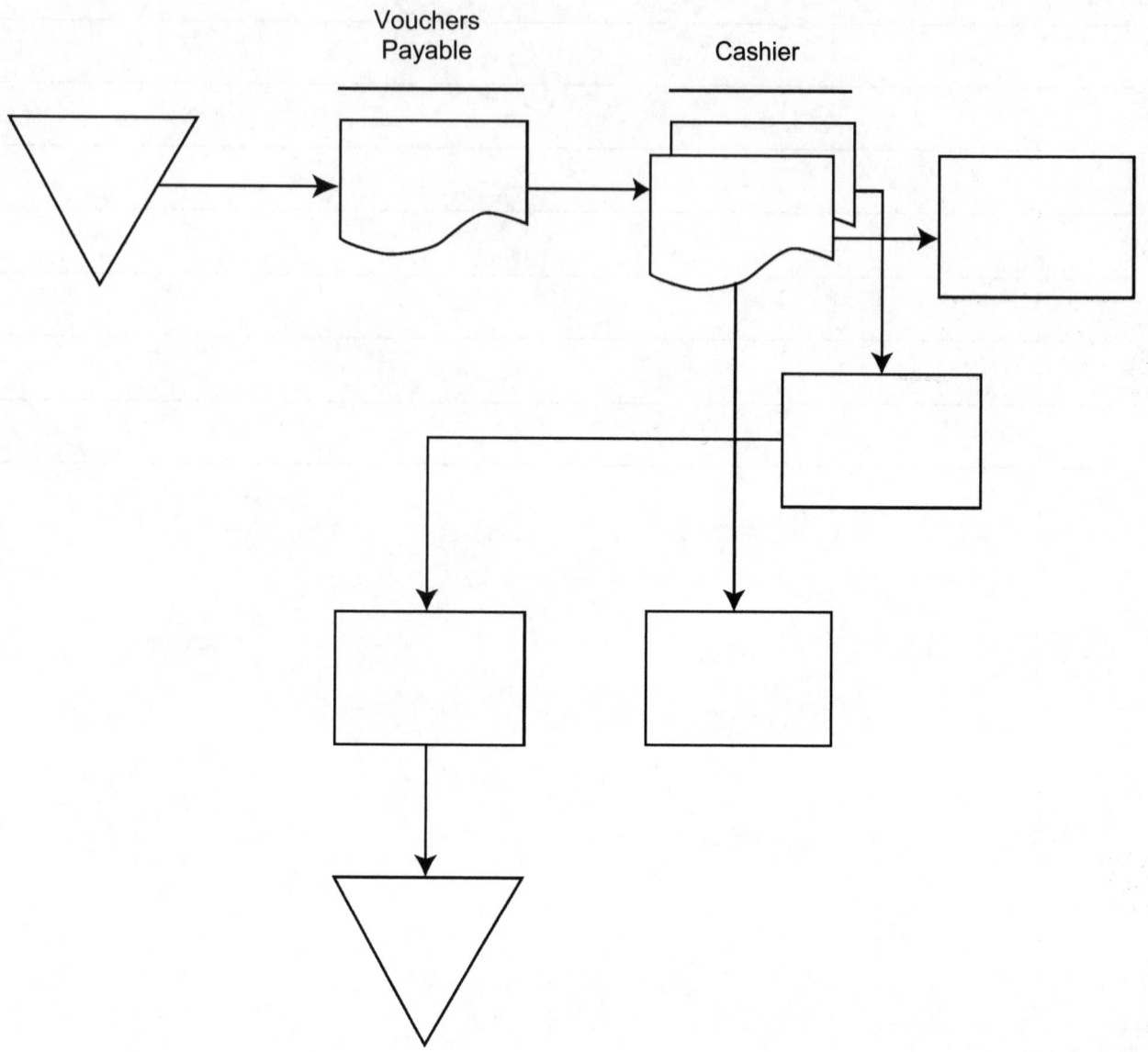

Problem 7Apx-4B

1. _____

_____

2. _____

_____

3. _____

_____

4. _____

_____

Exercise 8-1A

a. _____ regular hours × $10 per hour   _____

b. _____ overtime hours × $15 per hour   _____

c. Total gross wages   _____

d. Federal income tax withholding
   (from tax tables in Figure 8-4)   _____

e. Social Security withholding at 6.2%   _____

f. Medicare withholding at 1.45%   _____

g. Total withholding   _____

h. Net pay   _____

Exercise 8-2A

_____

_____

_____

_____

Exercise 8-3A

_____

_____

_____

_____

_____

_____

_____

Exercise 8-4A

	Marital Status	Total Weekly Earnings	Number of Allowances	Amount of Withholding
a.	S	$347.60	2	_____
b.	S	451.50	1	_____
c.	M	481.15	3	_____
d.	S	490.52	0	_____
e.	M	701.89	5	_____

Exercise 8-5A

Cumul. Pay Before Current Weekly Payroll	Current Gross Pay	Year-to-Date Earnings	Soc. Sec. Maximum	Amount Over Max. Soc. Sec.	Amount Subject to Soc. Sec.	Soc. Sec. Tax Withheld	Medicare Tax Withheld
$ 22,000	$1,700		$110,100				
54,000	4,200		110,100				
107,500	3,925		110,100				
109,500	4,600		110,100				

Exercise 8-6A

GENERAL JOURNAL   PAGE

	DATE		DESCRIPTION	POST. REF.	DEBIT	CREDIT	
1							1
2							2
3							3
4							4
5							5
6							6
7							7
8							8
9							9

Exercise 8-7A

GENERAL JOURNAL   PAGE

	DATE		DESCRIPTION	POST. REF.	DEBIT	CREDIT	
1							1
2							2
3							3
4							4
5							5
6							6
7							7
8							8
9							9

Problem 8-8A

1.

_____

_____

_____

_____

_____

_____

_____

_____

_____

_____

_____

_____

_____

_____

_____

_____

_____

_____

_____

2.

GENERAL JOURNAL

PAGE

	DATE		DESCRIPTION	POST. REF.	DEBIT	CREDIT	
1							1
2							2
3							3
4							4
5							5
6							6
7							7
8							8
9							9
10							10
11							11
12							12
13							13
14							14
15							15

Problem 8-9A

1.

PAYROLL REGISTER

	NAME	NO. ALLOW.	MARIT. STATUS	EARNINGS REGULAR		OVERTIME		TOTAL		CUMULATIVE TOTAL		TAXABLE EARNINGS UNEMPLOY. COMP.		SOCIAL SECURITY		
1																
2																
3																
4																
5																
6																
7																
8																
9																
10																
11																
12																
13																
14																

Problem 8-9A (Concluded)

FOR PERIOD ENDED _____ 20--

	FEDERAL INCOME TAX	SOCIAL SECURITY TAX	MEDICARE TAX	CITY TAX	HEALTH INSUR.	OTHER	TOTAL	NET PAY	CK. NO.
	DEDUCTIONS								
1									
2									
3									
4									
5									
6									
7									
8									
9									
10									
11									
12									
13									
14									

2.

GENERAL JOURNAL   PAGE ____

DATE	DESCRIPTION	POST. REF.	DEBIT	CREDIT	
					1
					2
					3
					4
					5
					6
					7
					8
					9
					10
					11
					12
					13
					14

Problem 8-10A

EMPLOYEE EARNINGS RECORD

20 -- PERIOD ENDED	EARNINGS				TAXABLE EARNINGS		DEDUCTIONS	
	REGULAR	OVERTIME	TOTAL	CUMULATIVE TOTAL	UNEMPLOY. COMP.	SOCIAL SECURITY	FEDERAL INCOME TAX	SOCIAL SECURITY TAX
GENDER	DEPARTMENT		OCCUPATION		SOCIAL SECURITY NO.		MARITAL STATUS	ALLOW-ANCES
M F								

Problem 8-10A (Concluded)

FOR PERIOD ENDED _____ 20--

MEDICARE TAX		CITY TAX		HEALTH INSURANCE	DEDUCTIONS OTHER			TOTAL		CK. NO.	AMOUNT	
PAY RATE		DATE OF BIRTH		DATE HIRED	NAME/ADDRESS							EMP. NO.

Exercise 8-1B

a. _____ regular hours × $12 per hour _____

b. _____ overtime hours × $18 per hour _____

c. Total gross wages _____

d. Federal income tax withholding
     (from tax tables in Figure 8-4) _____

e. Social Security withholding at 6.2% _____

f. Medicare withholding at 1.45% _____

g. Total withholding _____

h. Net pay _____

Exercise 8-2B

_____

_____

_____

_____

Exercise 8-3B

_____

_____

_____

_____

_____

_____

_____

_____

Exercise 8-4B

	Marital Status	Total Weekly Earnings	Number of Allowances	Amount of Withholding
a.	M	$546.00	4	_____
b.	M	390.00	3	_____
c.	S	461.39	2	_____
d.	M	522.88	2	_____
e.	S	612.00	0	_____

Exercise 8-5B

Cumul. Pay Before Current Weekly Payroll	Current Gross Pay	Year-to-Date Earnings	Soc. Sec. Maximum	Amount Over Max. Soc. Sec.	Amount Subject to Soc. Sec.	Soc. Sec. Tax Withheld	Medicare Tax Withheld
$ 31,000	$1,500		$110,100				
53,000	2,860		110,100				
107,200	3,140		110,100				
109,500	2,920		110,100				

Exercise 8-6B

GENERAL JOURNAL

PAGE

	DATE	DESCRIPTION	POST. REF.	DEBIT	CREDIT	
1						1
2						2
3						3
4						4
5						5
6						6
7						7
8						8
9						9
10						10
11						11
12						12
13						13
14						14
15						15
16						16
17						17
18						18
19						19
20						20
21						21
22						22

Exercise 8-7B

GENERAL JOURNAL

PAGE

	DATE	DESCRIPTION	POST. REF.	DEBIT	CREDIT	
1						1
2						2
3						3
4						4
5						5
6						6
7						7
8						8
9						9
10						10
11						11
12						12
13						13

Problem 8-8B

1.

Problem 8-8B (Concluded)

2.

PAGE

	DATE		DESCRIPTION	POST. REF.	DEBIT	CREDIT	
1							1
2							2
3							3
4							4
5							5
6							6
7							7
8							8
9							9
10							10
11							11
12							12
13							13
14							14
15							15
16							16
17							17
18							18
19							19
20							20
21							21
22							22
23							23
24							24
25							25
26							26
27							27
28							28
29							29
30							30
31							31
32							32
33							33
34							34
35							35

Problem 8-9B

1.

PAYROLL REGISTER

	NAME	NO. ALLOW.	MARIT. STATUS	EARNINGS							TAXABLE EARNINGS			
				REGULAR		OVERTIME		TOTAL		CUMULATIVE TOTAL		UNEMPLOY. COMP.		SOCIAL SECURITY	
1															
2															
3															
4															
5															
6															
7															
8															
9															
10															
11															
12															
13															
14															

Problem 8-9B (Concluded)

FOR PERIOD ENDED

20--

FEDERAL INCOME TAX	SOCIAL SECURITY TAX	MEDICARE TAX	CITY TAX	HEALTH INSUR.	OTHER		TOTAL	NET PAY	CK. NO.	
										1
										2
										3
										4
										5
										6
										7
										8
										9
										10
										11
										12
										13
										14

(DEDUCTIONS column spans Federal Income Tax through Total)

2.

GENERAL JOURNAL

PAGE

	DATE	DESCRIPTION	POST. REF.	DEBIT	CREDIT	
1						1
2						2
3						3
4						4
5						5
6						6
7						7
8						8
9						9
10						10
11						11
12						12
13						13
14						14

Problem 8-10B

EMPLOYEE EARNINGS RECORD

20 -- PERIOD ENDED	EARNINGS					TAXABLE EARNINGS				DEDUCTIONS				
	REGULAR		OVERTIME		TOTAL	CUMULATIVE TOTAL		UNEMPLOY. COMP.	SOCIAL SECURITY		FEDERAL INCOME TAX		SOCIAL SECURITY TAX	

GENDER	DEPARTMENT	OCCUPATION	SOCIAL SECURITY NO.	MARITAL STATUS	ALLOW-ANCES
M	F					

Problem 8-10B (Concluded)

FOR PERIOD ENDED _____   20--

MEDICARE TAX	CITY TAX	HEALTH INSURANCE	DEDUCTIONS				TOTAL	CK. NO.	AMOUNT	
			OTHER							
PAY RATE	DATE OF BIRTH	DATE HIRED	NAME/ADDRESS						EMP. NO.	

Mastery Problem

1.

PAYROLL REGISTER

	NAME	NO. ALLOW.	MARIT. STATUS	EARNINGS REGULAR	EARNINGS OVERTIME	EARNINGS TOTAL	CUMULATIVE TOTAL	TAXABLE EARNINGS UNEMPLOY. COMP.	TAXABLE EARNINGS SOCIAL SECURITY
1									
2									
3									
4									
5									
6									
7									
8									
9									
10									
11									
12									
13									
14									

3.

EMPLOYEE EARNINGS RECORD

20 -- PERIOD ENDED	EARNINGS REGULAR	EARNINGS OVERTIME	EARNINGS TOTAL	CUMULATIVE TOTAL	TAXABLE EARNINGS UNEMPLOY. COMP.	TAXABLE EARNINGS SOCIAL SECURITY	FEDERAL INCOME TAX
11/4	330 00	33 00	363 00	6,145 50	363 00	363 00	6 00
11/11	440 00	49 50	489 50	6,635 00	489 50	489 50	18 00
11/18							
11/25							

GENDER	DEPARTMENT	OCCUPATION	SOCIAL SECURITY NO.	MARITAL STATUS
M F				

Mastery Problem (Continued)

FOR PERIOD ENDED 20--

FEDERAL INCOME TAX		SOCIAL SECURITY TAX		MEDICARE TAX		STATE INCOME TAX		HEALTH INSURANCE		CREDIT UNION		TOTAL		NET PAY		CK. NO.	
																	1
																	2
																	3
																	4
																	5
																	6
																	7
																	8
																	9
																	10
																	11
																	12
																	13
																	14

FOR PERIOD ENDED 20--

SOCIAL SECURITY TAX		MEDICARE TAX		STATE INCOME TAX		HEALTH INSURANCE		CREDIT UNION		TOTAL		CK. NO.	AMOUNT	
22	51	5	26	12	71			72	60	119	08	121	243	92
30	35	7	10	17	13			97	90	170	48	229	319	02

ALLOWANCES	PAY RATE	DATE OF BIRTH	DATE HIRED	NAME/ADDRESS	EMP. NO.

Mastery Problem (Concluded)

2.

GENERAL JOURNAL   PAGE

DATE	DESCRIPTION	POST. REF.	DEBIT	CREDIT	
					1
					2
					3
					4
					5
					6
					7
					8
					9
					10
					11
					12
					13
					14
					15
					16
					17
					18
					19
					20
					21
					22
					23
					24
					25
					26
					27
					28
					29
					30
					31
					32
					33
					34
					35

Challenge Problem

1.

GENERAL JOURNAL

PAGE _____

	DATE		DESCRIPTION	POST. REF.	DEBIT	CREDIT	
1							1
2							2
3							3
4							4
5							5
6							6
7							7
8							8
9							9
10							10

2.

Exercise 9-1A

_____

_____

_____

_____

_____

GENERAL JOURNAL

PAGE _____

	DATE		DESCRIPTION	POST. REF.	DEBIT	CREDIT	
1							1
2							2
3							3
4							4
5							5
6							6
7							7

Exercise 9-2A

_____

_____

_____

_____

_____

_____

_____

_____

_____

GENERAL JOURNAL

PAGE _____

	DATE		DESCRIPTION	POST. REF.	DEBIT	CREDIT	
1							1
2							2
3							3
4							4
5							5
6							6
7							7

Exercise 9-3A

Name	Current Earnings	Taxable Earnings Unemploy. Comp.	Social Security
Jordahl			
Keesling			
Palmer			
Soltis			
Stout			
Xia			
Total			

GENERAL JOURNAL   PAGE _____

	DATE	DESCRIPTION	POST. REF.	DEBIT	CREDIT	
1						1
2						2
3						3
4						4
5						5
6						6
7						7

Exercise 9-4A

Exercise 9-5A

GENERAL JOURNAL

PAGE _____

	DATE		DESCRIPTION	POST. REF.	DEBIT	CREDIT	
1							1
2							2
3							3
4							4
5							5
6							6
7							7
8							8
9							9
10							10
11							11
12							12

Exercise 9-6A

1.

GENERAL JOURNAL

PAGE _____

	DATE	DESCRIPTION	POST. REF.	DEBIT	CREDIT	
1						1
2						2
3						3
4						4
5						5

2.

_____

_____

_____

_____

GENERAL JOURNAL

PAGE _____

	DATE		DESCRIPTION	POST. REF.	DEBIT	CREDIT	
1							1
2							2
3							3
4							4

Problem 9-7A

1.

		Taxable Earnings	
Name	**Current Earnings**	**Unemploy. Comp.**	**Social Security**
Click, Katelyn			
Coombs, Michelle			
Faus, Erin			
Lenihan, Marcus			
McMahon, Drew			
Newell, Marg			
Stevens, Matt			
Total			

2.

GENERAL JOURNAL

PAGE

	DATE	DESCRIPTION	POST. REF.	DEBIT	CREDIT	
1						1
2						2
3						3
4						4
5						5
6						6
7						7
8						8
9						9
10						10

Problem 9-8A

1.

GENERAL JOURNAL

PAGE _____

	DATE		DESCRIPTION	POST. REF.	DEBIT	CREDIT	
1							1
2							2
3							3
4							4
5							5
6							6
7							7
8							8
9							9
10							10
11							11
12							12
13							13
14							14
15							15
16							16
17							17
18							18
19							19
20							20
21							21
22							22
23							23
24							24
25							25
26							26
27							27
28							28
29							29
30							30
31							31
32							32
33							33
34							34
35							35
36							36

Problem 9-8A (Continued)

GENERAL JOURNAL   PAGE _____

	DATE		DESCRIPTION	POST. REF.	DEBIT	CREDIT	
1							1
2							2
3							3
4							4
5							5
6							6
7							7
8							8
9							9
10							10
11							11
12							12
13							13
14							14
15							15
16							16
17							17
18							18
19							19
20							20
21							21
22							22
23							23
24							24
25							25
26							26
27							27
28							28
29							29
30							30
31							31
32							32
33							33
34							34
35							35

Problem 9-8A (Concluded)

2.

Cash	101		Employee Federal Income Tax Payable 211

Social Security Tax Payable	212		Medicare Tax Payable	213

Savings Bond Deductions Payable	218		FUTA Tax Payable	221

SUTA Tax Payable	222		Wages and Salaries Expense	511

Payroll Taxes Expense	530

Problem 9-9A

1.

_____
_____
_____
_____
_____
_____
_____

GENERAL JOURNAL

PAGE _____

	DATE		DESCRIPTION	POST. REF.	DEBIT	CREDIT	
1							1
2							2
3							3
4							4
5							5
6							6

2.

_____
_____
_____
_____
_____
_____
_____

GENERAL JOURNAL

PAGE _____

	DATE		DESCRIPTION	POST. REF.	DEBIT	CREDIT	
1							1
2							2
3							3
4							4
5							5
6							6

Problem 9-9A (Concluded)

3.

_____
_____
_____
_____
_____
_____

GENERAL JOURNAL

PAGE _____

	DATE		DESCRIPTION	POST. REF.	DEBIT	CREDIT	
1							1
2							2
3							3
4							4
5							5

Exercise 9-1B

_____
_____
_____
_____
_____
_____

GENERAL JOURNAL

PAGE _____

	DATE		DESCRIPTION	POST. REF.	DEBIT	CREDIT	
1							1
2							2
3							3
4							4
5							5
6							6
7							7
8							8
9							9

Exercise 9-2B

_____

_____

_____

_____

_____

_____

_____

_____

_____

_____

GENERAL JOURNAL   PAGE _____

	DATE	DESCRIPTION	POST. REF.	DEBIT	CREDIT	
1						1
2						2
3						3
4						4
5						5
6						6
7						7
8						8

Exercise 9-3B

		Taxable Earnings	
Name	**Current Earnings**	**Unemploy. Comp.**	**Social Security**
Carlson	_____	_____	_____
Delgado	_____	_____	_____
Lewis	_____	_____	_____
Nixon	_____	_____	_____
Shippe	_____	_____	_____
Watts	_____	_____	_____
Total	_____	_____	_____

Exercise 9-3B (Concluded)

_____

_____

_____

_____

_____

GENERAL JOURNAL   PAGE _____

	DATE	DESCRIPTION	POST. REF.	DEBIT	CREDIT	
1						1
2						2
3						3
4						4
5						5
6						6
7						7

Exercise 9-4B: See page WP-302.

Exercise 9-5B

GENERAL JOURNAL   PAGE _____

	DATE	DESCRIPTION	POST. REF.	DEBIT	CREDIT	
1						1
2						2
3						3
4						4
5						5
6						6
7						7
8						8
9						9
10						10
11						11
12						12
13						13
14						14

Exercise 9-4B

_____

_____

_____

_____

_____

_____

_____

_____

Exercise 9-6B

1.

GENERAL JOURNAL

PAGE

	DATE		DESCRIPTION	POST. REF.	DEBIT	CREDIT	
1							1
2							2
3							3
4							4
5							5

2.

_____

_____

_____

_____

_____

GENERAL JOURNAL

PAGE

	DATE		DESCRIPTION	POST. REF.	DEBIT	CREDIT	
1							1
2							2
3							3
4							4
5							5

Problem 9-7B

1.

| | | | **Taxable Earnings** | |
Name	**Current Earnings**	**Unemploy. Comp.**	**Social Security**
Ackers, Alice	_____	_____	_____
Conley, Dorothy	_____	_____	_____
Davis, James	_____	_____	_____
Lawrence, Kevin	_____	_____	_____
Rawlings, Judy	_____	_____	_____
Tanaka, Sumio	_____	_____	_____
Vadillo, Raynette	_____	_____	_____
Total	_____	_____	_____

_____

_____

_____

_____

_____

_____

_____

_____

_____

_____

2.

GENERAL JOURNAL   PAGE _____

	DATE	DESCRIPTION	POST. REF.	DEBIT	CREDIT	
1						1
2						2
3						3
4						4
5						5
6						6
7						7
8						8
9						9
10						10
11						11
12						12

Problem 9-8B

1.

GENERAL JOURNAL

PAGE

	DATE	DESCRIPTION	POST. REF.	DEBIT	CREDIT	
1						1
2						2
3						3
4						4
5						5
6						6
7						7
8						8
9						9
10						10
11						11
12						12
13						13
14						14
15						15
16						16
17						17
18						18
19						19
20						20
21						21
22						22
23						23
24						24
25						25
26						26
27						27
28						28
29						29
30						30
31						31
32						32
33						33
34						34
35						35
36						36

Problem 9-8B (Continued)

GENERAL JOURNAL

PAGE _____

DATE	DESCRIPTION	POST. REF.	DEBIT	CREDIT	
					1
					2
					3
					4
					5
					6
					7
					8
					9
					10
					11
					12
					13
					14
					15
					16
					17
					18
					19
					20
					21
					22
					23
					24
					25
					26
					27
					28
					29
					30
					31
					32
					33
					34
					35

Problem 9-8B (Concluded)

2.

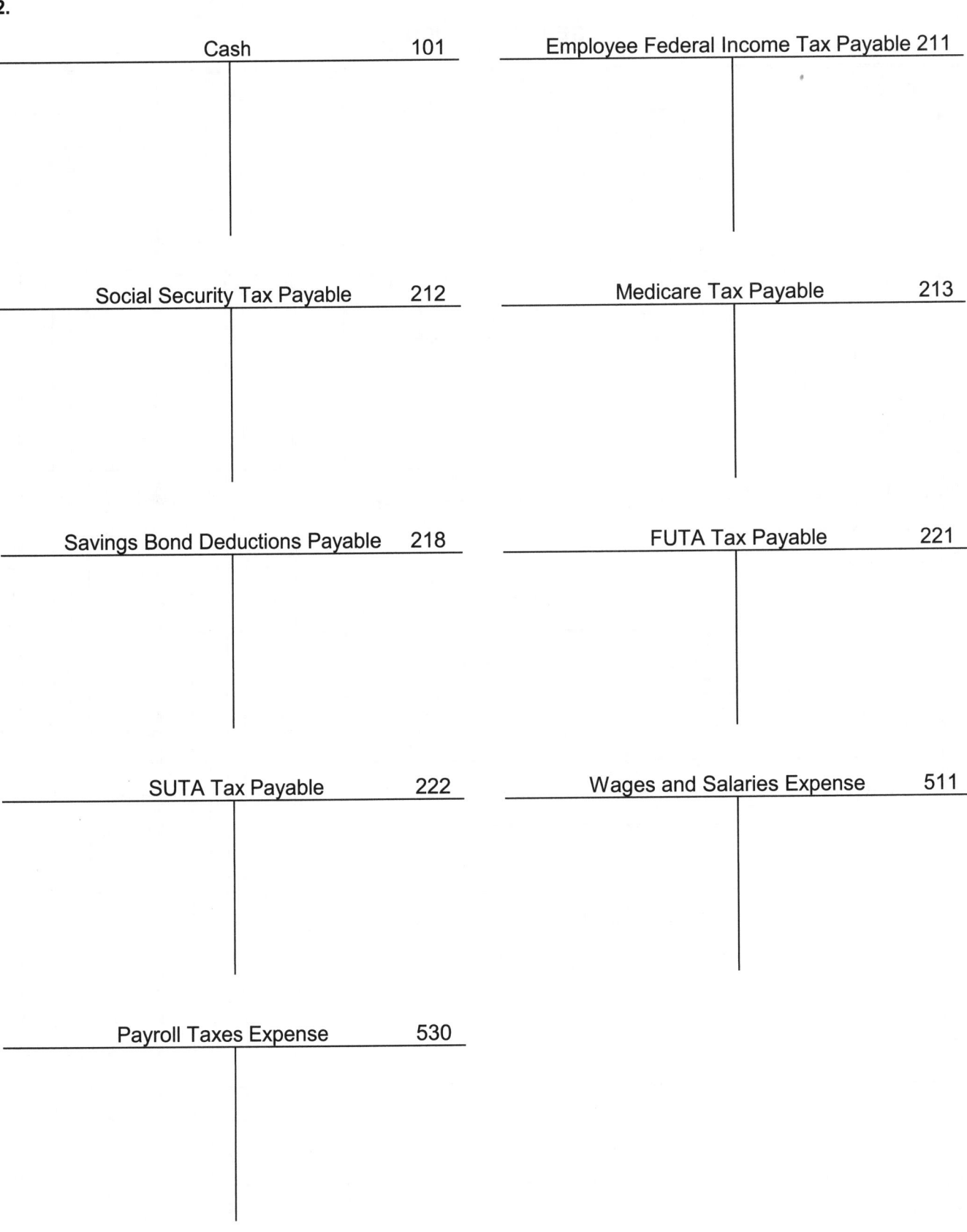

Cash 101	Employee Federal Income Tax Payable 211
Social Security Tax Payable 212	Medicare Tax Payable 213
Savings Bond Deductions Payable 218	FUTA Tax Payable 221
SUTA Tax Payable 222	Wages and Salaries Expense 511
Payroll Taxes Expense 530	

Problem 9-9B

1.

_____
_____
_____
_____
_____
_____

GENERAL JOURNAL

PAGE

	DATE		DESCRIPTION	POST. REF.	DEBIT	CREDIT	
1							1
2							2
3							3
4							4
5							5
6							6

2.

_____
_____
_____
_____
_____
_____

GENERAL JOURNAL

PAGE

	DATE		DESCRIPTION	POST. REF.	DEBIT	CREDIT	
1							1
2							2
3							3
4							4
5							5
6							6

Problem 9-9B (Concluded)

3.

GENERAL JOURNAL   PAGE

	DATE		DESCRIPTION	POST. REF.	DEBIT	CREDIT	
1							1
2							2
3							3
4							4

Mastery Problem
1., 2., and 3.

GENERAL JOURNAL

PAGE _____

	DATE		DESCRIPTION	POST. REF.	DEBIT	CREDIT	
1							1
2							2
3							3
4							4
5							5
6							6
7							7
8							8
9							9
10							10
11							11
12							12
13							13
14							14
15							15
16							16
17							17
18							18
19							19
20							20
21							21
22							22
23							23
24							24
25							25
26							26
27							27
28							28
29							29
30							30
31							31
32							32
33							33
34							34
35							35

Mastery Problem (Concluded)

GENERAL JOURNAL

PAGE

DATE	DESCRIPTION	POST. REF.	DEBIT	CREDIT
1				
2				
3				
4				
5				
6				
7				
8				
9				
10				
11				
12				
13				
14				
15				
16				
17				
18				
19				
20				
21				
22				
23				
24				
25				
26				
27				
28				
29				
30				
31				
32				
33				
34				
35				

Challenge Problem

1.

_____

_____

_____

_____

_____

_____

_____

2.

GENERAL JOURNAL   PAGE _____

DATE	DESCRIPTION	POST. REF.	DEBIT	CREDIT	
					1
					2
					3
					4
					5
					6
					7

3.

_____

_____

_____

_____

_____

Exercise 10-1A

1. _____

2. _____

3. _____

4. _____

5. _____

6. _____

Exercise 10-2A

1.

Cash	Accounts Receivable

Sales Tax Payable	Sales

Sales Returns and Allowances	Sales Discounts

2.

Cash	Accounts Receivable

Sales Tax Payable	Sales

Sales Returns and Allowances	Sales Discounts

Exercise 10-2A (Concluded)

3.

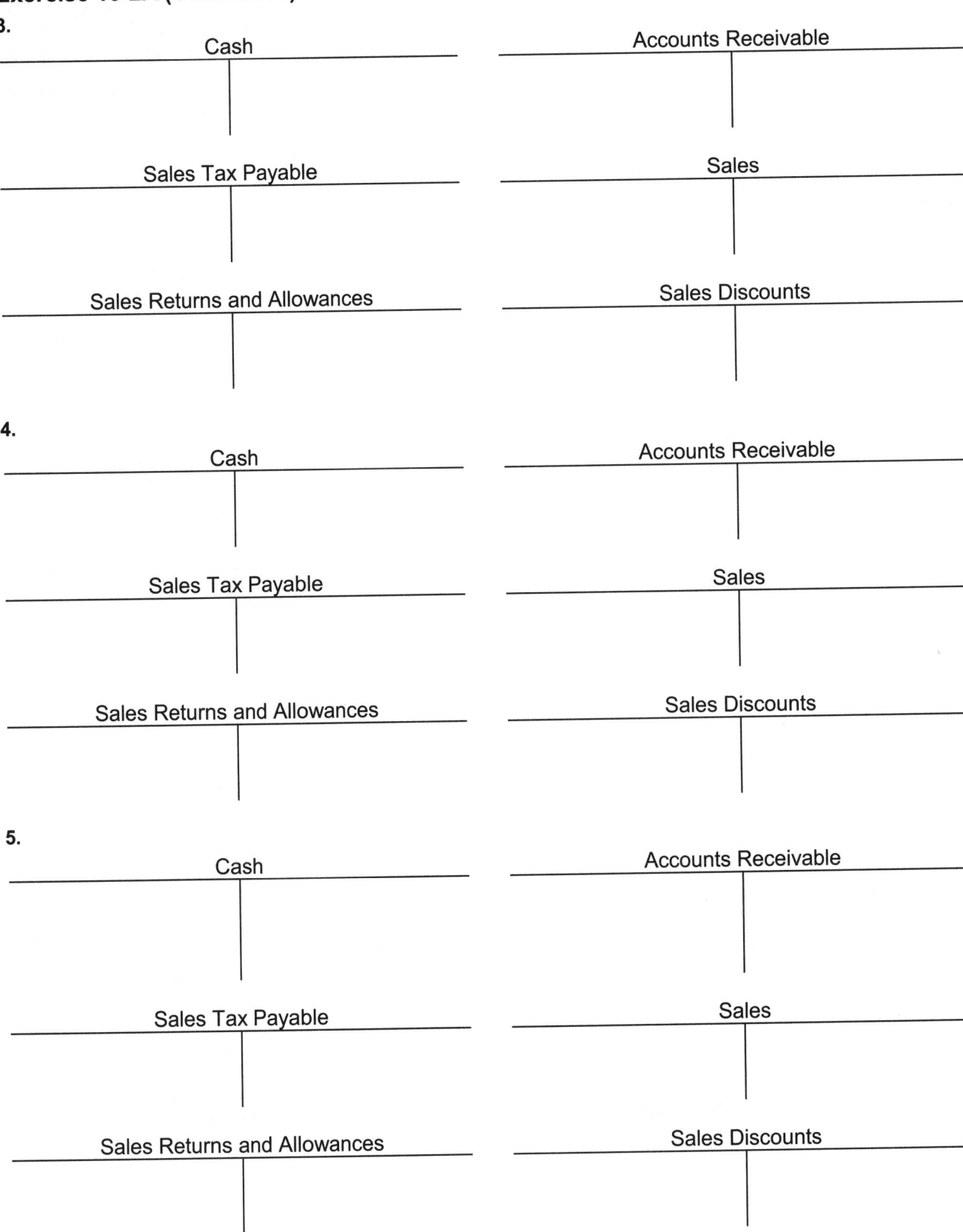

Cash	Accounts Receivable

Sales Tax Payable	Sales

Sales Returns and Allowances	Sales Discounts

4.

Cash	Accounts Receivable

Sales Tax Payable	Sales

Sales Returns and Allowances	Sales Discounts

5.

Cash	Accounts Receivable

Sales Tax Payable	Sales

Sales Returns and Allowances	Sales Discounts

Exercise 10-3A

_____
_____
_____
_____
_____
_____
_____
_____
_____

Exercise 10-4A

GENERAL JOURNAL

PAGE

	DATE	DESCRIPTION	POST. REF.	DEBIT	CREDIT	
1						1
2						2
3						3
4						4
5						5
6						6
7						7
8						8
9						9
10						10
11						11
12						12
13						13
14						14
15						15
16						16
17						17
18						18
19						19
20						20

Exercise 10-4A (Concluded)

GENERAL JOURNAL   PAGE

	DATE		DESCRIPTION	POST. REF.	DEBIT	CREDIT	
21							21
22							22
23							23
24							24
25							25
26							26
27							27
28							28

Exercise 10-5A

GENERAL JOURNAL   PAGE

	DATE		DESCRIPTION	POST. REF.	DEBIT	CREDIT	
1							1
2							2
3							3
4							4
5							5
6							6
7							7
8							8
9							9
10							10
11							11
12							12
13							13
14							14
15							15
16							16
17							17
18							18
19							19
20							20
21							21
22							22

Exercise 10-6A

GENERAL JOURNAL

	DATE		DESCRIPTION	POST. REF.	DEBIT	CREDIT	
1							1
2							2
3							3
4							4
5							5
6							6
7							7
8							8
9							9
10							10
11							11
12							12
13							13
14							14
15							15

GENERAL LEDGER

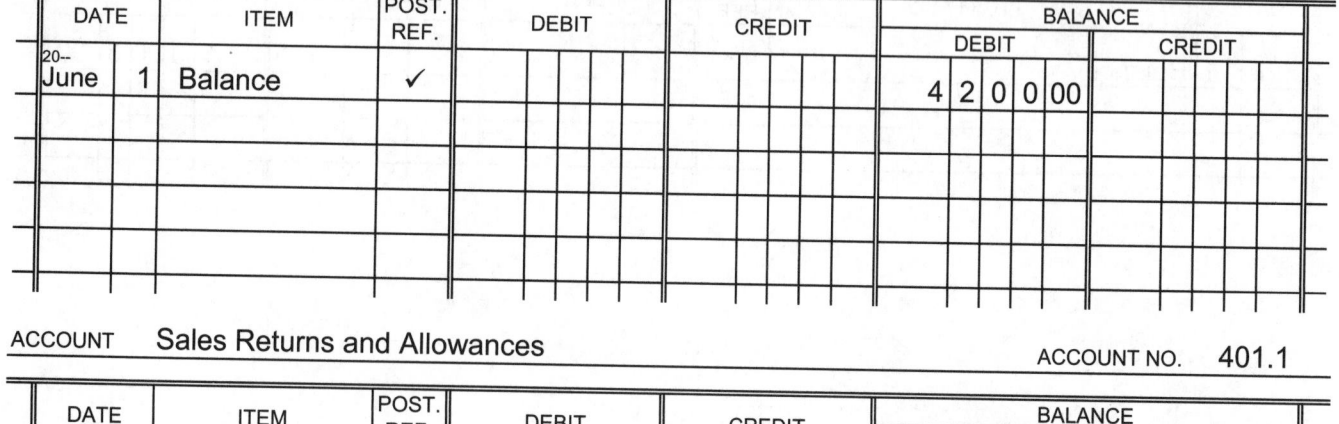

ACCOUNT   Accounts Receivable

ACCOUNT NO.   122

DATE		ITEM	POST. REF.	DEBIT	CREDIT	BALANCE DEBIT	BALANCE CREDIT
20-- June	1	Balance	✓			4 2 0 0 00	

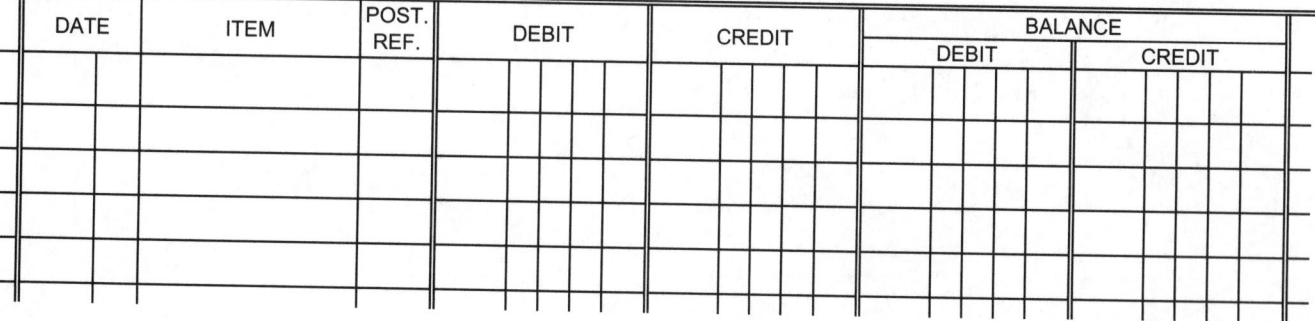

ACCOUNT   Sales Returns and Allowances

ACCOUNT NO.   401.1

DATE	ITEM	POST. REF.	DEBIT	CREDIT	BALANCE DEBIT	BALANCE CREDIT

Exercise 10-6A (Concluded)

ACCOUNTS RECEIVABLE LEDGER

NAME John B. Abramowitz

ADDRESS 3201 West Judkins Road, Seattle, WA 98201-1079

DATE		ITEM	POST. REF.	DEBIT	CREDIT	BALANCE
20-- June	1	Balance	✓			8 5 0 00

NAME L. B. Gruder

ADDRESS 44 Western Blvd., Spokane, WA 98601-4092

DATE		ITEM	POST. REF.	DEBIT	CREDIT	BALANCE
20-- June	1	Balance	✓			4 2 8 00

NAME Marie L. Perez

ADDRESS 158 West Adams Point, Bellevue, WA 98401-0663

DATE		ITEM	POST. REF.	DEBIT	CREDIT	BALANCE
20-- June	1	Balance	✓			1 0 1 8 00

Exercise 10-7A

GENERAL JOURNAL

PAGE _____

	DATE	DESCRIPTION	POST. REF.	DEBIT	CREDIT	
1						1
2						2
3						3
4						4
5						5
6						6
7						7
8						8
9						9
10						10
11						11
12						12
13						13
14						14
15						15
16						16
17						17
18						18
19						19
20						20
21						21
22						22

Exercise 10-8A

Problem 10-9A

1.

GENERAL JOURNAL   PAGE 15

DATE	DESCRIPTION	POST. REF.	DEBIT	CREDIT
1				
2				
3				
4				
5				
6				
7				
8				
9				
10				
11				
12				
13				
14				
15				
16				
17				
18				
19				
20				
21				
22				
23				
24				
25				
26				
27				
28				
29				
30				
31				
32				
33				
34				

Problem 10-9A (Continued)

2.

GENERAL LEDGER

ACCOUNT Accounts Receivable   ACCOUNT NO. 122

DATE	ITEM	POST. REF.	DEBIT	CREDIT	BALANCE DEBIT	BALANCE CREDIT

ACCOUNT Sales Tax Payable   ACCOUNT NO. 231

DATE	ITEM	POST. REF.	DEBIT	CREDIT	BALANCE DEBIT	BALANCE CREDIT

ACCOUNT Sales   ACCOUNT NO. 401

DATE	ITEM	POST. REF.	DEBIT	CREDIT	BALANCE DEBIT	BALANCE CREDIT

Problem 10-9A (Concluded)

ACCOUNTS RECEIVABLE LEDGER

NAME Hassad Co.

ADDRESS 1225 W. Temperance Street, Elletsville, IN 47429-9976

DATE	ITEM	POST. REF.	DEBIT	CREDIT	BALANCE

NAME Helsinki, Inc.

ADDRESS 125 Fishers Drive, Noblesville, IN 47870-8867

DATE	ITEM	POST. REF.	DEBIT	CREDIT	BALANCE

NAME Jung Manufacturing Co.

ADDRESS 8825 Old State Road, Bloomington, IN 47401-8823

DATE	ITEM	POST. REF.	DEBIT	CREDIT	BALANCE

NAME Ardis Myler

ADDRESS 2100 Greer Lane, Bedford, IN 47421-8876

DATE	ITEM	POST. REF.	DEBIT	CREDIT	BALANCE

Problem 10-10A

1.

GENERAL JOURNAL   PAGE 20

DATE	DESCRIPTION	POST. REF.	DEBIT	CREDIT
1				
2				
3				
4				
5				
6				
7				
8				
9				
10				
11				
12				
13				
14				
15				
16				
17				
18				
19				
20				
21				
22				
23				
24				
25				
26				
27				
28				
29				
30				
31				
32				
33				
34				

Problem 10-10A (Continued)

GENERAL JOURNAL

PAGE 21

DATE	DESCRIPTION	POST. REF.	DEBIT	CREDIT

Problem 10-10A (Continued)

2.

GENERAL LEDGER

ACCOUNT   Cash   ACCOUNT NO.   101

DATE		ITEM	POST. REF.	DEBIT	CREDIT	BALANCE DEBIT	BALANCE CREDIT
20-- Dec.	1	Balance	✓			9 8 6 2 00	

ACCOUNT   Accounts Receivable   ACCOUNT NO.   122

DATE		ITEM	POST. REF.	DEBIT	CREDIT	BALANCE DEBIT	BALANCE CREDIT
20-- Dec.	1	Balance	✓			9 3 5 2 00	

Problem 10-10A (Continued)

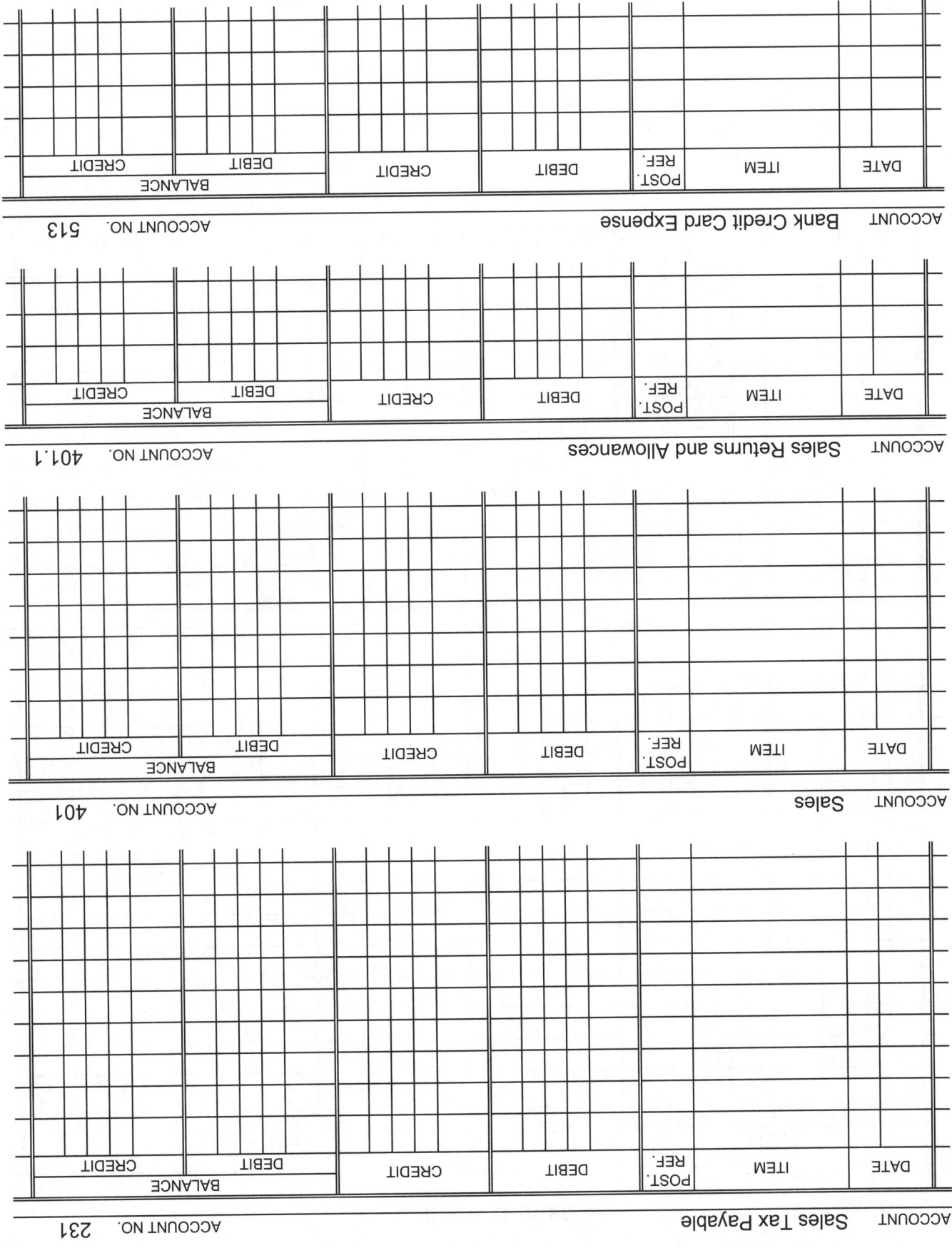

ACCOUNT Sales Tax Payable   ACCOUNT NO. 231

DATE	ITEM	POST. REF.	DEBIT	CREDIT	BALANCE DEBIT	BALANCE CREDIT

ACCOUNT Sales   ACCOUNT NO. 401

DATE	ITEM	POST. REF.	DEBIT	CREDIT	BALANCE DEBIT	BALANCE CREDIT

ACCOUNT Sales Returns and Allowances   ACCOUNT NO. 401.1

DATE	ITEM	POST. REF.	DEBIT	CREDIT	BALANCE DEBIT	BALANCE CREDIT

ACCOUNT Bank Credit Card Expense   ACCOUNT NO. 513

DATE	ITEM	POST. REF.	DEBIT	CREDIT	BALANCE DEBIT	BALANCE CREDIT

Problem 10-10A (Continued)

ACCOUNTS RECEIVABLE LEDGER

NAME Michael Anderson

ADDRESS 233 West 11th Avenue, Detroit, MI 59500-1154

DATE		ITEM	POST. REF.	DEBIT	CREDIT	BALANCE
20-- Dec.	1	Balance	✓			2 4 8 0 00

NAME Ansel Manufacturing

ADDRESS 284 West 88 Street, Detroit, MI 59522-1168

DATE		ITEM	POST. REF.	DEBIT	CREDIT	BALANCE
20-- Dec.	1	Balance	✓			9 8 2 00

NAME J. Gorbea

ADDRESS P.O. Box 864, Detroit, MI 59552-0864

DATE		ITEM	POST. REF.	DEBIT	CREDIT	BALANCE
20-- Dec.	1	Balance	✓			8 8 0 00

Problem 10-10A (Concluded)

NAME Rachel Carson

ADDRESS 11312 Fourteenth Avenue South, Detroit, MI 59221-1142

DATE		ITEM	POST. REF.	DEBIT	CREDIT	BALANCE
20-- Dec.	1	Balance	✓			3 2 0 0 00

NAME Tom Wilson

ADDRESS 100 NW Seward St., Detroit, MI 59210-1337

DATE		ITEM	POST. REF.	DEBIT	CREDIT	BALANCE
20-- Dec.	1	Balance	✓			1 8 1 0 00

Problem 10-11A

1.

GENERAL JOURNAL

DATE	DESCRIPTION	POST. REF.	DEBIT	CREDIT
1				
2				
3				
4				
5				
6				
7				
8				
9				
10				
11				
12				
13				
14				
15				
16				
17				
18				
19				
20				
21				
22				
23				
24				
25				
26				
27				
28				
29				
30				
31				
32				
33				
34				

Problem 10-11A (Continued)

GENERAL JOURNAL

PAGE 8

DATE	DESCRIPTION	POST. REF.	DEBIT	CREDIT	
					1
					2
					3
					4
					5
					6
					7
					8
					9
					10
					11
					12
					13
					14
					15
					16
					17
					18
					19
					20
					21
					22
					23
					24
					25
					26
					27
					28
					29
					30
					31
					32
					33
					34

Problem 10-11A (Continued)

GENERAL JOURNAL

	DATE	DESCRIPTION	POST. REF.	DEBIT	CREDIT	
1						1
2						2
3						3
4						4
5						5
6						6
7						7
8						8
9						9
10						10

2.

GENERAL LEDGER

ACCOUNT Cash

ACCOUNT NO. 101

DATE		ITEM	POST. REF.	DEBIT	CREDIT	BALANCE DEBIT	BALANCE CREDIT
20-- Mar.	1	Balance	✓			9 5 8 6 00	

Problem 10-11A (Continued)

ACCOUNT Accounts Receivable   ACCOUNT NO. 122

DATE		ITEM	POST. REF.	DEBIT	CREDIT	BALANCE	
						DEBIT	CREDIT
20-- Mar.	1	Balance	✓			1 0 1 6 00	

ACCOUNT Sales Tax Payable   ACCOUNT NO. 231

DATE	ITEM	POST. REF.	DEBIT	CREDIT	BALANCE	
					DEBIT	CREDIT

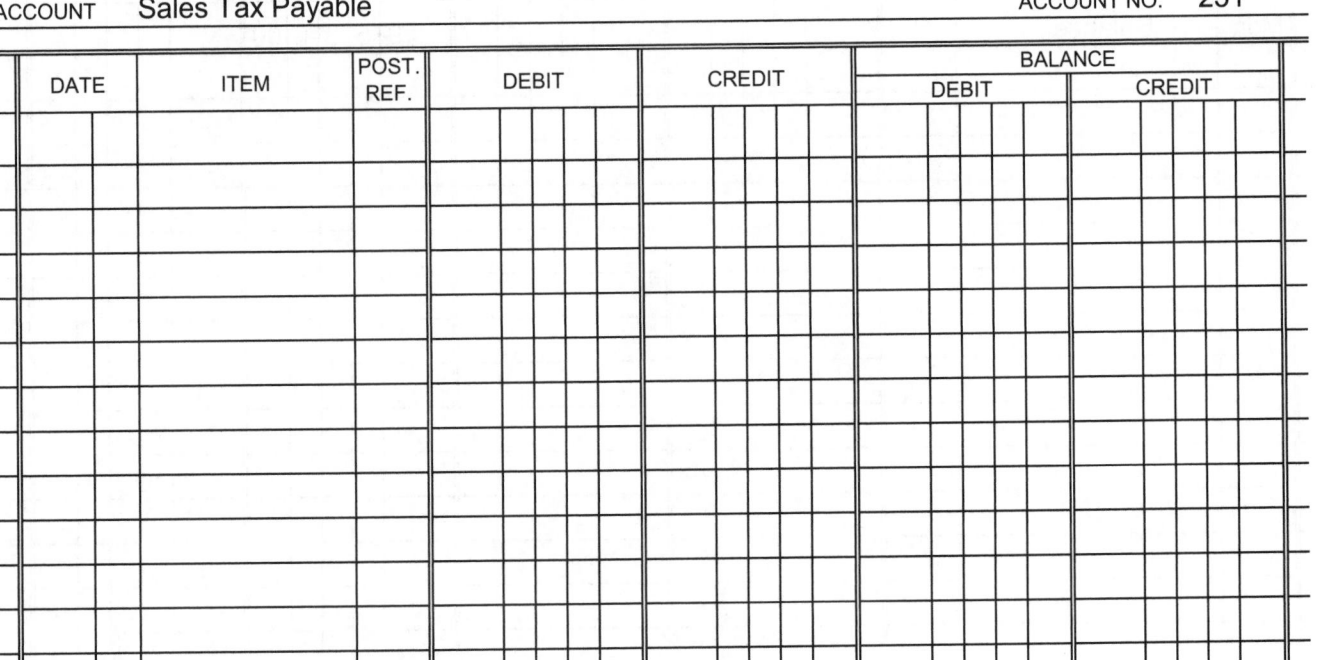

Problem 10-11A (Continued)

ACCOUNT   Sales   ACCOUNT NO.   401

DATE	ITEM	POST. REF.	DEBIT	CREDIT	BALANCE	
					DEBIT	CREDIT

ACCOUNT   Sales Returns and Allowances   ACCOUNT NO.   401.1

DATE	ITEM	POST. REF.	DEBIT	CREDIT	BALANCE	
					DEBIT	CREDIT

ACCOUNTS RECEIVABLE LEDGER

NAME Donachie & Co.

ADDRESS 1424 Jackson Creek Road, Nashville, IN 47448-2245

DATE	ITEM	POST. REF.	DEBIT	CREDIT	BALANCE

Problem 10-11A (Concluded)

NAME Eck Bakery

ADDRESS 6422 E. Bender Road, Bloomington, IN 47401-7756

DATE	ITEM	POST. REF.	DEBIT	CREDIT	BALANCE

NAME R. J. Kibubu, Inc.

ADDRESS 3315 Longview Avenue, Bloomington, IN 47401-7223

DATE	ITEM	POST. REF.	DEBIT	CREDIT	BALANCE

NAME Whitaker Group

ADDRESS 2300 E. National Road, Cumberland, IN 46229-4824

DATE		ITEM	POST. REF.	DEBIT	CREDIT	BALANCE
20-- Mar.	1	Balance	✓			1 0 1 6 00

Problem 10-12A

Exercise 10-1B

1. _____ 4. _____

2. _____ 5. _____

3. _____ 6. _____

Exercise 10-2B

1.

Cash	Accounts Receivable

Sales Tax Payable	Sales

Sales Returns and Allowances	Sales Discounts

2.

Cash	Accounts Receivable

Sales Tax Payable	Sales

Sales Returns and Allowances	Sales Discounts

Exercise 10-2B (Concluded)

3.

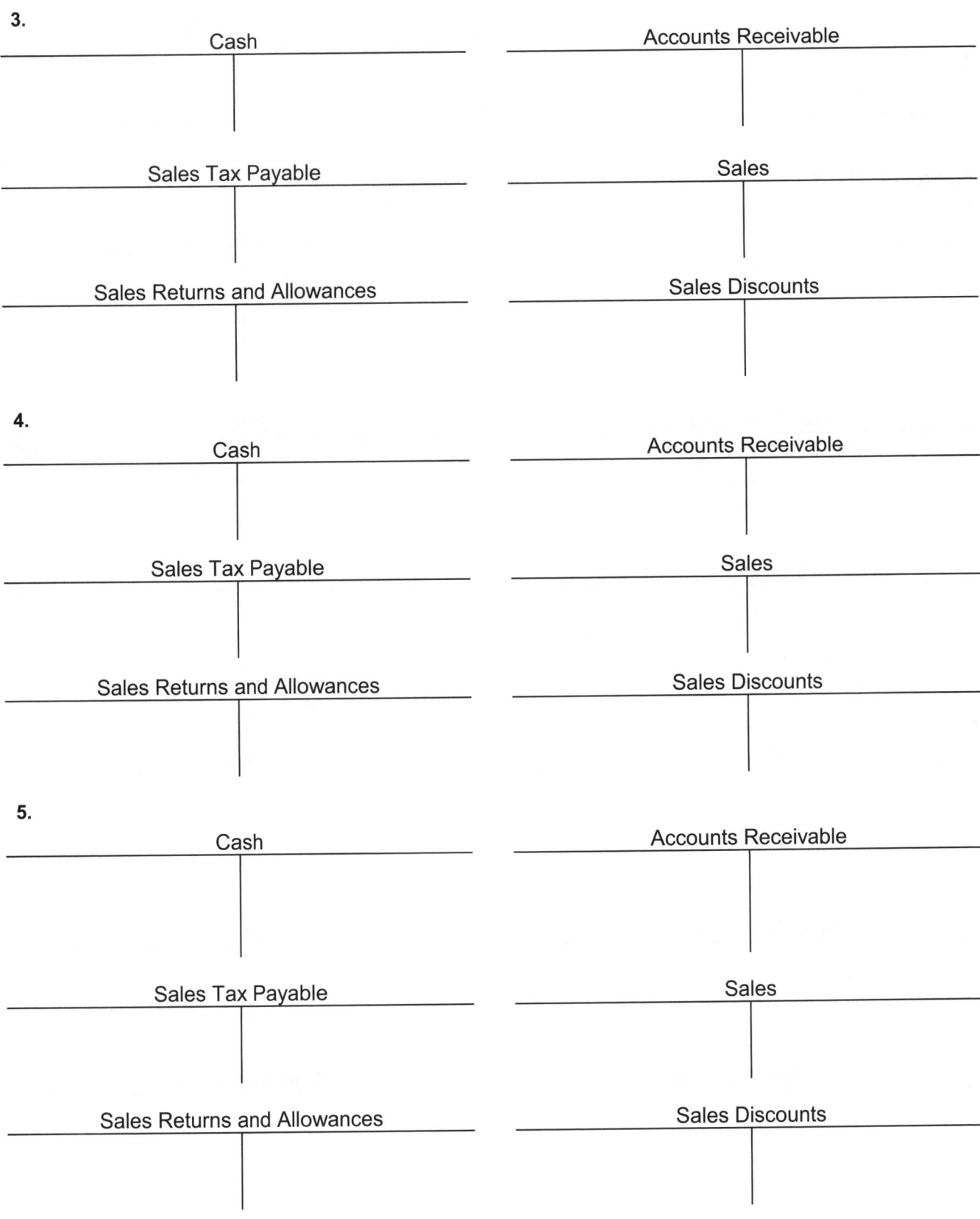

Cash	Accounts Receivable
Sales Tax Payable	Sales
Sales Returns and Allowances	Sales Discounts

4.

Cash	Accounts Receivable
Sales Tax Payable	Sales
Sales Returns and Allowances	Sales Discounts

5.

Cash	Accounts Receivable
Sales Tax Payable	Sales
Sales Returns and Allowances	Sales Discounts

Exercise 10-3B

_____
_____
_____
_____
_____
_____
_____
_____

Exercise 10-4B

GENERAL JOURNAL

PAGE _____

	DATE	DESCRIPTION	POST. REF.	DEBIT	CREDIT	
1						1
2						2
3						3
4						4
5						5
6						6
7						7
8						8
9						9
10						10
11						11
12						12
13						13
14						14
15						15
16						16
17						17
18						18
19						19
20						20

Exercise 10-4B (Concluded)

GENERAL JOURNAL   PAGE

	DATE		DESCRIPTION	POST. REF.	DEBIT	CREDIT	
21							21
22							22
23							23
24							24
25							25
26							26
27							27
28							28

Exercise 10-5B

GENERAL JOURNAL   PAGE

	DATE		DESCRIPTION	POST. REF.	DEBIT	CREDIT	
1							1
2							2
3							3
4							4
5							5
6							6
7							7
8							8
9							9
10							10
11							11
12							12
13							13
14							14
15							15
16							16
17							17
18							18
19							19
20							20
21							21
22							22

Exercise 10-6B

GENERAL JOURNAL

PAGE 60

	DATE		DESCRIPTION	POST. REF.	DEBIT	CREDIT	
1							1
2							2
3							3
4							4
5							5
6							6
7							7
8							8
9							9
10							10
11							11
12							12
13							13
14							14

GENERAL LEDGER

ACCOUNT Accounts Receivable   ACCOUNT NO. 122

DATE		ITEM	POST. REF.	DEBIT	CREDIT	BALANCE DEBIT	BALANCE CREDIT
20-- June	1	Balance	✓			3 9 0 0 00	

ACCOUNT Sales Returns and Allowances   ACCOUNT NO. 401.1

DATE	ITEM	POST. REF.	DEBIT	CREDIT	BALANCE DEBIT	BALANCE CREDIT

Exercise 10-6B (Concluded)

ACCOUNTS RECEIVABLE LEDGER

NAME John B. Adams

ADDRESS 127 Strawberry Lane, Manchester, CT 06040-0865

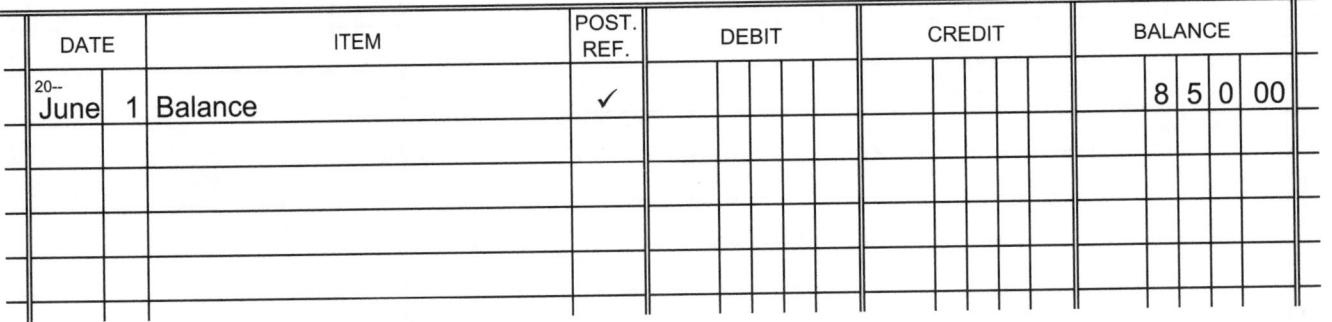

DATE		ITEM	POST. REF.	DEBIT	CREDIT	BALANCE
20-- June	1	Balance	✓			8 5 0 00

NAME L. B. Greene

ADDRESS 2254 Blackrock, Bronx, NY 10472-1974

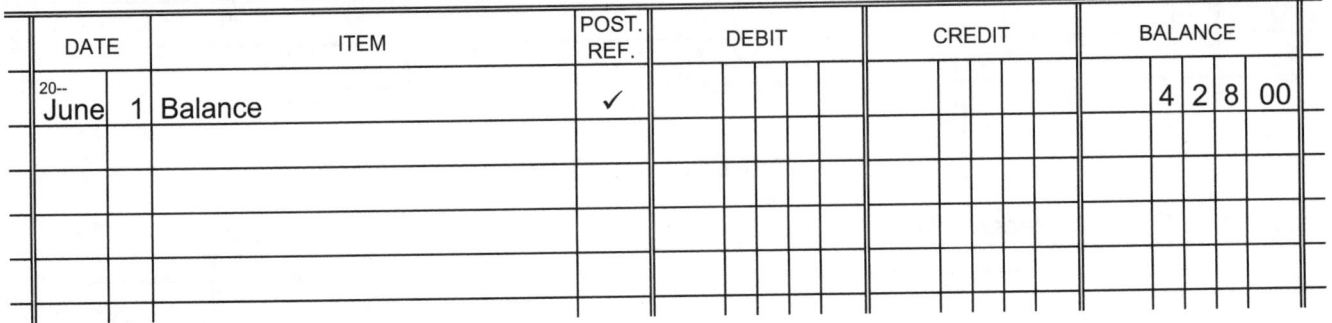

DATE		ITEM	POST. REF.	DEBIT	CREDIT	BALANCE
20-- June	1	Balance	✓			4 2 8 00

NAME Marie L. Phillips

ADDRESS 334 Fern St., W. Hartford, CT 06119-2314

DATE		ITEM	POST. REF.	DEBIT	CREDIT	BALANCE
20-- June	1	Balance	✓			1 0 1 8 00

Exercise 10-7B

GENERAL JOURNAL

	DATE	DESCRIPTION	POST. REF.	DEBIT	CREDIT	
1						1
2						2
3						3
4						4
5						5
6						6
7						7
8						8
9						9
10						10
11						11
12						12
13						13
14						14
15						15
16						16
17						17
18						18
19						19
20						20
21						21
22						22
23						23

Exercise 10-8B

Problem 10-9B

1.

GENERAL JOURNAL

DATE	DESCRIPTION	POST. REF.	DEBIT	CREDIT	
					1
					2
					3
					4
					5
					6
					7
					8
					9
					10
					11
					12
					13
					14
					15
					16
					17
					18
					19
					20
					21
					22
					23
					24
					25
					26
					27
					28
					29
					30
					31
					32
					33
					34

Problem 10-9B (Continued)

2.

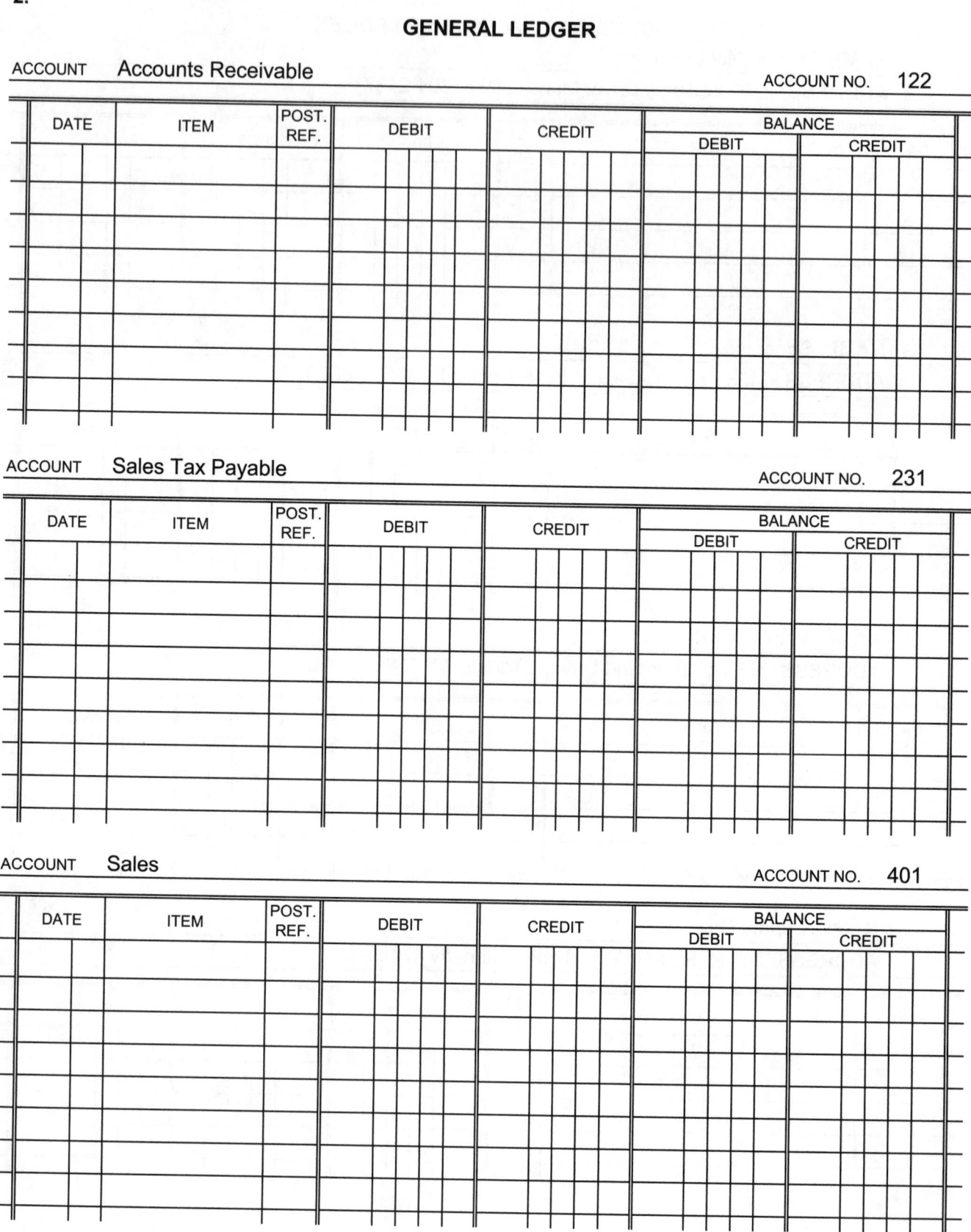

GENERAL LEDGER

ACCOUNT   Accounts Receivable   ACCOUNT NO.   122

DATE	ITEM	POST. REF.	DEBIT	CREDIT	BALANCE	
					DEBIT	CREDIT

ACCOUNT   Sales Tax Payable   ACCOUNT NO.   231

DATE	ITEM	POST. REF.	DEBIT	CREDIT	BALANCE	
					DEBIT	CREDIT

ACCOUNT   Sales   ACCOUNT NO.   401

DATE	ITEM	POST. REF.	DEBIT	CREDIT	BALANCE	
					DEBIT	CREDIT

Problem 10-9B (Concluded)

ACCOUNTS RECEIVABLE LEDGER

NAME Dvorak Manufacturing

ADDRESS 2105 Williams Drive, Muncie, IN 47304-2437

DATE	ITEM	POST. REF.	DEBIT	CREDIT	BALANCE

NAME Saga, Inc.

ADDRESS 1453 Parnell Avenue, Indianapolis, IN 46201-6870

DATE	ITEM	POST. REF.	DEBIT	CREDIT	BALANCE

NAME Vinnie Ward

ADDRESS 308 So. Muirhead Drive, Okemos, MI 48864-5356

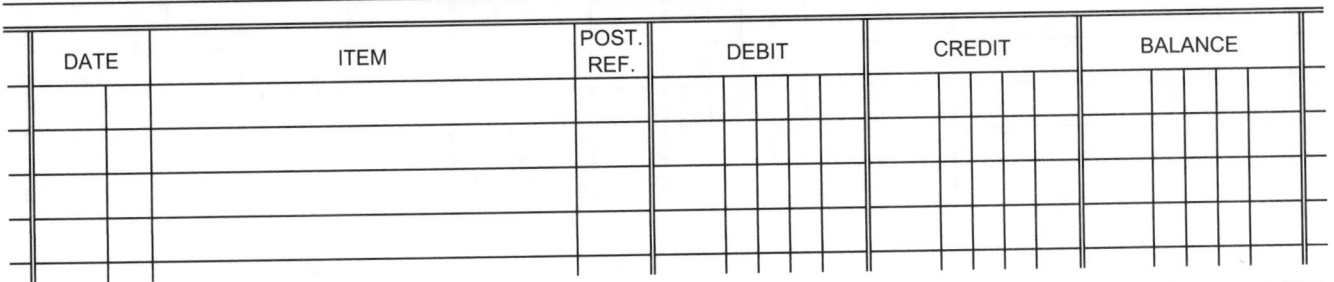

DATE	ITEM	POST. REF.	DEBIT	CREDIT	BALANCE

NAME Zapata Co.

ADDRESS 789 N. Stafford Dr., Bloomington, IN 47401-6201

DATE	ITEM	POST. REF.	DEBIT	CREDIT	BALANCE

Problem 10-10B

1.

GENERAL JOURNAL

	DATE		DESCRIPTION	POST. REF.	DEBIT	CREDIT	
1							1
2							2
3							3
4							4
5							5
6							6
7							7
8							8
9							9
10							10
11							11
12							12
13							13
14							14
15							15
16							16
17							17
18							18
19							19
20							20
21							21
22							22
23							23
24							24
25							25
26							26
27							27
28							28
29							29
30							30
31							31
32							32
33							33
34							34

Problem 10-10B (Continued)

GENERAL JOURNAL

	DATE	DESCRIPTION	POST. REF.	DEBIT	CREDIT	
1						1
2						2
3						3
4						4
5						5
6						6
7						7
8						8
9						9
10						10
11						11
12						12
13						13
14						14
15						15
16						16
17						17
18						18
19						19
20						20
21						21
22						22
23						23
24						24
25						25
26						26
27						27
28						28
29						29
30						30
31						31
32						32
33						33
34						34

Problem 10-10B (Continued)

2.

GENERAL LEDGER

ACCOUNT   Cash   ACCOUNT NO.   101

DATE		ITEM	POST. REF.	DEBIT	CREDIT	BALANCE	
						DEBIT	CREDIT
20-- Jan.	1	Balance	✓			2 8 9 0 75	

ACCOUNT   Accounts Receivable   ACCOUNT NO.   122

DATE		ITEM	POST. REF.	DEBIT	CREDIT	BALANCE	
						DEBIT	CREDIT
20-- Jan.	1	Balance	✓			6 3 0 0 00	

Problem 10-10B (Continued)

ACCOUNT Sales Tax Payable   ACCOUNT NO. 231

DATE	ITEM	POST. REF.	DEBIT	CREDIT	BALANCE DEBIT	BALANCE CREDIT

ACCOUNT Sales   ACCOUNT NO. 401

DATE	ITEM	POST. REF.	DEBIT	CREDIT	BALANCE DEBIT	BALANCE CREDIT

ACCOUNT Sales Returns and Allowances   ACCOUNT NO. 401.1

DATE	ITEM	POST. REF.	DEBIT	CREDIT	BALANCE DEBIT	BALANCE CREDIT

ACCOUNT Bank Credit Card Expense   ACCOUNT NO. 513

DATE	ITEM	POST. REF.	DEBIT	CREDIT	BALANCE DEBIT	BALANCE CREDIT

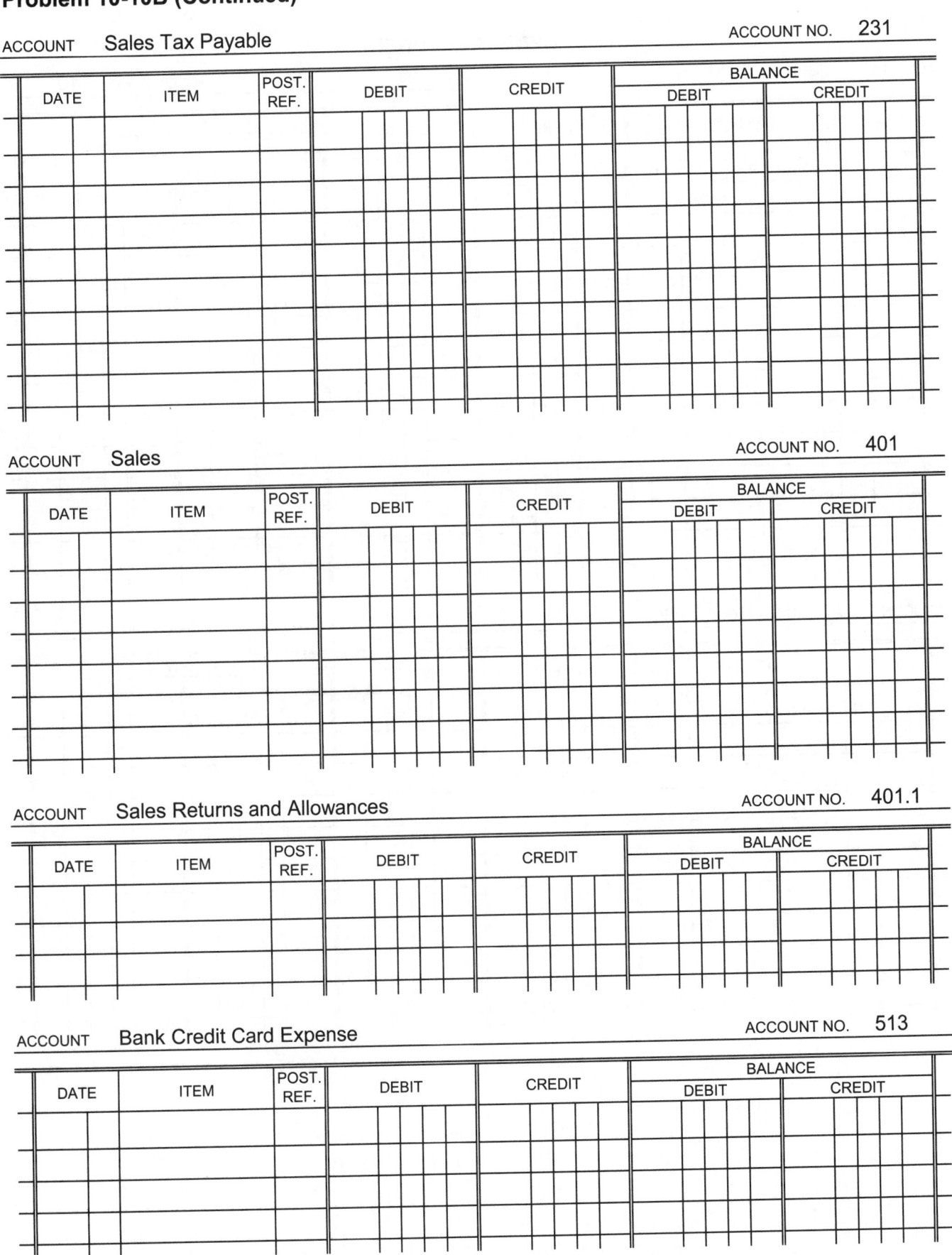

Problem 10-10B (Continued)

ACCOUNTS RECEIVABLE LEDGER

NAME Ray Boyd

ADDRESS 229 SE 65th Avenue, Portland, OR 97215-1451

DATE		ITEM	POST. REF.	DEBIT	CREDIT	BALANCE
20-- Jan.	1	Balance	✓			1 4 0 0 00

NAME Dazai Manufacturing

ADDRESS 447 6th Avenue, Flagstaff, AZ 86004-6842

DATE		ITEM	POST. REF.	DEBIT	CREDIT	BALANCE
20-- Jan.	1	Balance	✓			3 1 8 00

NAME Clint Hassell

ADDRESS 1462 N. Steves Blvd., Los Cruces, NM 88012-7791

DATE		ITEM	POST. REF.	DEBIT	CREDIT	BALANCE
20-- Jan.	1	Balance	✓			8 1 5 00

Problem 10-10B (Concluded)

NAME Jan Sowada

ADDRESS 5997 Blackgold Lane, Grapevine, TX 76051-2366

DATE		ITEM	POST. REF.	DEBIT	CREDIT	BALANCE
20-- Jan.	1	Balance	✓			1 4 8 1 00

NAME Robert Zehnle

ADDRESS 6881 Seneca Drive, San Diego, CA 92127-8671

DATE		ITEM	POST. REF.	DEBIT	CREDIT	BALANCE
20-- Jan.	1	Balance	✓			2 2 8 6 00

Problem 10-11B

1.

GENERAL JOURNAL

	DATE		DESCRIPTION	POST. REF.	DEBIT	CREDIT	
1							1
2							2
3							3
4							4
5							5
6							6
7							7
8							8
9							9
10							10
11							11
12							12
13							13
14							14
15							15
16							16
17							17
18							18
19							19
20							20
21							21
22							22
23							23
24							24
25							25
26							26
27							27
28							28
29							29
30							30
31							31
32							32
33							33
34							34

Problem 10-11B (Continued)

GENERAL JOURNAL

	DATE	DESCRIPTION	POST. REF.	DEBIT	CREDIT	
1						1
2						2
3						3
4						4
5						5
6						6
7						7
8						8
9						9
10						10
11						11
12						12
13						13
14						14
15						15
16						16
17						17
18						18
19						19
20						20
21						21
22						22
23						23
24						24
25						25
26						26
27						27
28						28
29						29
30						30
31						31
32						32
33						33
34						34

Problem 10-11B (Continued)

2.

GENERAL LEDGER

ACCOUNT Cash   ACCOUNT NO. 101

DATE	ITEM	POST. REF.	DEBIT	CREDIT	BALANCE DEBIT	BALANCE CREDIT
20-- Apr. 1	Balance	✓			2 8 6 4 54	

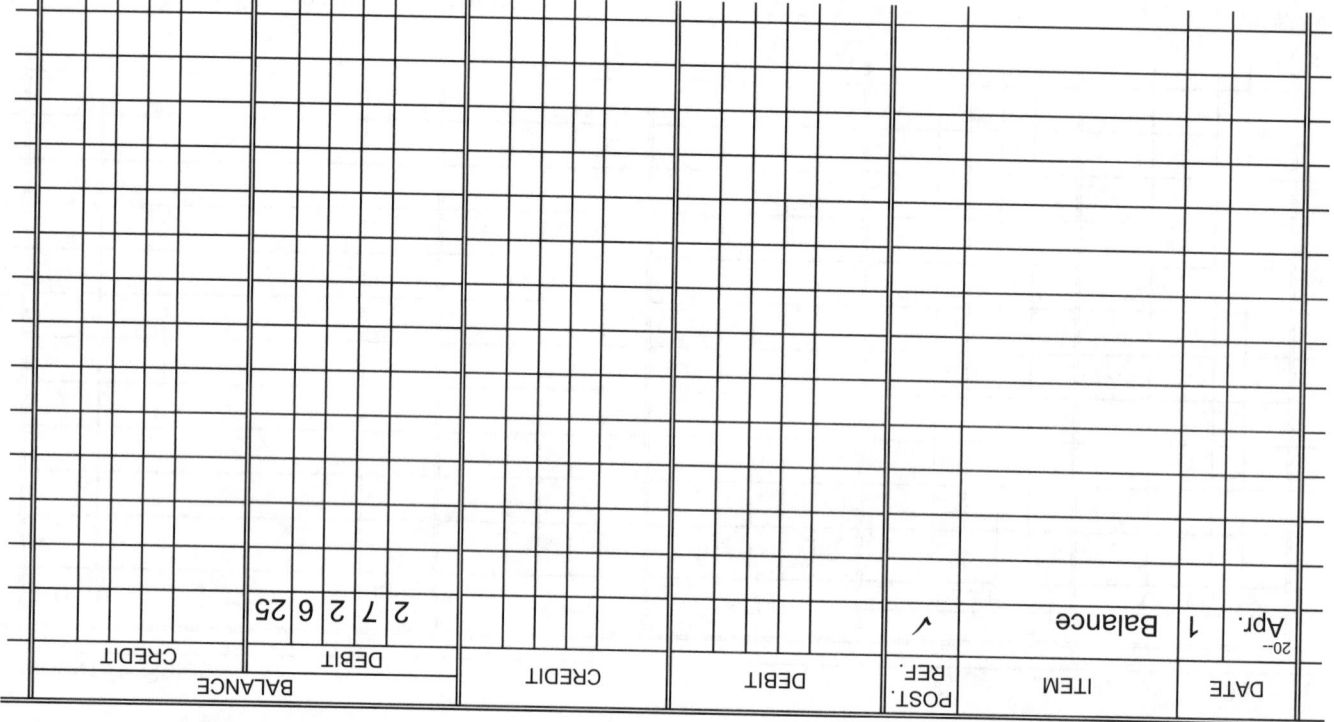

ACCOUNT Accounts Receivable   ACCOUNT NO. 122

DATE	ITEM	POST. REF.	DEBIT	CREDIT	BALANCE DEBIT	BALANCE CREDIT
20-- Apr. 1	Balance	✓			2 7 2 6 25	

Problem 10-11B (Continued)

ACCOUNT Sales Tax Payable   ACCOUNT NO. 231

DATE	ITEM	POST. REF.	DEBIT	CREDIT	BALANCE DEBIT	BALANCE CREDIT

ACCOUNT Sales   ACCOUNT NO. 401

DATE	ITEM	POST. REF.	DEBIT	CREDIT	BALANCE DEBIT	BALANCE CREDIT

ACCOUNT Sales Returns and Allowances   ACCOUNT NO. 401.1

DATE	ITEM	POST. REF.	DEBIT	CREDIT	BALANCE DEBIT	BALANCE CREDIT

Problem 10-11B (Concluded)

ACCOUNTS RECEIVABLE LEDGER

NAME O. L. Meyers

ADDRESS 119 Hartford Turnpike, Vernon, CT 06066-0113

DATE		ITEM	POST. REF.	DEBIT	CREDIT	BALANCE

NAME Kelsay Munkres

ADDRESS 233 Cambridge Dr., Branford, CT 06405-9276

DATE		ITEM	POST. REF.	DEBIT	CREDIT	BALANCE
20-- Apr.	1	Balance	✓			4 8 2 00

NAME Andrew Plaa

ADDRESS 51 Bissell Ave., Old Saybrook, CT 06475-0212

DATE		ITEM	POST. REF.	DEBIT	CREDIT	BALANCE

NAME Melissa Richfield

ADDRESS 1107 Silver Lane, East Hartford, CT 06108-1907

DATE		ITEM	POST. REF.	DEBIT	CREDIT	BALANCE
20-- Apr.	1	Balance	✓			2 2 4 4 25

Problem 10-12B

Name _____

Mastery Problem

1.

GENERAL JOURNAL

	DATE		DESCRIPTION	POST. REF.	DEBIT	CREDIT	
1							1
2							2
3							3
4							4
5							5
6							6
7							7
8							8
9							9
10							10
11							11
12							12
13							13
14							14
15							15
16							16
17							17
18							18
19							19
20							20
21							21
22							22
23							23
24							24
25							25
26							26
27							27
28							28
29							29
30							30
31							31
32							32
33							33
34							34

Mastery Problem (Continued)

GENERAL JOURNAL PAGE 8

	DATE	DESCRIPTION	POST. REF.	DEBIT	CREDIT	
1						1
2						2
3						3
4						4
5						5
6						6
7						7
8						8
9						9
10						10
11						11
12						12
13						13
14						14
15						15
16						16
17						17
18						18
19						19
20						20
21						21
22						22
23						23
24						24
25						25
26						26
27						27
28						28
29						29
30						30
31						31
32						32
33						33
34						34

Mastery Problem (Continued)

GENERAL JOURNAL

	DATE		DESCRIPTION	POST. REF.	DEBIT	CREDIT	
1							1
2							2
3							3
4							4
5							5
6							6
7							7
8							8
9							9
10							10
11							11
12							12
13							13
14							14
15							15
16							16
17							17
18							18
19							19
20							20
21							21
22							22
23							23
24							24
25							25
26							26
27							27
28							28
29							29
30							30
31							31
32							32
33							33
34							34

Mastery Problem (Continued)

GENERAL JOURNAL   PAGE 10

DATE	DESCRIPTION	POST. REF.	DEBIT	CREDIT	
					1
					2
					3
					4
					5
					6
					7
					8
					9
					10

2.

GENERAL LEDGER

ACCOUNT   Cash   ACCOUNT NO.   101

DATE	ITEM	POST. REF.	DEBIT	CREDIT	BALANCE DEBIT	BALANCE CREDIT
20-- Sept. 1	Balance	✓			23 5 0 0 25	

Mastery Problem (Continued)

ACCOUNT Accounts Receivable   ACCOUNT NO. 122

DATE		ITEM	POST. REF.	DEBIT	CREDIT	BALANCE DEBIT	BALANCE CREDIT
20-- Sept.	1	Balance	✓			8 5 0 7 5	

ACCOUNT Notes Payable   ACCOUNT NO. 201

DATE		ITEM	POST. REF.	DEBIT	CREDIT	BALANCE DEBIT	BALANCE CREDIT
20-- Sept.	1	Balance	✓				2 5 0 0 00

Mastery Problem (Continued)

ACCOUNT Sales Tax Payable   ACCOUNT NO. 231

DATE	ITEM	POST. REF.	DEBIT	CREDIT	BALANCE DEBIT	BALANCE CREDIT
20-- Sept. 1	Balance	✓				9 0 6 0 6

ACCOUNT Sales   ACCOUNT NO. 401

DATE	ITEM	POST. REF.	DEBIT	CREDIT	BALANCE DEBIT	BALANCE CREDIT
20-- Sept. 1	Balance	✓				1 3 0 5 0 48

Mastery Problem (Continued)

ACCOUNT   Sales Returns and Allowances   ACCOUNT NO.   401.1

DATE		ITEM	POST. REF.	DEBIT	CREDIT	BALANCE	
						DEBIT	CREDIT
20-- Sept.	1	Balance	✓			8 6 00	

ACCOUNT   Boarding and Grooming Revenue   ACCOUNT NO.   402

DATE		ITEM	POST. REF.	DEBIT	CREDIT	BALANCE	
						DEBIT	CREDIT
20-- Sept.	1	Balance	✓				2 1 1 5 00

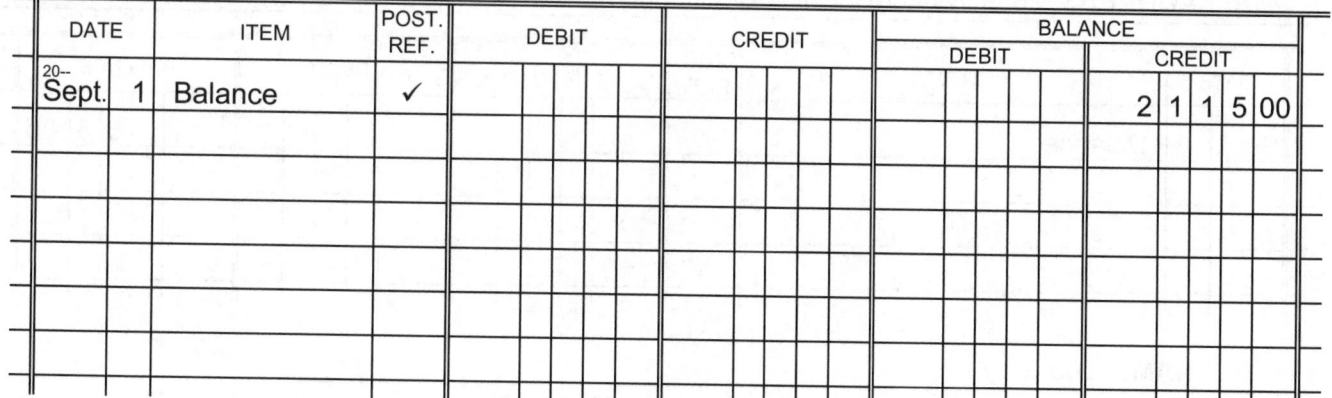

ACCOUNTS RECEIVABLE LEDGER

NAME All American Day Camp

ADDRESS 3025 Old Mill Run, Bloomington, IN 47408-1080

DATE	ITEM	POST. REF.	DEBIT	CREDIT	BALANCE

Mastery Problem (Continued)

NAME Rosa Alanso

ADDRESS 2541 East 2nd Street, Bloomington, IN 47401-5356

DATE		ITEM	POST. REF.	DEBIT	CREDIT	BALANCE
20-- Sept.	1	Balance	✓			4 5 6 00

NAME Ed Cochran

ADDRESS 2669 Windcrest Drive, Bloomington, IN 47401-5446

DATE		ITEM	POST. REF.	DEBIT	CREDIT	BALANCE
20-- Sept.	1	Balance	✓			6 3 25

NAME Joe Gloy

ADDRESS 1458 Parnell Avenue, Muncie, IN 47304-2682

DATE		ITEM	POST. REF.	DEBIT	CREDIT	BALANCE
20-- Sept.	1	Balance	✓			2 7 3 25

NAME Susan Hays

ADDRESS 1424 Jackson Creek Road, Nashville, IN 47448-2245

DATE	ITEM	POST. REF.	DEBIT	CREDIT	BALANCE

Mastery Problem (Continued)

NAME Ken Shank

ADDRESS 6422 E. Bender Road, Bloomington, IN 47401-7756

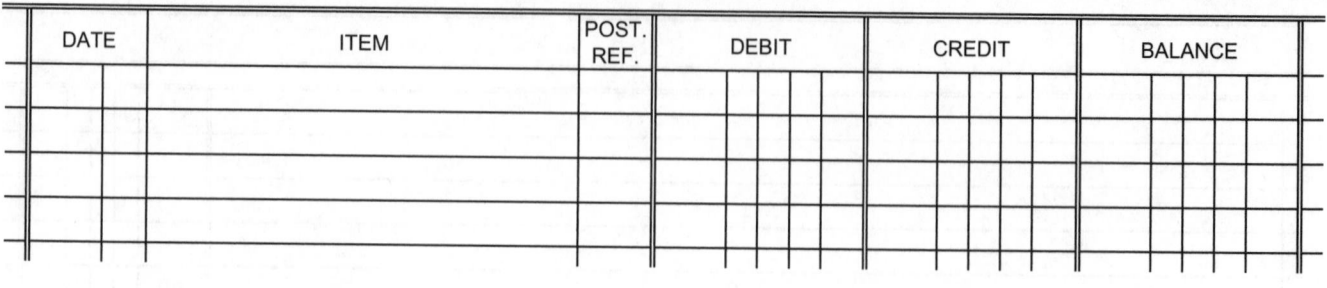

DATE	ITEM	POST. REF.	DEBIT	CREDIT	BALANCE

NAME Tully Shaw

ADDRESS 3315 Longview Avenue, Bloomington, IN 47401-7223

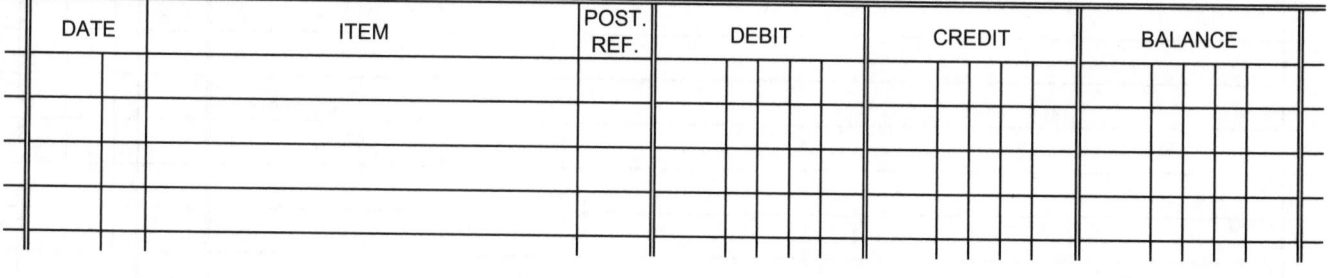

DATE	ITEM	POST. REF.	DEBIT	CREDIT	BALANCE

NAME Nancy Truelove

ADDRESS 2300 E. National Road, Cumberland, IN 46229-4824

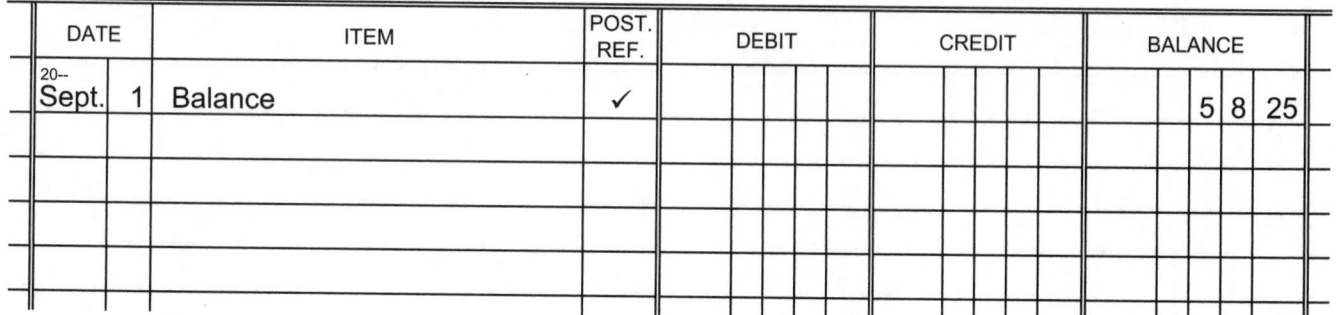

DATE		ITEM	POST. REF.	DEBIT	CREDIT	BALANCE
20-- Sept.	1	Balance	✓			5 8 25

NAME Jean Warkentin

ADDRESS 1813 Deep Well Court, Bloomington, IN 47401-5124

DATE	ITEM	POST. REF.	DEBIT	CREDIT	BALANCE

Mastery Problem (Concluded)

3.

4.

Challenge Problem

GENERAL JOURNAL

	DATE		DESCRIPTION	POST. REF.	DEBIT	CREDIT	
1							1
2							2
3							3
4							4
5							5
6							6
7							7
8							8
9							9
10							10
11							11
12							12
13							13
14							14
15							15
16							16
17							17
18							18
19							19
20							20
21							21
22							22
23							23
24							24
25							25
26							26
27							27
28							28
29							29
30							30
31							31
32							32
33							33
34							34

Exercise 11-1A

1. _____

2. Purchase order _____

3. _____

4. _____

Exercise 11-2A

1.

_____
_____
_____
_____

2.

_____
_____
_____
_____

3.

GENERAL JOURNAL

PAGE _____

	DATE		DESCRIPTION	POST. REF.	DEBIT	CREDIT	
1							1
2							2
3							3
4							4
5							5
6							6
7							7
8							8
9							9
10							10
11							11
12							12
13							13
14							14
15							15

Exercise 11-3A

1.

Cash		Accounts Payable

Purchases		Purchases Returns and Allowances

Purchases Discounts		Freight-In

2.

Cash		Accounts Payable

Purchases		Purchases Returns and Allowances

Purchases Discounts		Freight-In

Exercise 11-3A (Concluded)

3.

Cash		Accounts Payable

Purchases		Purchases Returns and Allowances

Purchases Discounts		Freight-In

4.

Cash		Accounts Payable

Purchases		Purchases Returns and Allowances

Purchases Discounts		Freight-In

Exercise 11-4A

Exercise 11-5A

GENERAL JOURNAL

PAGE _____

	DATE		DESCRIPTION	POST. REF.	DEBIT	CREDIT	
1							1
2							2
3							3
4							4
5							5
6							6
7							7
8							8
9							9
10							10
11							11
12							12
13							13
14							14
15							15
16							16
17							17
18							18
19							19
20							20
21							21
22							22
23							23
24							24
25							25
26							26
27							27
28							28
29							29
30							30
31							31
32							32
33							33
34							34

Exercise 11-6A

GENERAL JOURNAL   PAGE 3

	DATE	DESCRIPTION	POST. REF.	DEBIT	CREDIT	
1						1
2						2
3						3
4						4
5						5
6						6
7						7
8						8
9						9
10						10
11						11
12						12

GENERAL LEDGER

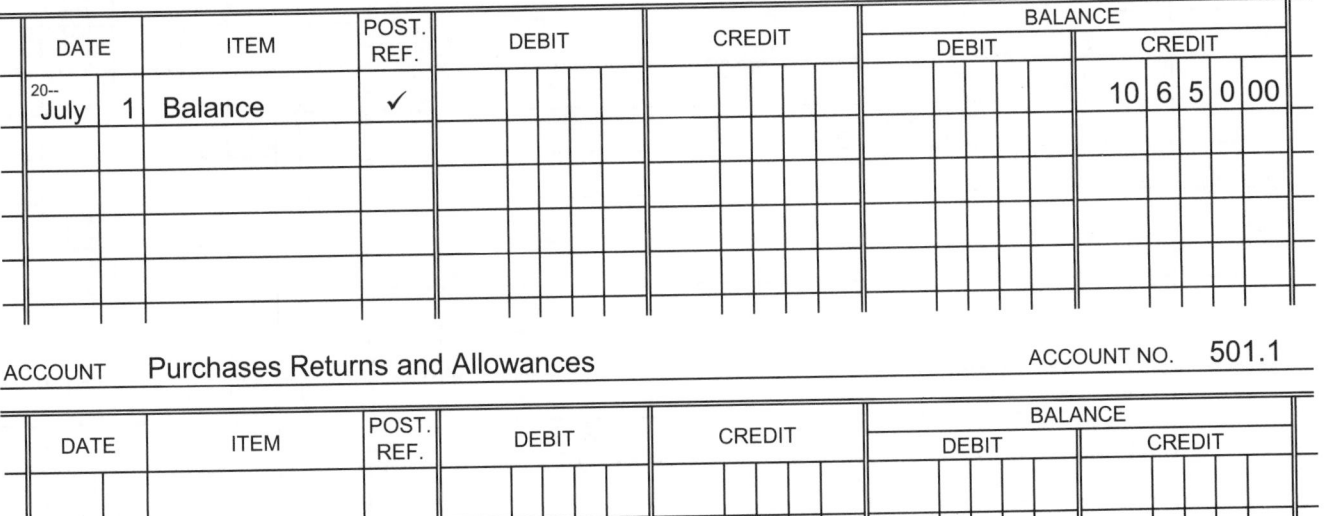

ACCOUNT   Accounts Payable   ACCOUNT NO.   202

DATE	ITEM	POST. REF.	DEBIT	CREDIT	BALANCE DEBIT	BALANCE CREDIT
20-- July 1	Balance	✓				10 6 5 0 00

ACCOUNT   Purchases Returns and Allowances   ACCOUNT NO.   501.1

DATE	ITEM	POST. REF.	DEBIT	CREDIT	BALANCE DEBIT	BALANCE CREDIT

Exercise 11-6A (Concluded)

ACCOUNTS PAYABLE LEDGER

NAME Datamagic
ADDRESS

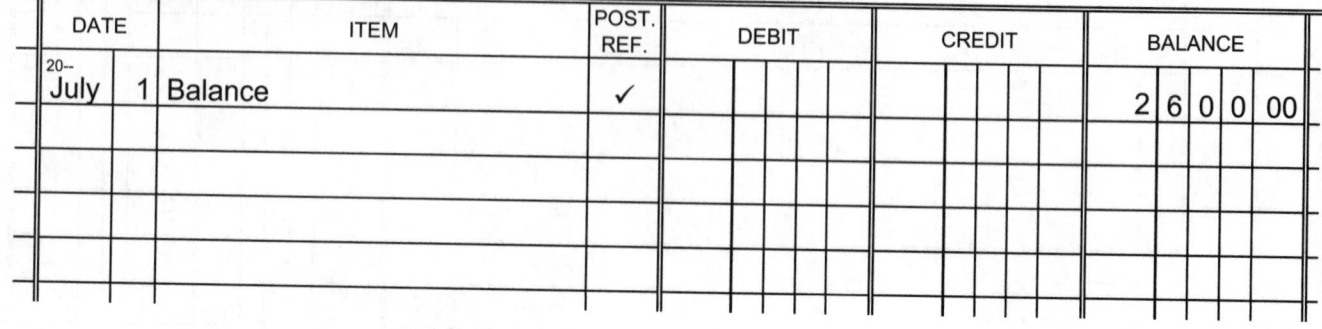

DATE		ITEM	POST. REF.	DEBIT	CREDIT	BALANCE
20-- July	1	Balance	✓			2 6 0 0 00

NAME Starcraft Industries
ADDRESS

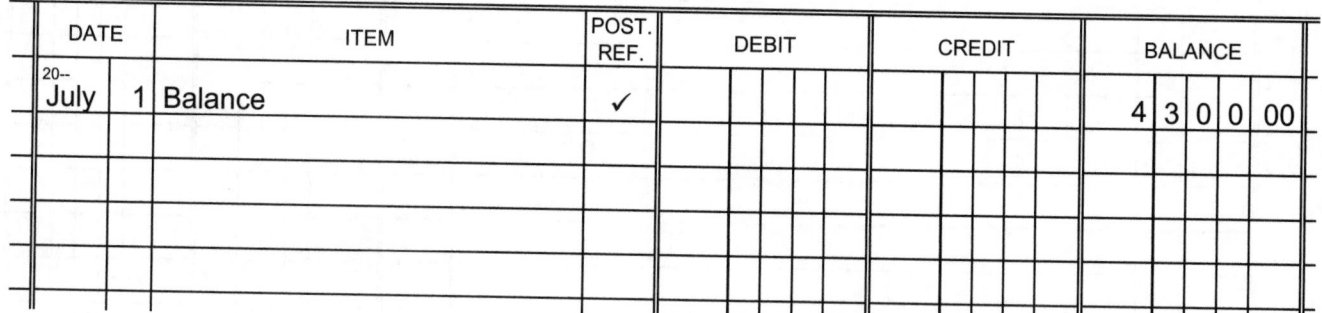

DATE		ITEM	POST. REF.	DEBIT	CREDIT	BALANCE
20-- July	1	Balance	✓			4 3 0 0 00

NAME XYZ, Inc.
ADDRESS

DATE		ITEM	POST. REF.	DEBIT	CREDIT	BALANCE
20-- July	1	Balance	✓			3 7 5 0 00

Exercise 11-7A

	DATE	DESCRIPTION	POST. REF.	DEBIT	CREDIT	
1						1
2						2
3						3
4						4
5						5
6						6
7						7
8						8
9						9
10						10
11						11
12						12
13						13
14						14
15						15
16						16
17						17
18						18
19						19
20						20
21						21

Exercise 11-8A

Problem 11-9A

1.

GENERAL JOURNAL

	DATE	DESCRIPTION	POST. REF.	DEBIT	CREDIT	
1						1
2						2
3						3
4						4
5						5
6						6
7						7
8						8
9						9
10						10
11						11
12						12
13						13
14						14
15						15
16						16
17						17
18						18
19						19
20						20
21						21
22						22
23						23
24						24
25						25
26						26
27						27
28						28
29						29
30						30
31						31
32						32
33						33
34						34

Problem 11-9A (Continued)

2.

GENERAL LEDGER

ACCOUNT   Accounts Payable   ACCOUNT NO.   202

DATE	ITEM	POST. REF.	DEBIT	CREDIT	BALANCE DEBIT	BALANCE CREDIT

ACCOUNT   Purchases   ACCOUNT NO.   501

DATE	ITEM	POST. REF.	DEBIT	CREDIT	BALANCE DEBIT	BALANCE CREDIT

ACCOUNTS PAYABLE LEDGER

NAME

ADDRESS

DATE	ITEM	POST. REF.	DEBIT	CREDIT	BALANCE

Problem 11-9A (Concluded)

NAME _____
ADDRESS _____

DATE		ITEM	POST. REF.	DEBIT	CREDIT	BALANCE

NAME _____
ADDRESS _____

DATE		ITEM	POST. REF.	DEBIT	CREDIT	BALANCE

NAME _____
ADDRESS _____

DATE		ITEM	POST. REF.	DEBIT	CREDIT	BALANCE

NAME _____
ADDRESS _____

DATE		ITEM	POST. REF.	DEBIT	CREDIT	BALANCE

Problem 11-10A

1.

GENERAL JOURNAL

PAGE 9

	DATE	DESCRIPTION	POST. REF.	DEBIT	CREDIT	
1						1
2						2
3						3
4						4
5						5
6						6
7						7
8						8
9						9
10						10
11						11
12						12
13						13
14						14
15						15
16						16
17						17
18						18
19						19
20						20
21						21
22						22
23						23
24						24
25						25
26						26
27						27
28						28
29						29
30						30
31						31
32						32
33						33
34						34

Problem 11-10A (Continued)

GENERAL JOURNAL

	DATE		DESCRIPTION	POST. REF.	DEBIT	CREDIT	
1							1
2							2
3							3
4							4
5							5

2.

GENERAL LEDGER

ACCOUNT Cash   ACCOUNT NO. 101

DATE		ITEM	POST. REF.	DEBIT	CREDIT	BALANCE DEBIT	BALANCE CREDIT
20-- May	1	Balance	✓			40 0 0 0 00	

ACCOUNT Accounts Payable   ACCOUNT NO. 202

DATE		ITEM	POST. REF.	DEBIT	CREDIT	BALANCE DEBIT	BALANCE CREDIT
20-- May	1	Balance	✓				20 0 0 0 00

Problem 11-10A (Continued)

ACCOUNT Purchases ACCOUNT NO. 501

DATE	ITEM	POST. REF.	DEBIT	CREDIT	BALANCE DEBIT	BALANCE CREDIT

ACCOUNT Purchases Discounts ACCOUNT NO. 501.2

DATE	ITEM	POST. REF.	DEBIT	CREDIT	BALANCE DEBIT	BALANCE CREDIT

ACCOUNT Freight-In ACCOUNT NO. 502

DATE	ITEM	POST. REF.	DEBIT	CREDIT	BALANCE DEBIT	BALANCE CREDIT

ACCOUNT Rent Expense ACCOUNT NO. 521

DATE	ITEM	POST. REF.	DEBIT	CREDIT	BALANCE DEBIT	BALANCE CREDIT

ACCOUNT Utilities Expense ACCOUNT NO. 533

DATE	ITEM	POST. REF.	DEBIT	CREDIT	BALANCE DEBIT	BALANCE CREDIT

Problem 11-10A (Concluded)

ACCOUNTS PAYABLE LEDGER

NAME Fantastic Toys

ADDRESS

DATE		ITEM	POST. REF.	DEBIT	CREDIT	BALANCE
20-- May	1	Balance	✓			5 2 0 0 00

NAME Goya Outlet

ADDRESS

DATE		ITEM	POST. REF.	DEBIT	CREDIT	BALANCE
20-- May	1	Balance	✓			3 8 0 0 00

NAME Mueller's Distributors

ADDRESS

DATE		ITEM	POST. REF.	DEBIT	CREDIT	BALANCE
20-- May	1	Balance	✓			3 6 0 0 00

NAME Van Kooning

ADDRESS

DATE		ITEM	POST. REF.	DEBIT	CREDIT	BALANCE
20-- May	1	Balance	✓			7 4 0 0 00

Problem 11-11A

1.

GENERAL JOURNAL

	DATE		DESCRIPTION	POST. REF.	DEBIT	CREDIT	
1							1
2							2
3							3
4							4
5							5
6							6
7							7
8							8
9							9
10							10
11							11
12							12
13							13
14							14
15							15
16							16
17							17
18							18
19							19
20							20
21							21
22							22
23							23
24							24
25							25
26							26
27							27
28							28
29							29
30							30
31							31
32							32
33							33
34							34

Name _____

Problem 11-11A (Continued)

GENERAL JOURNAL

	DATE		DESCRIPTION	POST. REF.	DEBIT	CREDIT	
1							1
2							2
3							3
4							4
5							5
6							6
7							7
8							8
9							9
10							10
11							11
12							12
13							13
14							14
15							15
16							16
17							17
18							18
19							19
20							20
21							21
22							22
23							23
24							24
25							25
26							26
27							27
28							28
29							29
30							30
31							31
32							32
33							33
34							34

Problem 11-11A (Continued)

2.

GENERAL LEDGER

ACCOUNT   Cash   ACCOUNT NO.   101

DATE		ITEM	POST. REF.	DEBIT	CREDIT	BALANCE DEBIT	BALANCE CREDIT
20-- July	1	Balance	✓			21 0 0 0 00	

ACCOUNT   Accounts Payable   ACCOUNT NO.   202

DATE	ITEM	POST. REF.	DEBIT	CREDIT	BALANCE DEBIT	BALANCE CREDIT

Problem 11-11A (Continued)

ACCOUNT   Purchases   ACCOUNT NO.   501

DATE		ITEM	POST. REF.	DEBIT	CREDIT	BALANCE	
						DEBIT	CREDIT

ACCOUNT   Purchases Returns and Allowances   ACCOUNT NO.   501.1

DATE		ITEM	POST. REF.	DEBIT	CREDIT	BALANCE	
						DEBIT	CREDIT

ACCOUNT   Purchases Discounts   ACCOUNT NO.   501.2

DATE		ITEM	POST. REF.	DEBIT	CREDIT	BALANCE	
						DEBIT	CREDIT

ACCOUNT   Rent Expense   ACCOUNT NO.   521

DATE		ITEM	POST. REF.	DEBIT	CREDIT	BALANCE	
						DEBIT	CREDIT

Problem 11-11A (Concluded)

ACCOUNTS PAYABLE LEDGER

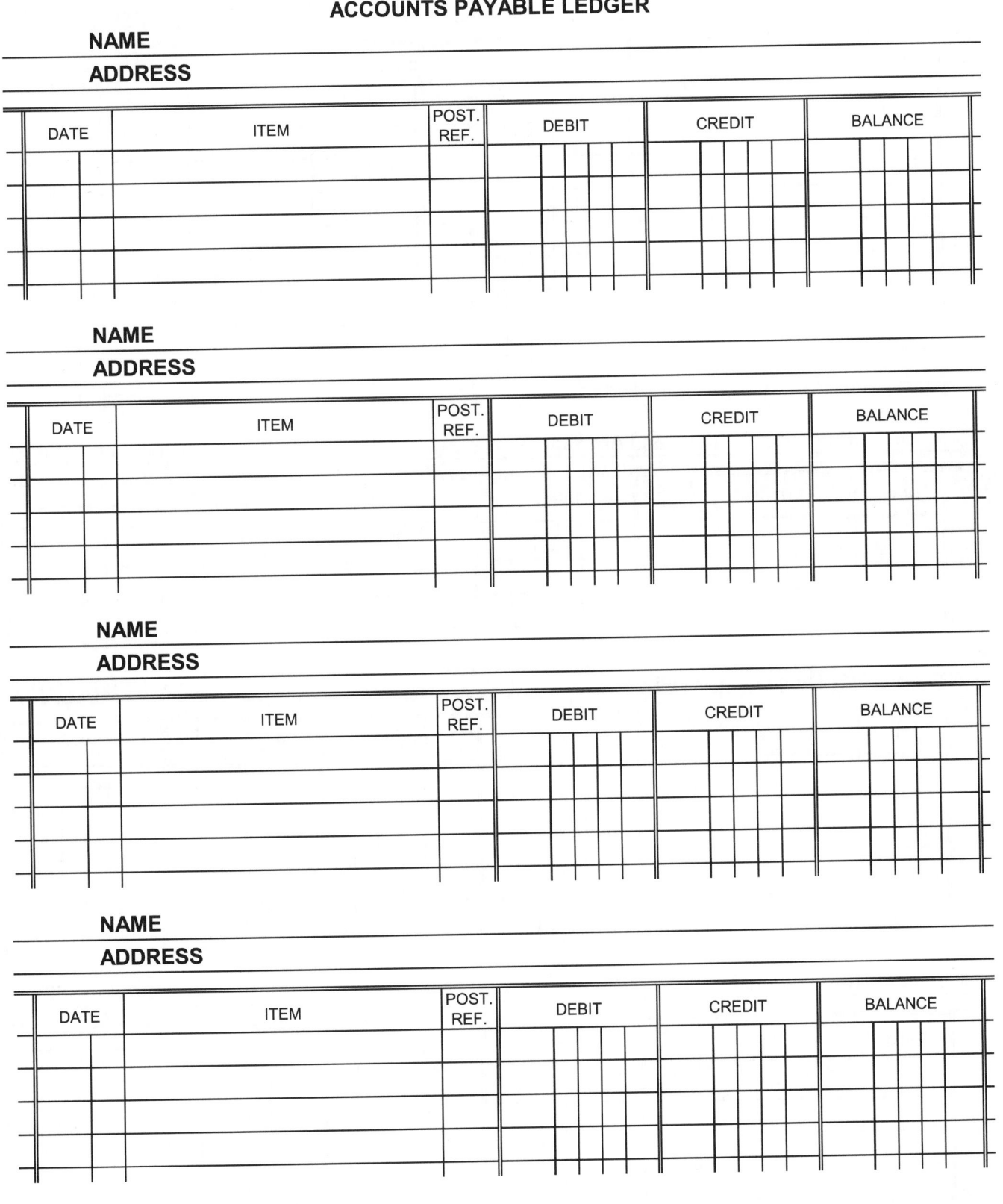

NAME

ADDRESS

DATE	ITEM	POST. REF.	DEBIT	CREDIT	BALANCE

NAME

ADDRESS

DATE	ITEM	POST. REF.	DEBIT	CREDIT	BALANCE

NAME

ADDRESS

DATE	ITEM	POST. REF.	DEBIT	CREDIT	BALANCE

NAME

ADDRESS

DATE	ITEM	POST. REF.	DEBIT	CREDIT	BALANCE

Problem 11-12A

Exercise 11-1B

1. _____

2. _____

3. _____

4. _____

Exercise 11-2B

1.

_____
_____
_____
_____
_____

2.

_____
_____
_____
_____
_____

3.

GENERAL JOURNAL   PAGE _____

DATE	DESCRIPTION	POST. REF.	DEBIT	CREDIT	
					1
					2
					3
					4
					5
					6
					7
					8
					9
					10
					11
					12
					13
					15

Exercise 11-3B

1.

Cash	Accounts Payable

Purchases	Purchases Returns and Allowances

Purchases Discounts	Freight-In

2.

Cash	Accounts Payable

Purchases	Purchases Returns and Allowances

Purchases Discounts	Freight-In

Exercise 11-3B (Concluded)

3.

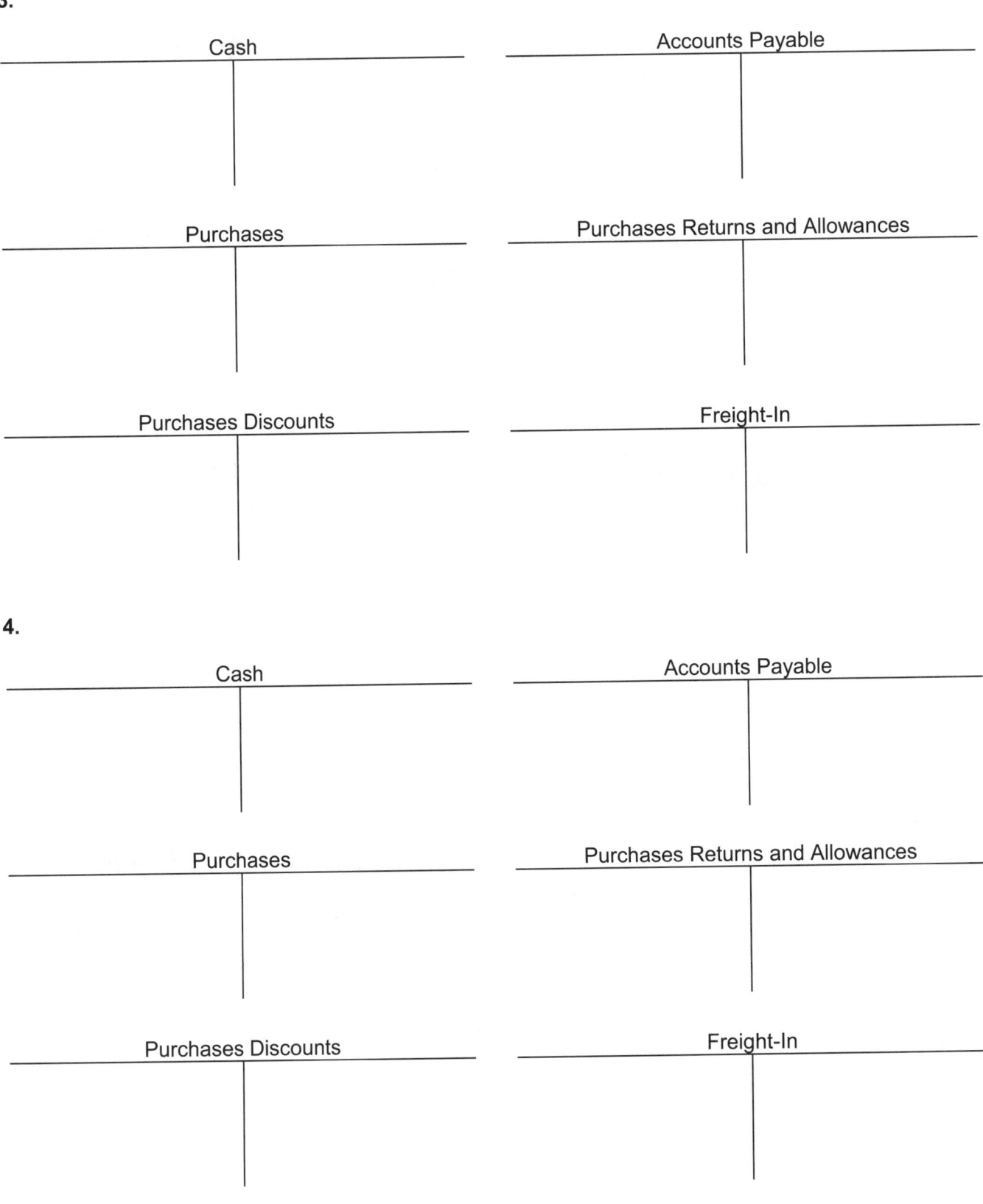

Cash	Accounts Payable

Purchases	Purchases Returns and Allowances

Purchases Discounts	Freight-In

4.

Cash	Accounts Payable

Purchases	Purchases Returns and Allowances

Purchases Discounts	Freight-In

Exercise 11-4B

Exercise 11-5B

GENERAL JOURNAL

PAGE

DATE	DESCRIPTION	POST. REF.	DEBIT	CREDIT

Exercise 11-6B

GENERAL JOURNAL

	DATE		DESCRIPTION	POST. REF.	DEBIT	CREDIT	
1							1
2							2
3							3
4							4
5							5
6							6
7							7
8							8
9							9
10							10
11							11
12							12

GENERAL LEDGER

ACCOUNT Accounts Payable ACCOUNT NO. 202

DATE		ITEM	POST. REF.	DEBIT	CREDIT	BALANCE DEBIT	BALANCE CREDIT
20-- Mar.	1	Balance	✓				8 3 5 0 00

ACCOUNT Purchases Returns and Allowances ACCOUNT NO. 501.1

DATE	ITEM	POST. REF.	DEBIT	CREDIT	BALANCE DEBIT	BALANCE CREDIT

Exercise 11-6B (Concluded)

ACCOUNTS PAYABLE LEDGER

NAME A & D Arms

ADDRESS

DATE		ITEM	POST. REF.	DEBIT	CREDIT	BALANCE
20-- Mar.	1	Balance	✓			2 3 0 0 00

NAME Mighty Mansion

ADDRESS

DATE		ITEM	POST. REF.	DEBIT	CREDIT	BALANCE
20-- Mar.	1	Balance	✓			1 4 5 0 00

NAME Tower Industries

ADDRESS

DATE		ITEM	POST. REF.	DEBIT	CREDIT	BALANCE
20-- Mar.	1	Balance	✓			4 6 0 0 00

Exercise 11-7B

GENERAL JOURNAL

	DATE		DESCRIPTION	POST. REF.	DEBIT	CREDIT	
1							1
2							2
3							3
4							4
5							5
6							6
7							7
8							8
9							9
10							10
11							11
12							12
13							13
14							14
15							15
16							16
17							17
18							18
19							19
20							20
21							21

Exercise 11-8B

Problem 11-9B

1.

<table>
<tr><th colspan="2"></th><th></th><th></th><th></th><th>GENERAL JOURNAL</th><th colspan="3"></th><th></th><th colspan="4"></th><th colspan="2">PAGE 16</th></tr>
</table>

	DATE		DESCRIPTION	POST. REF.	DEBIT	CREDIT	
1							1
2							2
3							3
4							4
5							5
6							6
7							7
8							8
9							9
10							10
11							11
12							12
13							13
14							14
15							15
16							16
17							17
18							18
19							19
20							20
21							21
22							22
23							23
24							24
25							25
26							26
27							27
28							28
29							29
30							30
31							31
32							32
33							33
34							34

Problem 11-9B (Continued)

2.

GENERAL LEDGER

ACCOUNT   Accounts Payable   ACCOUNT NO.   202

DATE	ITEM	POST. REF.	DEBIT	CREDIT	BALANCE DEBIT	BALANCE CREDIT

ACCOUNT   Purchases   ACCOUNT NO.   501

DATE	ITEM	POST. REF.	DEBIT	CREDIT	BALANCE DEBIT	BALANCE CREDIT

ACCOUNTS PAYABLE LEDGER

NAME

ADDRESS

DATE	ITEM	POST. REF.	DEBIT	CREDIT	BALANCE

Problem 11-9B (Concluded)

NAME

ADDRESS

DATE	ITEM	POST. REF.	DEBIT	CREDIT	BALANCE

NAME

ADDRESS

DATE	ITEM	POST. REF.	DEBIT	CREDIT	BALANCE

NAME

ADDRESS

DATE	ITEM	POST. REF.	DEBIT	CREDIT	BALANCE

NAME

ADDRESS

DATE	ITEM	POST. REF.	DEBIT	CREDIT	BALANCE

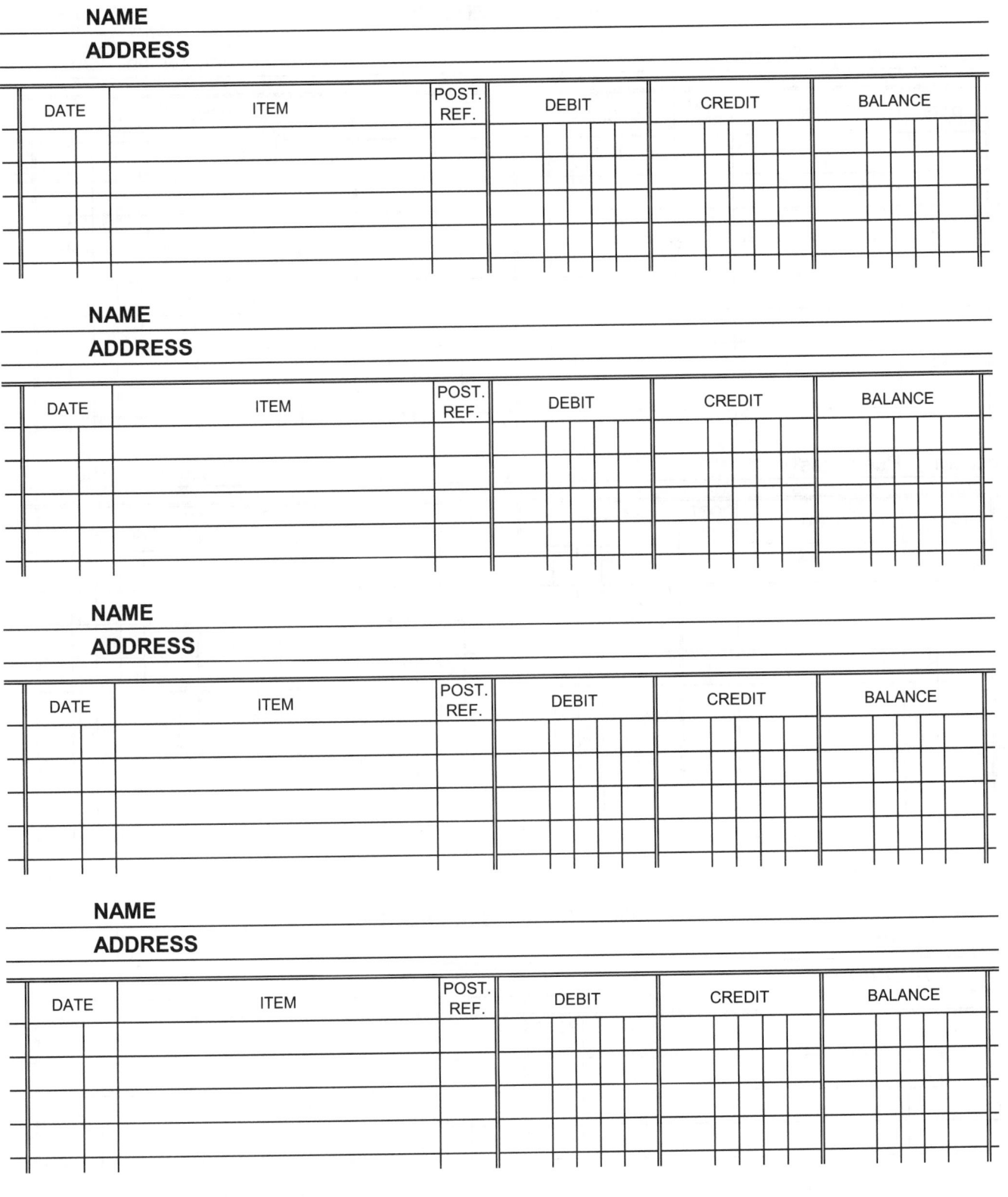

Problem 11-10B

1.

GENERAL JOURNAL

PAGE 9

	DATE		DESCRIPTION	POST. REF.	DEBIT	CREDIT	
1							1
2							2
3							3
4							4
5							5
6							6
7							7
8							8
9							9
10							10
11							11
12							12
13							13
14							14
15							15
16							16
17							17
18							18
19							19
20							20
21							21
22							22
23							23
24							24
25							25
26							26
27							27
28							28
29							29
30							30
31							31
32							32
33							33
34							34

Problem 11-10B (Continued)

GENERAL JOURNAL

	DATE	DESCRIPTION	POST. REF.	DEBIT	CREDIT	
1						1
2						2
3						3
4						4
5						5

2.

GENERAL LEDGER

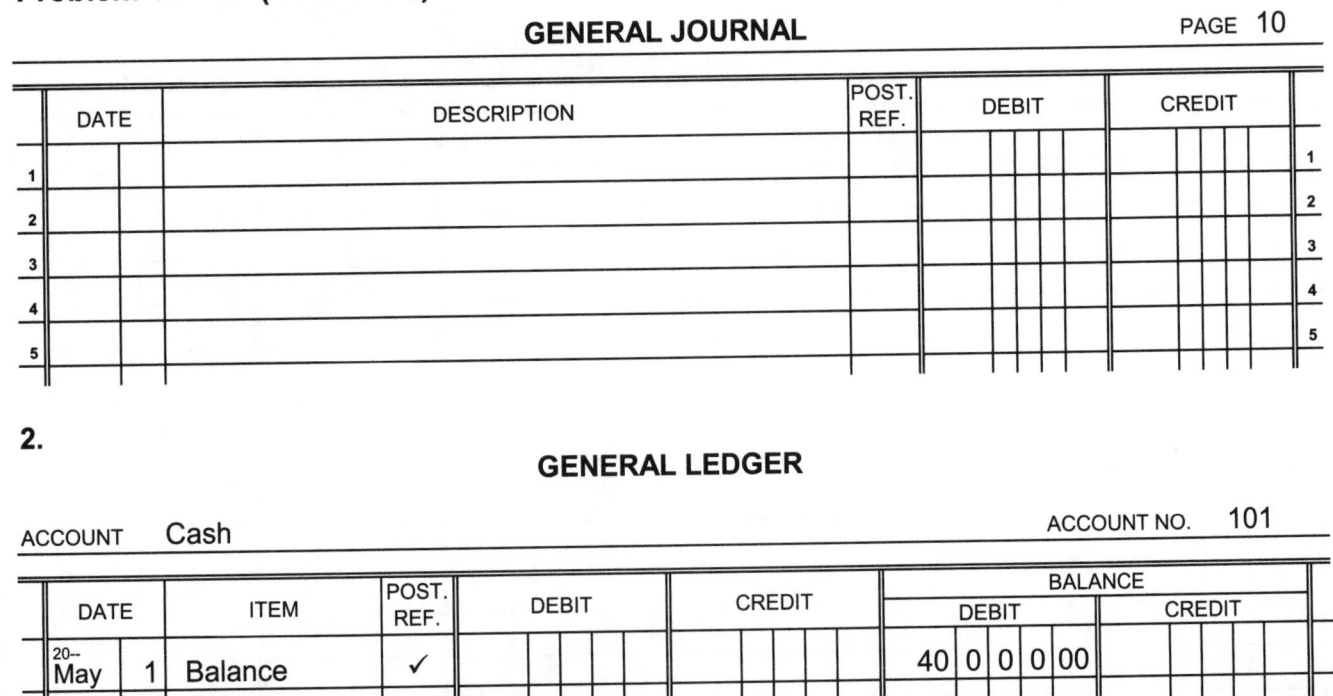

ACCOUNT Cash   ACCOUNT NO. 101

DATE		ITEM	POST. REF.	DEBIT	CREDIT	BALANCE DEBIT	BALANCE CREDIT
20-- May	1	Balance	✓			40 0 0 0 00	

ACCOUNT Accounts Payable   ACCOUNT NO. 202

DATE		ITEM	POST. REF.	DEBIT	CREDIT	BALANCE DEBIT	BALANCE CREDIT
20-- May	1	Balance	✓				20 0 0 0 00

Problem 11-10B (Continued)

ACCOUNT Purchases   ACCOUNT NO. 501

DATE		ITEM	POST. REF.	DEBIT	CREDIT	BALANCE	
						DEBIT	CREDIT

ACCOUNT Purchases Discounts   ACCOUNT NO. 501.2

DATE		ITEM	POST. REF.	DEBIT	CREDIT	BALANCE	
						DEBIT	CREDIT

ACCOUNT Freight-In   ACCOUNT NO. 502

DATE		ITEM	POST. REF.	DEBIT	CREDIT	BALANCE	
						DEBIT	CREDIT

ACCOUNT Rent Expense   ACCOUNT NO. 521

DATE		ITEM	POST. REF.	DEBIT	CREDIT	BALANCE	
						DEBIT	CREDIT

ACCOUNT Utilities Expense   ACCOUNT NO. 533

DATE		ITEM	POST. REF.	DEBIT	CREDIT	BALANCE	
						DEBIT	CREDIT

Problem 11-10B (Concluded)

ACCOUNTS PAYABLE LEDGER

NAME Cortez Distributors

ADDRESS

DATE		ITEM	POST. REF.	DEBIT	CREDIT	BALANCE
20-- May	1	Balance	✓			4 2 0 0 00

NAME Indra & Velga

ADDRESS

DATE		ITEM	POST. REF.	DEBIT	CREDIT	BALANCE
20-- May	1	Balance	✓			6 8 0 0 00

NAME Toy Corner

ADDRESS

DATE		ITEM	POST. REF.	DEBIT	CREDIT	BALANCE
20-- May	1	Balance	✓			4 6 0 0 00

NAME Troutman Outlet

ADDRESS

DATE		ITEM	POST. REF.	DEBIT	CREDIT	BALANCE
20-- May	1	Balance	✓			4 4 0 0 00

Problem 11-11B

1.

GENERAL JOURNAL

	DATE	DESCRIPTION	POST. REF.	DEBIT	CREDIT	
1						1
2						2
3						3
4						4
5						5
6						6
7						7
8						8
9						9
10						10
11						11
12						12
13						13
14						14
15						15
16						16
17						17
18						18
19						19
20						20
21						21
22						22
23						23
24						24
25						25
26						26
27						27
28						28
29						29
30						30
31						31
32						32
33						33
34						34

Problem 11-11B (Continued)

GENERAL JOURNAL

	DATE	DESCRIPTION	POST. REF.	DEBIT	CREDIT	
1						1
2						2
3						3
4						4
5						5
6						6
7						7
8						8
9						9
10						10
11						11
12						12
13						13
14						14
15						15
16						16
17						17
18						18
19						19
20						20
21						21
22						22
23						23
24						24
25						25
26						26
27						27
28						28
29						29
30						30
31						31
32						32
33						33
34						34

Problem 11-11B (Continued)

2.

GENERAL LEDGER

ACCOUNT   Cash   ACCOUNT NO.   101

DATE		ITEM	POST. REF.	DEBIT	CREDIT	BALANCE	
						DEBIT	CREDIT
20-- July	1	Balance	✓			20 0 0 0 00	

ACCOUNT   Accounts Payable   ACCOUNT NO.   202

DATE		ITEM	POST. REF.	DEBIT	CREDIT	BALANCE	
						DEBIT	CREDIT

Problem 11-11B (Continued)

ACCOUNT Purchases   ACCOUNT NO. 501

DATE	ITEM	POST. REF.	DEBIT	CREDIT	BALANCE DEBIT	BALANCE CREDIT

ACCOUNT Purchases Returns and Allowances   ACCOUNT NO. 501.1

DATE	ITEM	POST. REF.	DEBIT	CREDIT	BALANCE DEBIT	BALANCE CREDIT

ACCOUNT Purchases Discounts   ACCOUNT NO. 501.2

DATE	ITEM	POST. REF.	DEBIT	CREDIT	BALANCE DEBIT	BALANCE CREDIT

ACCOUNT Rent Expense   ACCOUNT NO. 521

DATE	ITEM	POST. REF.	DEBIT	CREDIT	BALANCE DEBIT	BALANCE CREDIT

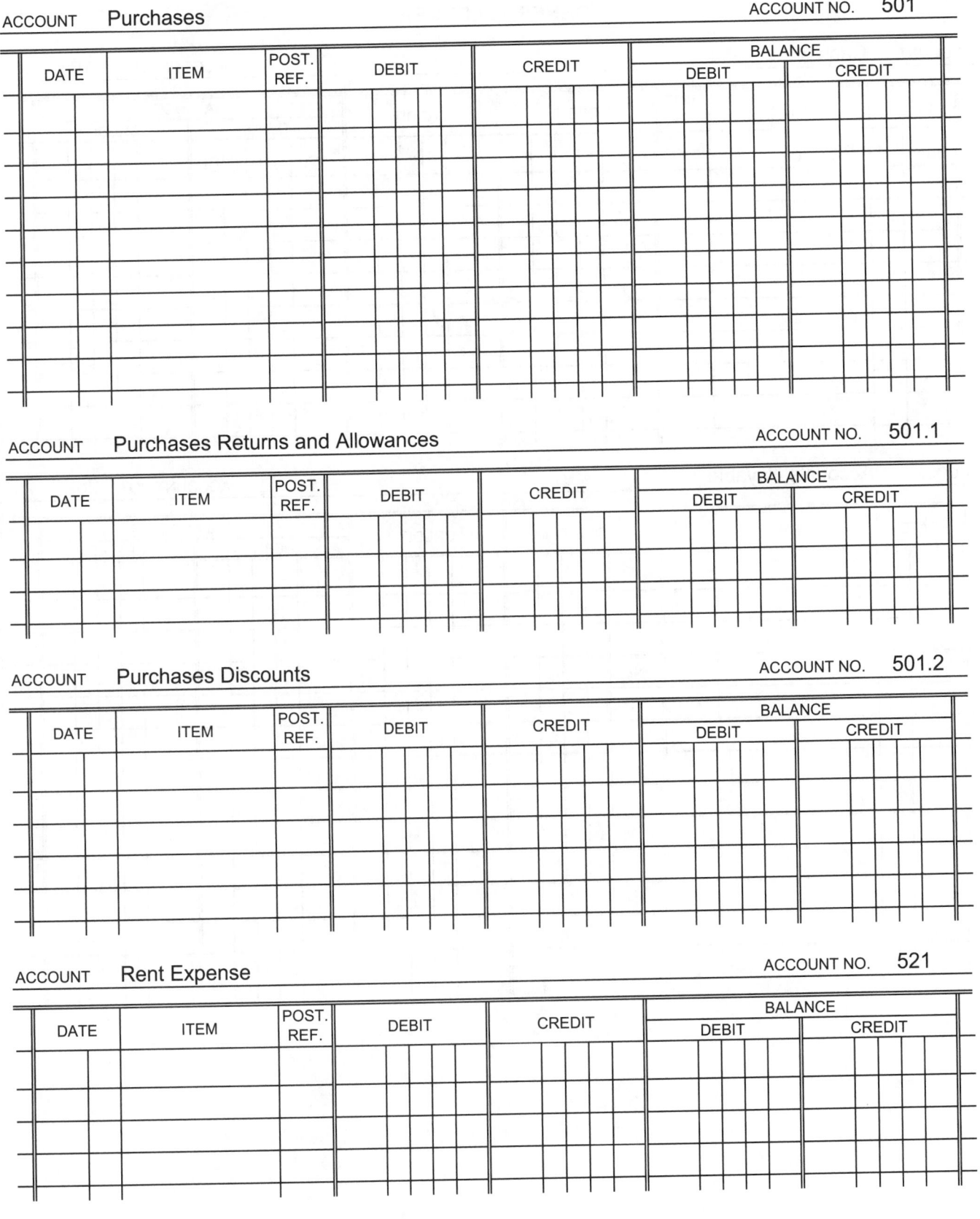

Problem 11-11B (Concluded)

ACCOUNTS PAYABLE LEDGER

NAME _____

ADDRESS _____

DATE		ITEM	POST. REF.	DEBIT	CREDIT	BALANCE

NAME _____

ADDRESS _____

DATE		ITEM	POST. REF.	DEBIT	CREDIT	BALANCE

NAME _____

ADDRESS _____

DATE		ITEM	POST. REF.	DEBIT	CREDIT	BALANCE

NAME _____

ADDRESS _____

DATE		ITEM	POST. REF.	DEBIT	CREDIT	BALANCE

Problem 11-12B

Mastery Problem

1.

GENERAL JOURNAL

	DATE		DESCRIPTION	POST. REF.	DEBIT	CREDIT	
1							1
2							2
3							3
4							4
5							5
6							6
7							7
8							8
9							9
10							10
11							11
12							12
13							13
14							14
15							15
16							16
17							17
18							18
19							19
20							20
21							21
22							22
23							23
24							24
25							25
26							26
27							27
28							28
29							29
30							30
31							31
32							32
33							33
34							34

Mastery Problem (Continued)

GENERAL JOURNAL

	DATE		DESCRIPTION	POST. REF.	DEBIT	CREDIT	
1							1
2							2
3							3
4							4
5							5
6							6
7							7
8							8
9							9
10							10
11							11
12							12
13							13
14							14
15							15
16							16
17							17
18							18
19							19
20							20
21							21
22							22
23							23
24							24
25							25
26							26
27							27
28							28
29							29
30							30
31							31
32							32
33							33
34							34

Mastery Problem (Continued)

2.

GENERAL LEDGER

ACCOUNT Cash   ACCOUNT NO. 101

DATE		ITEM	POST. REF.	DEBIT	CREDIT	BALANCE	
						DEBIT	CREDIT
20-- June	1	Balance	✓			32 2 0 0 00	

ACCOUNT Accounts Payable   ACCOUNT NO. 202

DATE		ITEM	POST. REF.	DEBIT	CREDIT	BALANCE	
						DEBIT	CREDIT
20-- June	1	Balance	✓				2 0 0 0 00

Mastery Problem (Continued)

ACCOUNT   M. French, Drawing   ACCOUNT NO.   312

DATE		ITEM	POST. REF.	DEBIT	CREDIT	BALANCE DEBIT	BALANCE CREDIT
20-- June	1	Balance	✓			18 0 0 0 00	

ACCOUNT   Purchases   ACCOUNT NO.   501

DATE		ITEM	POST. REF.	DEBIT	CREDIT	BALANCE DEBIT	BALANCE CREDIT
20-- June	1	Balance	✓			67 0 2 1 66	

ACCOUNT   Purchases Returns and Allowances   ACCOUNT NO.   501.1

DATE		ITEM	POST. REF.	DEBIT	CREDIT	BALANCE DEBIT	BALANCE CREDIT
20-- June	1	Balance	✓				2 3 1 5 23

ACCOUNT   Purchases Discounts   ACCOUNT NO.   501.2

DATE		ITEM	POST. REF.	DEBIT	CREDIT	BALANCE DEBIT	BALANCE CREDIT
20-- June	1	Balance	✓				9 0 5 00

Mastery Problem (Continued)

ACCOUNT Freight-In   ACCOUNT NO. 502

DATE		ITEM	POST. REF.	DEBIT	CREDIT	BALANCE	
						DEBIT	CREDIT
20-- June	1	Balance	✓			5 2 2 60	

ACCOUNT Rent Expense   ACCOUNT NO. 521

DATE		ITEM	POST. REF.	DEBIT	CREDIT	BALANCE	
						DEBIT	CREDIT
20-- June	1	Balance	✓			3 1 2 5 00	

ACCOUNT Utilities Expense   ACCOUNT NO. 533

DATE		ITEM	POST. REF.	DEBIT	CREDIT	BALANCE	
						DEBIT	CREDIT
20-- June	1	Balance	✓			1 5 2 2 87	

ACCOUNTS PAYABLE LEDGER

NAME Broadway Publishing, Inc.

ADDRESS 2300 Goodman, Cincinnati, OH 45219-2901

DATE		ITEM	POST. REF.	DEBIT	CREDIT	BALANCE

Mastery Problem (Continued)

NAME Irving Publishing Company
ADDRESS 5200 N. Keystone Ave., Indianapolis, IN 46220-1986

DATE	ITEM	POST. REF.	DEBIT	CREDIT	BALANCE

NAME Northeastern Publishing Co.
ADDRESS 874 Crescent Drive, Flint, MI 48503-7564

DATE		ITEM	POST. REF.	DEBIT	CREDIT	BALANCE
20-- June	1	Balance	✓			2 0 0 0 00

NAME Riley Publishing Co.
ADDRESS 5675 Pulaski Road, Chicago, IL 60629-6705

DATE	ITEM	POST. REF.	DEBIT	CREDIT	BALANCE

Mastery Problem (Concluded)

3.

4.

Challenge Problem

GENERAL JOURNAL

	DATE		DESCRIPTION	POST. REF.	DEBIT	CREDIT	
1							1
2							2
3							3
4							4
5							5
6							6
7							7
8							8
9							9
10							10
11							11
12							12
13							13
14							14
15							15
16							16
17							17
18							18
19							19
20							20
21							21
22							22
23							23
24							24
25							25
26							26
27							27
28							28
29							29
30							30
31							31
32							32
33							33
34							34

Exercise 11Apx-1A

1.

GENERAL JOURNAL

	DATE	DESCRIPTION	POST. REF.	DEBIT	CREDIT	
1						1
2						2
3						3
4						4
5						5
6						6
7						7
8						8
9						9
10						10
11						11
12						12
13						13
14						14
15						15
16						16

2.

1						1
2						2
3						3
4						4
5						5
6						6
7						7
8						8
9						9
10						10
11						11
12						12
13						13
14						14
15						15
16						16

Exercise 11Apx-1B

1.

GENERAL JOURNAL

	DATE		DESCRIPTION	POST. REF.	DEBIT	CREDIT	
1							1
2							2
3							3
4							4
5							5
6							6
7							7
8							8
9							9
10							10
11							11
12							12
13							13
14							14
15							15
16							16

2.

1							1
2							2
3							3
4							4
5							5
6							6
7							7
8							8
9							9
10							10
11							11
12							12
13							13
14							14
15							15
16							16

Exercise 12-1A

Journal (underlined, right side)

Journal

a. Sold merchandise on account. _____

b. Purchased delivery truck on account for use in the business. _____

c. Received payment from customer on account. _____

d. Purchased merchandise on account. _____

e. Issued check in payment of electric bill. _____

f. Recorded depreciation on factory building. _____

Exercise 12-2A

SALES JOURNAL

PAGE

DATE	SALE NO.	TO WHOM SOLD	POST. REF.	ACCOUNTS RECEIVABLE DEBIT	SALES CREDIT	SALES TAX PAYABLE CREDIT

Exercise 12-3A

CASH RECEIPTS JOURNAL

PAGE

	DATE	ACCOUNT CREDITED	POST. REF.	GENERAL CREDIT	ACCOUNTS RECEIVABLE CREDIT	SALES CREDIT	SALES TAX PAYABLE CREDIT	CASH DEBIT	
1									1
2									2
3									3
4									4
5									5
6									6
7									7
8									8
9									9
10									10
11									11

Exercise 12-4A

PURCHASES JOURNAL

PAGE

DATE	INVOICE NO.	FROM WHOM PURCHASED	POST. REF.	PURCHASES DEBIT ACCTS. PAY. CREDIT	
1					1
2					2
3					3
4					4
5					5
6					6
7					7
8					8
9					9
10					10
11					11

Exercise 12-5A

CASH PAYMENTS JOURNAL

PAGE

DATE	CK. NO.	ACCOUNT DEBITED	POST. REF.	GENERAL DEBIT	ACCOUNTS PAYABLE DEBIT	PURCHASES DEBIT	PURCHASES DISCOUNTS CREDIT	CASH CREDIT	
1									1
2									2
3									3
4									4
5									5
6									6
7									7
8									8
9									9
10									10
11									11
12									12
13									13

Problem 12-6A

1.

SALES JOURNAL

DATE	SALE NO.	TO WHOM SOLD	POST. REF.	ACCOUNTS RECEIVABLE DEBIT	SALES CREDIT	SALES TAX PAYABLE CREDIT

2.

GENERAL LEDGER

ACCOUNT Accounts Receivable   ACCOUNT NO. 122

DATE	ITEM	POST. REF.	DEBIT	CREDIT	BALANCE DEBIT	BALANCE CREDIT

ACCOUNT Sales Tax Payable   ACCOUNT NO. 231

DATE	ITEM	POST. REF.	DEBIT	CREDIT	BALANCE DEBIT	BALANCE CREDIT

Problem 12-6A (Concluded)

ACCOUNT Sales   ACCOUNT NO. 401

DATE	ITEM	POST. REF.	DEBIT	CREDIT	BALANCE DEBIT	BALANCE CREDIT

ACCOUNTS RECEIVABLE LEDGER

NAME Hassan Co.

ADDRESS 1225 W. Temperance Street, Ellettsville, IN 47429-9976

DATE	ITEM	POST. REF.	DEBIT	CREDIT	BALANCE

NAME Habrock, Inc.

ADDRESS 125 Fishers Dr., Noblesville, IN 47870-8867

DATE	ITEM	POST. REF.	DEBIT	CREDIT	BALANCE

NAME Jeter Manufacturing Co.

ADDRESS 8825 Old State Road, Bloomington, IN 47401-8823

DATE	ITEM	POST. REF.	DEBIT	CREDIT	BALANCE

NAME Seth Mowbray

ADDRESS 2100 Greer Lane, Bedford, IN 47421-8876

DATE	ITEM	POST. REF.	DEBIT	CREDIT	BALANCE

Problem 12-7A

1.

GENERAL JOURNAL

	DATE		DESCRIPTION	POST. REF.	DEBIT	CREDIT	
1							1
2							2
3							3
4							4
5							5
6							6
7							7
8							8
9							9
10							10
11							11
12							12
13							13
14							14
15							15
16							16
17							17
18							18
19							19
20							20
21							21
22							22
23							23
24							24
25							25
26							26
27							27
28							28
29							29
30							30
31							31
32							32
33							33
34							34

Problem 12-7A (Continued)

CASH RECEIPTS JOURNAL

	DATE	ACCOUNT CREDITED	POST. REF.	GENERAL CREDIT	ACCOUNTS RECEIVABLE CREDIT
1					
2					
3					
4					
5					
6					
7					
8					
9					
10					
11					
12					
13					
14					
15					
16					
17					
18					
19					
20					
21					
22					
23					
24					
25					
26					
27					
28					

Problem 12-7A (Continued)

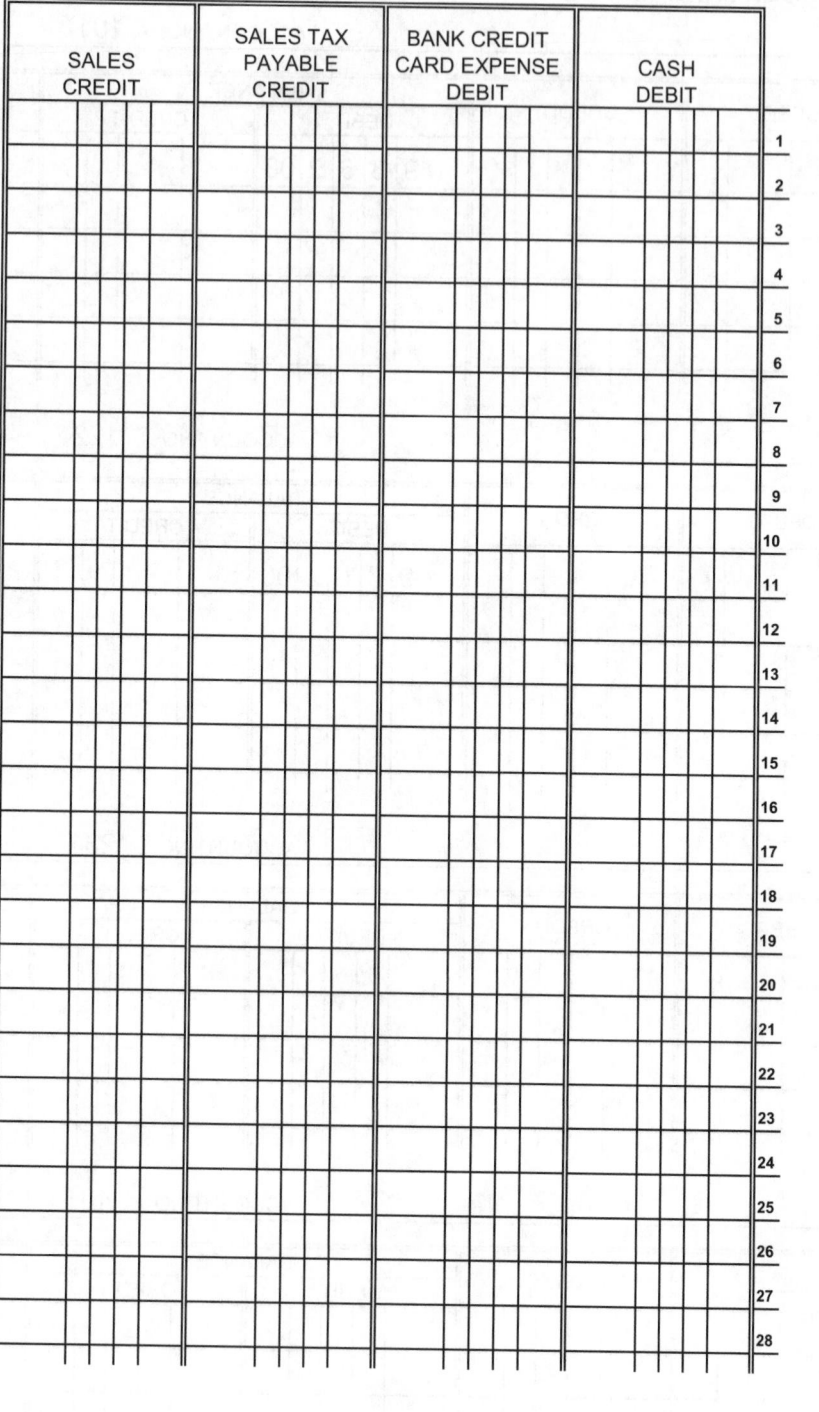

SALES CREDIT	SALES TAX PAYABLE CREDIT	BANK CREDIT CARD EXPENSE DEBIT	CASH DEBIT	
				1
				2
				3
				4
				5
				6
				7
				8
				9
				10
				11
				12
				13
				14
				15
				16
				17
				18
				19
				20
				21
				22
				23
				24
				25
				26
				27
				28

Problem 12-7A (Continued)

2.

GENERAL LEDGER

ACCOUNT   Cash   ACCOUNT NO.   101

DATE		ITEM	POST. REF.	DEBIT	CREDIT	BALANCE	
						DEBIT	CREDIT
20-- Dec.	1	Balance	✓			9 8 6 2 00	

ACCOUNT   Accounts Receivable   ACCOUNT NO.   122

DATE		ITEM	POST. REF.	DEBIT	CREDIT	BALANCE	
						DEBIT	CREDIT
20-- Dec.	1	Balance	✓			9 3 5 2 00	

ACCOUNT   Sales Tax Payable   ACCOUNT NO.   231

DATE	ITEM	POST. REF.	DEBIT	CREDIT	BALANCE	
					DEBIT	CREDIT

ACCOUNT   Sales   ACCOUNT NO.   401

DATE	ITEM	POST. REF.	DEBIT	CREDIT	BALANCE	
					DEBIT	CREDIT

Problem 12-7A (Continued)

ACCOUNT   Sales Returns and Allowances   ACCOUNT NO.   401.1

DATE		ITEM	POST. REF.	DEBIT	CREDIT	BALANCE	
						DEBIT	CREDIT

ACCOUNT   Bank Credit Card Expense   ACCOUNT NO.   513

DATE		ITEM	POST. REF.	DEBIT	CREDIT	BALANCE	
						DEBIT	CREDIT

ACCOUNTS RECEIVABLE LEDGER

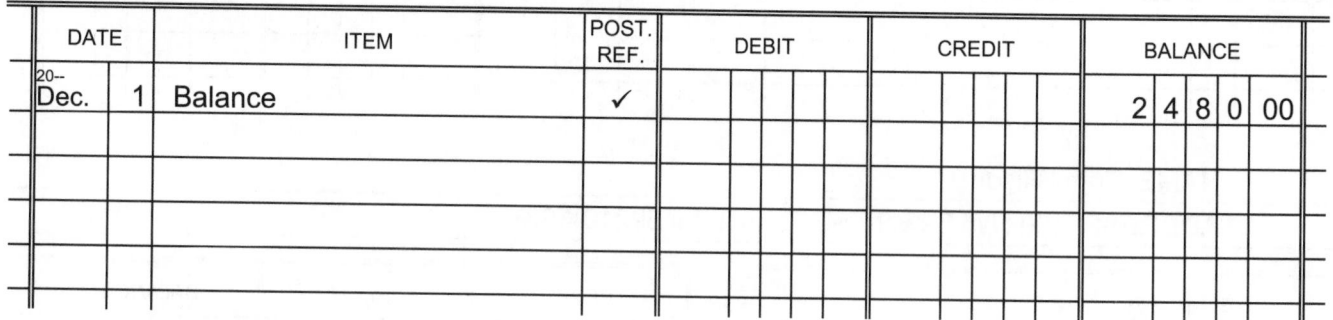

NAME Michael Anderson

ADDRESS 233 West 11th Avenue, Detroit, MI 59500-1154

DATE		ITEM	POST. REF.	DEBIT	CREDIT	BALANCE
20-- Dec.	1	Balance	✓			2 4 8 0 00

NAME Ansel Manufacturing

ADDRESS 284 West 88 Street, Detroit, MI 59522-1168

DATE		ITEM	POST. REF.	DEBIT	CREDIT	BALANCE
20-- Dec.	1	Balance	✓			9 8 2 00

Problem 12-7A (Concluded)

NAME J. Gorbea

ADDRESS P.O. Box 864, Detroit, MI 59552-0864

DATE		ITEM	POST. REF.	DEBIT	CREDIT	BALANCE
20-- Dec.	1	Balance	✓			8 8 0 00

NAME Rachel Carson

ADDRESS 11312 Fourteenth Avenue South, Detroit, MI 59221-1142

DATE		ITEM	POST. REF.	DEBIT	CREDIT	BALANCE
20-- Dec.	1	Balance	✓			3 2 0 0 00

NAME Tom Wilson

ADDRESS 100 NW Seward St., Detroit, MI 59210-1337

DATE		ITEM	POST. REF.	DEBIT	CREDIT	BALANCE
20-- Dec.	1	Balance	✓			1 8 1 0 00

Problem 12-8A

1.

SALES JOURNAL

	DATE	SALE NO.	TO WHOM SOLD	POST. REF.	ACCOUNTS RECEIVABLE DEBIT	SALES CREDIT	SALES TAX PAYABLE CREDIT

CASH RECEIPTS JOURNAL

	DATE	ACCOUNT CREDITED	POST. REF.	GENERAL CREDIT	ACCOUNTS RECEIVABLE CREDIT	SALES CREDIT	SALES TAX PAYABLE CREDIT	CASH DEBIT	
1									1
2									2
3									3
4									4
5									5
6									6
7									7
8									8
9									9

Problem 12-8A (Continued)

GENERAL JOURNAL

	DATE	DESCRIPTION	POST. REF.	DEBIT	CREDIT	
1						1
2						2
3						3
4						4
5						5
6						6
7						7
8						8
9						9
10						10
11						11
12						12
13						13
14						14

2.

GENERAL LEDGER

ACCOUNT   Cash   ACCOUNT NO.   101

DATE		ITEM	POST. REF.	DEBIT	CREDIT	BALANCE DEBIT	BALANCE CREDIT
20-- Mar.	1	Balance	✓			9 7 4 1 00	

ACCOUNT   Accounts Receivable   ACCOUNT NO.   122

DATE		ITEM	POST. REF.	DEBIT	CREDIT	BALANCE DEBIT	BALANCE CREDIT
20-- Mar.	1	Balance	✓			1 0 5 8 25	

Problem 12-8A (Continued)

ACCOUNT   Sales Tax Payable   ACCOUNT NO.   231

DATE	ITEM	POST. REF.	DEBIT	CREDIT	BALANCE	
					DEBIT	CREDIT

ACCOUNT   Sales   ACCOUNT NO.   401

DATE	ITEM	POST. REF.	DEBIT	CREDIT	BALANCE	
					DEBIT	CREDIT

ACCOUNT   Sales Returns and Allowances   ACCOUNT NO.   401.1

DATE	ITEM	POST. REF.	DEBIT	CREDIT	BALANCE	
					DEBIT	CREDIT

Problem 12-8A (Concluded)

ACCOUNTS RECEIVABLE LEDGER

NAME Able & Co.

ADDRESS 1424 Jackson Creek Road, Nashville, IN 47448-2245

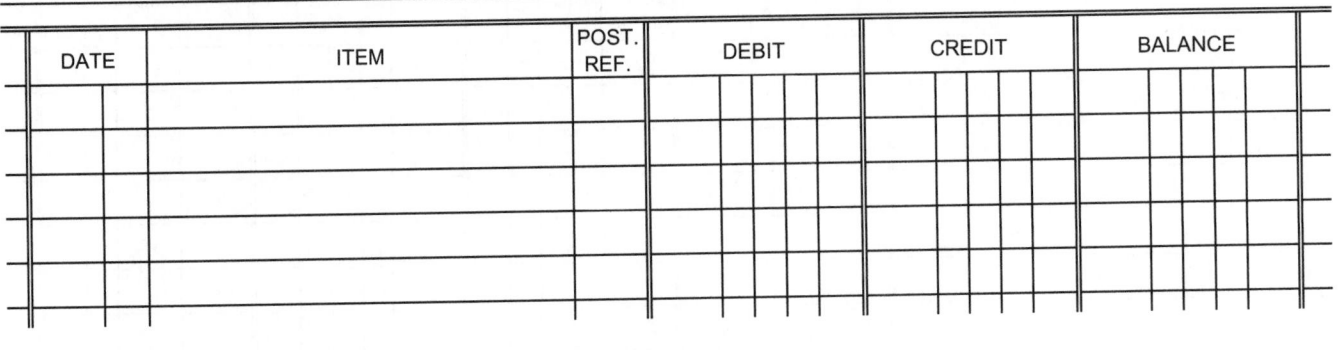

DATE	ITEM	POST. REF.	DEBIT	CREDIT	BALANCE

NAME Blevins Bakery

ADDRESS 6422 E. Bender Road, Bloomington, IN 47401-7756

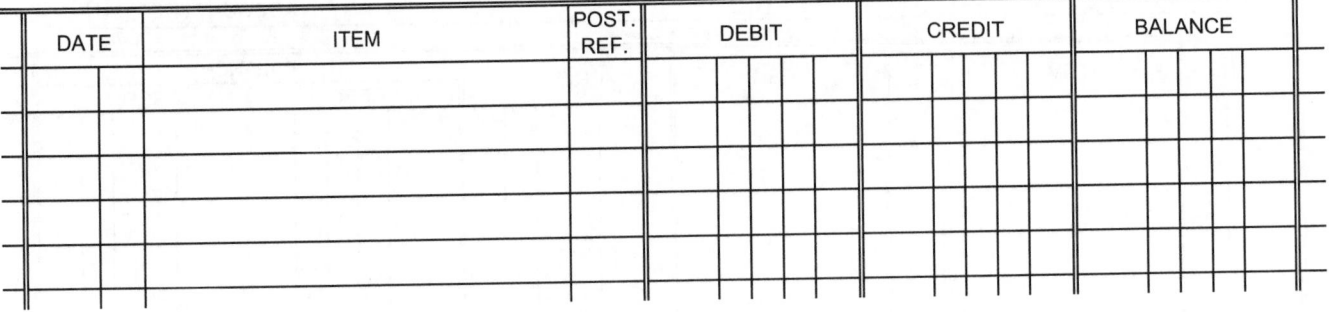

DATE	ITEM	POST. REF.	DEBIT	CREDIT	BALANCE

NAME R. J. Kalas, Inc.

ADDRESS 3315 Longview Avenue, Bloomington, IN 47401-7223

DATE	ITEM	POST. REF.	DEBIT	CREDIT	BALANCE

NAME Thompson Group

ADDRESS 2300 E. National Road, Cumberland, IN 46229-4824

DATE		ITEM	POST. REF.	DEBIT	CREDIT	BALANCE
20-- Mar.	1	Balance	✓			1 0 5 8 25

Problem 12-9A

1.

PURCHASES JOURNAL

	DATE	INVOICE NO.	FROM WHOM PURCHASED	POST. REF.	PURCHASES DEBIT ACCTS. PAY. CREDIT	
1						1
2						2
3						3
4						4
5						5
6						6
7						7
8						8
9						9
10						10
11						11
12						12
13						13
14						14

2.

GENERAL LEDGER

ACCOUNT   Accounts Payable   ACCOUNT NO.   202

DATE	ITEM	POST. REF.	DEBIT	CREDIT	BALANCE DEBIT	BALANCE CREDIT

ACCOUNT   Purchases   ACCOUNT NO.   501

DATE	ITEM	POST. REF.	DEBIT	CREDIT	BALANCE DEBIT	BALANCE CREDIT

Problem 12-9A (Concluded)

ACCOUNTS PAYABLE LEDGER

NAME

ADDRESS

DATE	ITEM	POST. REF.	DEBIT	CREDIT	BALANCE

NAME

ADDRESS

DATE	ITEM	POST. REF.	DEBIT	CREDIT	BALANCE

NAME

ADDRESS

DATE	ITEM	POST. REF.	DEBIT	CREDIT	BALANCE

NAME

ADDRESS

DATE	ITEM	POST. REF.	DEBIT	CREDIT	BALANCE

NAME

ADDRESS

DATE	ITEM	POST. REF.	DEBIT	CREDIT	BALANCE

Problem 12-10A

1.

GENERAL LEDGER

ACCOUNT Accounts Payable   ACCOUNT NO. 202

DATE	ITEM	POST. REF.	DEBIT	CREDIT	BALANCE DEBIT	BALANCE CREDIT

ACCOUNT Purchases   ACCOUNT NO. 501

DATE	ITEM	POST. REF.	DEBIT	CREDIT	BALANCE DEBIT	BALANCE CREDIT

2.

ACCOUNTS PAYABLE LEDGER

NAME
ADDRESS

DATE	ITEM	POST. REF.	DEBIT	CREDIT	BALANCE

NAME
ADDRESS

DATE	ITEM	POST. REF.	DEBIT	CREDIT	BALANCE

Problem 12-10A (Concluded)

NAME

ADDRESS

DATE	ITEM	POST. REF.	DEBIT	CREDIT	BALANCE

NAME

ADDRESS

DATE	ITEM	POST. REF.	DEBIT	CREDIT	BALANCE

NAME

ADDRESS

DATE	ITEM	POST. REF.	DEBIT	CREDIT	BALANCE

Problem 12-11A

1.

CASH PAYMENTS JOURNAL

PAGE 6

	DATE	CK. NO.	ACCOUNT DEBITED	POST. REF.	GENERAL DEBIT	ACCOUNTS PAYABLE DEBIT	PURCHASES DEBIT	PURCHASES DISCOUNTS CREDIT	CASH CREDIT	
1										1
2										2
3										3
4										4
5										5
6										6
7										7
8										8
9										9
10										10
11										11
12										12

_____

_____

_____

_____

2.

GENERAL LEDGER

ACCOUNT Cash

ACCOUNT NO. 101

DATE		ITEM	POST. REF.	DEBIT	CREDIT	BALANCE DEBIT	BALANCE CREDIT
20-- May	1	Balance	✓			40 0 0 0 00	

ACCOUNT Accounts Payable

ACCOUNT NO. 202

DATE		ITEM	POST. REF.	DEBIT	CREDIT	BALANCE DEBIT	BALANCE CREDIT
20-- May	1	Balance	✓				20 0 0 0 00

Problem 12-11A (Continued)

ACCOUNT Purchases   ACCOUNT NO. 501

DATE	ITEM	POST. REF.	DEBIT	CREDIT	BALANCE DEBIT	BALANCE CREDIT

ACCOUNT Purchases Discounts   ACCOUNT NO. 501.2

DATE	ITEM	POST. REF.	DEBIT	CREDIT	BALANCE DEBIT	BALANCE CREDIT

ACCOUNT Freight-In   ACCOUNT NO. 502

DATE	ITEM	POST. REF.	DEBIT	CREDIT	BALANCE DEBIT	BALANCE CREDIT

ACCOUNT Rent Expense   ACCOUNT NO. 521

DATE	ITEM	POST. REF.	DEBIT	CREDIT	BALANCE DEBIT	BALANCE CREDIT

ACCOUNT Utilities Expense   ACCOUNT NO. 533

DATE	ITEM	POST. REF.	DEBIT	CREDIT	BALANCE DEBIT	BALANCE CREDIT

Problem 12-11A (Concluded)

ACCOUNTS PAYABLE LEDGER

NAME Fantastic Toys
ADDRESS

DATE		ITEM	POST. REF.	DEBIT	CREDIT	BALANCE
20-- May	1	Balance	✓			5 2 0 0 00

NAME Goya Outlet
ADDRESS

DATE		ITEM	POST. REF.	DEBIT	CREDIT	BALANCE
20-- May	1	Balance	✓			3 8 0 0 00

NAME Mueller's Distributors
ADDRESS

DATE		ITEM	POST. REF.	DEBIT	CREDIT	BALANCE
20-- May	1	Balance	✓			3 6 0 0 00

NAME Van Kooning
ADDRESS

DATE		ITEM	POST. REF.	DEBIT	CREDIT	BALANCE
20-- May	1	Balance	✓			7 4 0 0 00

Problem 12-12A

1.

PURCHASES JOURNAL

DATE	INVOICE NO.	FROM WHOM PURCHASED	POST. REF.	PURCHASES DEBIT ACCTS. PAY. CREDIT	
					1
					2
					3
					4
					5
					6
					7
					8
					9
					10

CASH PAYMENTS JOURNAL

DATE	CK. NO.	ACCOUNT DEBITED	POST. REF.	GENERAL DEBIT	ACCOUNTS PAYABLE DEBIT	PURCHASES DEBIT	PURCHASES DISCOUNTS CREDIT	CASH CREDIT	
									1
									2
									3
									4
									5
									6
									7
									8
									9
									10
									11
									12

Problem 12-12A (Continued)

GENERAL JOURNAL

	DATE		DESCRIPTION	POST. REF.	DEBIT	CREDIT	
1							1
2							2
3							3
4							4
5							5
6							6
7							7
8							8
9							9
10							10

2.

GENERAL LEDGER

ACCOUNT   Cash

ACCOUNT NO.   101

DATE		ITEM	POST. REF.	DEBIT	CREDIT	BALANCE DEBIT	BALANCE CREDIT
20-- July	1	Balance	✓			20 0 0 0 00	

ACCOUNT   Accounts Payable

ACCOUNT NO.   202

DATE		ITEM	POST. REF.	DEBIT	CREDIT	BALANCE DEBIT	BALANCE CREDIT

Problem 12-12A (Continued)

ACCOUNT   F. Flint, Drawing   ACCOUNT NO.   312

DATE	ITEM	POST. REF.	DEBIT	CREDIT	BALANCE DEBIT	BALANCE CREDIT

ACCOUNT   Purchases   ACCOUNT NO.   501

DATE	ITEM	POST. REF.	DEBIT	CREDIT	BALANCE DEBIT	BALANCE CREDIT

ACCOUNT   Purchases Returns and Allowances   ACCOUNT NO.   501.1

DATE	ITEM	POST. REF.	DEBIT	CREDIT	BALANCE DEBIT	BALANCE CREDIT

ACCOUNT   Purchases Discounts   ACCOUNT NO.   501.2

DATE	ITEM	POST. REF.	DEBIT	CREDIT	BALANCE DEBIT	BALANCE CREDIT

ACCOUNT   Rent Expense   ACCOUNT NO.   521

DATE	ITEM	POST. REF.	DEBIT	CREDIT	BALANCE DEBIT	BALANCE CREDIT

Problem 12-12A (Concluded)

ACCOUNTS PAYABLE LEDGER

NAME _____
ADDRESS _____

DATE	ITEM	POST. REF.	DEBIT	CREDIT	BALANCE

NAME _____
ADDRESS _____

DATE	ITEM	POST. REF.	DEBIT	CREDIT	BALANCE

NAME _____
ADDRESS _____

DATE	ITEM	POST. REF.	DEBIT	CREDIT	BALANCE

NAME _____
ADDRESS _____

DATE	ITEM	POST. REF.	DEBIT	CREDIT	BALANCE

Exercise 12-1B

Journal

a.   Issued credit memo to customer for merchandise returned.   _____

b.   Sold merchandise for cash.   _____

c.   Purchased merchandise on account.   _____

d.   Issued checks to employees in payment of wages.   _____

e.   Purchased factory supplies on account.   _____

f.   Sold merchandise on account.   _____

Exercise 12-2B

SALES JOURNAL

PAGE

DATE	SALE NO.	TO WHOM SOLD	POST. REF.	ACCOUNTS RECEIVABLE DEBIT	SALES CREDIT	SALES TAX PAYABLE CREDIT

Exercise 12-3B

CASH RECEIPTS JOURNAL

PAGE

DATE	ACCOUNT CREDITED	POST. REF.	GENERAL CREDIT	ACCOUNTS RECEIVABLE CREDIT	SALES CREDIT	SALES TAX PAYABLE CREDIT	CASH DEBIT	
1								1
2								2
3								3
4								4
5								5
6								6
7								7
8								8
9								9
10								10
11								11

Exercise 12-4B

PURCHASES JOURNAL

PAGE _____

	DATE	INVOICE NO.	FROM WHOM PURCHASED	POST. REF.	PURCHASES DEBIT ACCTS. PAY. CREDIT	
1						1
2						2
3						3
4						4
5						5
6						6
7						7
8						8
9						9
10						10
11						11

Exercise 12-5B

CASH PAYMENTS JOURNAL

PAGE _____

	DATE	CK. NO.	ACCOUNT DEBITED	POST. REF.	GENERAL DEBIT	ACCOUNTS PAYABLE DEBIT	PURCHASES DEBIT	PURCHASES DISCOUNTS CREDIT	CASH CREDIT	
1										1
2										2
3										3
4										4
5										5
6										6
7										7
8										8
9										9
10										10
11										11
12										12
13										13

Problem 12-6B

1.

				SALES JOURNAL					PAGE 8

DATE	SALE NO.	TO WHOM SOLD	POST. REF.	ACCOUNTS RECEIVABLE DEBIT	SALES CREDIT	SALES TAX PAYABLE CREDIT

2.

GENERAL LEDGER

ACCOUNT Accounts Receivable   ACCOUNT NO. 122

DATE	ITEM	POST. REF.	DEBIT	CREDIT	BALANCE DEBIT	BALANCE CREDIT

ACCOUNT Sales Tax Payable   ACCOUNT NO. 231

DATE	ITEM	POST. REF.	DEBIT	CREDIT	BALANCE DEBIT	BALANCE CREDIT

Problem 12-6B (Concluded)

ACCOUNT Sales

ACCOUNT NO. 401

DATE		ITEM	POST. REF.	DEBIT	CREDIT	BALANCE	
						DEBIT	CREDIT

ACCOUNTS RECEIVABLE LEDGER

NAME Dvorak Manufacturing Co.

ADDRESS 2105 Williams Drive, Muncie, IN 47304-2437

DATE		ITEM	POST. REF.	DEBIT	CREDIT	BALANCE

NAME Saga, Inc.

ADDRESS 1453 Parnell Avenue, Indianapolis, IN 46201-6870

DATE		ITEM	POST. REF.	DEBIT	CREDIT	BALANCE

NAME Vinnie Ward

ADDRESS 308 So. Muirhead Drive, Okemos, MI 48864-5356

DATE		ITEM	POST. REF.	DEBIT	CREDIT	BALANCE

NAME Zapata Co.

ADDRESS 789 N. Stafford Dr., Bloomington, IN 47401-6201

DATE		ITEM	POST. REF.	DEBIT	CREDIT	BALANCE

Problem 12-7B

1.

CASH RECEIPTS JOURNAL

	DATE		ACCOUNT CREDITED	POST. REF.	GENERAL CREDIT					ACCOUNTS RECEIVABLE CREDIT				
1														
2														
3														
4														
5														
6														
7														
8														
9														
10														
11														
12														
13														
14														
15														
16														
17														
18														
19														
20														
21														
22														
23														
24														
25														
26														
27														
28														

Problem 12-7B (Continued)

PAGE 10

	SALES CREDIT	SALES TAX PAYABLE CREDIT	BANK CREDIT CARD EXPENSE DEBIT	CASH DEBIT

Problem 12-7B (Continued)

GENERAL JOURNAL

PAGE 8

	DATE		DESCRIPTION	POST. REF.	DEBIT	CREDIT	
1							1
2							2
3							3
4							4
5							5
6							6
7							7
8							8
9							9
10							10
11							11
12							12
13							13
14							14
15							15
16							16
17							17
18							18
19							19
20							20
21							21
22							22
23							23
24							24
25							25
26							26
27							27
28							28
29							29
30							30
31							31
32							32
33							33
34							34

Problem 12-7B (Continued)

2.

GENERAL LEDGER

ACCOUNT Cash   ACCOUNT NO. 101

DATE		ITEM	POST. REF.	DEBIT	CREDIT	BALANCE	
						DEBIT	CREDIT
20-- Jan.	1	Balance	✓			2 8 9 0 75	

ACCOUNT Accounts Receivable   ACCOUNT NO. 122

DATE		ITEM	POST. REF.	DEBIT	CREDIT	BALANCE	
						DEBIT	CREDIT
20-- Jan.	1	Balance	✓			6 3 0 0 00	

ACCOUNT Sales Tax Payable   ACCOUNT NO. 231

DATE	ITEM	POST. REF.	DEBIT	CREDIT	BALANCE	
					DEBIT	CREDIT

ACCOUNT Sales   ACCOUNT NO. 401

DATE	ITEM	POST. REF.	DEBIT	CREDIT	BALANCE	
					DEBIT	CREDIT

Problem 12-7B (Continued)

ACCOUNT Sales Returns and Allowances   ACCOUNT NO. 401.1

DATE	ITEM	POST. REF.	DEBIT	CREDIT	BALANCE DEBIT	BALANCE CREDIT

ACCOUNT Bank Credit Card Expense   ACCOUNT NO. 513

DATE	ITEM	POST. REF.	DEBIT	CREDIT	BALANCE DEBIT	BALANCE CREDIT

ACCOUNTS RECEIVABLE LEDGER

NAME Ray Boyd
ADDRESS 229 SE 65th Avenue, Portland, OR 97215-1451

DATE	ITEM	POST. REF.	DEBIT	CREDIT	BALANCE
20-- Jan. 1	Balance	✓			1 4 0 0 00

NAME Dazai Manufacturing
ADDRESS 447 6th Avenue, Flagstaff, AZ 86004-6842

DATE	ITEM	POST. REF.	DEBIT	CREDIT	BALANCE
20-- Jan. 1	Balance	✓			3 1 8 00

Problem 12-7B (Concluded)

NAME Clint Hassell

ADDRESS 1462 N. Steves Blvd., Los Cruces, NM 88012-7791

DATE		ITEM	POST. REF.	DEBIT	CREDIT	BALANCE
20-- Jan.	1	Balance	✓			8 1 5 00

NAME Jan Sowada

ADDRESS 5997 Blackgold Lane, Grapevine, TX 76051-2366

DATE		ITEM	POST. REF.	DEBIT	CREDIT	BALANCE
20-- Jan.	1	Balance	✓			1 4 8 1 00

NAME Robert Zehnle

ADDRESS 6881 Seneca Drive, San Diego, CA 92127-8671

DATE		ITEM	POST. REF.	DEBIT	CREDIT	BALANCE
20-- Jan.	1	Balance	✓			2 2 8 6 00

Problem 12-8B

1.

SALES JOURNAL   PAGE 6

DATE	SALE NO.	TO WHOM SOLD	POST. REF.	ACCOUNTS RECEIVABLE DEBIT	SALES CREDIT	SALES TAX PAYABLE CREDIT

CASH RECEIPTS JOURNAL   PAGE 9

	DATE	ACCOUNT CREDITED	POST. REF.	GENERAL CREDIT	ACCOUNTS RECEIVABLE CREDIT	SALES CREDIT	SALES TAX PAYABLE CREDIT	CASH DEBIT	
1									1
2									2
3									3
4									4
5									5
6									6
7									7
8									8
9									9

Problem 12-8B (Continued)

GENERAL JOURNAL

PAGE 5

	DATE	DESCRIPTION	POST. REF.	DEBIT	CREDIT	
1						1
2						2
3						3
4						4
5						5
6						6
7						7
8						8
9						9
10						10
11						11
12						12
13						13
14						14

2.

GENERAL LEDGER

ACCOUNT   Cash   ACCOUNT NO.   101

DATE		ITEM	POST. REF.	DEBIT	CREDIT	BALANCE DEBIT	BALANCE CREDIT
20-- Apr.	1	Balance	✓			2 8 6 4 54	

ACCOUNT   Accounts Receivable   ACCOUNT NO.   122

DATE		ITEM	POST. REF.	DEBIT	CREDIT	BALANCE DEBIT	BALANCE CREDIT
20-- Apr.	1	Balance	✓			2 7 2 6 25	

Problem 12-8B (Continued)

ACCOUNT Sales Tax Payable ACCOUNT NO. 231

DATE	ITEM	POST. REF.	DEBIT	CREDIT	BALANCE	
					DEBIT	CREDIT

ACCOUNT Sales ACCOUNT NO. 401

DATE	ITEM	POST. REF.	DEBIT	CREDIT	BALANCE	
					DEBIT	CREDIT

ACCOUNT Sales Returns and Allowances ACCOUNT NO. 401.1

DATE	ITEM	POST. REF.	DEBIT	CREDIT	BALANCE	
					DEBIT	CREDIT

Problem 12-8B (Concluded)

ACCOUNTS RECEIVABLE LEDGER

NAME O. L. Meyers

ADDRESS 119 Hartford Turnpike, Vernon, CT 06066-0113

DATE		ITEM	POST. REF.	DEBIT	CREDIT	BALANCE
20-- Apr.	1	Balance	✓			2 1 8 6 00

NAME Kelsay Munkres

ADDRESS 233 Cambridge Dr., Branford, CT 06405-9276

DATE		ITEM	POST. REF.	DEBIT	CREDIT	BALANCE
20-- Apr.	1	Balance	✓			4 8 2 00

NAME Andrew Plaa

ADDRESS 51 Bissell Ave., Old Saybrook, CT 06475-0212

DATE		ITEM	POST. REF.	DEBIT	CREDIT	BALANCE

NAME Melissa Richfield

ADDRESS 1107 Silver Lane, East Hartford, CT 06108-1907

DATE		ITEM	POST. REF.	DEBIT	CREDIT	BALANCE
20-- Apr.	1	Balance	✓			5 8 25

Problem 12-9B

1.

| | | | PURCHASES JOURNAL | | PAGE 7 | | | | | |

PURCHASES JOURNAL   PAGE 7

	DATE	INVOICE NO.	FROM WHOM PURCHASED	POST. REF.	PURCHASES DEBIT ACCTS. PAY. CREDIT		
1							1
2							2
3							3
4							4
5							5
6							6
7							7
8							8
9							9
10							10
11							11
12							12
13							13
14							14

2.

GENERAL LEDGER

ACCOUNT   Accounts Payable   ACCOUNT NO. 202

DATE	ITEM	POST. REF.	DEBIT	CREDIT	BALANCE DEBIT	BALANCE CREDIT

ACCOUNT   Purchases   ACCOUNT NO. 501

DATE	ITEM	POST. REF.	DEBIT	CREDIT	BALANCE DEBIT	BALANCE CREDIT

Problem 12-9B (Concluded)

ACCOUNTS PAYABLE LEDGER

NAME

ADDRESS

DATE	ITEM	POST. REF.	DEBIT	CREDIT	BALANCE

NAME

ADDRESS

DATE	ITEM	POST. REF.	DEBIT	CREDIT	BALANCE

NAME

ADDRESS

DATE	ITEM	POST. REF.	DEBIT	CREDIT	BALANCE

NAME

ADDRESS

DATE	ITEM	POST. REF.	DEBIT	CREDIT	BALANCE

NAME

ADDRESS

DATE	ITEM	POST. REF.	DEBIT	CREDIT	BALANCE

Problem 12-10B

1.

GENERAL LEDGER

ACCOUNT   Accounts Payable   ACCOUNT NO.   202

DATE	ITEM	POST. REF.	DEBIT	CREDIT	BALANCE DEBIT	BALANCE CREDIT

ACCOUNT   Purchases   ACCOUNT NO.   501

DATE	ITEM	POST. REF.	DEBIT	CREDIT	BALANCE DEBIT	BALANCE CREDIT

2.

ACCOUNTS PAYABLE LEDGER

NAME

ADDRESS

DATE	ITEM	POST. REF.	DEBIT	CREDIT	BALANCE

NAME

ADDRESS

DATE	ITEM	POST. REF.	DEBIT	CREDIT	BALANCE

Problem 12-10B (Concluded)

NAME _____

ADDRESS _____

DATE	ITEM	POST. REF.	DEBIT	CREDIT	BALANCE

NAME _____

ADDRESS _____

DATE	ITEM	POST. REF.	DEBIT	CREDIT	BALANCE

NAME _____

ADDRESS _____

DATE	ITEM	POST. REF.	DEBIT	CREDIT	BALANCE

Problem 12-11B

1.

CASH PAYMENTS JOURNAL

PAGE 6

	DATE	CK. NO.	ACCOUNT DEBITED	POST. REF.	GENERAL DEBIT	ACCOUNTS PAYABLE DEBIT	PURCHASES DEBIT	PURCHASES DISCOUNTS CREDIT	CASH CREDIT	
1										1
2										2
3										3
4										4
5										5
6										6
7										7
8										8
9										9
10										10
11										11
12										12

2.

GENERAL LEDGER

ACCOUNT   Cash

ACCOUNT NO.   101

DATE		ITEM	POST. REF.	DEBIT	CREDIT	BALANCE DEBIT	BALANCE CREDIT
20-- May	1	Balance	✓			40 0 0 0 00	

ACCOUNT   Accounts Payable

ACCOUNT NO.   202

DATE		ITEM	POST. REF.	DEBIT	CREDIT	BALANCE DEBIT	BALANCE CREDIT
20-- May	1	Balance	✓				20 0 0 0 00

Problem 12-11B (Continued)

ACCOUNT   Purchases   ACCOUNT NO.   501

DATE	ITEM	POST. REF.	DEBIT	CREDIT	BALANCE	
					DEBIT	CREDIT

ACCOUNT   Purchases Discounts   ACCOUNT NO.   501.2

DATE	ITEM	POST. REF.	DEBIT	CREDIT	BALANCE	
					DEBIT	CREDIT

ACCOUNT   Freight-In   ACCOUNT NO.   502

DATE	ITEM	POST. REF.	DEBIT	CREDIT	BALANCE	
					DEBIT	CREDIT

ACCOUNT   Rent Expense   ACCOUNT NO.   521

DATE	ITEM	POST. REF.	DEBIT	CREDIT	BALANCE	
					DEBIT	CREDIT

ACCOUNT   Utilities Expense   ACCOUNT NO.   533

DATE	ITEM	POST. REF.	DEBIT	CREDIT	BALANCE	
					DEBIT	CREDIT

Problem 12-11B (Concluded)

ACCOUNTS PAYABLE LEDGER

NAME Cortez Distributors

ADDRESS

DATE		ITEM	POST. REF.	DEBIT	CREDIT	BALANCE
20-- May	1	Balance	✓			4 2 0 0 00

NAME Indra & Velga

ADDRESS

DATE		ITEM	POST. REF.	DEBIT	CREDIT	BALANCE
20-- May	1	Balance	✓			6 8 0 0 00

NAME Toy Corner

ADDRESS

DATE		ITEM	POST. REF.	DEBIT	CREDIT	BALANCE
20-- May	1	Balance	✓			4 6 0 0 00

NAME Troutman Outlet

ADDRESS

DATE		ITEM	POST. REF.	DEBIT	CREDIT	BALANCE
20-- May	1	Balance	✓			4 4 0 0 00

Problem 12-12B

1.

PURCHASES JOURNAL

	DATE	INVOICE NO.	FROM WHOM PURCHASED	POST. REF.	PURCHASES DEBIT ACCTS. PAY. CREDIT	
1						1
2						2
3						3
4						4
5						5
6						6
7						7
8						8
9						9
10						10

CASH PAYMENTS JOURNAL

	DATE	CK. NO.	ACCOUNT DEBITED	POST. REF.	GENERAL DEBIT	ACCOUNTS PAYABLE DEBIT	PURCHASES DEBIT	PURCHASES DISCOUNTS CREDIT	CASH CREDIT	
1										1
2										2
3										3
4										4
5										5
6										6
7										7
8										8
9										9
10										10
11										11
12										12

Problem 12-12B (Continued)

GENERAL JOURNAL

	DATE	DESCRIPTION	POST. REF.	DEBIT	CREDIT	
1						1
2						2
3						3
4						4
5						5
6						6
7						7
8						8
9						9
10						10

2.

GENERAL LEDGER

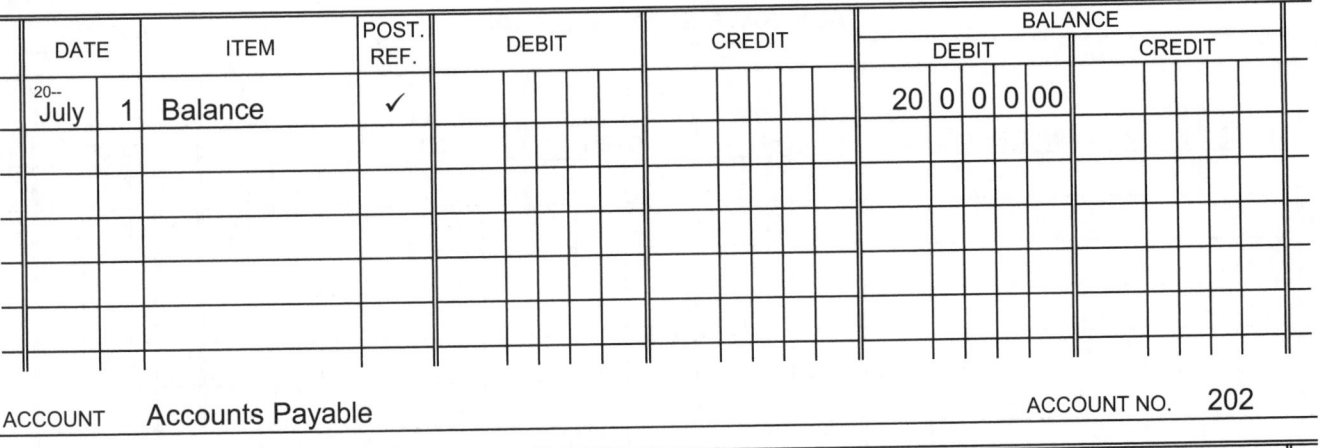

ACCOUNT Cash   ACCOUNT NO. 101

DATE		ITEM	POST. REF.	DEBIT	CREDIT	BALANCE DEBIT	BALANCE CREDIT
20-- July	1	Balance	✓			20 0 0 0 00	

ACCOUNT Accounts Payable   ACCOUNT NO. 202

DATE	ITEM	POST. REF.	DEBIT	CREDIT	BALANCE DEBIT	BALANCE CREDIT

Problem 12-12B (Continued)

ACCOUNT   D. Mueller, Drawing   ACCOUNT NO.   312

DATE	ITEM	POST. REF.	DEBIT	CREDIT	BALANCE	
					DEBIT	CREDIT

ACCOUNT   Purchases   ACCOUNT NO.   501

DATE	ITEM	POST. REF.	DEBIT	CREDIT	BALANCE	
					DEBIT	CREDIT

ACCOUNT   Purchases Returns and Allowances   ACCOUNT NO.   501.1

DATE	ITEM	POST. REF.	DEBIT	CREDIT	BALANCE	
					DEBIT	CREDIT

ACCOUNT   Purchases Discounts   ACCOUNT NO.   501.2

DATE	ITEM	POST. REF.	DEBIT	CREDIT	BALANCE	
					DEBIT	CREDIT

ACCOUNT   Rent Expense   ACCOUNT NO.   521

DATE	ITEM	POST. REF.	DEBIT	CREDIT	BALANCE	
					DEBIT	CREDIT

Problem 12-12B (Concluded)

ACCOUNTS PAYABLE LEDGER

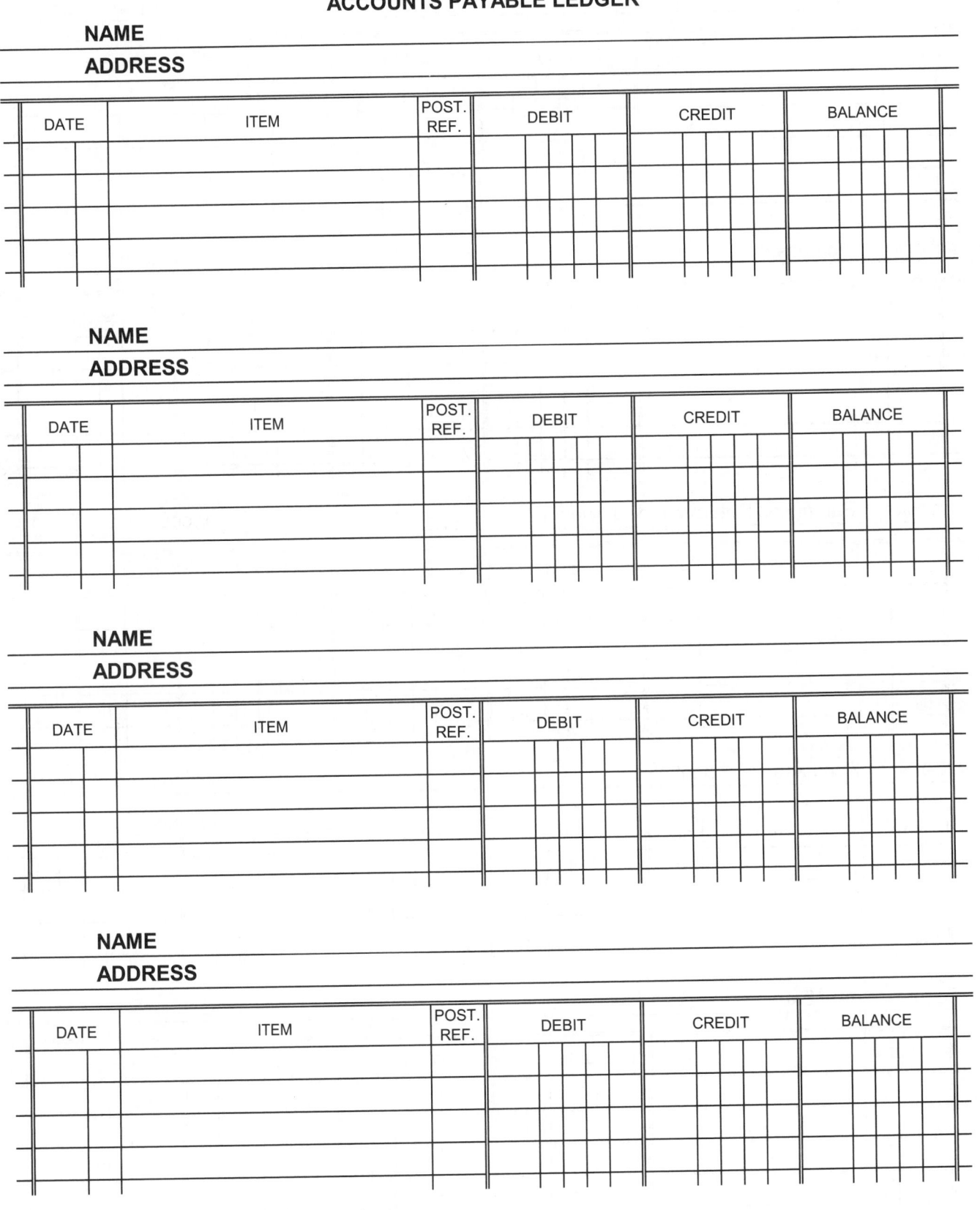

NAME

ADDRESS

DATE	ITEM	POST. REF.	DEBIT	CREDIT	BALANCE

NAME

ADDRESS

DATE	ITEM	POST. REF.	DEBIT	CREDIT	BALANCE

NAME

ADDRESS

DATE	ITEM	POST. REF.	DEBIT	CREDIT	BALANCE

NAME

ADDRESS

DATE	ITEM	POST. REF.	DEBIT	CREDIT	BALANCE

Mastery Problem

1.

SALES JOURNAL

	DATE	SALE NO.	TO WHOM SOLD	POST. REF.	ACCOUNTS RECEIVABLE DEBIT	SALES CREDIT	SALES TAX PAYABLE CREDIT	
1								1
2								2
3								3
4								4
5								5
6								6
7								7
8								8

CASH RECEIPTS JOURNAL

	DATE	ACCOUNT CREDITED	POST. REF.	GENERAL CREDIT	ACCOUNTS RECEIVABLE CREDIT	SALES CREDIT	SALES TAX PAYABLE CREDIT	CASH DEBIT	
1									1
2									2
3									3
4									4
5									5
6									6
7									7
8									8
9									9
10									10
11									11
12									12
13									13

Mastery Problem (Continued)

PURCHASES JOURNAL

PAGE 6

	DATE	INVOICE NO.	FROM WHOM PURCHASED	POST. REF.	PURCHASES DEBIT ACCTS. PAY. CREDIT	
1						1
2						2
3						3
4						4
5						5
6						6
7						7
8						8
9						9
10						10
11						11

CASH PAYMENTS JOURNAL

PAGE 11

	DATE	CK. NO.	ACCOUNT DEBITED	POST. REF.	GENERAL DEBIT	ACCOUNTS PAYABLE DEBIT	PURCHASES DEBIT	PURCHASES DISCOUNTS CREDIT	CASH CREDIT	
1										1
2										2
3										3
4										4
5										5
6										6
7										7
8										8
9										9
10										10
11										11
12										12
13										13

Mastery Problem (Continued)

GENERAL JOURNAL

PAGE 5

	DATE	DESCRIPTION	POST. REF.	DEBIT	CREDIT	
1						1
2						2
3						3
4						4
5						5
6						6
7						7
8						8
9						9
10						10
11						11
12						12

2.

GENERAL LEDGER

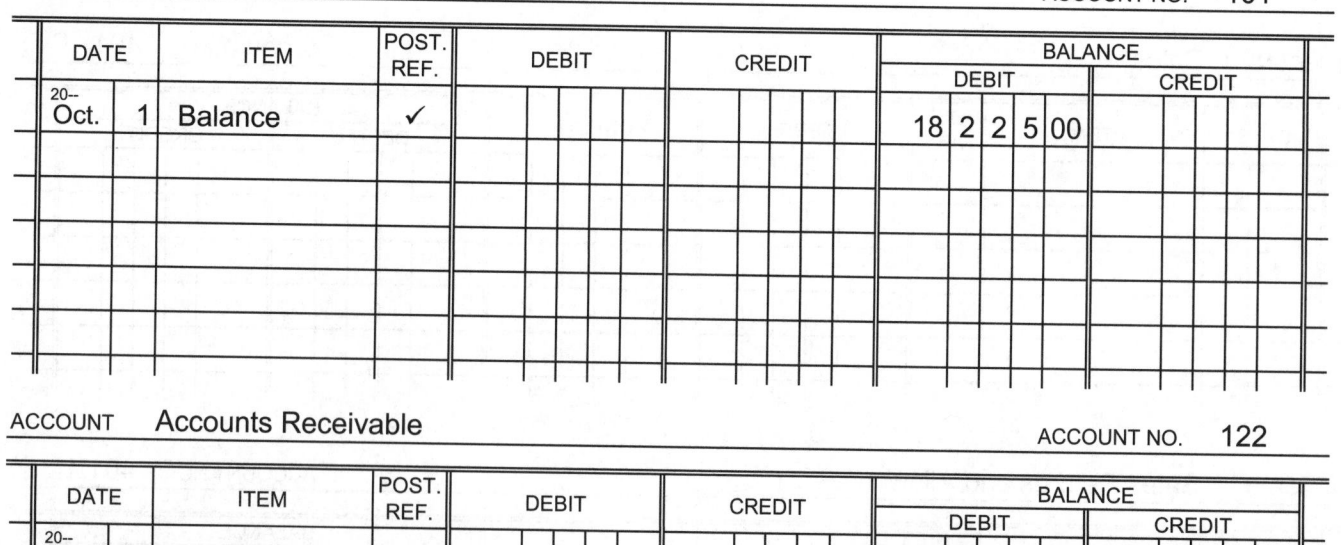

ACCOUNT Cash   ACCOUNT NO. 101

DATE		ITEM	POST. REF.	DEBIT	CREDIT	BALANCE DEBIT	BALANCE CREDIT
20-- Oct.	1	Balance	✓			18 2 2 5 00	

ACCOUNT Accounts Receivable   ACCOUNT NO. 122

DATE		ITEM	POST. REF.	DEBIT	CREDIT	BALANCE DEBIT	BALANCE CREDIT
20-- Oct.	1	Balance	✓			9 6 1 9 00	

Mastery Problem (Continued)

ACCOUNT Accounts Payable   ACCOUNT NO. 202

DATE	ITEM	POST. REF.	DEBIT	CREDIT	BALANCE DEBIT	BALANCE CREDIT
20-- Oct. 1	Balance	✓				5 1 2 0 00

ACCOUNT Sales Tax Payable   ACCOUNT NO. 231

DATE	ITEM	POST. REF.	DEBIT	CREDIT	BALANCE DEBIT	BALANCE CREDIT

ACCOUNT Sales   ACCOUNT NO. 401

DATE	ITEM	POST. REF.	DEBIT	CREDIT	BALANCE DEBIT	BALANCE CREDIT

ACCOUNT Sales Returns and Allowances   ACCOUNT NO. 401.1

DATE	ITEM	POST. REF.	DEBIT	CREDIT	BALANCE DEBIT	BALANCE CREDIT

Mastery Problem (Continued)

ACCOUNT Purchases   ACCOUNT NO. 501

DATE	ITEM	POST. REF.	DEBIT	CREDIT	BALANCE	
					DEBIT	CREDIT

ACCOUNT Purchases Returns and Allowances   ACCOUNT NO. 501.1

DATE	ITEM	POST. REF.	DEBIT	CREDIT	BALANCE	
					DEBIT	CREDIT

ACCOUNT Purchases Discounts   ACCOUNT NO. 501.2

DATE	ITEM	POST. REF.	DEBIT	CREDIT	BALANCE	
					DEBIT	CREDIT

ACCOUNT Wages Expense   ACCOUNT NO. 511

DATE	ITEM	POST. REF.	DEBIT	CREDIT	BALANCE	
					DEBIT	CREDIT

ACCOUNT Telephone Expense   ACCOUNT NO. 525

DATE	ITEM	POST. REF.	DEBIT	CREDIT	BALANCE	
					DEBIT	CREDIT

Mastery Problem (Continued)

ACCOUNTS RECEIVABLE LEDGER

NAME David's Decorating

ADDRESS 12 Jude Lane, Hartford, CT 06117

DATE		ITEM	POST. REF.	DEBIT	CREDIT	BALANCE
20-- Oct.	1	Balance	✓			3 3 4 0 00

NAME Meg Johnson

ADDRESS 700 Hobbes Dr., Avon, CT 06108

DATE		ITEM	POST. REF.	DEBIT	CREDIT	BALANCE
20-- Oct.	1	Balance	✓			4 0 0 0 00

NAME Elizabeth Shoemaker

ADDRESS 52 Juniper Road, Hartford, CT 06118

DATE		ITEM	POST. REF.	DEBIT	CREDIT	BALANCE
20-- Oct.	1	Balance	✓			2 7 9 00

NAME Leigh Summers

ADDRESS 5200 Hamilton Ave., Hartford, CT 06111

DATE		ITEM	POST. REF.	DEBIT	CREDIT	BALANCE
20-- Oct.	1	Balance	✓			2 0 0 0 00

Mastery Problem (Concluded)

ACCOUNTS PAYABLE LEDGER

NAME Flower Wholesalers

ADDRESS 43 Lucky Lane, Bristol, CT 06007

DATE		ITEM	POST. REF.	DEBIT	CREDIT	BALANCE
20-- Oct.	1	Balance	✓			1 5 0 0 00

NAME Jill Hand

ADDRESS 1009 Drake Rd., Farmington, CT 06082

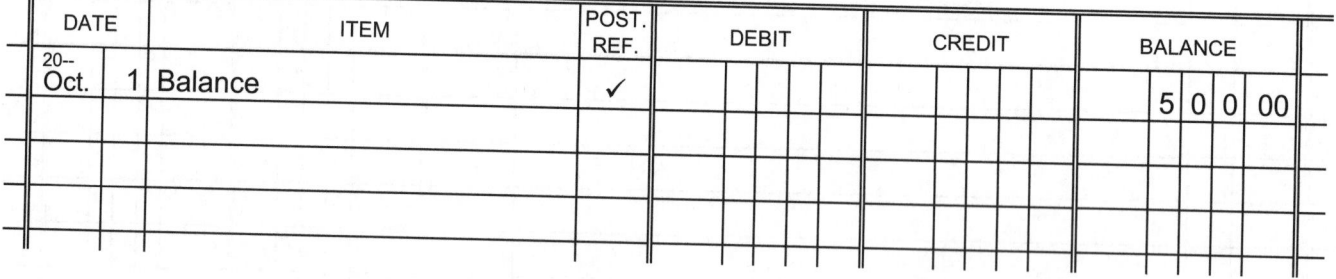

DATE		ITEM	POST. REF.	DEBIT	CREDIT	BALANCE
20-- Oct.	1	Balance	✓			5 0 0 00

NAME Seidl Enterprises

ADDRESS 888 Anders Street, Newington, CT 06789

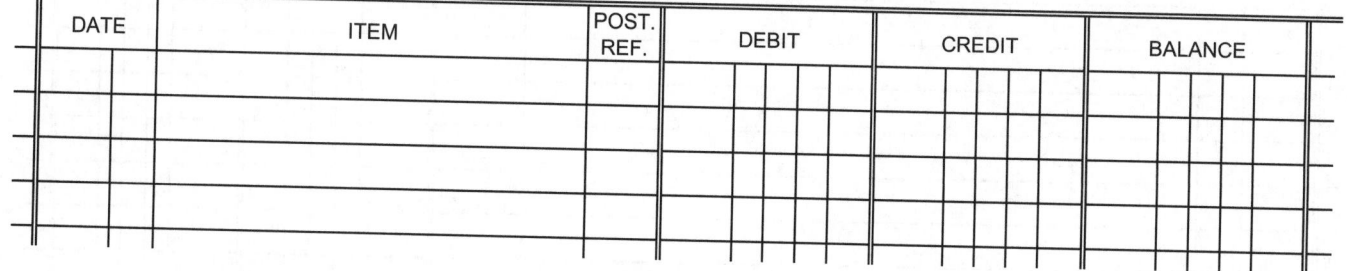

DATE		ITEM	POST. REF.	DEBIT	CREDIT	BALANCE

NAME Vases Etc.

ADDRESS 34 Harry Ave., East Hartford, CT 05234

DATE		ITEM	POST. REF.	DEBIT	CREDIT	BALANCE
20-- Oct.	1	Balance	✓			3 1 2 0 00

Challenge Problem

1.

GENERAL JOURNAL

PAGE

	DATE	DESCRIPTION	POST. REF.	DEBIT	CREDIT	
1						1
2						2
3						3
4						4
5						5
6						6
7						7
8						8
9						9
10						10
11						11
12						12
13						13
14						14
15						15
16						16
17						17
18						18
19						19
20						20
21						21
22						22
23						23
24						24
25						25
26						26
27						27
28						28
29						29
30						30
31						31
32						32
33						33
34						34

Challenge Problem (Continued)

GENERAL JOURNAL

PAGE _____

DATE	DESCRIPTION	POST. REF.	DEBIT	CREDIT	
					1
					2
					3
					4
					5
					6
					7
					8
					9
					10
					11
					12
					13
					14
					15
					16
					17
					18
					19
					20
					21
					22
					23
					24
					25
					26
					27
					28
					29
					30
					31
					32
					33
					34

Challenge Problem (Continued)

GENERAL JOURNAL

PAGE

	DATE	DESCRIPTION	POST. REF.	DEBIT	CREDIT	
1						1
2						2
3						3
4						4
5						5
6						6
7						7
8						8
9						9
10						10
11						11
12						12
13						13
14						14
15						15
16						16
17						17
18						18
19						19
20						20
21						21
22						22
23						23
24						24
25						25
26						26
27						27
28						28
29						29
30						30
31						31
32						32
33						33
34						34

Challenge Problem (Concluded)

2.

SALES JOURNAL

PAGE

CASH RECEIPTS JOURNAL

PAGE

PURCHASES JOURNAL

PAGE

CASH PAYMENTS JOURNAL

PAGE

Exercise 13-1A

	Year 1	Year 2
Ending merchandise inventory	_____	_____
Beginning merchandise inventory	_____	_____
Cost of goods sold	_____	_____
Gross profit	_____	_____
Net income	_____	_____
Ending owner's capital	_____	_____

Exercise 13-2A

GENERAL JOURNAL

PAGE ____

	DATE		DESCRIPTION	POST. REF.	DEBIT	CREDIT	
1							1
2							2
3							3
4							4
5							5
6							6
7							7
8							8
9							9
10							10
11							11
12							12
13							13
14							14
15							15
16							16
17							17
18							18
19							19
20							20
21							21
22							22
23							23

Exercise 13-3A

GENERAL JOURNAL   PAGE

	DATE	DESCRIPTION	POST. REF.	DEBIT	CREDIT	
1						1
2						2
3						3
4						4
5						5
6						6
7						7
8						8
9						9
10						10
11						11
12						12
13						13
14						14
15						15
16						16
17						17
18						18
19						19
20						20
21						21
22						22
23						23

Exercise 13-4A

Name _____

Exercise 13-5A

Problem 13-6A

1. FIFO Inventory Method

Date 20-1/ 20-2		Cost of Goods Sold			Cost of Ending Inventory		
		Units	Unit Price	Total	Units	Unit Price	Total

2. LIFO Inventory Method

Date 20-1/ 20-2		Cost of Goods Sold			Cost of Ending Inventory		
		Units	Unit Price	Total	Units	Unit Price	Total

Problem 13-6A (Concluded)

3. _____

_____

_____

_____

_____

_____

_____

_____

_____

_____

_____

_____

_____

_____

_____

_____

_____

_____

_____

4. **Specific Identification Method**

Date 20-1/ 20-2		Cost of Goods Sold			Cost of Ending Inventory		
		Units	Unit Price	Total	Units	Unit Price	Total

Problem 13-7A

1.

a. FIFO Inventory Method

Date 20--		Cost of Goods Sold			Cost of Ending Inventory		
		Units	Unit Price	Total	Units	Unit Price	Total

b. LIFO Inventory Method

Date 20--		Cost of Goods Sold			Cost of Ending Inventory		
		Units	Unit Price	Total	Units	Unit Price	Total

Problem 13-7A (Concluded)

Problem 13-8A

Problem 13-9A

1. and 2.

	Cost	Retail

Exercise 13-1B

	Year 1	Year 2
Ending merchandise inventory		
Beginning merchandise inventory		
Cost of goods sold		
Gross profit		
Net income		
Ending owner's capital		

Exercise 13-2B

GENERAL JOURNAL

	DATE		DESCRIPTION	POST. REF.	DEBIT	CREDIT	
1							1
2							2
3							3
4							4
5							5
6							6
7							7
8							8
9							9
10							10
11							11
12							12
13							13
14							14
15							15
16							16
17							17
18							18
19							19
20							20
21							21
22							22
23							23
24							24
25							25
26							26
27							27
28							28
29							29
30							30
31							31
32							32
33							33
34							34
35							35

Exercise 13-3B

	GENERAL JOURNAL				PAGE

	DATE		DESCRIPTION	POST. REF.	DEBIT	CREDIT	
1							1
2							2
3							3
4							4
5							5
6							6
7							7
8							8
9							9
10							10
11							11
12							12
13							13
14							14
15							15
16							16
17							17
18							18
19							19
20							20
21							21
22							22
23							23

Exercise 13-4B

Name _____

Exercise 13-5B

Problem 13-6B

1. FIFO Inventory Method

Date 20-1/ 20-2		Cost of Goods Sold Unit			Cost of Ending Inventory Unit		
		Units	Price	Total	Units	Price	Total

2. LIFO Inventory Method

Date 20-1/ 20-2		Cost of Goods Sold Unit			Cost of Ending Inventory Unit		
		Units	Price	Total	Units	Price	Total

Problem 13-6B (Concluded)

3. _____

_____

_____

_____

_____

_____

_____

_____

_____

_____

_____

_____

_____

_____

4. Specific Identification Method

Date 20-1/ 20-2		Cost of Goods Sold	Unit		Cost of Ending Inventory	Unit	
		Units	Price	Total	Units	Price	Total

Problem 13-7B

1.

a. FIFO Inventory Method

Date 20--		Cost of Goods Sold			Cost of Ending Inventory		
		Units	Unit Price	Total	Units	Unit Price	Total

b. LIFO Inventory Method

Date 20--		Cost of Goods Sold			Cost of Ending Inventory		
		Units	Unit Price	Total	Units	Unit Price	Total

Problem 13-7B (Concluded)

Problem 13-8B

Problem 13-9B

1. and 2.

	Cost	Retail

Mastery Problem

1.

a. FIFO Inventory Method

Date 20-2		Cost of Goods Sold			Cost of Ending Inventory		
		Units	Unit Price	Total	Units	Unit Price	Total

b. LIFO Inventory Method

Date 20-2		Cost of Goods Sold			Cost of Ending Inventory		
		Units	Unit Price	Total	Units	Unit Price	Total

Mastery Problem (Concluded)

Challenge Problem

20-1	FIFO			LIFO		
	Units	Cost/Unit	Cost	Units	Cost/Unit	Cost

Details of Cost of Goods Sold 20-1	FIFO			LIFO		
	Units	Cost/Unit	Cost	Units	Cost/Unit	Cost

Challenge Problem (Concluded)

20-2	FIFO Units	FIFO Cost/Unit	FIFO Cost	LIFO Units	LIFO Cost/Unit	LIFO Cost

Details of Cost of Goods Sold 20-2	FIFO Units	FIFO Cost/Unit	FIFO Cost	LIFO Units	LIFO Cost/Unit	LIFO Cost

APPENDIX: PERPETUAL INVENTORY METHOD: LIFO AND MOVING-AVERAGE METHODS

Exercise 13Apx-1A

1. Perpetual LIFO

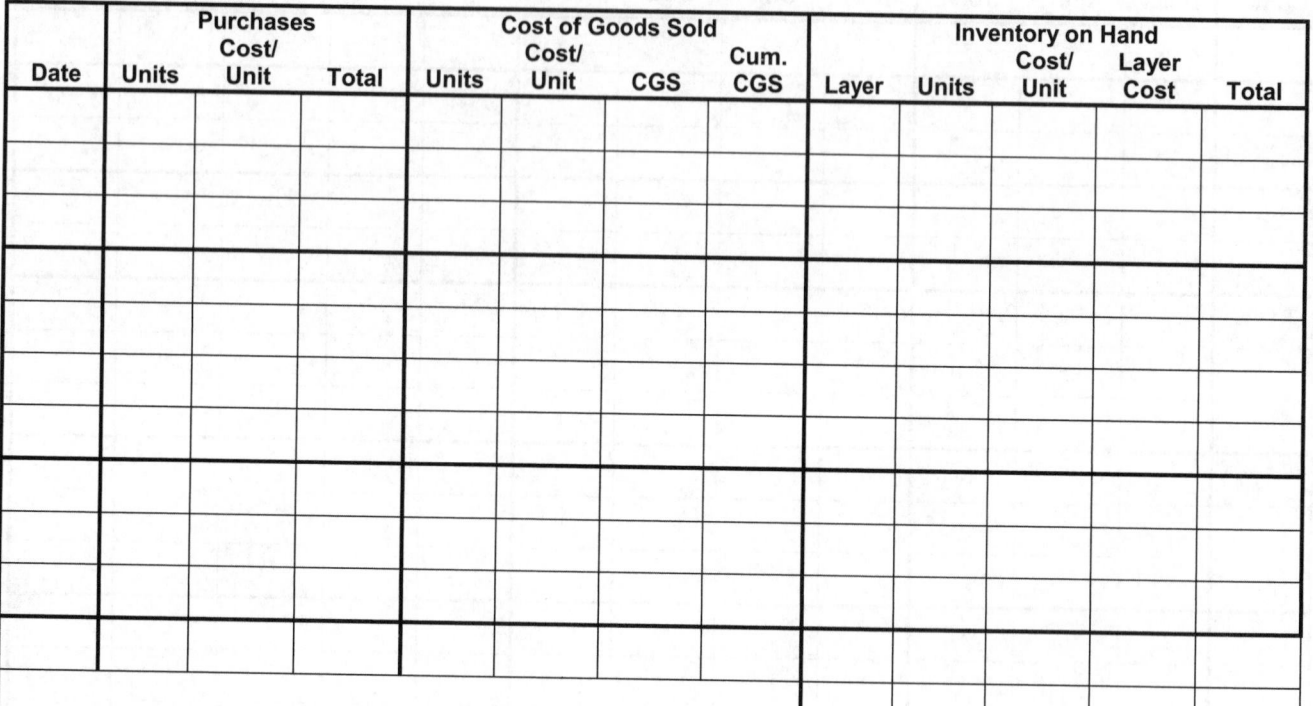

Date	Purchases Units	Purchases Cost/ Unit	Purchases Total	Cost of Goods Sold Units	Cost of Goods Sold Cost/ Unit	Cost of Goods Sold CGS	Cost of Goods Sold Cum. CGS	Inventory on Hand Layer	Inventory on Hand Units	Inventory on Hand Cost/ Unit	Inventory on Hand Layer Cost	Inventory on Hand Total

2. Perpetual Moving-Average

Date	Purchases Units	Purchases Cost/ Unit	Purchases Total	Cost of Goods Sold Units	Cost of Goods Sold Cost/ Unit	Cost of Goods Sold CGS	Cost of Goods Sold Cum. CGS	Inventory on Hand and Average Cost per Unit Cost of Purchase or (Sale)	Cost of Inventory on Hand	Units on Hand	Average Cost/ Unit

Problem 13Apx-2A

1. Perpetual LIFO

Date	Purchases			Cost of Goods Sold				Inventory on Hand				
	Units	Cost/ Unit	Total	Units	Cost/ Unit	CGS	Cum. CGS	Layer	Units	Cost/ Unit	Layer Cost	Total

Problem 13Apx-2A (Concluded)

2. Perpetual Moving-Average

Date	Purchases			Cost of Goods Sold				Inventory on Hand and Average Cost per Unit			
	Units	Cost/ Unit	Total	Units	Cost/ Unit	CGS	Cum. CGS	Cost of Purchase or (Sale)	Cost of Inventory on Hand	Units on Hand	Average Cost/ Unit

Exercise 13Apx-1B

1. Perpetual LIFO

Date	Purchases			Cost of Goods Sold				Inventory on Hand				
	Units	Cost/ Unit	Total	Units	Cost/ Unit	CGS	Cum. CGS	Layer	Units	Cost/ Unit	Layer Cost	Total

2. Perpetual Moving-Average

Date	Purchases			Cost of Goods Sold				Inventory on Hand and Average Cost per Unit			
	Units	Cost/ Unit	Total	Units	Cost/ Unit	CGS	Cum. CGS	Cost of Purchase or (Sale)	Cost of Inventory on Hand	Units on Hand	Average Cost/ Unit

Problem 13Apx-2B

1. Perpetual LIFO

Date	Purchases			Cost of Goods Sold					Inventory on Hand				
	Units	Cost/ Unit	Total	Units	Cost/ Unit	CGS	Cum. CGS		Layer	Units	Cost/ Unit	Layer Cost	Total

Problem 13Apx-2B (Concluded)

2. Perpetual Moving-Average

Date	Purchases			Cost of Goods Sold				Inventory on Hand and Average Cost per Unit		
	Units	Cost/ Unit	Total	Units	Cost/ Unit	CGS	Cum. CGS	Cost of Purchase or (Sale)	Cost of Inventory on Hand	Units on Hand	Average Cost/ Unit

Exercise 14-1A

Merchandise Inventory	Income Summary

Exercise 14-2A

Exercise 14-3A

Cash	Unearned Ticket Revenue

Ticket Revenue

Exercise 14-4A

1., 2., and 3.

Kevin's

Work

For Year Ended

	ACCOUNT TITLE	TRIAL BALANCE										ADJUSTMENTS										
		DEBIT					CREDIT					DEBIT					CREDIT					
1	Merchandise Inventory	40	0	0	0	00																
12	Income Summary																					
13	Purchases	90	0	0	0	00																
14	Purchases Returns and Allow.						2	0	0	0	00											
15	Purchases Discounts						3	0	0	0	00											
16	Freight-In		5	0	0	00																
17																						
18																						

Exercise 14-4A (Concluded)

Gift Shop

Sheet (Partial)

December 31, 20--

ADJUSTED TRIAL BALANCE		INCOME STATEMENT		BALANCE SHEET		
DEBIT	CREDIT	DEBIT	CREDIT	DEBIT	CREDIT	
						1
						12
						13
						14
						15
						16
						17
						18

4.

Exercise 14-5A

Exercise 14-6A

GENERAL JOURNAL   PAGE ____

	DATE	DESCRIPTION	POST. REF.	DEBIT	CREDIT	
1						1
2						2
3						3
4						4
5						5
6						6
7						7
8						8
9						9
10						10
11						11
12						12
13						13
14						14
15						15
16						16
17						17
18						18
19						19
20						20
21						21
22						22
23						23
24						24
25						25
26						26
27						27

Exercise 14-7A

GENERAL JOURNAL

PAGE _____

	DATE		DESCRIPTION	POST. REF.	DEBIT	CREDIT	
1							1
2							2
3							3
4							4
5							5
6							6
7							7
8							8
9							9
10							10
11							11
12							12
13							13
14							14
15							15
16							16
17							17
18							18
19							19

Exercise 14-8A

GENERAL JOURNAL

PAGE _____

	DATE		DESCRIPTION	POST. REF.	DEBIT	CREDIT	
1							1
2							2
3							3
4							4
5							5
6							6
7							7
8							8
9							9
10							10
11							11

Problem 14-9A

1. and 2.

Venice Beach

Work

For Year Ended

	ACCOUNT TITLE	TRIAL BALANCE DEBIT					TRIAL BALANCE CREDIT					ADJUSTMENTS DEBIT					ADJUSTMENTS CREDIT					
1	Cash	20	0	0	0	00																
2	Accounts Receivable	14	0	0	0	00																
3	Merchandise Inventory	25	0	0	0	00																
4	Supplies	8	0	0	0	00																
5	Prepaid Insurance	5	4	0	0	00																
6	Land	30	0	0	0	00																
7	Building	50	0	0	0	00																
8	Accumulated Depr.—Building						20	0	0	0	00											
9	Store Equipment	35	0	0	0	00																
10	Accumulated Depr.—Store Equip.						14	0	0	0	00											
11	Accounts Payable						9	6	0	0	00											
12	Wages Payable																					
13	Sales Tax Payable						5	9	0	0	00											
14	Unearned Rent Revenue						8	9	0	0	00											
15	Mortgage Payable						45	0	0	0	00											
16	M. Young, Capital						65	4	1	0	00											
17	M. Young, Drawing	26	0	0	0	00																
18	Income Summary																					
19	Sales						118	0	0	0	00											
20	Sales Returns and Allowances	1	7	0	0	00																
21	Rent Revenue																					
22	Purchases	27	0	0	0	00																
23	Purchases Returns and Allow.						1	4	0	0	00											
24	Purchases Discounts						1	8	0	0	00											
25	Freight-In	2	1	0	0	00																
26	Wages Expense	32	0	0	0	00																
27	Advertising Expense	3	6	0	0	00																
28	Supplies Expense																					
29	Telephone Expense	1	3	5	0	00																
30	Utilities Expense	8	0	0	0	00																
31	Insurance Expense																					
32	Depreciation Expense—Building																					
33	Depreciation Exp.—Store Equip.																					
34	Miscellaneous Expense		8	6	0	00																
35		290	0	1	0	00	290	0	1	0	00											
36																						
37																						
38																						

Problem 14-9A (Continued)

Kite Shop

Sheet

December 31, 20--

ADJUSTED TRIAL BALANCE		INCOME STATEMENT		BALANCE SHEET		
DEBIT	CREDIT	DEBIT	CREDIT	DEBIT	CREDIT	
						1
						2
						3
						4
						5
						6
						7
						8
						9
						10
						11
						12
						13
						14
						15
						16
						17
						18
						19
						20
						21
						22
						23
						24
						25
						26
						27
						28
						29
						30
						31
						32
						33
						34
						35
						36
						37
						38

Problem 14-9A (Concluded)

3.

GENERAL JOURNAL   PAGE

	DATE	DESCRIPTION	POST. REF.	DEBIT	CREDIT	
1						1
2						2
3						3
4						4
5						5
6						6
7						7
8						8
9						9
10						10
11						11
12						12
13						13
14						14
15						15
16						16
17						17
18						18
19						19
20						20
21						21
22						22
23						23
24						24
25						25
26						26
27						27
28						28
29						29
30						30
31						31
32						32
33						33
34						34

Problem 14-10A
1. and 2. (See pages 518 and 519.)
3.

GENERAL JOURNAL

PAGE

	DATE		DESCRIPTION	POST. REF.	DEBIT	CREDIT	
1							1
2							2
3							3
4							4
5							5
6							6
7							7
8							8
9							9
10							10
11							11
12							12
13							13
14							14
15							15
16							16
17							17
18							18
19							19
20							20
21							21
22							22
23							23
24							24
25							25
26							26
27							27
28							28
29							29
30							30
31							31
32							32
33							33
34							34

Problem 14-10A (Continued)

1. and 2.

Cascade Bicycle
Work
For Year Ended

	ACCOUNT TITLE	TRIAL BALANCE DEBIT					TRIAL BALANCE CREDIT					ADJUSTMENTS DEBIT					ADJUSTMENTS CREDIT					
1	Cash	23	0	0	0	00																
2	Accounts Receivable	15	0	0	0	00																
3	Merchandise Inventory	31	0	0	0	00																
4	Supplies	7	2	0	0	00																
5	Prepaid Insurance	4	6	0	0	00																
6	Land	28	0	0	0	00																
7	Building	53	0	0	0	00																
8	Accumulated Depr.—Building						17	0	0	0	00											
9	Store Equipment	27	0	0	0	00																
10	Accumulated Depr.—Store Equip.						9	0	0	0	00											
11	Accounts Payable						3	8	0	0	00											
12	Wages Payable																					
13	Sales Tax Payable						3	0	5	0	00											
14	Unearned Storage Revenue						5	6	0	0	00											
15	Mortgage Payable						42	0	0	0	00											
16	D. Lamond, Capital						165	7	6	0	00											
17	D. Lamond, Drawing	33	0	0	0	00																
18	Income Summary																					
19	Sales						51	0	0	0	00											
20	Sales Returns and Allowances	2	4	0	0	00																
21	Storage Revenue																					
22	Purchases	21	0	0	0	00																
23	Purchases Returns and Allow.						1	3	0	0	00											
24	Purchases Discounts						1	9	0	0	00											
25	Freight-In	1	8	0	0	00																
26	Wages Expense	35	0	0	0	00																
27	Advertising Expense	5	7	0	0	00																
28	Supplies Expense																					
29	Telephone Expense	2	2	0	0	00																
30	Utilities Expense	9	6	0	0	00																
31	Insurance Expense																					
32	Depreciation Expense—Building																					
33	Depreciation Exp.—Store Equip.																					
34	Miscellaneous Expense		9	1	0	00																
35		300	4	1	0	00	300	4	1	0	00											
36																						
37																						
38																						

Problem 14-10A (Concluded)

Shop _____

Sheet _____

December 31, 20-- _____

	ADJUSTED TRIAL BALANCE		INCOME STATEMENT		BALANCE SHEET		
	DEBIT	CREDIT	DEBIT	CREDIT	DEBIT	CREDIT	
							1
							2
							3
							4
							5
							6
							7
							8
							9
							10
							11
							12
							13
							14
							15
							16
							17
							18
							19
							20
							21
							22
							23
							24
							25
							26
							27
							28
							29
							30
							31
							32
							33
							34
							35
							36
							37
							38

Problem 14-11A

1.

Stark Street Computers

Work Sheet (Partial)

For Year Ended December 31, 20--

	ACCOUNT TITLE	TRIAL BALANCE DEBIT	TRIAL BALANCE CREDIT	ADJUSTMENTS DEBIT	ADJUSTMENTS CREDIT	ADJUSTED TRIAL BALANCE DEBIT	ADJUSTED TRIAL BALANCE CREDIT	
1	Cash	18 0 0 0 00				18 0 0 0 00		1
2	Accounts Receivable	11 0 0 0 00				11 0 0 0 00		2
3	Merchandise Inventory	25 0 0 0 00				35 0 0 0 00		3
4	Supplies	8 0 0 0 00				2 8 2 0 00		4
5	Prepaid Insurance	5 4 0 0 00				1 2 2 5 00		5
6	Land	27 0 0 0 00				27 0 0 0 00		6
7	Building	48 0 0 0 00				48 0 0 0 00		7
8	Accum. Depr.—Building		20 0 0 0 00				27 0 0 0 00	8
9	Store Equipment	33 0 0 0 00				33 0 0 0 00		9
10	Accum. Depr.—Store Equip.		8 7 0 0 00				12 8 0 0 00	10
11	Accounts Payable		6 4 0 0 00				6 4 0 0 00	11
12	Wages Payable						1 3 0 0 00	12
13	Sales Tax Payable		5 7 0 0 00				5 7 0 0 00	13
14	Unearned Repair Rev.		8 2 0 0 00				1 8 0 0 00	14
15	Mortgage Payable		44 0 0 0 00				44 0 0 0 00	15
16	L. Cowart, Capital		80 0 2 5 00				80 0 2 5 00	16
17	L. Cowart, Drawing	35 0 0 0 00				35 0 0 0 00		17
18	Income Summary					25 0 0 0 00	35 0 0 0 00	18
19	Sales		122 0 0 0 00				122 0 0 0 00	19
20	Sales Returns and Allow.	2 2 5 0 00				2 2 5 0 00		20
21	Repair Revenue						6 4 0 0 00	21
22	Purchases	29 7 5 0 00				29 7 5 0 00		22
23	Purchases Ret. and Allow.		1 8 5 0 00				1 8 5 0 00	23
24	Purchases Discounts		1 4 2 5 00				1 4 2 5 00	24
25	Freight-In	3 2 0 0 00				3 2 0 0 00		25
26	Wages Expense	37 0 0 0 00				38 3 0 0 00		26
27	Advertising Expense	4 1 2 5 00				4 1 2 5 00		27
28	Supplies Expense					5 1 8 0 00		28
29	Telephone Expense	1 6 5 0 00				1 6 5 0 00		29
30	Utilities Expense	9 1 5 0 00				9 1 5 0 00		30
31	Insurance Expense					4 1 7 5 00		31
32	Depr. Exp.—Building					7 0 0 0 00		32
33	Depr. Exp.—Store Equip.					4 1 0 0 00		33
34	Miscellaneous Expense	7 7 5 00				7 7 5 00		34
35		298 3 0 0 00	298 3 0 0 00			345 7 0 0 00	345 7 0 0 00	35
36								36
37								37
38								38

Problem 14-11A (Concluded)

2.

GENERAL JOURNAL   PAGE _____

	DATE	DESCRIPTION	POST. REF.	DEBIT	CREDIT	
1						1
2						2
3						3
4						4
5						5
6						6
7						7
8						8
9						9
10						10
11						11
12						12
13						13
14						14
15						15
16						16
17						17
18						18
19						19
20						20
21						21
22						22
23						23
24						24
25						25
26						26
27						27
28						28
29						29
30						30
31						31
32						32
33						33
34						34
35						35

Problem 14-12A

1.

Lewis Music

Work

For Year Ended

	ACCOUNT TITLE	TRIAL BALANCE										ADJUSTMENTS									
		DEBIT					CREDIT					DEBIT					CREDIT				
1	Cash	27	0	0	0	00															
2	Accounts Receivable	13	3	0	0	00															
3	Merchandise Inventory	34	0	0	0	00															
4	Supplies	5	3	0	0	00															
5	Prepaid Insurance	6	1	0	0	00															
6	Land	31	0	0	0	00															
7	Building	52	0	0	0	00															
8	Accumulated Depr.—Building						17	0	0	0	00										
9	Store Equipment	39	0	0	0	00															
10	Accumulated Depr.—Store Equip.						11	9	0	0	00										
11	Accounts Payable						6	2	5	0	00										
12	Wages Payable																				
13	Sales Tax Payable						6	2	0	0	00										
14	Unearned Rent Revenue						7	4	0	0	00										
15	Mortgage Payable						46	0	0	0	00										
16	H. Lewis, Capital						111	6	2	0	00										
17	H. Lewis, Drawing	37	0	0	0	00															
18	Income Summary																				
19	Sales						136	0	0	0	00										
20	Sales Returns and Allowances	3	5	0	0	00															
21	Rent Revenue																				
22	Purchases	39	0	0	0	00															
23	Purchases Returns and Allow.						2	5	3	0	00										
24	Purchases Discounts						1	9	7	5	00										
25	Freight-In	2	6	5	0	00															
26	Wages Expense	42	0	0	0	00															
27	Advertising Expense	4	1	7	5	00															
28	Supplies Expense																				
29	Telephone Expense	1	9	8	0	00															
30	Utilities Expense	7	9	4	5	00															
31	Insurance Expense																				
32	Depreciation Expense—Building																				
33	Depreciation Exp.—Store Equip.																				
34	Miscellaneous Expense		9	2	5	00															
35		346	8	7	5	00	346	8	7	5	00										
36	Net Income																				
37																					
38																					

Problem 14-12A (Continued)

Store _____

Sheet _____

December 31, 20--

	ADJUSTED TRIAL BALANCE		INCOME STATEMENT		BALANCE SHEET		
	DEBIT	CREDIT	DEBIT	CREDIT	DEBIT	CREDIT	
1					27 0 0 0 00		
2					13 3 0 0 00		
3					38 0 0 0 00		
4					1 5 0 0 00		
5					1 7 8 5 00		
6					31 0 0 0 00		
7					52 0 0 0 00		
8						21 1 4 5 00	
9					39 0 0 0 00		
10						14 8 7 5 00	
11						6 2 5 0 00	
12						8 7 5 00	
13						6 2 0 0 00	
14						3 1 7 5 00	
15						46 0 0 0 00	
16						111 6 2 0 00	
17					37 0 0 0 00		
18			34 0 0 0 00	38 0 0 0 00			
19				136 0 0 0 00			
20			3 5 0 0 00				
21				4 2 2 5 00			
22			39 0 0 0 00				
23				2 5 3 0 00			
24				1 9 7 5 00			
25			2 6 5 0 00				
26			42 8 7 5 00				
27			4 1 7 5 00				
28			3 8 0 0 00				
29			1 9 8 0 00				
30			7 9 4 5 00				
31			4 3 1 5 00				
32			4 1 4 5 00				
33			2 9 7 5 00				
34			9 2 5 00				
35			152 2 8 5 00	182 7 3 0 00	240 5 8 5 00	210 1 4 0 00	
36			30 4 4 5 00			30 4 4 5 00	
37			182 7 3 0 00	182 7 3 0 00	240 5 8 5 00	240 5 8 5 00	
38							

Problem 14-12A (Continued)

2.

GENERAL JOURNAL

PAGE

DATE	DESCRIPTION	POST. REF.	DEBIT	CREDIT
1				
2				
3				
4				
5				
6				
7				
8				
9				
10				
11				
12				
13				
14				
15				
16				
17				
18				
19				
20				
21				
22				
23				
24				
25				
26				
27				
28				
29				
30				
31				
32				
33				
34				

Problem 14-12A (Concluded)

3.

Exercise 14-1B

Merchandise Inventory	Income Summary

Exercise 14-2B

Exercise 14-3B

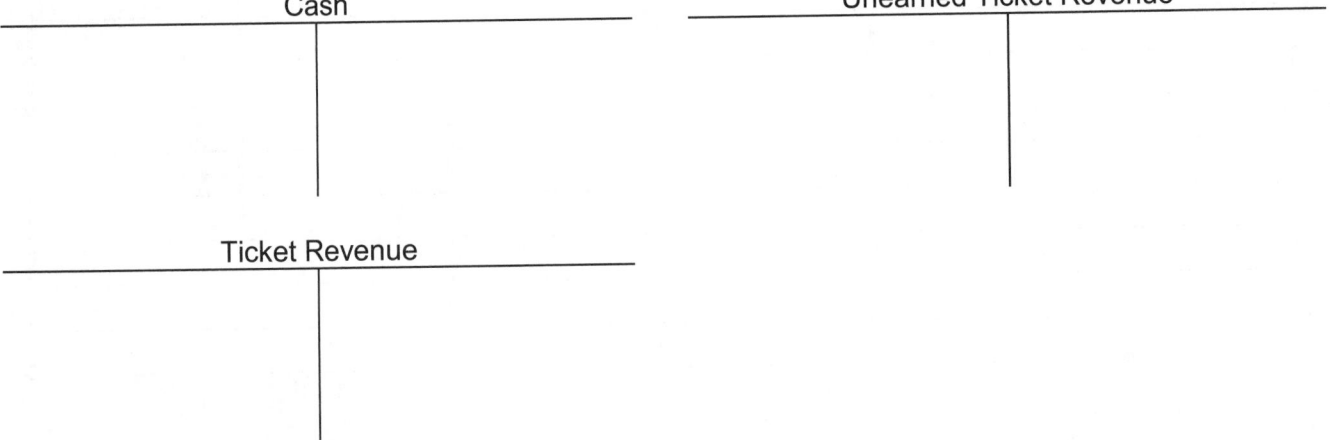

Cash	Unearned Ticket Revenue

Ticket Revenue

Exercise 14-4B

1., 2., 3., and 4. (See pages 528 and 529.)

Exercise 14-5B

_____

_____

_____

_____

Exercise 14-6B

GENERAL JOURNAL

PAGE

	DATE		DESCRIPTION	POST. REF.	DEBIT	CREDIT	
1							1
2							2
3							3
4							4
5							5
6							6
7							7
8							8
9							9
10							10
11							11
12							12
13							13
14							14
15							15
16							16
17							17
18							18
19							19
20							20
21							21
22							22
23							23
24							24
25							25
26							26
27							27

Exercise 14-4B
1., 2., and 3.

Nicole's

Work

For Year Ended

	ACCOUNT TITLE	TRIAL BALANCE DEBIT	TRIAL BALANCE CREDIT	ADJUSTMENTS DEBIT	ADJUSTMENTS CREDIT	
1	Merchandise Inventory	30 0 0 0 00				
12	Income Summary					
13	Purchases	85 0 0 0 00				
14	Purchases Returns and Allow.		2 2 0 0 00			
15	Purchases Discounts		2 5 0 0 00			
16	Freight-In	1 0 0 00				
17						
18						

Exercise 14-4B (Concluded)

Gift Shop

Sheet (Partial)

December 31, 20--

ADJUSTED TRIAL BALANCE		INCOME STATEMENT		BALANCE SHEET		
DEBIT	CREDIT	DEBIT	CREDIT	DEBIT	CREDIT	
						1
						12
						13
						14
						15
						16
						17
						18

4.

Exercise 14-7B

GENERAL JOURNAL

PAGE

	DATE	DESCRIPTION	POST. REF.	DEBIT	CREDIT	
1						1
2						2
3						3
4						4
5						5
6						6
7						7
8						8
9						9
10						10
11						11
12						12
13						13
14						14
15						15
16						16
17						17
18						18
19						19
20						20
21						21

Exercise 14-8B

GENERAL JOURNAL

PAGE

	DATE	DESCRIPTION	POST. REF.	DEBIT	CREDIT	
1						1
2						2
3						3
4						4
5						5
6						6
7						7
8						8
9						9
10						10

Problem 14-9B

1. and 2. (See pages 532 and 533.)

3.

GENERAL JOURNAL

	DATE		DESCRIPTION	POST. REF.	DEBIT	CREDIT	
1							1
2							2
3							3
4							4
5							5
6							6
7							7
8							8
9							9
10							10
11							11
12							12
13							13
14							14
15							15
16							16
17							17
18							18
19							19
20							20
21							21
22							22
23							23
24							24
25							25
26							26
27							27
28							28
29							29
30							30
31							31
32							32
33							33
34							34

Problem 14-9B (Continued)
1. and 2.

Basket

Work

For Year Ended

	ACCOUNT TITLE	TRIAL BALANCE		ADJUSTMENTS	
		DEBIT	CREDIT	DEBIT	CREDIT
1	Cash	25 0 0 0 00			
2	Accounts Receivable	8 1 0 0 00			
3	Merchandise Inventory	32 0 0 0 00			
4	Supplies	7 1 0 0 00			
5	Prepaid Insurance	3 6 0 0 00			
6	Land	40 0 0 0 00			
7	Building	45 0 0 0 00			
8	Accumulated Depr.—Building		16 0 0 0 00		
9	Store Equipment	27 0 0 0 00			
10	Accumulated Depr.—Store Equip.		5 5 0 0 00		
11	Accounts Payable		3 6 0 0 00		
12	Wages Payable				
13	Sales Tax Payable		6 2 0 0 00		
14	Unearned Decorating Revenue		6 3 0 0 00		
15	Mortgage Payable		36 0 0 0 00		
16	L. Palermo, Capital		112 0 5 0 00		
17	L. Palermo, Drawing	31 0 0 0 00			
18	Income Summary				
19	Sales		125 0 0 0 00		
20	Sales Returns and Allowances	2 6 0 0 00			
21	Decorating Revenue				
22	Purchases	38 0 0 0 00			
23	Purchases Returns and Allow.		2 2 0 0 00		
24	Purchases Discounts		1 7 0 0 00		
25	Freight-In	1 9 0 0 00			
26	Wages Expense	38 0 0 0 00			
27	Advertising Expense	4 2 0 0 00			
28	Supplies Expense				
29	Telephone Expense	1 8 7 0 00			
30	Utilities Expense	8 4 0 0 00			
31	Insurance Expense				
32	Depreciation Expense—Building				
33	Depreciation Exp.—Store Equip.				
34	Miscellaneous Expense	7 8 0 00			
35		314 5 5 0 00	314 5 5 0 00		
36					
37					
38					

Problem 14-9B (Concluded)

Corner _____

Sheet _____

December 31, 20-- _____

ADJUSTED TRIAL BALANCE		INCOME STATEMENT		BALANCE SHEET		
DEBIT	CREDIT	DEBIT	CREDIT	DEBIT	CREDIT	
						1
						2
						3
						4
						5
						6
						7
						8
						9
						10
						11
						12
						13
						14
						15
						16
						17
						18
						19
						20
						21
						22
						23
						24
						25
						26
						27
						28
						29
						30
						31
						32
						33
						34
						35
						36
						37
						38

Problem 14-10B

1. and 2.

Oregon Bike

Work

For Year Ended

	ACCOUNT TITLE	TRIAL BALANCE										ADJUSTMENTS							
		DEBIT					CREDIT					DEBIT			CREDIT				
1	Cash	27	0	0	0	00													
2	Accounts Receivable	12	0	0	0	00													
3	Merchandise Inventory	39	0	0	0	00													
4	Supplies	6	2	0	0	00													
5	Prepaid Insurance	5	8	0	0	00													
6	Land	32	0	0	0	00													
7	Building	58	0	0	0	00													
8	Accumulated Depr.—Building						27	0	0	0	00								
9	Store Equipment	31	0	0	0	00													
10	Accumulated Depr.—Store Equip.						14	0	0	0	00								
11	Accounts Payable						4	9	0	0	00								
12	Wages Payable																		
13	Sales Tax Payable						2	9	0	0	00								
14	Unearned Rent Revenue						6	1	0	0	00								
15	Mortgage Payable						49	0	0	0	00								
16	C. Moody, Capital						169	5	0	0	00								
17	C. Moody, Drawing	36	0	0	0	00													
18	Income Summary																		
19	Sales						58	0	0	0	00								
20	Sales Returns and Allowances	3	3	0	0	00													
21	Rent Revenue																		
22	Purchases	19	0	0	0	00													
23	Purchases Returns and Allow.							9	0	0	00								
24	Purchases Discounts						1	4	5	0	00								
25	Freight-In		8	0	0	00													
26	Wages Expense	47	0	0	0	00													
27	Advertising Expense	6	2	0	0	00													
28	Supplies Expense																		
29	Telephone Expense	1	8	6	0	00													
30	Utilities Expense	8	1	0	0	00													
31	Insurance Expense																		
32	Depreciation Expense—Building																		
33	Depreciation Exp.—Store Equip.																		
34	Miscellaneous Expense		4	9	0	00													
35		333	7	5	0	00	333	7	5	0	00								
36																			
37																			
38																			

Problem 14-10B (Continued)

Company _____

Sheet _____

December 31, 20-- _____

	ADJUSTED TRIAL BALANCE		INCOME STATEMENT		BALANCE SHEET		
	DEBIT	CREDIT	DEBIT	CREDIT	DEBIT	CREDIT	
							1
							2
							3
							4
							5
							6
							7
							8
							9
							10
							11
							12
							13
							14
							15
							16
							17
							18
							19
							20
							21
							22
							23
							24
							25
							26
							27
							28
							29
							30
							31
							32
							33
							34
							35
							36
							37
							38

Problem 14-10B (Concluded)

3.

GENERAL JOURNAL

PAGE ____

DATE	DESCRIPTION	POST. REF.	DEBIT	CREDIT	
					1
					2
					3
					4
					5
					6
					7
					8
					9
					10
					11
					12
					13
					14
					15
					16
					17
					18
					19
					20
					21
					22
					23
					24
					25
					26
					27
					28
					29
					30
					31
					32
					33
					34

Name _____

Problem 14-11B

1.

Burnside Auto Parts

Work Sheet (Partial)

For Year Ended December 31, 20--

	ACCOUNT TITLE	TRIAL BALANCE DEBIT	TRIAL BALANCE CREDIT	ADJUSTMENTS DEBIT	ADJUSTMENTS CREDIT	ADJ. TRIAL BALANCE DEBIT	ADJ. TRIAL BALANCE CREDIT	
1	Cash	21 0 0 0 00				21 0 0 0 00		1
2	Accounts Receivable	8 3 0 0 00				8 3 0 0 00		2
3	Merchandise Inventory	32 0 0 0 00				36 0 0 0 00		3
4	Supplies	6 1 5 0 00				1 8 6 5 00		4
5	Prepaid Insurance	5 9 2 5 00				1 8 3 5 00		5
6	Land	41 7 5 0 00				41 7 5 0 00		6
7	Building	43 0 0 0 00				43 0 0 0 00		7
8	Accum. Depr.—Building		24 0 0 0 00				27 5 0 0 00	8
9	Store Equipment	25 4 0 0 00				25 4 0 0 00		9
10	Accum. Depr.—Store Equip.		12 4 0 0 00				14 7 5 0 00	10
11	Accounts Payable		8 1 0 0 00				8 1 0 0 00	11
12	Wages Payable						9 8 0 00	12
13	Sales Tax Payable		5 2 0 0 00				5 2 0 0 00	13
14	Unearn. Rent-A-Junk Rev.		7 9 5 0 00				2 3 5 0 00	14
15	Mortgage Payable		26 0 0 0 00				26 0 0 0 00	15
16	B. Davis, Capital		109 1 3 0 00				109 1 3 0 00	16
17	B. Davis, Drawing	40 0 0 0 00				40 0 0 0 00		17
18	Income Summary					32 0 0 0 00	36 0 0 0 00	18
19	Sales		123 5 0 0 00				123 5 0 0 00	19
20	Sales Returns and Allow.	2 8 6 0 00				2 8 6 0 00		20
21	Rent-A-Junk Revenue						5 6 0 0 00	21
22	Purchases	32 5 2 5 00				32 5 2 5 00		22
23	Purchases Ret. and Allow.		2 1 5 0 00				2 1 5 0 00	23
24	Purchases Discounts		2 4 0 0 00				2 4 0 0 00	24
25	Freight-In	3 1 7 5 00				3 1 7 5 00		25
26	Wages Expense	44 1 7 5 00				45 1 5 5 00		26
27	Advertising Expense	3 2 7 5 00				3 2 7 5 00		27
28	Supplies Expense					4 2 8 5 00		28
29	Telephone Expense	2 2 0 0 00				2 2 0 0 00		29
30	Utilities Expense	8 2 5 0 00				8 2 5 0 00		30
31	Insurance Expense					4 0 9 0 00		31
32	Depr. Exp.—Building					3 5 0 0 00		32
33	Depr. Exp.—Store Equip.					2 3 5 0 00		33
34	Miscellaneous Expense	8 4 5 00				8 4 5 00		34
35		320 8 3 0 00	320 8 3 0 00			363 6 6 0 00	363 6 6 0 00	35
36								36
37								37
38								38

Problem 14-11B (Concluded)

2.

GENERAL JOURNAL

PAGE

	DATE	DESCRIPTION	POST. REF.	DEBIT	CREDIT	
1						1
2						2
3						3
4						4
5						5
6						6
7						7
8						8
9						9
10						10
11						11
12						12
13						13
14						14
15						15
16						16
17						17
18						18
19						19
20						20
21						21
22						22
23						23
24						24
25						25
26						26
27						27
28						28
29						29
30						30
31						31
32						32
33						33
34						34

Problem 14-12B
1. (See pages 540 and 541.)
2.

GENERAL JOURNAL

PAGE

	DATE		DESCRIPTION	POST. REF.	DEBIT	CREDIT	
1							1
2							2
3							3
4							4
5							5
6							6
7							7
8							8
9							9
10							10
11							11
12							12
13							13
14							14
15							15
16							16
17							17
18							18
19							19
20							20
21							21
22							22
23							23
24							24
25							25
26							26
27							27
28							28
29							29
30							30
31							31
32							32
33							33
34							34

Problem 14-12B (Continued)

1.

Diamond Music

Work

For Year Ended

	ACCOUNT TITLE	TRIAL BALANCE DEBIT	TRIAL BALANCE CREDIT	ADJUSTMENTS DEBIT	ADJUSTMENTS CREDIT
1	Cash	31 0 0 0 00			
2	Accounts Receivable	11 9 8 0 00			
3	Merchandise Inventory	33 6 0 0 00			
4	Supplies	7 1 4 0 00			
5	Prepaid Insurance	5 9 8 5 00			
6	Land	36 2 0 0 00			
7	Building	51 8 5 0 00			
8	Accumulated Depr.—Building		13 5 9 0 00		
9	Store Equipment	32 6 7 5 00			
10	Accumulated Depr.—Store Equip.		10 2 9 0 00		
11	Accounts Payable		5 8 9 5 00		
12	Wages Payable				
13	Sales Tax Payable		6 3 7 5 00		
14	Unearned Rent Revenue		8 8 5 0 00		
15	Mortgage Payable		42 4 0 0 00		
16	N. Diamond, Capital		116 3 5 0 00		
17	N. Diamond, Drawing	39 5 0 0 00			
18	Income Summary				
19	Sales		148 0 0 0 00		
20	Sales Returns and Allowances	2 8 0 0 00			
21	Rent Revenue				
22	Purchases	40 7 0 0 00			
23	Purchases Returns and Allow.		2 7 7 5 00		
24	Purchases Discounts		2 3 2 5 00		
25	Freight-In	1 8 7 5 00			
26	Wages Expense	47 0 0 0 00			
27	Advertising Expense	4 6 9 5 00			
28	Supplies Expense				
29	Telephone Expense	2 2 5 0 00			
30	Utilities Expense	6 8 2 5 00			
31	Insurance Expense				
32	Depreciation Expense—Building				
33	Depreciation Exp.—Store Equip.				
34	Miscellaneous Expense	7 7 5 00			
35		356 8 5 0 00	356 8 5 0 00		
36	Net Income				
37					
38					

Problem 14-12B (Continued)

Store _____
Sheet _____
December 31, 20--

	ADJUSTED TRIAL BALANCE		INCOME STATEMENT		BALANCE SHEET		
	DEBIT	CREDIT	DEBIT	CREDIT	DEBIT	CREDIT	
1					31 0 0 0 00		
2					11 9 8 0 00		
3					39 1 0 0 00		
4					1 9 6 5 00		
5					1 2 3 5 00		
6					36 2 0 0 00		
7					51 8 5 0 00		
8						18 8 7 5 00	
9					32 6 7 5 00		
10						14 7 5 5 00	
11						5 8 9 5 00	
12						1 2 5 0 00	
13						6 3 7 5 00	
14						2 9 3 0 00	
15						42 4 0 0 00	
16						116 3 5 0 00	
17					39 5 0 0 00		
18			33 6 0 0 00	39 1 0 0 00			
19				148 0 0 0 00			
20			2 8 0 0 00				
21				5 9 2 0 00			
22			40 7 0 0 00				
23				2 7 7 5 00			
24				2 3 2 5 00			
25			1 8 7 5 00				
26			48 2 5 0 00				
27			4 6 9 5 00				
28			5 1 7 5 00				
29			2 2 5 0 00				
30			6 8 2 5 00				
31			4 7 5 0 00				
32			5 2 8 5 00				
33			4 4 6 5 00				
34			7 7 5 00				
35			161 4 4 5 00	198 1 2 0 00	245 5 0 5 00	208 8 3 0 00	
36			36 6 7 5 00			36 6 7 5 00	
37			198 1 2 0 00	198 1 2 0 00	245 5 0 5 00	245 5 0 5 00	
38							

Problem 14-12B (Concluded)

3.

Mastery Problem

1. (See pages 544 and 545 for work sheet.)
2.

GENERAL JOURNAL

PAGE _____

	DATE		DESCRIPTION	POST. REF.	DEBIT	CREDIT	
1							1
2							2
3							3
4							4
5							5
6							6
7							7
8							8
9							9
10							10
11							11
12							12
13							13
14							14
15							15
16							16
17							17
18							18
19							19
20							20
21							21
22							22
23							23
24							24
25							25
26							26
27							27
28							28
29							29
30							30
31							31
32							32
33							33
34							34

Mastery Problem (Continued)

1.

Waikiki Surf

Work

For Year Ended

	ACCOUNT TITLE	TRIAL BALANCE DEBIT					TRIAL BALANCE CREDIT					ADJUSTMENTS DEBIT					ADJUSTMENTS CREDIT				
1	Cash	30	0	0	0	00															
2	Accounts Receivable	22	5	0	0	00															
3	Merchandise Inventory	57	0	0	0	00															
4	Supplies	2	7	0	0	00															
5	Prepaid Insurance	3	6	0	0	00															
6	Land	15	0	0	0	00															
7	Building	135	0	0	0	00															
8	Accumulated Depr.—Building						24	0	0	0	00										
9	Store Equipment	75	0	0	0	00															
10	Accumulated Depr.—Store Equip.						22	5	0	0	00										
11	Notes Payable						7	5	0	0	00										
12	Accounts Payable						15	0	0	0	00										
13	Wages Payable																				
14	Unearned Boat Rental Revenue						33	0	0	0	00										
15	J. Neff, Capital						233	7	0	0	00										
16	J. Neff, Drawing	30	0	0	0	00															
17	Income Summary																				
18	Sales						300	7	5	0	00										
19	Sales Returns and Allowances	1	8	0	0	00															
20	Boat Rental Revenue																				
21	Purchases	157	5	0	0	00															
22	Purchases Returns and Allow.						1	2	0	0	00										
23	Purchases Discounts						1	5	0	0	00										
24	Freight-In		4	5	0	00															
25	Wages Expense	63	0	0	0	00															
26	Advertising Expense	11	2	5	0	00															
27	Supplies Expense																				
28	Telephone Expense	5	2	5	0	00															
29	Utilities Expense	18	0	0	0	00															
30	Insurance Expense																				
31	Depreciation Expense—Building																				
32	Depreciation Exp.—Store Equip.																				
33	Miscellaneous Expense	10	8	7	5	00															
34	Interest Expense		2	2	5	00															
35		639	1	5	0	00	639	1	5	0	00										
36																					
37																					
38																					

Mastery Problem (Concluded)

Shop _____

Sheet _____

December 31, 20-- _____

ADJUSTED TRIAL BALANCE		INCOME STATEMENT		BALANCE SHEET		
DEBIT	CREDIT	DEBIT	CREDIT	DEBIT	CREDIT	
						1
						2
						3
						4
						5
						6
						7
						8
						9
						10
						11
						12
						13
						14
						15
						16
						17
						18
						19
						20
						21
						22
						23
						24
						25
						26
						27
						28
						29
						30
						31
						32
						33
						34
						35
						36
						37
						38

Challenge Problem

APPENDIX: EXPENSE METHOD OF ACCOUNTING FOR PREPAID EXPENSES

Exercise 14Apx-1A

GENERAL JOURNAL

PAGE

	DATE		DESCRIPTION	POST. REF.	DEBIT	CREDIT	
1							1
2							2
3							3
4							4
5							5
6							6
7							7
8							8
9							9
10							10
11							11
12							12

Exercise 14Apx-1B

GENERAL JOURNAL

PAGE

	DATE		DESCRIPTION	POST. REF.	DEBIT	CREDIT	
1							1
2							2
3							3
4							4
5							5
6							6
7							7
8							8
9							9
10							10
11							11
12							12

Name _____

Exercise 15-1A

Exercise 15-2A

Exercise 15-3A

Exercise 15-4A

Exercise 15-5A

1.

GENERAL JOURNAL

PAGE

	DATE		DESCRIPTION	POST. REF.	DEBIT	CREDIT	
1							1
2							2
3							3
4							4
5							5
6							6
7							7
8							8
9							9
10							10
11							11
12							12
13							13
14							14
15							15
16							16
17							17
18							18
19							19
20							20
21							21
22							22
23							23
24							24
25							25
26							26
27							27
28							28
29							29
30							30
31							31
32							32
33							33
34							34

Exercise 15-5A (Concluded)

2.

J. M. Gimbel, Capital

Exercise 15-6A

GENERAL JOURNAL PAGE

	DATE	DESCRIPTION	POST. REF.	DEBIT	CREDIT	
1						1
2						2
3						3
4						4
5						5

Exercise 15-7A

DATE	WITHOUT REVERSING ENTRY	WITH REVERSING ENTRY
Adjusting Entry:		
Closing Entry:		
Reversing Entry:		
Payment of Payroll:		

Wages Expense

Wages Expense

Wages Payable

Wages Payable

Cash

Cash

Problem 15-8A

1.

Problem 15-8A (Continued)

2.

Problem 15-8A (Concluded)

3.

Problem 15-9A

Problem 15-10A
1. (See pages 562 and 563)
2., 3., and 5.

GENERAL JOURNAL

PAGE _____

	DATE	DESCRIPTION	POST. REF.	DEBIT	CREDIT	
1						1
2						2
3						3
4						4
5						5
6						6
7						7
8						8
9						9
10						10
11						11
12						12
13						13
14						14
15						15
16						16
17						17
18						18
19						19
20						20
21						21
22						22
23						23
24						24
25						25
26						26
27						27
28						28
29						29
30						30
31						31
32						32
33						33
34						34

Problem 15-10A (Continued)

2., 3., and 5.

GENERAL JOURNAL

PAGE _____

	DATE	DESCRIPTION	POST. REF.	DEBIT	CREDIT	
1						1
2						2
3						3
4						4
5						5
6						6
7						7
8						8
9						9
10						10
11						11
12						12
13						13
14						14
15						15
16						16
17						17
18						18
19						19
20						20
21						21
22						22
23						23
24						24
25						25
26						26
27						27
28						28
29						29
30						30
31						31
32						32
33						33
34						34

Problem 15-10A (Continued)

4.

ACCOUNT	DEBIT BALANCE	CREDIT BALANCE

Problem 15-10A (Continued)

1.

Vicki's Fabric

Work

For Year Ended

		TRIAL BALANCE			ADJUSTMENTS	
		DEBIT	CREDIT		DEBIT	CREDIT
1	Cash	28 0 0 0 00				
2	Accounts Receivable	14 2 0 0 00				
3	Merchandise Inventory	33 0 0 0 00				
4	Supplies	1 6 0 0 00				
5	Prepaid Insurance	9 0 0 00				
6	Equipment	6 6 0 0 00				
7	Accumulated Depr.—Equipment		1 0 0 0 00			
8	Accounts Payable		15 6 2 0 00			
9	Wages Payable					
10	Sales Tax Payable		8 5 0 00			
11	Unearned Revenue		5 0 0 0 00			
12	Vicki Roberts, Capital		71 2 0 0 00			
13	Vicki Roberts, Drawing	21 6 1 0 00				
14	Income Summary					
15	Sales		74 5 0 0 00			
16	Sales Returns and Allowances	1 8 5 0 00				
17	Interest Revenue		1 2 0 0 00			
18	Purchases	41 5 0 0 00				
19	Purchases Returns and Allow.		1 8 0 0 00			
20	Purchases Discounts		8 3 0 00			
21	Freight-In	6 6 0 00				
22	Wages Expense	14 8 8 0 00				
23	Advertising Expense	8 1 0 00				
24	Supplies Expense					
25	Telephone Expense	1 2 1 0 00				
26	Utilities Expense	3 2 4 0 00				
27	Insurance Expense					
28	Depreciation Expense—Equip.					
29	Miscellaneous Expense	9 2 0 00				
30	Interest Expense	1 0 2 0 00				
31		172 0 0 0 00	172 0 0 0 00			
32						
33						

Problem 15-10A (Concluded)

Store

Sheet

December 31, 20-1

	ADJUSTED TRIAL BALANCE		INCOME STATEMENT		BALANCE SHEET	
	DEBIT	CREDIT	DEBIT	CREDIT	DEBIT	CREDIT
1						
2						
3						
4						
5						
6						
7						
8						
9						
10						
11						
12						
13						
14						
15						
16						
17						
18						
19						
20						
21						
22						
23						
24						
25						
26						
27						
28						
29						
30						
31						
32						
33						

Exercise 15-1B

Exercise 15-2B

Name _____

Exercise 15-3B

Exercise 15-4B

Exercise 15-5B

1.

GENERAL JOURNAL

PAGE _____

	DATE		DESCRIPTION	POST. REF.	DEBIT	CREDIT	
1							1
2							2
3							3
4							4
5							5
6							6
7							7
8							8
9							9
10							10
11							11
12							12
13							13
14							14
15							15
16							16
17							17
18							18
19							19
20							20
21							21
22							22
23							23
24							24
25							25
26							26
27							27
28							28
29							29
30							30
31							31
32							32
33							33
34							34

Exercise 15-5B (Concluded)

2.

L. Marlow, Capital

Exercise 15-6B

GENERAL JOURNAL

PAGE

	DATE	DESCRIPTION	POST. REF.	DEBIT	CREDIT	
1						1
2						2
3						3
4						4
5						5

Exercise 15-7B

DATE	WITHOUT REVERSING ENTRY	WITH REVERSING ENTRY
Adjusting Entry:		
Closing Entry:		
Reversing Entry:		
Payment of Payroll:		

Wages Expense   Wages Expense

Wages Payable   Wages Payable

Cash   Cash

Problem 15-8B

1.

Problem 15-8B (Continued)

2.

Problem 15-8B (Concluded)

3.

Problem 15-9B

Problem 15-10B

1.

Darby Kite

Work

For Year Ended

| | TRIAL BALANCE | | ADJUSTMENTS | |
	DEBIT	CREDIT	DEBIT	CREDIT
1 Cash	11 7 0 0 00			
2 Accounts Receivable	11 2 0 0 00			
3 Merchandise Inventory	25 0 0 0 00			
4 Supplies	1 2 0 0 00			
5 Prepaid Insurance	8 0 0 00			
6 Equipment	5 4 0 0 00			
7 Accumulated Depr.—Equipment		8 0 0 00		
8 Accounts Payable		7 1 0 0 00		
9 Wages Payable				
10 Sales Tax Payable		2 5 0 00		
11 Unearned Revenue		3 0 0 0 00		
12 M. D. Akins, Capital		50 0 0 0 00		
13 M. D. Akins, Drawing	10 5 0 0 00			
14 Income Summary				
15 Sales		55 4 9 0 00		
16 Sales Returns and Allowances	1 4 5 0 00			
17 Purchases	34 5 0 0 00			
18 Purchases Returns and Allow.		1 1 0 0 00		
19 Purchases Discounts		6 3 0 00		
20 Freight-In	3 6 0 00			
21 Wages Expense	10 8 8 0 00			
22 Advertising Expense	7 4 0 00			
23 Supplies Expense				
24 Telephone Expense	1 1 0 0 00			
25 Utilities Expense	2 3 0 0 00			
26 Insurance Expense				
27 Depreciation Expense—Equip.				
28 Miscellaneous Expense	3 2 0 00			
29 Interest Expense	9 2 0 00			
30	118 3 7 0 00	118 3 7 0 00		
31				
33				

Problem 15-10B (Continued)

Store _____

Sheet _____

December 31, 20-1

ADJUSTED TRIAL BALANCE		INCOME STATEMENT		BALANCE SHEET		
DEBIT	CREDIT	DEBIT	CREDIT	DEBIT	CREDIT	
						1
						2
						3
						4
						5
						6
						7
						8
						9
						10
						11
						12
						13
						14
						15
						16
						17
						18
						19
						20
						21
						22
						23
						24
						25
						26
						27
						28
						29
						30
						31
						32

Problem 15-10B (Continued)

2., 3., and 5.

GENERAL JOURNAL

PAGE

	DATE		DESCRIPTION	POST. REF.	DEBIT	CREDIT	
1							1
2							2
3							3
4							4
5							5
6							6
7							7
8							8
9							9
10							10
11							11
12							12
13							13
14							14
15							15
16							16
17							17
18							18
19							19
20							20
21							21
22							22
23							23
24							24
25							25
26							26
27							27
28							28
29							29
30							30
31							31
32							32
33							33
34							34

Problem 15-10B (Continued)

GENERAL JOURNAL

PAGE

	DATE	DESCRIPTION	POST. REF.	DEBIT	CREDIT	
1						1
2						2
3						3
4						4
5						5
6						6
7						7
8						8
9						9
10						10
11						11
12						12
13						13
14						14
15						15
16						16
17						17
18						18
19						19
20						20
21						21
22						22
23						23
24						24
25						25
26						26
27						27
28						28
29						29
30						30
31						31
32						32
33						33
34						34

Problem 15-10B (Concluded)

4.

ACCOUNT	DEBIT BALANCE	CREDIT BALANCE

Name _____

Mastery Problem

1.

Mastery Problem (Continued)

2.

Mastery Problem (Continued)

3.

Mastery Problem (Continued)

4.

Mastery Problem (Continued)

5.

GENERAL JOURNAL

	DATE		DESCRIPTION	POST. REF.	DEBIT	CREDIT	
1							1
2							2
3							3
4							4
5							5
6							6
7							7
8							8
9							9
10							10
11							11
12							12
13							13
14							14
15							15
16							16
17							17
18							18
19							19
20							20
21							21
22							22

Should the adjustment be reversed?

_____

_____

_____

_____

_____

_____

_____

_____

Mastery Problem (Concluded)

6. and 7.

GENERAL JOURNAL

	DATE	DESCRIPTION	POST. REF.	DEBIT	CREDIT	
1						1
2						2
3						3
4						4
5						5
6						6
7						7
8						8
9						9
10						10
11						11
12						12
13						13
14						14
15						15
16						16
17						17
18						18
19						19
20						20
21						21
22						22
23						23
24						24
25						25
26						26
27						27
28						28
29						29
30						30
31						31
32						32
33						33
34						34
35						35

Challenge Problem

Comprehensive Problem 2—General Journal Based, Part 1

Requirements 2. and 3. **GENERAL JOURNAL** PAGE 3

	DATE	DESCRIPTION	POST. REF.	DEBIT	CREDIT	
1						1
2						2
3						3
4						4
5						5
6						6
7						7
8						8
9						9
10						10
11						11
12						12
13						13
14						14
15						15
16						16
17						17
18						18
19						19
20						20
21						21
22						22
23						23
24						24
25						25
26						26
27						27
28						28
29						29
30						30
31						31
32						32
33						33
34						34
35						35
36						36
37						37
38						38
39						39
40						40
41						41

Comprehensive Problem 2—General Journal Based, Part 1 (Requirements 2. and 3. Concluded)

GENERAL JOURNAL
PAGE 4

DATE	DESCRIPTION	POST. REF.	DEBIT	CREDIT	
					1
					2
					3
					4
					5
					6
					7
					8
					9
					10
					11
					12
					13
					14
					15
					16
					17

Requirements 1., 2., 3., 6., 7., and 9.

GENERAL LEDGER

ACCOUNT Cash   ACCOUNT NO. 101

DATE		ITEM	POST. REF.	DEBIT	CREDIT	BALANCE DEBIT	BALANCE CREDIT
20-1 Dec.	16	Balance	✓			9 7 0 5 00	

Comprehensive Problem 2—General Journal Based, Part 1
(Requirements 1., 2., 3., 6., 7., and 9. Continued)

ACCOUNT **Accounts Receivable** ACCOUNT NO. 122

DATE		ITEM	POST. REF.	DEBIT	CREDIT	BALANCE DEBIT	BALANCE CREDIT
20-1 Dec.	16	Balance	✓			10 2 5 6 00	

ACCOUNT **Merchandise Inventory** ACCOUNT NO. 131

DATE		ITEM	POST. REF.	DEBIT	CREDIT	BALANCE DEBIT	BALANCE CREDIT
20-1 Dec.	16	Balance	✓			21 8 0 0 00	

ACCOUNT **Supplies** ACCOUNT NO. 141

DATE		ITEM	POST. REF.	DEBIT	CREDIT	BALANCE DEBIT	BALANCE CREDIT
20-1 Dec.	16	Balance	✓			1 0 3 5 00	

ACCOUNT **Prepaid Insurance** ACCOUNT NO. 145

DATE		ITEM	POST. REF.	DEBIT	CREDIT	BALANCE DEBIT	BALANCE CREDIT
20-1 Dec.	16	Balance	✓			1 3 8 0 00	

Comprehensive Problem 2—General Journal Based, Part 1
(Requirements 1., 2., 3., 6., 7., and 9. Continued)

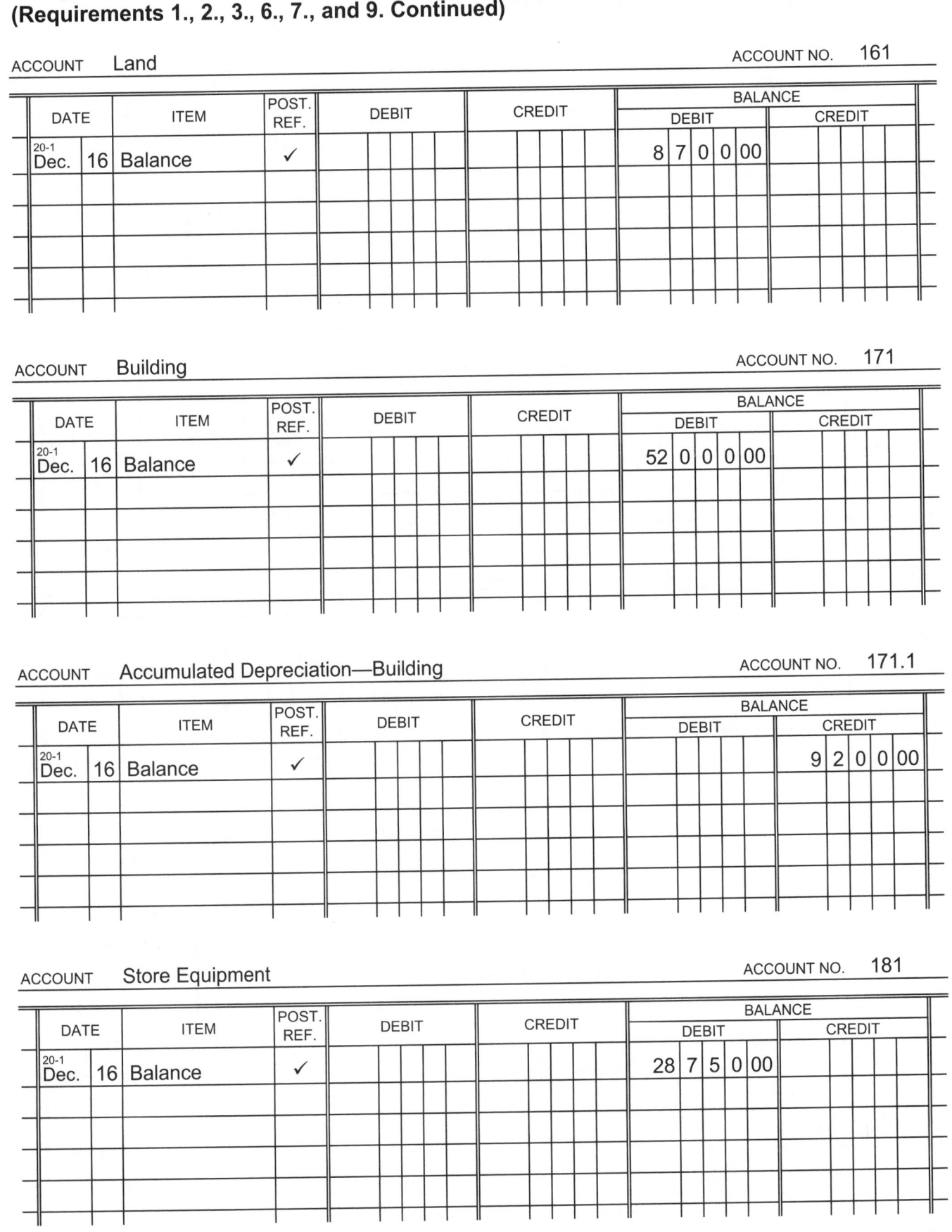

ACCOUNT Land   ACCOUNT NO. 161

DATE		ITEM	POST. REF.	DEBIT	CREDIT	BALANCE DEBIT	BALANCE CREDIT
20-1 Dec.	16	Balance	✓			8 7 0 0 00	

ACCOUNT Building   ACCOUNT NO. 171

DATE		ITEM	POST. REF.	DEBIT	CREDIT	BALANCE DEBIT	BALANCE CREDIT
20-1 Dec.	16	Balance	✓			52 0 0 0 00	

ACCOUNT Accumulated Depreciation—Building   ACCOUNT NO. 171.1

DATE		ITEM	POST. REF.	DEBIT	CREDIT	BALANCE DEBIT	BALANCE CREDIT
20-1 Dec.	16	Balance	✓				9 2 0 0 00

ACCOUNT Store Equipment   ACCOUNT NO. 181

DATE		ITEM	POST. REF.	DEBIT	CREDIT	BALANCE DEBIT	BALANCE CREDIT
20-1 Dec.	16	Balance	✓			28 7 5 0 00	

Comprehensive Problem 2—General Journal Based, Part 1
(Requirements 1., 2., 3., 6., 7., and 9. Continued)

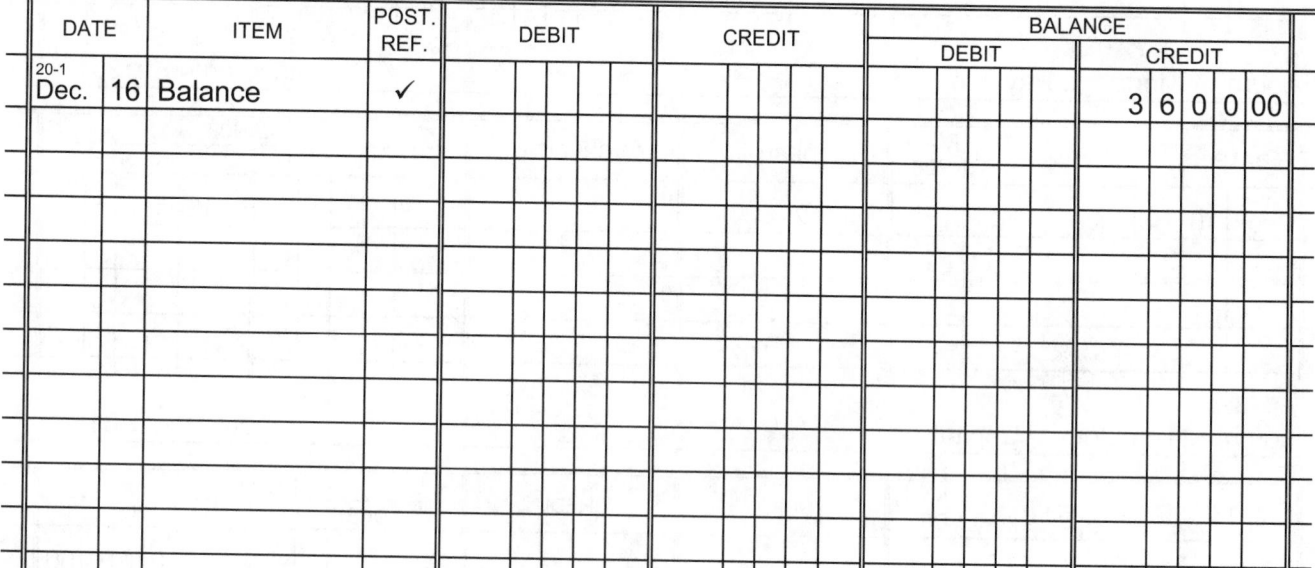

ACCOUNT Accumulated Depreciation—Store Equipment   ACCOUNT NO. 181.1

DATE		ITEM	POST. REF.	DEBIT	CREDIT	BALANCE DEBIT	BALANCE CREDIT
20-1 Dec.	16	Balance	✓				9 3 0 0 00

ACCOUNT Accounts Payable   ACCOUNT NO. 202

DATE		ITEM	POST. REF.	DEBIT	CREDIT	BALANCE DEBIT	BALANCE CREDIT
20-1 Dec.	16	Balance	✓				3 6 0 0 00

ACCOUNT Wages Payable   ACCOUNT NO. 219

DATE		ITEM	POST. REF.	DEBIT	CREDIT	BALANCE DEBIT	BALANCE CREDIT

Comprehensive Problem 2—General Journal Based, Part 1
(Requirements 1., 2., 3., 6., 7., and 9. Continued)

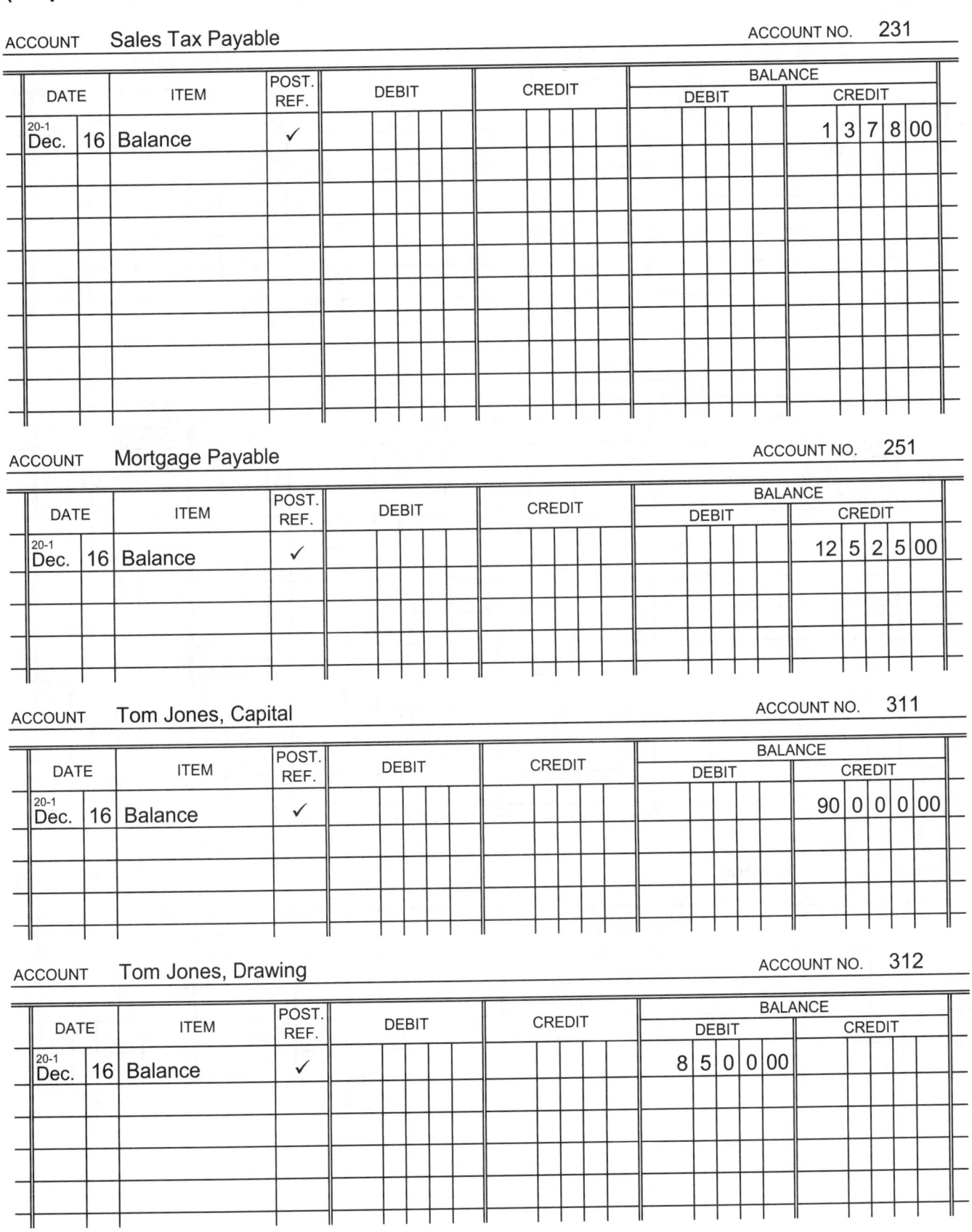

ACCOUNT Sales Tax Payable   **ACCOUNT NO.** 231

DATE		ITEM	POST. REF.	DEBIT	CREDIT	BALANCE	
						DEBIT	CREDIT
20-1 Dec.	16	Balance	✓				1 3 7 8 00

ACCOUNT Mortgage Payable   **ACCOUNT NO.** 251

DATE		ITEM	POST. REF.	DEBIT	CREDIT	BALANCE	
						DEBIT	CREDIT
20-1 Dec.	16	Balance	✓				12 5 2 5 00

ACCOUNT Tom Jones, Capital   **ACCOUNT NO.** 311

DATE		ITEM	POST. REF.	DEBIT	CREDIT	BALANCE	
						DEBIT	CREDIT
20-1 Dec.	16	Balance	✓				90 0 0 0 00

ACCOUNT Tom Jones, Drawing   **ACCOUNT NO.** 312

DATE		ITEM	POST. REF.	DEBIT	CREDIT	BALANCE	
						DEBIT	CREDIT
20-1 Dec.	16	Balance	✓			8 5 0 0 00	

Comprehensive Problem 2—General Journal Based, Part 1
(Requirements 1., 2., 3., 6., 7., and 9. Continued)

ACCOUNT Income Summary   ACCOUNT NO. 313

DATE	ITEM	POST. REF.	DEBIT	CREDIT	BALANCE DEBIT	BALANCE CREDIT

ACCOUNT Sales   ACCOUNT NO. 401

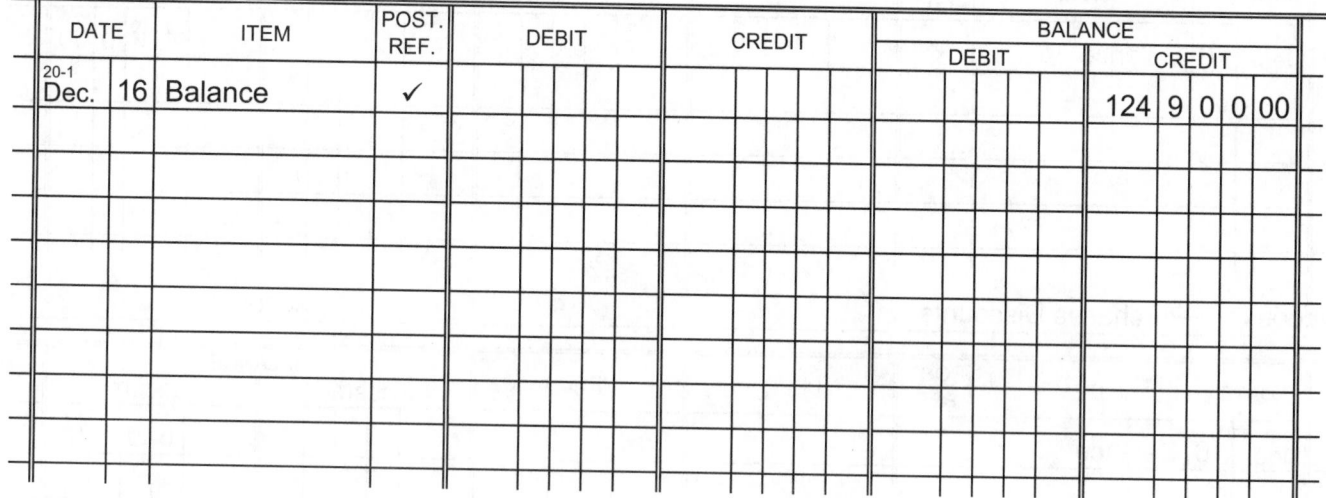

DATE	ITEM	POST. REF.	DEBIT	CREDIT	BALANCE DEBIT	BALANCE CREDIT
20-1 Dec. 16	Balance	✓				124 9 0 0 00

ACCOUNT Sales Returns and Allowances   ACCOUNT NO. 401.1

DATE	ITEM	POST. REF.	DEBIT	CREDIT	BALANCE DEBIT	BALANCE CREDIT
20-1 Dec. 16	Balance	✓			1 4 3 0 00	

Comprehensive Problem 2—General Journal Based, Part 1 (Requirements 1., 2., 3., 6., 7., and 9. Continued)

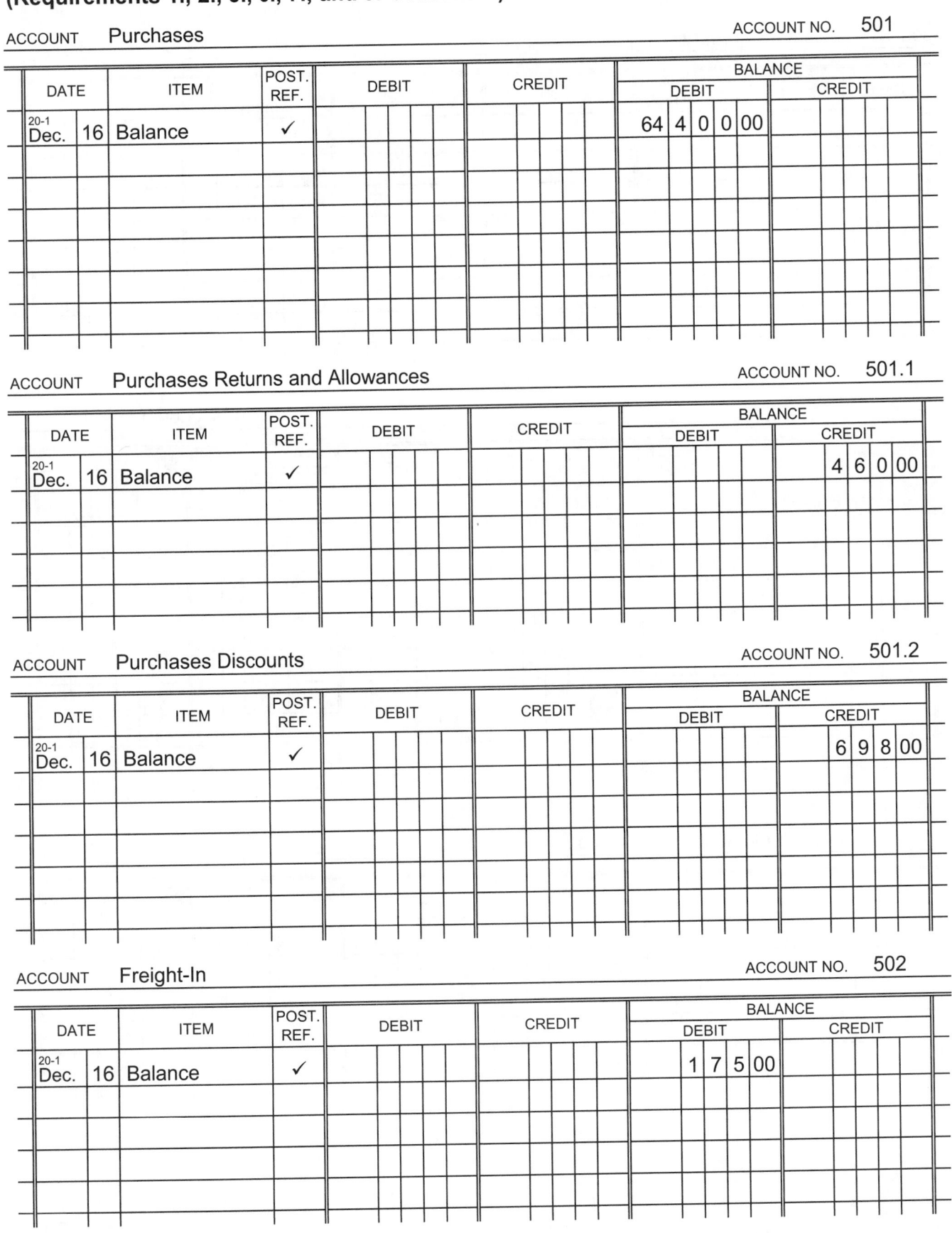

ACCOUNT Purchases   ACCOUNT NO. 501

DATE		ITEM	POST. REF.	DEBIT	CREDIT	BALANCE DEBIT	BALANCE CREDIT
20-1 Dec.	16	Balance	✓			64 4 0 0 00	

ACCOUNT Purchases Returns and Allowances   ACCOUNT NO. 501.1

DATE		ITEM	POST. REF.	DEBIT	CREDIT	BALANCE DEBIT	BALANCE CREDIT
20-1 Dec.	16	Balance	✓				4 6 0 00

ACCOUNT Purchases Discounts   ACCOUNT NO. 501.2

DATE		ITEM	POST. REF.	DEBIT	CREDIT	BALANCE DEBIT	BALANCE CREDIT
20-1 Dec.	16	Balance	✓				6 9 8 00

ACCOUNT Freight-In   ACCOUNT NO. 502

DATE		ITEM	POST. REF.	DEBIT	CREDIT	BALANCE DEBIT	BALANCE CREDIT
20-1 Dec.	16	Balance	✓			1 7 5 00	

Comprehensive Problem 2—General Journal Based, Part 1
(Requirements 1., 2., 3., 6., 7., and 9. Continued)

ACCOUNT Wages Expense   ACCOUNT NO. 511

DATE		ITEM	POST. REF.	DEBIT	CREDIT	BALANCE	
						DEBIT	CREDIT
20-1 Dec.	16	Balance	✓			26 1 0 0 00	

ACCOUNT Advertising Expense   ACCOUNT NO. 512

DATE		ITEM	POST. REF.	DEBIT	CREDIT	BALANCE	
						DEBIT	CREDIT
20-1 Dec.	16	Balance	✓			4 7 0 0 00	

ACCOUNT Supplies Expense   ACCOUNT NO. 524

DATE		ITEM	POST. REF.	DEBIT	CREDIT	BALANCE	
						DEBIT	CREDIT

ACCOUNT Telephone Expense   ACCOUNT NO. 525

DATE		ITEM	POST. REF.	DEBIT	CREDIT	BALANCE	
						DEBIT	CREDIT
20-1 Dec.	16	Balance	✓			2 1 8 0 00	

Comprehensive Problem 2—General Journal Based, Part 1
(Requirements 1., 2., 3., 6., 7., and 9. Continued)

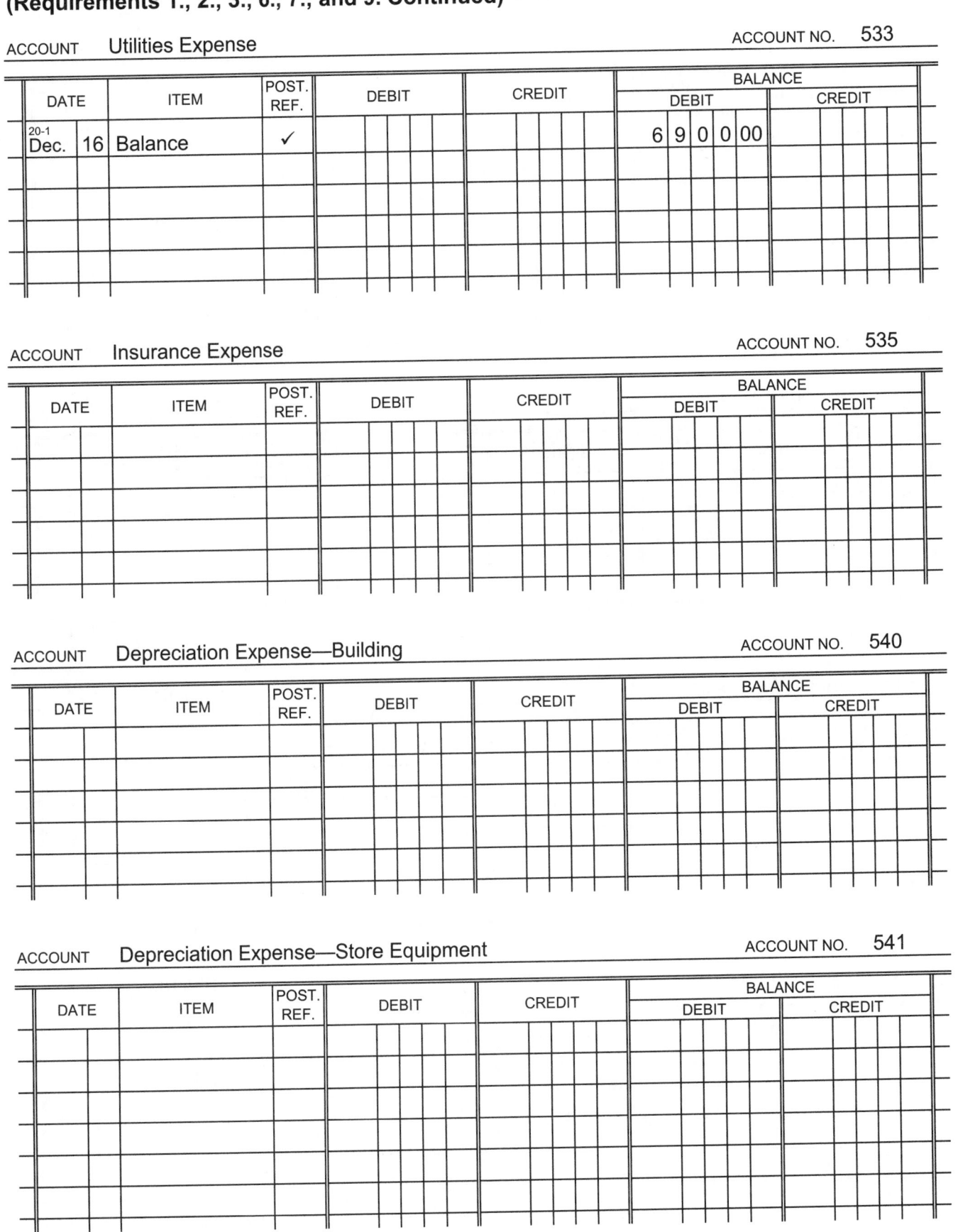

ACCOUNT Utilities Expense   ACCOUNT NO. 533

DATE		ITEM	POST. REF.	DEBIT	CREDIT	BALANCE DEBIT	BALANCE CREDIT
20-1 Dec.	16	Balance	✓			6 9 0 0 00	

ACCOUNT Insurance Expense   ACCOUNT NO. 535

DATE	ITEM	POST. REF.	DEBIT	CREDIT	BALANCE DEBIT	BALANCE CREDIT

ACCOUNT Depreciation Expense—Building   ACCOUNT NO. 540

DATE	ITEM	POST. REF.	DEBIT	CREDIT	BALANCE DEBIT	BALANCE CREDIT

ACCOUNT Depreciation Expense—Store Equipment   ACCOUNT NO. 541

DATE	ITEM	POST. REF.	DEBIT	CREDIT	BALANCE DEBIT	BALANCE CREDIT

Comprehensive Problem 2—General Journal Based, Part 1
(Requirements 1., 2., 3., 6., 7., and 9. Continued)

ACCOUNT   Miscellaneous Expense   ACCOUNT NO. 549

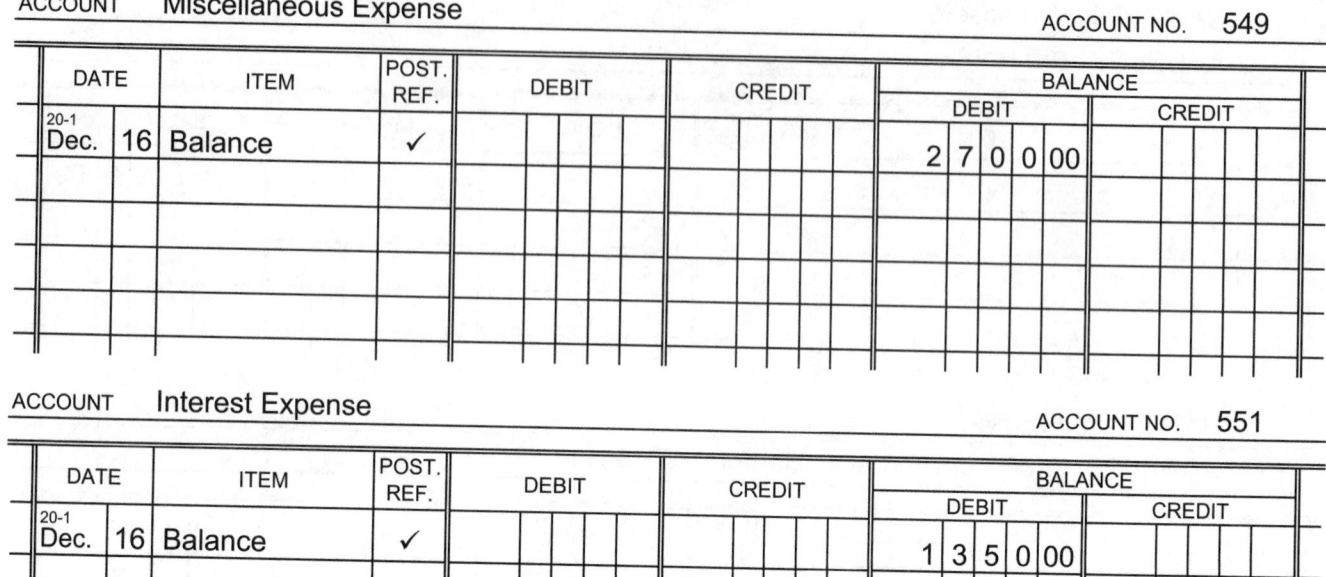

DATE		ITEM	POST. REF.	DEBIT	CREDIT	BALANCE DEBIT	BALANCE CREDIT
20-1 Dec.	16	Balance	✓			2 7 0 0 00	

ACCOUNT   Interest Expense   ACCOUNT NO. 551

DATE		ITEM	POST. REF.	DEBIT	CREDIT	BALANCE DEBIT	BALANCE CREDIT
20-1 Dec.	16	Balance	✓			1 3 5 0 00	

ACCOUNTS RECEIVABLE LEDGER

NAME Martha Boyle

ADDRESS 12 Jude Lane, Hartford, CT 06117

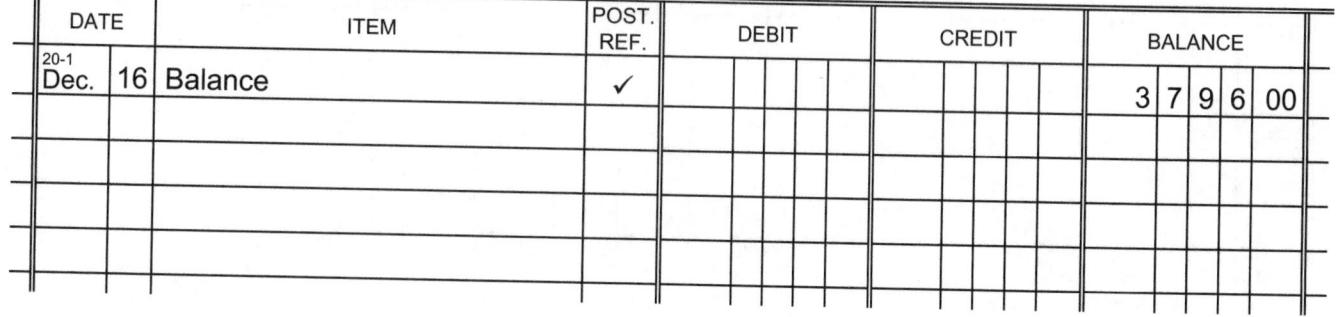

DATE		ITEM	POST. REF.	DEBIT	CREDIT	BALANCE
20-1 Dec.	16	Balance	✓			3 7 9 6 00

NAME Anne Clark

ADDRESS 52 Juniper Road, Hartford, CT 06118

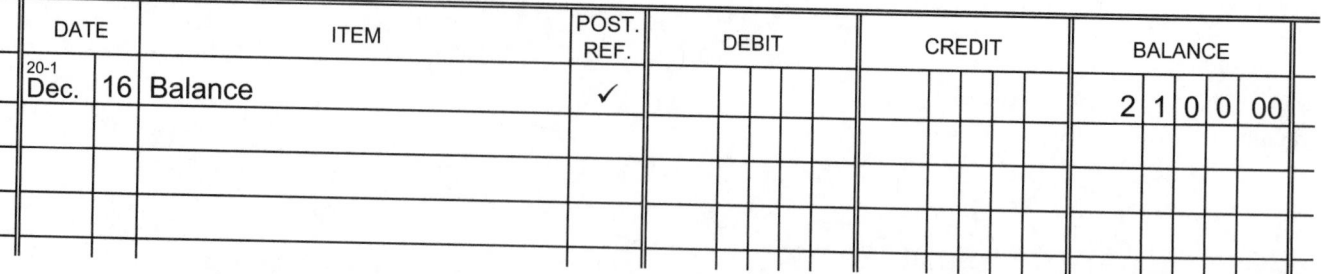

DATE		ITEM	POST. REF.	DEBIT	CREDIT	BALANCE
20-1 Dec.	16	Balance	✓			2 1 0 0 00

Comprehensive Problem 2—General Journal Based, Part 1
(Requirements 1., 2., 3., 6., 7., and 9. Continued)

NAME John Dempsey
ADDRESS 700 Hobbes Dr., Avon, CT 06108

DATE		ITEM	POST. REF.	DEBIT	CREDIT	BALANCE
20-1 Dec.	16	Balance	✓			1 5 6 0 00

NAME Kim Fields
ADDRESS 5200 Hamilton Ave., Hartford, CT 06117

DATE		ITEM	POST. REF.	DEBIT	CREDIT	BALANCE
20-1 Dec.	16	Balance	✓			

NAME Lucy Greene
ADDRESS 236 Bally Lane, Simsbury, CT 06123

DATE		ITEM	POST. REF.	DEBIT	CREDIT	BALANCE
20-1 Dec.	16	Balance	✓			2 8 0 0 00

Comprehensive Problem 2—General Journal Based, Part 1 (Requirements 1., 2., 3., 6., 7., and 9. Concluded)

ACCOUNTS PAYABLE LEDGER

NAME Evans Essentials

ADDRESS 34 Harry Ave., East Hartford, CT 05234

DATE		ITEM	POST. REF.	DEBIT	CREDIT	BALANCE
20-1 Dec.	16	Balance	✓			3 6 0 0 00

NAME Nathen Co.

ADDRESS 1009 Drake Rd., Farmington, CT 06082

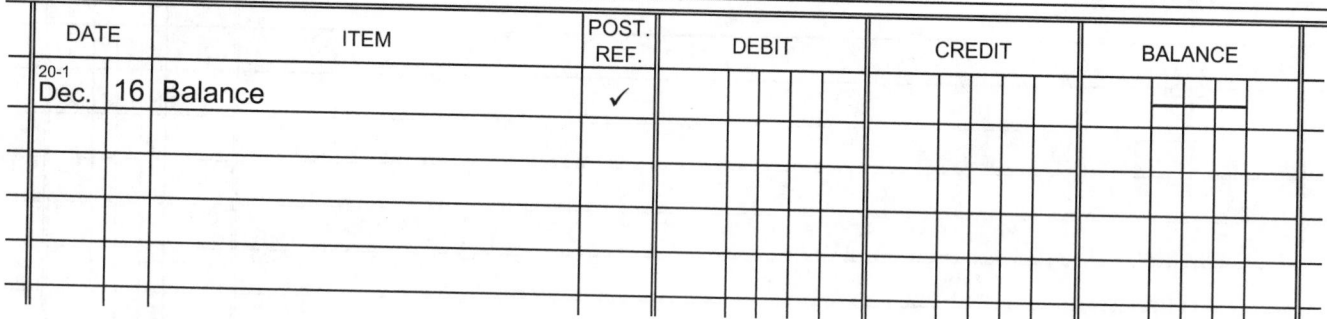

DATE		ITEM	POST. REF.	DEBIT	CREDIT	BALANCE
20-1 Dec.	16	Balance	✓			

NAME Owen Enterprises

ADDRESS 43 Lucky Lane, Bristol, CT 06007

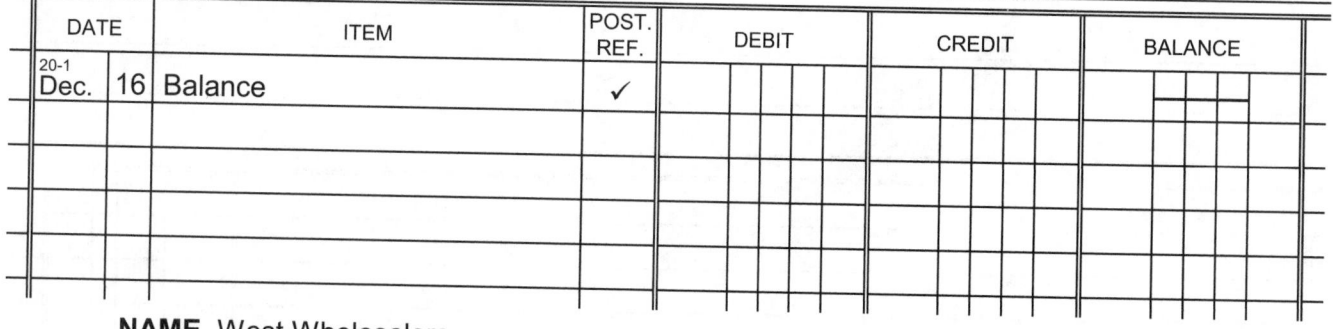

DATE		ITEM	POST. REF.	DEBIT	CREDIT	BALANCE
20-1 Dec.	16	Balance	✓			

NAME West Wholesalers

ADDRESS 888 Anders Street, Newington, CT 06789

DATE		ITEM	POST. REF.	DEBIT	CREDIT	BALANCE
20-1 Dec.	16	Balance	✓			

Comprehensive Problem 2—General Journal Based, Part 1

Requirement 4.

This page intentionally left blank.

Comprehensive Problem 2—General Journal Based, Part 1

Requirement 5.

	TRIAL BALANCE		ADJUSTMENTS	
	DEBIT	CREDIT	DEBIT	CREDIT
1				
2				
3				
4				
5				
6				
7				
8				
9				
10				
11				
12				
13				
14				
15				
16				
17				
18				
19				
20				
21				
22				
23				
24				
25				
26				
27				
28				
29				
30				
31				
32				
33				
34				
35				
36				

Comprehensive Problem 2—General Journal Based, Part 1
(Requirement 5. Continued)

ADJUSTED TRIAL BALANCE		INCOME STATEMENT		BALANCE SHEET		
DEBIT	CREDIT	DEBIT	CREDIT	DEBIT	CREDIT	
						1
						2
						3
						4
						5
						6
						7
						8
						9
						10
						11
						12
						13
						14
						15
						16
						17
						18
						19
						20
						21
						22
						23
						24
						25
						26
						27
						28
						29
						30
						31
						32
						33
						34
						35
						36

Comprehensive Problem 2—General Journal Based, Part 1
(Requirement 5. Continued)

Comprehensive Problem 2—General Journal Based, Part 1
(Requirement 5. Continued)

Comprehensive Problem 2—General Journal Based, Part 1
(Requirement 5. Concluded)

Comprehensive Problem 2—General Journal Based, Part 1

Requirement 6.

GENERAL JOURNAL

	DATE		DESCRIPTION	POST. REF.	DEBIT	CREDIT	
1							1
2							2
3							3
4							4
5							5
6							6
7							7
8							8
9							9
10							10
11							11
12							12
13							13
14							14
15							15
16							16
17							17
18							18
19							19
20							20
21							21
22							22
23							23
24							24
25							25
26							26
27							27
28							28
29							29
30							30
31							31
32							32
33							33
34							34

Comprehensive Problem 2—General Journal Based, Part 1

Requirements 7. and 9.

GENERAL JOURNAL

PAGE 6

	DATE		DESCRIPTION	POST. REF.	DEBIT	CREDIT	
1							1
2							2
3							3
4							4
5							5
6							6
7							7
8							8
9							9
10							10
11							11
12							12
13							13
14							14
15							15
16							16
17							17
18							18
19							19
20							20
21							21
22							22
23							23
24							24
25							25
26							26
27							27
28							28
29							29
30							30
31							31
32							32
33							33
34							34

Comprehensive Problem 2—General Journal Based, Part 1

Requirement 8.

ACCOUNT	DEBIT BALANCE	CREDIT BALANCE

Comprehensive Problem 2—General Journal Based, Part 2
Requirements 2. and 3.

GENERAL JOURNAL

	DATE		DESCRIPTION	POST. REF.	DEBIT	CREDIT	
1							1
2							2
3							3
4							4
5							5
6							6
7							7
8							8
9							9
10							10
11							11
12							12
13							13
14							14
15							15
16							16
17							17
18							18
19							19
20							20
21							21
22							22
23							23
24							24
25							25
26							26
27							27
28							28
29							29
30							30
31							31
32							32
33							33
34							34
35							35
36							36
37							37
38							38
39							39

Comprehensive Problem 2—General Journal Based, Part 2
(Requirements 2. and 3. Concluded)

GENERAL JOURNAL

PAGE 2

	DATE		DESCRIPTION	POST. REF.	DEBIT	CREDIT	
1							1
2							2
3							3
4							4
5							5
6							6
7							7
8							8
9							9
10							10
11							11
12							12
13							13
14							14
15							15
16							16
17							17
18							18
19							19
20							20
21							21
22							22
23							23
24							24
25							25
26							26
27							27
28							28
29							29
30							30
31							31
32							32
33							33
34							34
35							35
36							36
37							37
38							38
39							39

Comprehensive Problem 2—General Journal Based, Part 2

Requirements 1., 2., 3., 6., and 7.

GENERAL LEDGER

ACCOUNT Cash

ACCOUNT NO. 101

DATE		ITEM	POST. REF.	DEBIT	CREDIT	BALANCE DEBIT	BALANCE CREDIT
20-2 Jan.	1	Balance	✓			12 5 4 8 00	

ACCOUNT Accounts Receivable

ACCOUNT NO. 122

DATE		ITEM	POST. REF.	DEBIT	CREDIT	BALANCE DEBIT	BALANCE CREDIT
20-2 Jan.	1	Balance	✓			7 2 0 3 00	

Comprehensive Problem 2—General Journal Based, Part 2
(Requirements 1., 2., 3., 6., and 7. Continued)

ACCOUNT Merchandise Inventory   ACCOUNT NO. 131

DATE		ITEM	POST. REF.	DEBIT	CREDIT	BALANCE DEBIT	BALANCE CREDIT
20-2 Jan.	1	Balance	✓			19 7 0 0 00	

ACCOUNT Supplies   ACCOUNT NO. 141

DATE		ITEM	POST. REF.	DEBIT	CREDIT	BALANCE DEBIT	BALANCE CREDIT
20-2 Jan.	1	Balance	✓			5 2 5 00	

ACCOUNT Prepaid Insurance   ACCOUNT NO. 145

DATE		ITEM	POST. REF.	DEBIT	CREDIT	BALANCE DEBIT	BALANCE CREDIT
20-2 Jan.	1	Balance	✓			1 0 0 0 00	

ACCOUNT Land   ACCOUNT NO. 161

DATE		ITEM	POST. REF.	DEBIT	CREDIT	BALANCE DEBIT	BALANCE CREDIT
20-2 Jan.	1	Balance	✓			8 7 0 0 00	

Comprehensive Problem 2—General Journal Based, Part 2
(Requirements 1., 2., 3., 6., and 7. Continued)

ACCOUNT **Building** ACCOUNT NO. 171

DATE		ITEM	POST. REF.	DEBIT	CREDIT	BALANCE DEBIT	BALANCE CREDIT
20-2 Jan.	1	Balance	✓			52 0 0 0 00	

ACCOUNT **Accumulated Depreciation—Building** ACCOUNT NO. 171.1

DATE		ITEM	POST. REF.	DEBIT	CREDIT	BALANCE DEBIT	BALANCE CREDIT
20-2 Jan.	1	Balance	✓				10 0 0 0 00

ACCOUNT **Store Equipment** ACCOUNT NO. 181

DATE		ITEM	POST. REF.	DEBIT	CREDIT	BALANCE DEBIT	BALANCE CREDIT
20-2 Jan.	1	Balance	✓			28 7 5 0 00	

Comprehensive Problem 2—General Journal Based, Part 2
(Requirements 1., 2., 3., 6., and 7. Continued)

ACCOUNT Accumulated Depreciation—Store Equipment   ACCOUNT NO. 181.1

DATE		ITEM	POST. REF.	DEBIT	CREDIT	BALANCE DEBIT	BALANCE CREDIT
20-2 Jan.	1	Balance	✓				9 7 5 0 00

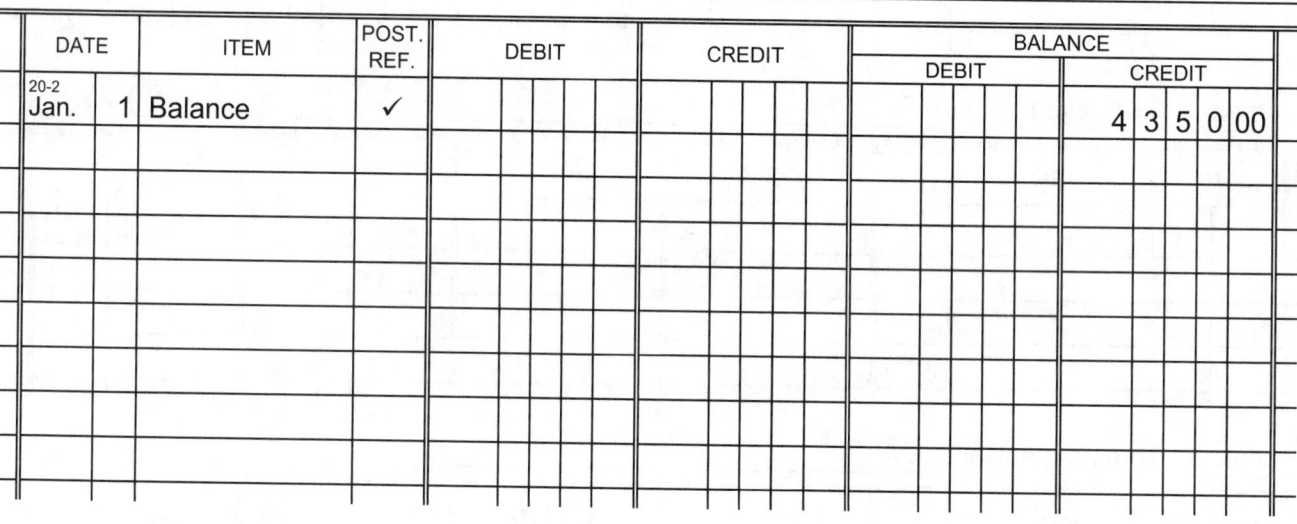

ACCOUNT Accounts Payable   ACCOUNT NO. 202

DATE		ITEM	POST. REF.	DEBIT	CREDIT	BALANCE DEBIT	BALANCE CREDIT
20-2 Jan.	1	Balance	✓				4 3 5 0 00

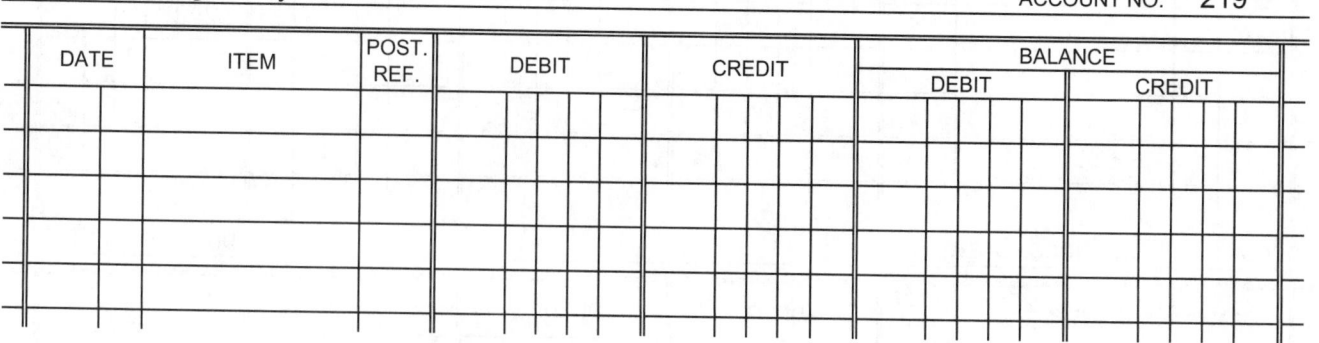

ACCOUNT Wages Payable   ACCOUNT NO. 219

DATE	ITEM	POST. REF.	DEBIT	CREDIT	BALANCE DEBIT	BALANCE CREDIT

Comprehensive Problem 2—General Journal Based, Part 2
(Requirements 1., 2., 3., 6., and 7. Continued)

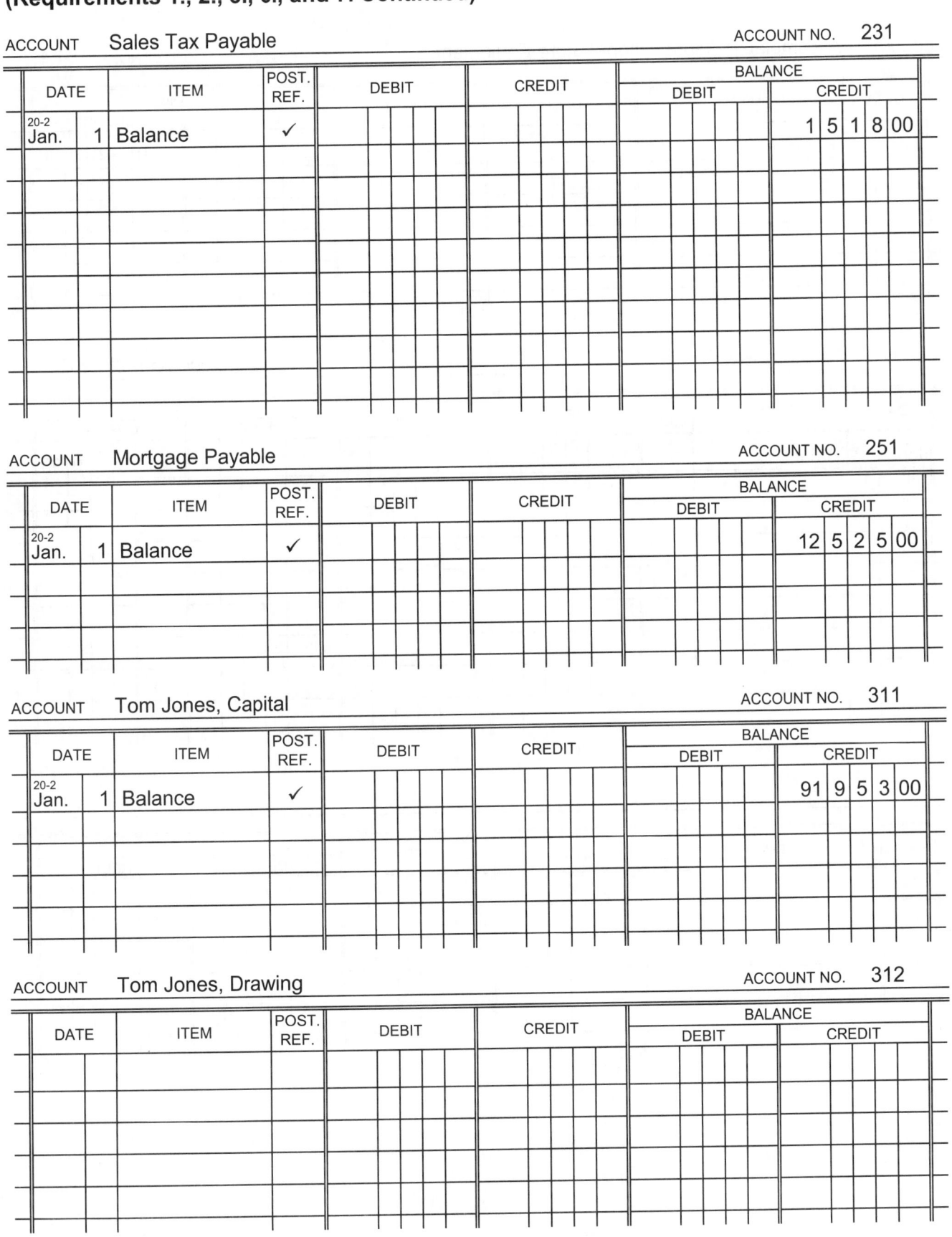

ACCOUNT Sales Tax Payable   ACCOUNT NO. 231

DATE		ITEM	POST. REF.	DEBIT	CREDIT	BALANCE DEBIT	BALANCE CREDIT
20-2 Jan.	1	Balance	✓				1 5 1 8 00

ACCOUNT Mortgage Payable   ACCOUNT NO. 251

DATE		ITEM	POST. REF.	DEBIT	CREDIT	BALANCE DEBIT	BALANCE CREDIT
20-2 Jan.	1	Balance	✓				12 5 2 5 00

ACCOUNT Tom Jones, Capital   ACCOUNT NO. 311

DATE		ITEM	POST. REF.	DEBIT	CREDIT	BALANCE DEBIT	BALANCE CREDIT
20-2 Jan.	1	Balance	✓				91 9 5 3 00

ACCOUNT Tom Jones, Drawing   ACCOUNT NO. 312

DATE		ITEM	POST. REF.	DEBIT	CREDIT	BALANCE DEBIT	BALANCE CREDIT

Comprehensive Problem 2—General Journal Based, Part 2
(Requirements 1., 2., 3., 6., and 7. Continued)

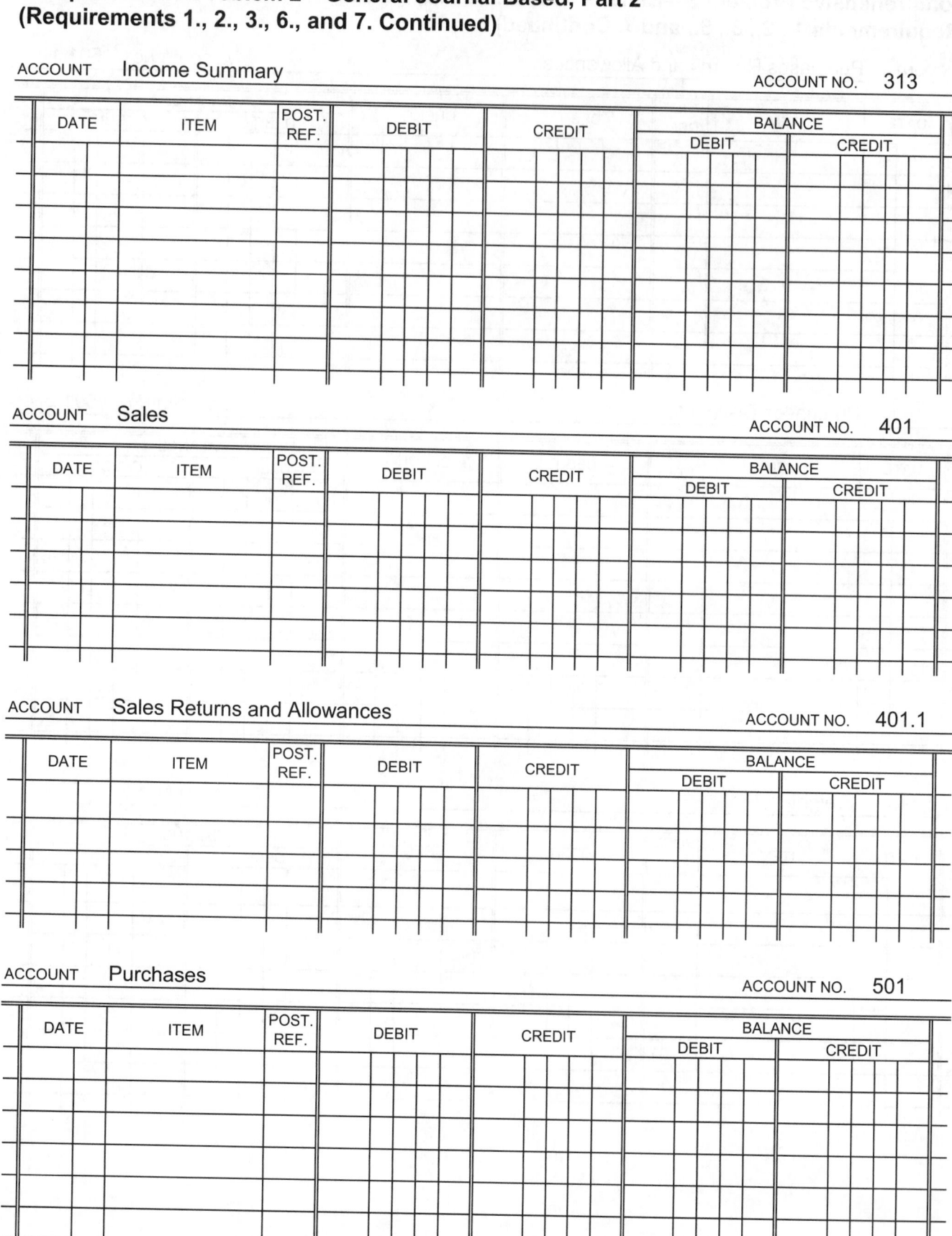

ACCOUNT Income Summary   **ACCOUNT NO.** 313

DATE	ITEM	POST. REF.	DEBIT	CREDIT	BALANCE DEBIT	BALANCE CREDIT

ACCOUNT Sales   **ACCOUNT NO.** 401

DATE	ITEM	POST. REF.	DEBIT	CREDIT	BALANCE DEBIT	BALANCE CREDIT

ACCOUNT Sales Returns and Allowances   **ACCOUNT NO.** 401.1

DATE	ITEM	POST. REF.	DEBIT	CREDIT	BALANCE DEBIT	BALANCE CREDIT

ACCOUNT Purchases   **ACCOUNT NO.** 501

DATE	ITEM	POST. REF.	DEBIT	CREDIT	BALANCE DEBIT	BALANCE CREDIT

Comprehensive Problem 2—General Journal Based, Part 2
(Requirements 1., 2., 3., 6., and 7. Continued)

ACCOUNT Purchases Returns and Allowances ACCOUNT NO. 501.1

DATE	ITEM	POST. REF.	DEBIT	CREDIT	BALANCE	
					DEBIT	CREDIT

ACCOUNT Purchases Discounts ACCOUNT NO. 501.2

DATE	ITEM	POST. REF.	DEBIT	CREDIT	BALANCE	
					DEBIT	CREDIT

ACCOUNT Freight-In ACCOUNT NO. 502

DATE	ITEM	POST. REF.	DEBIT	CREDIT	BALANCE	
					DEBIT	CREDIT

Comprehensive Problem 2—General Journal Based, Part 2
(Requirements 1., 2., 3., 6., and 7. Continued)

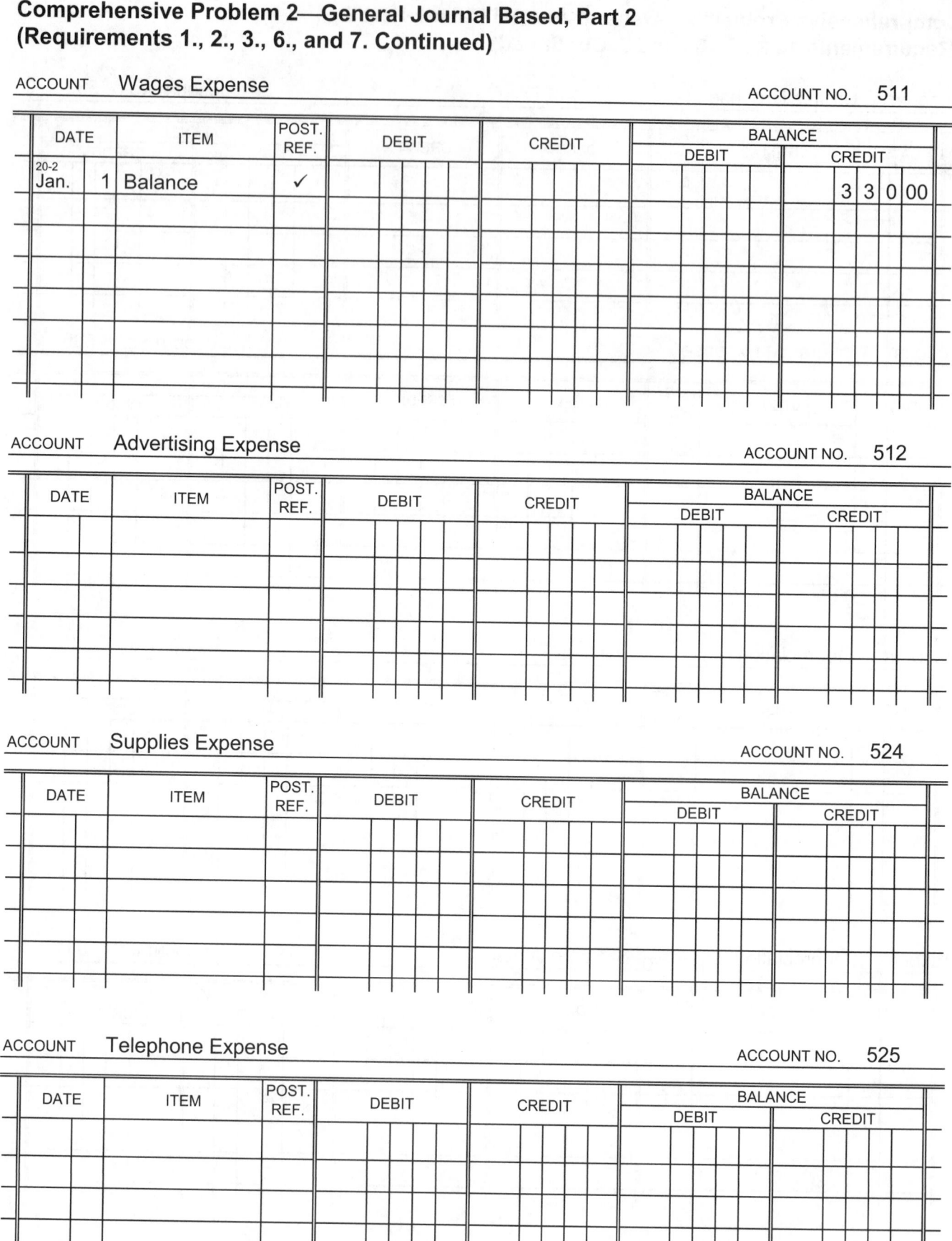

ACCOUNT   Wages Expense   ACCOUNT NO.   511

DATE		ITEM	POST. REF.	DEBIT	CREDIT	BALANCE DEBIT	BALANCE CREDIT
20-2 Jan.	1	Balance	✓				3 3 0 00

ACCOUNT   Advertising Expense   ACCOUNT NO.   512

DATE	ITEM	POST. REF.	DEBIT	CREDIT	BALANCE DEBIT	BALANCE CREDIT

ACCOUNT   Supplies Expense   ACCOUNT NO.   524

DATE	ITEM	POST. REF.	DEBIT	CREDIT	BALANCE DEBIT	BALANCE CREDIT

ACCOUNT   Telephone Expense   ACCOUNT NO.   525

DATE	ITEM	POST. REF.	DEBIT	CREDIT	BALANCE DEBIT	BALANCE CREDIT

Comprehensive Problem 2—General Journal Based, Part 2
(Requirements 1., 2., 3., 6., and 7. Continued)

ACCOUNT   Utilities Expense   ACCOUNT NO.   533

DATE	ITEM	POST. REF.	DEBIT	CREDIT	BALANCE DEBIT	BALANCE CREDIT

ACCOUNT   Insurance Expense   ACCOUNT NO.   535

DATE	ITEM	POST. REF.	DEBIT	CREDIT	BALANCE DEBIT	BALANCE CREDIT

ACCOUNT   Depreciation Expense—Building   ACCOUNT NO.   540

DATE	ITEM	POST. REF.	DEBIT	CREDIT	BALANCE DEBIT	BALANCE CREDIT

ACCOUNT   Depreciation Expense—Store Equipment   ACCOUNT NO.   541

DATE	ITEM	POST. REF.	DEBIT	CREDIT	BALANCE DEBIT	BALANCE CREDIT

Comprehensive Problem 2—General Journal Based, Part 2
(Requirements 1., 2., 3., 6., and 7. Continued)

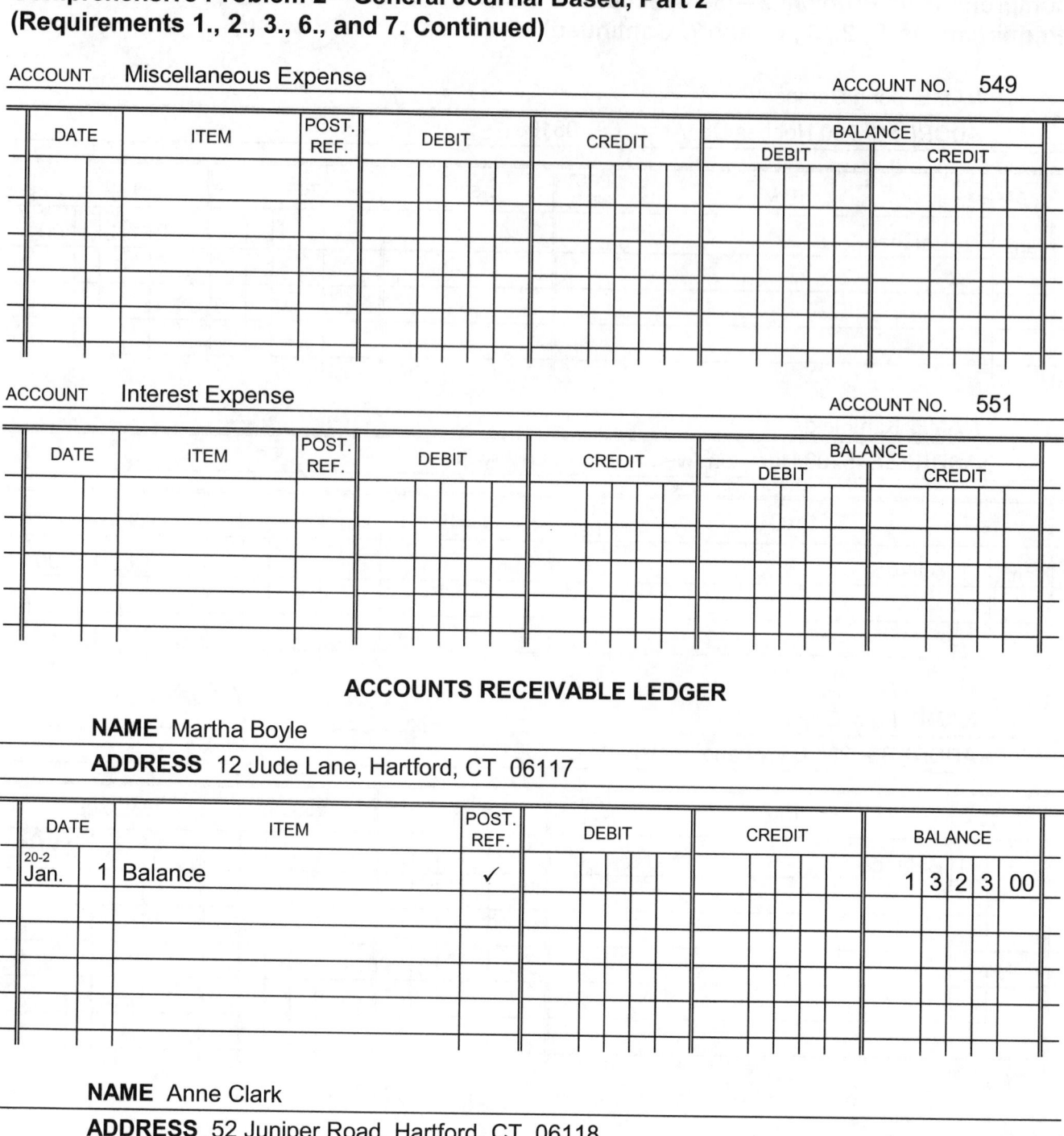

ACCOUNT Miscellaneous Expense   ACCOUNT NO. 549

DATE	ITEM	POST. REF.	DEBIT	CREDIT	BALANCE DEBIT	BALANCE CREDIT

ACCOUNT Interest Expense   ACCOUNT NO. 551

DATE	ITEM	POST. REF.	DEBIT	CREDIT	BALANCE DEBIT	BALANCE CREDIT

ACCOUNTS RECEIVABLE LEDGER

NAME Martha Boyle

ADDRESS 12 Jude Lane, Hartford, CT 06117

DATE		ITEM	POST. REF.	DEBIT	CREDIT	BALANCE
20-2 Jan.	1	Balance	✓			1 3 2 3 00

NAME Anne Clark

ADDRESS 52 Juniper Road, Hartford, CT 06118

DATE		ITEM	POST. REF.	DEBIT	CREDIT	BALANCE
20-2 Jan.	1	Balance	✓			2 1 0 0 00

Comprehensive Problem 2—General Journal Based, Part 2 (Requirements 1., 2., 3., 6., and 7. Continued)

NAME John Dempsey

ADDRESS 700 Hobbes Dr., Avon, CT 06108

DATE		ITEM	POST. REF.	DEBIT	CREDIT	BALANCE
20-2 Jan.	1	Balance	✓			2 1 2 1 00

NAME Kim Fields

ADDRESS 5200 Hamilton Ave., Hartford, CT 06117

DATE		ITEM	POST. REF.	DEBIT	CREDIT	BALANCE
20-2 Jan.	1	Balance	✓			1 6 8 00

NAME Lucy Greene

ADDRESS 236 Bally Lane, Simsbury, CT 06123

DATE		ITEM	POST. REF.	DEBIT	CREDIT	BALANCE
20-2 Jan.	1	Balance	✓			1 4 9 1 00

Comprehensive Problem 2—General Journal Based, Part 2
(Requirements 1., 2., 3., 6., and 7. Concluded)

ACCOUNTS PAYABLE LEDGER

NAME Evans Essentials

ADDRESS 34 Harry Ave., East Hartford, CT 05234

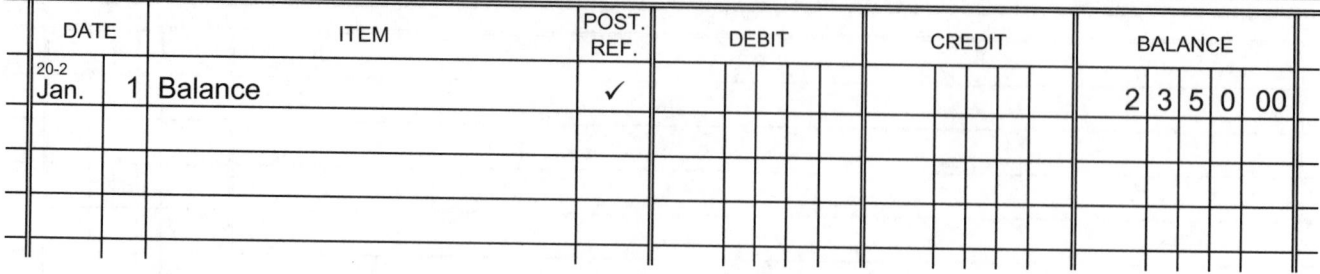

DATE		ITEM	POST. REF.	DEBIT	CREDIT	BALANCE
20-2 Jan.	1	Balance	✓			2 3 5 0 00

NAME Nathen Co.

ADDRESS 1009 Drake Rd., Farmington, CT 06082

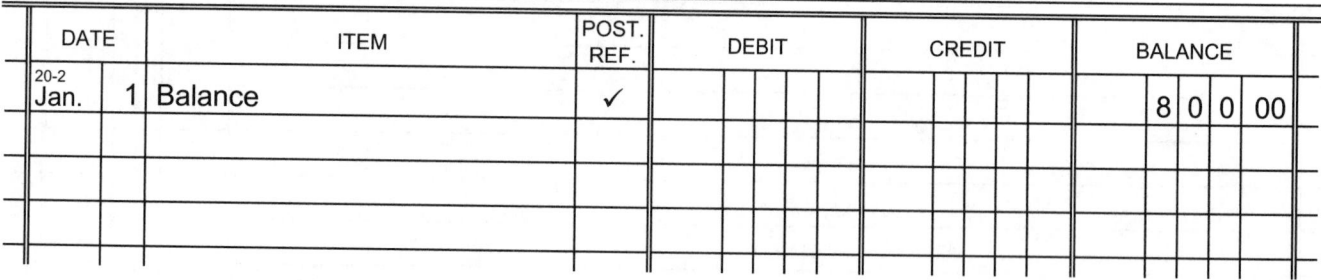

DATE		ITEM	POST. REF.	DEBIT	CREDIT	BALANCE
20-2 Jan.	1	Balance	✓			8 0 0 00

NAME Owen Enterprises

ADDRESS 43 Lucky Lane, Bristol, CT 06007

DATE	ITEM	POST. REF.	DEBIT	CREDIT	BALANCE

NAME West Wholesalers

ADDRESS 888 Anders Street, Newington, CT 06789

DATE		ITEM	POST. REF.	DEBIT	CREDIT	BALANCE
20-2 Jan.	1	Balance	✓			1 2 0 0 00

Comprehensive Problem 2—General Journal Based, Part 2

Requirement 4.

This page intentionally left blank.

COMPREHENSIVE PROBLEM

Comprehensive Problem 2—General Journal Based, Part 2

Requirement 5.

	TRIAL BALANCE		ADJUSTMENTS	
	DEBIT	CREDIT	DEBIT	CREDIT
1				
2				
3				
4				
5				
6				
7				
8				
9				
10				
11				
12				
13				
14				
15				
16				
17				
18				
19				
20				
21				
22				
23				
24				
25				
26				
27				
28				
29				
30				
31				
32				
33				
34				
35				
36				

Comprehensive Problem 2—General Journal Based, Part 2 (Requirement 5. Continued)

	ADJUSTED TRIAL BALANCE		INCOME STATEMENT		BALANCE SHEET	
	DEBIT	CREDIT	DEBIT	CREDIT	DEBIT	CREDIT
1						
2						
3						
4						
5						
6						
7						
8						
9						
10						
11						
12						
13						
14						
15						
16						
17						
18						
19						
20						
21						
22						
23						
24						
25						
26						
27						
28						
29						
30						
31						
32						
33						
34						
35						
36						

(Requirement 5. Continued)

Comprehensive Problem 2—General Journal Based, Part 2

**Comprehensive Problem 2—General Journal Based, Part 2
(Requirement 5. Continued)**

Comprehensive Problem 2—General Journal Based, Part 2
(Requirement 5. Concluded)

Comprehensive Problem 2—General Journal Based, Part 2

Requirement 6.

GENERAL JOURNAL

PAGE 3

	DATE		DESCRIPTION	POST. REF.	DEBIT	CREDIT	
1							1
2							2
3							3
4							4
5							5
6							6
7							7
8							8
9							9
10							10
11							11
12							12
13							13
14							14
15							15
16							16
17							17
18							18
19							19
20							20
21							21
22							22
23							23
24							24
25							25
26							26
27							27
28							28
29							29
30							30
31							31
32							32
33							33
34							34

Comprehensive Problem 2—General Journal Based, Part 2

GENERAL JOURNAL

PAGE 4

DATE	DESCRIPTION	POST. REF.	DEBIT	CREDIT	
					1
					2
					3
					4
					5
					6
					7
					8
					9
					10
					11
					12
					13
					14
					15
					16
					17
					18
					19
					20
					21
					22
					23
					24
					25
					26
					27
					28
					29
					30
					31
					32
					33
					34

ACCOUNT	DEBIT BALANCE	CREDIT BALANCE

Requirement 8.

Comprehensive Problem 2—General Journal Based, Part 2

Comprehensive Problem 2—Special Journals Based, Part 1

Requirements 2. and 3.

SALES JOURNAL

PAGE 6

DATE		SALE NO.	TO WHOM SOLD	POST. REF.	ACCOUNTS RECEIVABLE DEBIT	SALES CREDIT	SALES TAX PAYABLE CREDIT
20-1 Dec.	1-15		Cumulative Amount	✓	4 2 6 3 00	4 0 6 0 00	2 0 3 00

CASH RECEIPTS JOURNAL

PAGE 9

	DATE		ACCOUNT CREDITED	POST. REF.	GENERAL CREDIT	ACCOUNTS RECEIVABLE CREDIT	SALES CREDIT	SALES TAX PAYABLE CREDIT	CASH DEBIT	
1	20-1 Dec.	1-15	Cumulative Amt	✓		1 8 3 0 00	4 8 4 0 00	2 4 2 00	6 9 1 2 00	1
2										2
3										3
4										4
5										5
6										6
7										7

Comprehensive Problem 2—Special Journals Based, Part 1 (Requirements 2. and 3. Continued)

PURCHASES JOURNAL

	DATE	INVOICE NO.	FROM WHOM PURCHASED	POST. REF.	PURCHASES DEBIT ACCTS. PAY. CREDIT	
1	20-1 Dec. 1-15		Cumulative Amount	✓	3 9 0 0 00	1
2						2
3						3
4						4
5						5
6						6

CASH PAYMENTS JOURNAL

	DATE	CK. NO.	ACCOUNT DEBITED	POST. REF.	GENERAL DEBIT	ACCOUNTS PAYABLE DEBIT	PURCHASES DEBIT	PURCHASES DISCOUNTS CREDIT	CASH CREDIT	
1	20-1 Dec. 1-15		Cumulative Amount	✓	1 6 8 0 00	7 1 5 0 00		1 2 3 00	8 7 0 7 00	1
2										2
3										3
4										4
5										5
6										6
7										7
8										8
9										9
10										10
11										11
12										12
13										13
14										14
15										15

Comprehensive Problem 2—Special Journals Based, Part 1
(Requirements 2. and 3. Concluded)

GENERAL JOURNAL

PAGE 3

	DATE	DESCRIPTION	POST. REF.	DEBIT	CREDIT	
1						1
2						2
3						3
4						4
5						5
6						6
7						7
8						8
9						9
10						10
11						11
12						12

Requirements 1., 2., 3., 6., 7., and 9.

GENERAL LEDGER

ACCOUNT   Cash

ACCOUNT NO. 101

DATE		ITEM	POST. REF.	DEBIT	CREDIT	BALANCE DEBIT	BALANCE CREDIT
20-1 Dec.	16	Balance	✓			11 5 0 0 00	

ACCOUNT   Accounts Receivable

ACCOUNT NO. 122

DATE		ITEM	POST. REF.	DEBIT	CREDIT	BALANCE DEBIT	BALANCE CREDIT
20-1 Dec.	16	Balance	✓			7 8 2 3 00	

Comprehensive Problem 2—Special Journals Based, Part 1 (Requirements 1., 2., 3., 6., 7., and 9. Continued)

ACCOUNT Merchandise Inventory   **ACCOUNT NO.** 131

DATE		ITEM	POST. REF.	DEBIT	CREDIT	BALANCE	
						DEBIT	CREDIT
20-1 Dec.	16	Balance	✓			21 8 0 0 00	

ACCOUNT Supplies   **ACCOUNT NO.** 141

DATE		ITEM	POST. REF.	DEBIT	CREDIT	BALANCE	
						DEBIT	CREDIT
20-1 Dec.	16	Balance	✓			1 0 3 5 00	

ACCOUNT Prepaid Insurance   **ACCOUNT NO.** 145

DATE		ITEM	POST. REF.	DEBIT	CREDIT	BALANCE	
						DEBIT	CREDIT
20-1 Dec.	16	Balance	✓			1 3 8 0 00	

ACCOUNT Land   **ACCOUNT NO.** 161

DATE		ITEM	POST. REF.	DEBIT	CREDIT	BALANCE	
						DEBIT	CREDIT
20-1 Dec.	16	Balance	✓			8 7 0 0 00	

Comprehensive Problem 2—Special Journals Based, Part 1
(Requirements 1., 2., 3., 6., 7., and 9. Continued)

ACCOUNT Building

ACCOUNT NO. 171

DATE		ITEM	POST. REF.	DEBIT	CREDIT	BALANCE	
						DEBIT	CREDIT
20-1 Dec.	16	Balance	✓			52 0 0 0 00	

ACCOUNT Accumulated Depreciation—Building

ACCOUNT NO. 171.1

DATE		ITEM	POST. REF.	DEBIT	CREDIT	BALANCE	
						DEBIT	CREDIT
20-1 Dec.	16	Balance	✓				9 2 0 0 00

ACCOUNT Store Equipment

ACCOUNT NO. 181

DATE		ITEM	POST. REF.	DEBIT	CREDIT	BALANCE	
						DEBIT	CREDIT
20-1 Dec.	16	Balance	✓			28 7 5 0 00	

ACCOUNT Accumulated Depreciation—Store Equipment

ACCOUNT NO. 181.1

DATE		ITEM	POST. REF.	DEBIT	CREDIT	BALANCE	
						DEBIT	CREDIT
20-1 Dec.	16	Balance	✓				9 3 0 0 00

Comprehensive Problem 2—Special Journals Based, Part 1
(Requirements 1., 2., 3., 6., 7., and 9. Continued)

ACCOUNT Accounts Payable   ACCOUNT NO. 202

DATE		ITEM	POST. REF.	DEBIT	CREDIT	BALANCE DEBIT	BALANCE CREDIT
20-1 Dec.	16	Balance	✓				6 8 5 0 00

ACCOUNT Wages Payable   ACCOUNT NO. 219

DATE	ITEM	POST. REF.	DEBIT	CREDIT	BALANCE DEBIT	BALANCE CREDIT

ACCOUNT Sales Tax Payable   ACCOUNT NO. 231

DATE		ITEM	POST. REF.	DEBIT	CREDIT	BALANCE DEBIT	BALANCE CREDIT
20-1 Dec.	16	Balance	✓				9 3 3 00

ACCOUNT Mortgage Payable   ACCOUNT NO. 251

DATE		ITEM	POST. REF.	DEBIT	CREDIT	BALANCE DEBIT	BALANCE CREDIT
20-1 Dec.	16	Balance	✓				12 5 2 5 00

Comprehensive Problem 2—Special Journals Based, Part 1
(Requirements 1., 2., 3., 6., 7., and 9. Continued)

ACCOUNT Tom Jones, Capital   ACCOUNT NO. 311

DATE		ITEM	POST. REF.	DEBIT	CREDIT	BALANCE DEBIT	BALANCE CREDIT
20-1 Dec.	16	Balance	✓				90 0 0 0 00

ACCOUNT Tom Jones, Drawing   ACCOUNT NO. 312

DATE		ITEM	POST. REF.	DEBIT	CREDIT	BALANCE DEBIT	BALANCE CREDIT
20-1 Dec.	16	Balance	✓			8 5 0 0 00	

ACCOUNT Income Summary   ACCOUNT NO. 313

DATE		ITEM	POST. REF.	DEBIT	CREDIT	BALANCE DEBIT	BALANCE CREDIT

ACCOUNT Sales   ACCOUNT NO. 401

DATE		ITEM	POST. REF.	DEBIT	CREDIT	BALANCE DEBIT	BALANCE CREDIT
20-1 Dec.	16	Balance	✓				116 0 0 0 00

Comprehensive Problem 2—Special Journals Based, Part 1
(Requirements 1., 2., 3., 6., 7., and 9. Continued)

ACCOUNT Sales Returns and Allowances   ACCOUNT NO. 401.1

DATE		ITEM	POST. REF.	DEBIT	CREDIT	BALANCE DEBIT	BALANCE CREDIT
20-1 Dec.	16	Balance	✓			1 4 3 0 00	

ACCOUNT Purchases   ACCOUNT NO. 501

DATE		ITEM	POST. REF.	DEBIT	CREDIT	BALANCE DEBIT	BALANCE CREDIT
20-1 Dec.	16	Balance	✓			60 5 0 0 00	

ACCOUNT Purchases Returns and Allowances   ACCOUNT NO. 501.1

DATE		ITEM	POST. REF.	DEBIT	CREDIT	BALANCE DEBIT	BALANCE CREDIT
20-1 Dec.	16	Balance	✓				4 6 0 00

ACCOUNT Purchases Discounts   ACCOUNT NO. 501.2

DATE		ITEM	POST. REF.	DEBIT	CREDIT	BALANCE DEBIT	BALANCE CREDIT
20-1 Dec.	16	Balance	✓				5 7 5 00

Comprehensive Problem 2—Special Journals Based, Part 1
(Requirements 1., 2., 3., 6., 7., and 9. Continued)

ACCOUNT   Freight-In   ACCOUNT NO.   502

DATE		ITEM	POST. REF.	DEBIT	CREDIT	BALANCE	
						DEBIT	CREDIT
20-1 Dec.	16	Balance	✓			1 7 5 00	

ACCOUNT   Wages Expense   ACCOUNT NO.   511

DATE		ITEM	POST. REF.	DEBIT	CREDIT	BALANCE	
						DEBIT	CREDIT
20-1 Dec.	16	Balance	✓			26 1 0 0 00	

ACCOUNT   Advertising Expense   ACCOUNT NO.   512

DATE		ITEM	POST. REF.	DEBIT	CREDIT	BALANCE	
						DEBIT	CREDIT
20-1 Dec.	16	Balance	✓			4 7 0 0 00	

ACCOUNT   Supplies Expense   ACCOUNT NO.   524

DATE	ITEM	POST. REF.	DEBIT	CREDIT	BALANCE	
					DEBIT	CREDIT

Comprehensive Problem 2—Special Journals Based, Part 1
(Requirements 1., 2., 3., 6., 7., and 9. Continued)

ACCOUNT   Telephone Expense   ACCOUNT NO. 525

DATE		ITEM	POST. REF.	DEBIT	CREDIT	BALANCE DEBIT	BALANCE CREDIT
20-1 Dec.	16	Balance	✓			2 1 8 0 00	

ACCOUNT   Utilities Expense   ACCOUNT NO. 533

DATE		ITEM	POST. REF.	DEBIT	CREDIT	BALANCE DEBIT	BALANCE CREDIT
20-1 Dec.	16	Balance	✓			6 9 0 0 00	

ACCOUNT   Insurance Expense   ACCOUNT NO. 535

DATE		ITEM	POST. REF.	DEBIT	CREDIT	BALANCE DEBIT	BALANCE CREDIT

ACCOUNT   Depreciation Expense—Building   ACCOUNT NO. 540

DATE	ITEM	POST. REF.	DEBIT	CREDIT	BALANCE DEBIT	BALANCE CREDIT

Comprehensive Problem 2—Special Journals Based, Part 1
(Requirements 1., 2., 3., 6., 7., and 9. Continued)

ACCOUNT   Depreciation Expense—Store Equipment   ACCOUNT NO.   541

DATE	ITEM	POST. REF.	DEBIT	CREDIT	BALANCE DEBIT	BALANCE CREDIT

ACCOUNT   Miscellaneous Expense   ACCOUNT NO.   549

DATE		ITEM	POST. REF.	DEBIT	CREDIT	BALANCE DEBIT	BALANCE CREDIT
20-1 Dec.	16	Balance	✓			2 7 0 0 00	

ACCOUNT   Interest Expense   ACCOUNT NO.   551

DATE		ITEM	POST. REF.	DEBIT	CREDIT	BALANCE DEBIT	BALANCE CREDIT
20-1 Dec.	16	Balance	✓			1 3 5 0 00	

ACCOUNTS RECEIVABLE LEDGER

NAME Martha Boyle

ADDRESS 12 Jude Lane, Hartford, CT 06117

DATE		ITEM	POST. REF.	DEBIT	CREDIT	BALANCE
20-1 Dec.	16	Balance	✓			3 7 9 6 00

Comprehensive Problem 2—Special Journals Based, Part 1
(Requirements 1., 2., 3., 6., 7., and 9. Continued)

NAME Anne Clark

ADDRESS 52 Juniper Road, Hartford, CT 06118

DATE		ITEM	POST. REF.	DEBIT	CREDIT	BALANCE
20-1 Dec.	16	Balance	✓			2 1 0 0 00

NAME John Dempsey

ADDRESS 700 Hobbes Dr., Avon, CT 06108

DATE		ITEM	POST. REF.	DEBIT	CREDIT	BALANCE
20-1 Dec.	16	Balance	✓			1 5 6 0 00

NAME Kim Fields

ADDRESS 5200 Hamilton Ave., Hartford, CT 06117

DATE		ITEM	POST. REF.	DEBIT	CREDIT	BALANCE
20-1 Dec.	16	Balance	✓			

NAME Lucy Greene

ADDRESS 236 Bally Lane, Simsbury, CT 06123

DATE		ITEM	POST. REF.	DEBIT	CREDIT	BALANCE
20-1 Dec.	16	Balance	✓			2 8 0 0 00

Comprehensive Problem 2—Special Journals Based, Part 1
(Requirements 1., 2., 3., 6., 7., and 9. Continued)

ACCOUNTS PAYABLE LEDGER

NAME Evans Essentials

ADDRESS 34 Harry Ave., East Hartford, CT 05234

DATE		ITEM	POST. REF.	DEBIT	CREDIT	BALANCE
20-1 Dec.	16	Balance	✓			3 6 0 0 00

NAME Nathen Co.

ADDRESS 1009 Drake Rd., Farmington, CT 06082

DATE		ITEM	POST. REF.	DEBIT	CREDIT	BALANCE
20-1 Dec.	16	Balance	✓			

Comprehensive Problem 2—Special Journals Based, Part 1
(Requirements 1., 2., 3., 6., 7., and 9. Concluded)

NAME Owen Enterprises

ADDRESS 43 Lucky Lane, Bristol, CT 06007

DATE		ITEM	POST. REF.	DEBIT	CREDIT	BALANCE
20-1 Dec.	16	Balance	✓			

NAME West Wholesalers

ADDRESS 888 Anders Street, Newington, CT 06789

DATE		ITEM	POST. REF.	DEBIT	CREDIT	BALANCE
20-1 Dec.	16	Balance	✓			

Comprehensive Problem 2—Special Journals Based, Part 1

Requirement 4.

Comprehensive Problem 2—Special Journals Based, Part 1

Requirement 5.

	TRIAL BALANCE		ADJUSTMENTS	
	DEBIT	CREDIT	DEBIT	CREDIT
1				
2				
3				
4				
5				
6				
7				
8				
9				
10				
11				
12				
13				
14				
15				
16				
17				
18				
19				
20				
21				
22				
23				
24				
25				
26				
27				
28				
29				
30				
31				
32				
33				
34				
35				
36				

Comprehensive Problem 2—Special Journals Based, Part 1 (Requirement 5. Continued)

	ADJUSTED TRIAL BALANCE		INCOME STATEMENT		BALANCE SHEET	
	DEBIT	CREDIT	DEBIT	CREDIT	DEBIT	CREDIT
1						
2						
3						
4						
5						
6						
7						
8						
9						
10						
11						
12						
13						
14						
15						
16						
17						
18						
19						
20						
21						
22						
23						
24						
25						
26						
27						
28						
29						
30						
31						
32						
33						
34						
35						
36						

Comprehensive Problem 2—Special Journals Based, Part 1

(Requirement 5. Continued)

Comprehensive Problem 2—Special Journals Based, Part 1
(Requirement 5. Continued)

(Requirement 5. Concluded)

Comprehensive Problem 2—Special Journals Based, Part 1

COMPREHENSIVE PROBLEM

Name _____

Comprehensive Problem 2—Special Journals Based, Part 1

Requirement 6.

GENERAL JOURNAL

	DATE	DESCRIPTION	POST. REF.	DEBIT	CREDIT	
1						1
2						2
3						3
4						4
5						5
6						6
7						7
8						8
9						9
10						10
11						11
12						12
13						13
14						14
15						15
16						16
17						17
18						18
19						19
20						20
21						21
22						22
23						23
24						24
25						25
26						26
27						27
28						28
29						29
30						30
31						31
32						32
33						33
34						34

Comprehensive Problem 2—Special Journals Based, Part 1

Requirements 7. and 9.

GENERAL JOURNAL

PAGE 6

	DATE	DESCRIPTION	POST. REF.	DEBIT	CREDIT	
1						1
2						2
3						3
4						4
5						5
6						6
7						7
8						8
9						9
10						10
11						11
12						12
13						13
14						14
15						15
16						16
17						17
18						18
19						19
20						20
21						21
22						22
23						23
24						24
25						25
26						26
27						27
28						28
29						29
30						30
31						31
32						32
33						33
34						34

Comprehensive Problem 2—Special Journals Based, Part 1

Requirement 8.

ACCOUNT	DEBIT BALANCE	CREDIT BALANCE

Comprehensive Problem 2—Special Journals Based, Part 2

Requirements 2. and 3.

SALES JOURNAL   PAGE 7

DATE	SALE NO.	TO WHOM SOLD	POST. REF.	ACCOUNTS RECEIVABLE DEBIT	SALES CREDIT	SALES TAX PAYABLE CREDIT

CASH RECEIPTS JOURNAL   PAGE 10

	DATE	ACCOUNT CREDITED	POST. REF.	GENERAL CREDIT	ACCOUNTS RECEIVABLE CREDIT	SALES CREDIT	SALES TAX PAYABLE CREDIT	CASH DEBIT	
1									1
2									2
3									3
4									4
5									5
6									6
7									7
8									8
9									9

Comprehensive Problem 2—Special Journals Based, Part 2
(Requirements 2. and 3. Continued)

PURCHASES JOURNAL

	DATE	INVOICE NO.	FROM WHOM PURCHASED	POST. REF.	PURCHASES DEBIT ACCTS. PAY. CREDIT	
1						1
2						2
3						3
4						4
5						5
6						6
7						7
8						8
9						9

CASH PAYMENTS JOURNAL

	DATE	CK. NO.	ACCOUNT DEBITED	POST. REF.	GENERAL DEBIT	ACCOUNTS PAYABLE DEBIT	PURCHASES DEBIT	PURCHASES DISCOUNTS CREDIT	CASH CREDIT	
1										1
2										2
3										3
4										4
5										5
6										6
7										7
8										8
9										9
10										10
11										11
12										12
13										13

Comprehensive Problem 2—Special Journals Based, Part 2
(Requirements 2. and 3. Concluded)

GENERAL JOURNAL PAGE 1

	DATE	DESCRIPTION	POST. REF.	DEBIT	CREDIT	
1						1
2						2
3						3
4						4
5						5
6						6
7						7
8						8
9						9
10						10
11						11
12						12

Requirements 1., 2., 3., 6., and 7.

GENERAL LEDGER

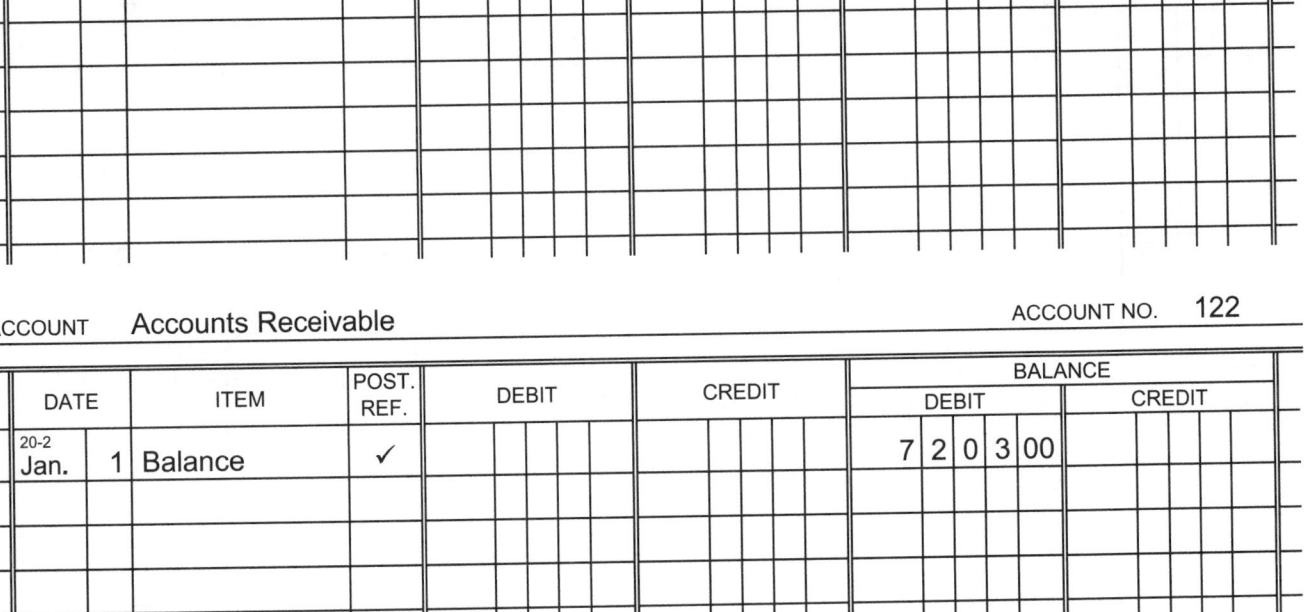

ACCOUNT Cash   ACCOUNT NO. 101

DATE	ITEM	POST. REF.	DEBIT	CREDIT	BALANCE DEBIT	BALANCE CREDIT
20-2 Jan. 1	Balance	✓			12 5 4 8 00	

ACCOUNT Accounts Receivable   ACCOUNT NO. 122

DATE	ITEM	POST. REF.	DEBIT	CREDIT	BALANCE DEBIT	BALANCE CREDIT
20-2 Jan. 1	Balance	✓			7 2 0 3 00	

Name _____

Comprehensive Problem 2—Special Journals Based, Part 2
(Requirements 1., 2., 3., 6., and 7. Continued)

ACCOUNT **Merchandise Inventory** ACCOUNT NO. 131

DATE		ITEM	POST. REF.	DEBIT	CREDIT	BALANCE DEBIT	BALANCE CREDIT
20-2 Jan.	1	Balance	✓			19 7 0 0 00	

ACCOUNT **Supplies** ACCOUNT NO. 141

DATE		ITEM	POST. REF.	DEBIT	CREDIT	BALANCE DEBIT	BALANCE CREDIT
20-2 Jan.	1	Balance	✓			5 2 5 00	

ACCOUNT **Prepaid Insurance** ACCOUNT NO. 145

DATE		ITEM	POST. REF.	DEBIT	CREDIT	BALANCE DEBIT	BALANCE CREDIT
20-2 Jan.	1	Balance	✓			1 0 0 0 00	

ACCOUNT **Land** ACCOUNT NO. 161

DATE		ITEM	POST. REF.	DEBIT	CREDIT	BALANCE DEBIT	BALANCE CREDIT
20-2 Jan.	1	Balance	✓			8 7 0 0 00	

Comprehensive Problem 2—Special Journals Based, Part 2
(Requirements 1., 2., 3., 6., and 7. Continued)

ACCOUNT **Building**   ACCOUNT NO. **171**

DATE		ITEM	POST. REF.	DEBIT	CREDIT	BALANCE DEBIT	BALANCE CREDIT
20-2 Jan.	1	Balance	✓			52 0 0 0 00	

ACCOUNT **Accumulated Depreciation—Building**   ACCOUNT NO. **171.1**

DATE		ITEM	POST. REF.	DEBIT	CREDIT	BALANCE DEBIT	BALANCE CREDIT
20-2 Jan.	1	Balance	✓				10 0 0 0 00

ACCOUNT **Store Equipment**   ACCOUNT NO. **181**

DATE		ITEM	POST. REF.	DEBIT	CREDIT	BALANCE DEBIT	BALANCE CREDIT
20-2 Jan.	1	Balance	✓			28 7 5 0 00	

ACCOUNT **Accumulated Depreciation—Store Equipment**   ACCOUNT NO. **181.1**

DATE		ITEM	POST. REF.	DEBIT	CREDIT	BALANCE DEBIT	BALANCE CREDIT
20-2 Jan.	1	Balance	✓				9 7 5 0 00

Comprehensive Problem 2—Special Journals Based, Part 2
(Requirements 1., 2., 3., 6., and 7. Continued)

ACCOUNT Accounts Payable   ACCOUNT NO. 202

DATE		ITEM	POST. REF.	DEBIT	CREDIT	BALANCE	
						DEBIT	CREDIT
20-2 Jan.	1	Balance	✓				4 3 5 0 00

ACCOUNT Wages Payable   ACCOUNT NO. 219

DATE	ITEM	POST. REF.	DEBIT	CREDIT	BALANCE	
					DEBIT	CREDIT

ACCOUNT Sales Tax Payable   ACCOUNT NO. 231

DATE		ITEM	POST. REF.	DEBIT	CREDIT	BALANCE	
						DEBIT	CREDIT
20-2 Jan.	1	Balance	✓				1 5 1 8 00

ACCOUNT Mortgage Payable   ACCOUNT NO. 251

DATE		ITEM	POST. REF.	DEBIT	CREDIT	BALANCE	
						DEBIT	CREDIT
20-2 Jan.	1	Balance	✓				12 5 2 5 00

Comprehensive Problem 2—Special Journals Based, Part 2
(Requirements 1., 2., 3., 6., and 7. Continued)

ACCOUNT Tom Jones, Capital   ACCOUNT NO. 311

DATE		ITEM	POST. REF.	DEBIT	CREDIT	BALANCE DEBIT	BALANCE CREDIT
20-2 Jan.	1	Balance	✓				91 9 5 3 00

ACCOUNT Tom Jones, Drawing   ACCOUNT NO. 312

DATE	ITEM	POST. REF.	DEBIT	CREDIT	BALANCE DEBIT	BALANCE CREDIT

ACCOUNT Income Summary   ACCOUNT NO. 313

DATE	ITEM	POST. REF.	DEBIT	CREDIT	BALANCE DEBIT	BALANCE CREDIT

ACCOUNT Sales   ACCOUNT NO. 401

DATE	ITEM	POST. REF.	DEBIT	CREDIT	BALANCE DEBIT	BALANCE CREDIT

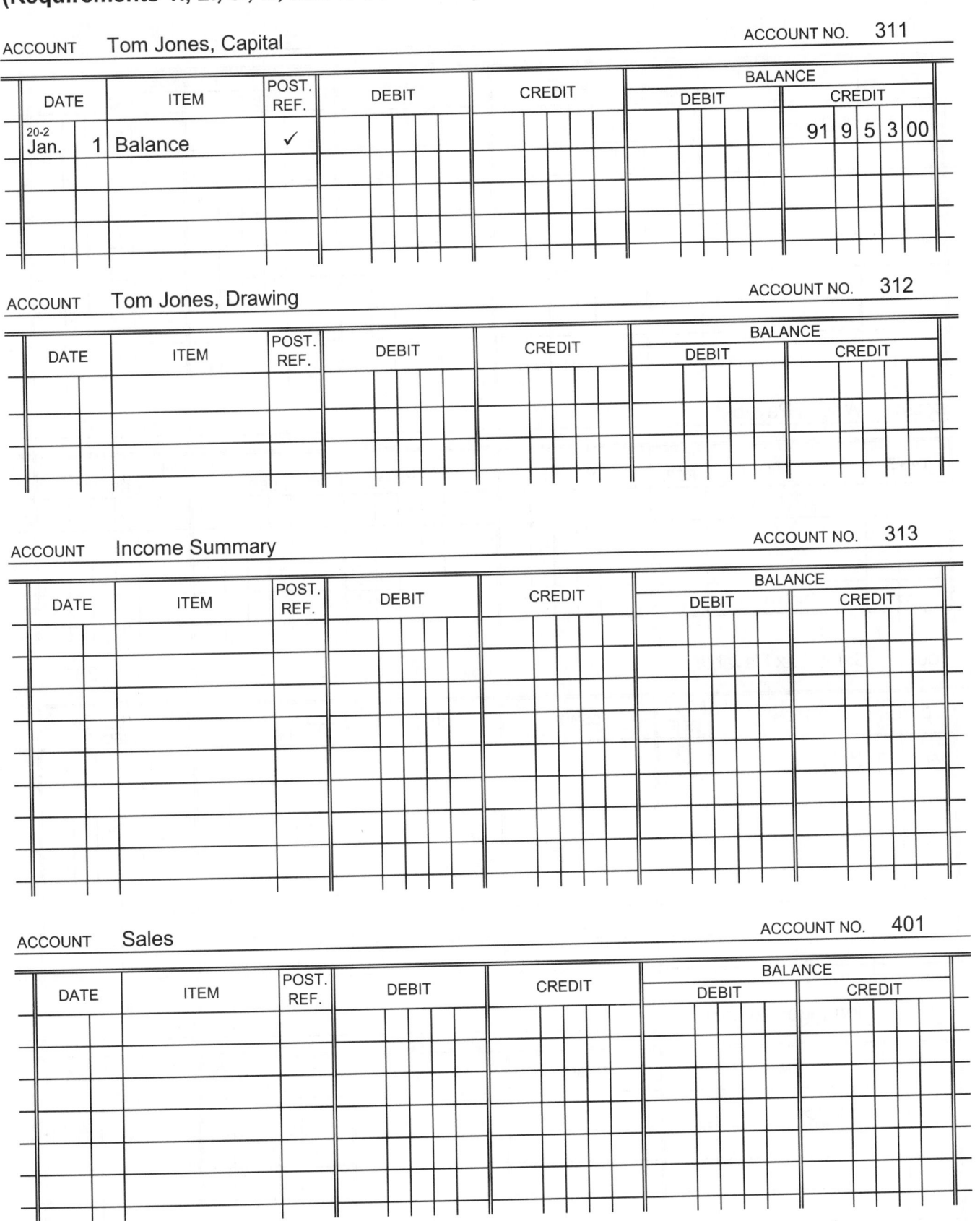

Comprehensive Problem 2—Special Journals Based, Part 2
(Requirements 1., 2., 3., 6., and 7. Continued)

ACCOUNT   Sales Returns and Allowances   ACCOUNT NO.   401.1

DATE	ITEM	POST. REF.	DEBIT	CREDIT	BALANCE DEBIT	BALANCE CREDIT

ACCOUNT   Purchases   ACCOUNT NO.   501

DATE	ITEM	POST. REF.	DEBIT	CREDIT	BALANCE DEBIT	BALANCE CREDIT

ACCOUNT   Purchases Returns and Allowances   ACCOUNT NO.   501.1

DATE	ITEM	POST. REF.	DEBIT	CREDIT	BALANCE DEBIT	BALANCE CREDIT

ACCOUNT   Purchases Discounts   ACCOUNT NO.   501.2

DATE	ITEM	POST. REF.	DEBIT	CREDIT	BALANCE DEBIT	BALANCE CREDIT

Comprehensive Problem 2—Special Journals Based, Part 2
(Requirements 1., 2., 3., 6., and 7. Continued)

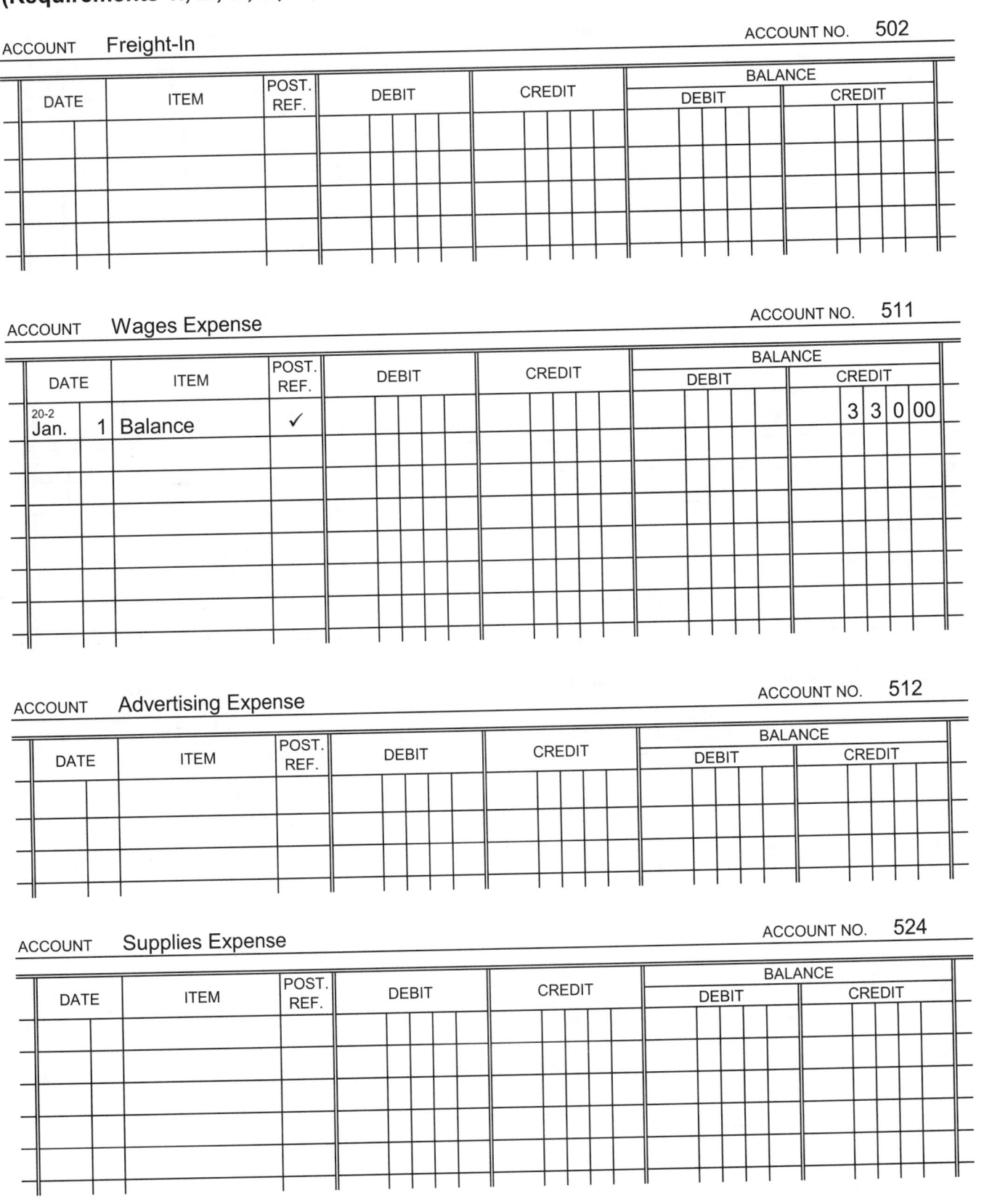

ACCOUNT Freight-In   ACCOUNT NO. 502

DATE	ITEM	POST. REF.	DEBIT	CREDIT	BALANCE DEBIT	BALANCE CREDIT

ACCOUNT Wages Expense   ACCOUNT NO. 511

DATE		ITEM	POST. REF.	DEBIT	CREDIT	BALANCE DEBIT	BALANCE CREDIT
20-2 Jan.	1	Balance	✓				3 3 0 0 00

ACCOUNT Advertising Expense   ACCOUNT NO. 512

DATE	ITEM	POST. REF.	DEBIT	CREDIT	BALANCE DEBIT	BALANCE CREDIT

ACCOUNT Supplies Expense   ACCOUNT NO. 524

DATE	ITEM	POST. REF.	DEBIT	CREDIT	BALANCE DEBIT	BALANCE CREDIT

Comprehensive Problem 2—Special Journals Based, Part 2
(Requirements 1., 2., 3., 6., and 7. Continued)

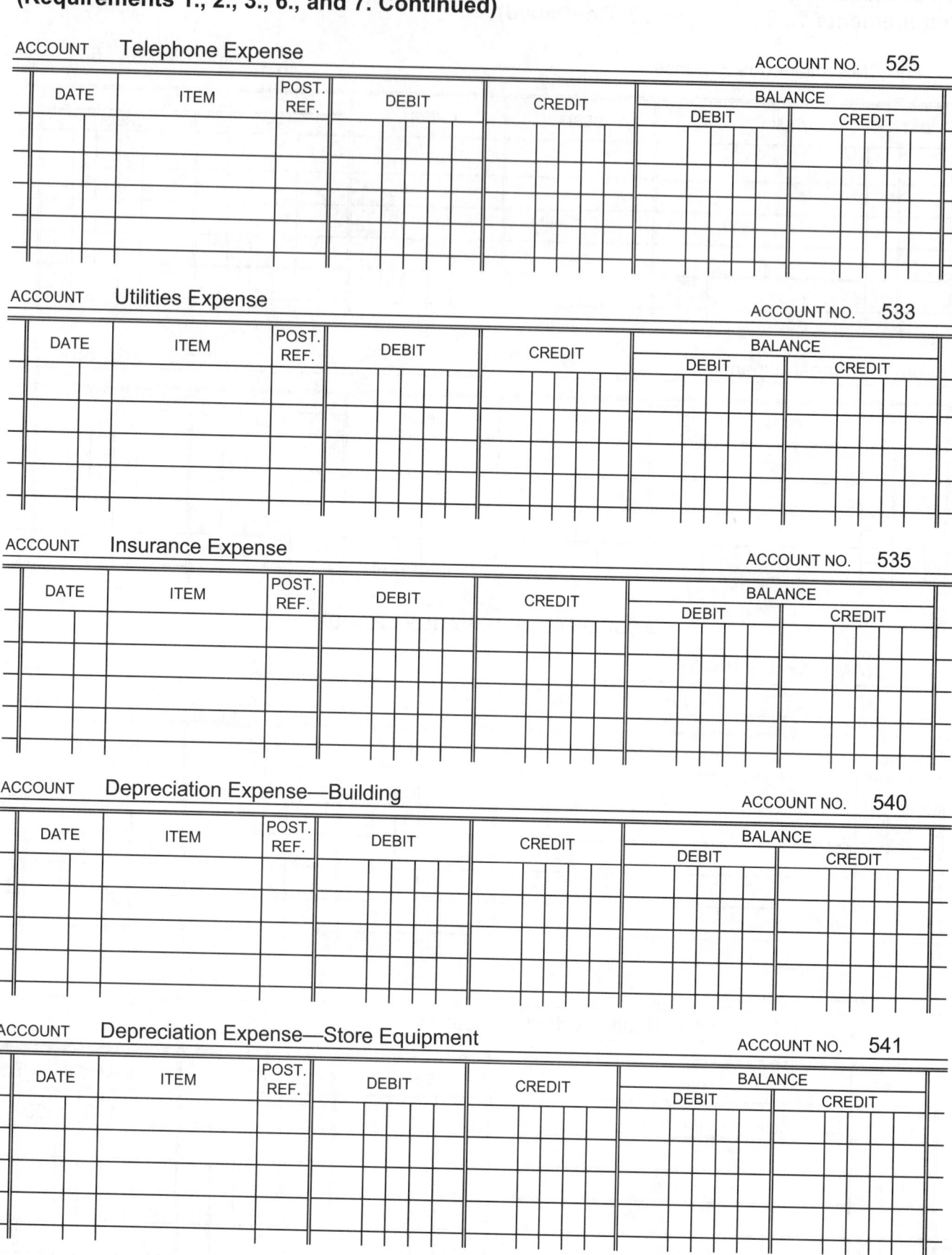

ACCOUNT   Telephone Expense   ACCOUNT NO.   525

DATE	ITEM	POST. REF.	DEBIT	CREDIT	BALANCE	
					DEBIT	CREDIT

ACCOUNT   Utilities Expense   ACCOUNT NO.   533

DATE	ITEM	POST. REF.	DEBIT	CREDIT	BALANCE	
					DEBIT	CREDIT

ACCOUNT   Insurance Expense   ACCOUNT NO.   535

DATE	ITEM	POST. REF.	DEBIT	CREDIT	BALANCE	
					DEBIT	CREDIT

ACCOUNT   Depreciation Expense—Building   ACCOUNT NO.   540

DATE	ITEM	POST. REF.	DEBIT	CREDIT	BALANCE	
					DEBIT	CREDIT

ACCOUNT   Depreciation Expense—Store Equipment   ACCOUNT NO.   541

DATE	ITEM	POST. REF.	DEBIT	CREDIT	BALANCE	
					DEBIT	CREDIT

Comprehensive Problem 2—Special Journals Based, Part 2
(Requirements 1., 2., 3., 6., and 7. Continued)

ACCOUNT Miscellaneous Expense   **ACCOUNT NO.** 549

DATE	ITEM	POST. REF.	DEBIT	CREDIT	BALANCE DEBIT	BALANCE CREDIT

ACCOUNT Interest Expense   **ACCOUNT NO.** 551

DATE	ITEM	POST. REF.	DEBIT	CREDIT	BALANCE DEBIT	BALANCE CREDIT

ACCOUNTS RECEIVABLE LEDGER

NAME Martha Boyle

ADDRESS 12 Jude Lane, Hartford, CT 06117

DATE		ITEM	POST. REF.	DEBIT	CREDIT	BALANCE
20-2 Jan.	1	Balance	✓			1 3 2 3 00

NAME Anne Clark

ADDRESS 52 Juniper Road, Hartford, CT 06118

DATE		ITEM	POST. REF.	DEBIT	CREDIT	BALANCE
20-2 Jan.	1	Balance	✓			2 1 0 0 00

**Comprehensive Problem 2—Special Journals Based, Part 2
(Requirements 1., 2., 3., 6., and 7. Continued)**

NAME John Dempsey

ADDRESS 700 Hobbes Dr., Avon, CT 06108

DATE		ITEM	POST. REF.	DEBIT	CREDIT	BALANCE
20-2 Jan.	1	Balance	✓			2 1 2 1 00

NAME Kim Fields

ADDRESS 5200 Hamilton Ave., Hartford, CT 06117

DATE		ITEM	POST. REF.	DEBIT	CREDIT	BALANCE
20-2 Jan.	1	Balance	✓			1 6 8 00

NAME Lucy Greene

ADDRESS 236 Bally Lane, Simsbury, CT 06123

DATE		ITEM	POST. REF.	DEBIT	CREDIT	BALANCE
20-2 Jan.	1	Balance	✓			1 4 9 1 00

Comprehensive Problem 2—Special Journals Based, Part 2
(Requirements 1., 2., 3., 6., and 7. Concluded)

ACCOUNTS PAYABLE LEDGER

NAME Evans Essentials

ADDRESS 34 Harry Ave., East Hartford, CT 05234

DATE		ITEM	POST. REF.	DEBIT	CREDIT	BALANCE
20-2 Jan.	1	Balance	✓			2 3 5 0 00

NAME Nathen Co.

ADDRESS 1009 Drake Rd., Farmington, CT 06082

DATE		ITEM	POST. REF.	DEBIT	CREDIT	BALANCE
20-2 Jan.	1	Balance	✓			8 0 0 00

NAME Owen Enterprises

ADDRESS 43 Lucky Lane, Bristol, CT 06007

DATE		ITEM	POST. REF.	DEBIT	CREDIT	BALANCE

NAME West Wholesalers

ADDRESS 888 Anders Street, Newington, CT 06789

DATE		ITEM	POST. REF.	DEBIT	CREDIT	BALANCE
20-2 Jan.	1	Balance	✓			1 2 0 0 00

Comprehensive Problem 2—Special Journals Based, Part 2

Requirement 4.

Comprehensive Problem 2—Special Journals Based, Part 2

Requirement 5.

	TRIAL BALANCE		ADJUSTMENTS	
	DEBIT	CREDIT	DEBIT	CREDIT
1				
2				
3				
4				
5				
6				
7				
8				
9				
10				
11				
12				
13				
14				
15				
16				
17				
18				
19				
20				
21				
22				
23				
24				
25				
26				
27				
28				
29				
30				
31				
32				
33				
34				
35				
36				

Comprehensive Problem 2—Special Journals Based, Part 2
(Requirement 5. Continued)

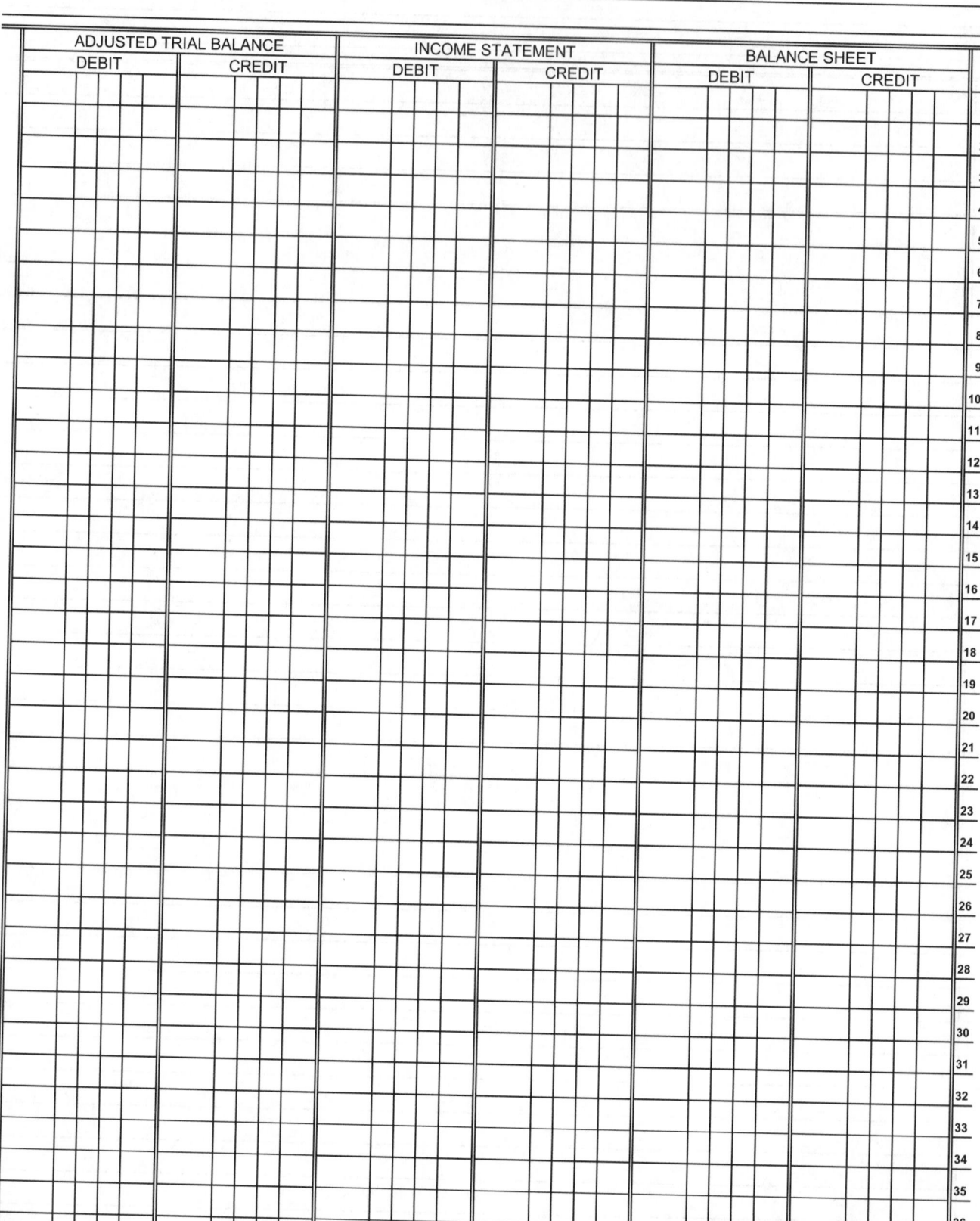

ADJUSTED TRIAL BALANCE		INCOME STATEMENT		BALANCE SHEET		
DEBIT	CREDIT	DEBIT	CREDIT	DEBIT	CREDIT	
						1
						2
						3
						4
						5
						6
						7
						8
						9
						10
						11
						12
						13
						14
						15
						16
						17
						18
						19
						20
						21
						22
						23
						24
						25
						26
						27
						28
						29
						30
						31
						32
						33
						34
						35
						36

Comprehensive Problem 2—Special Journals Based, Part 2
(Requirement 5. Continued)

Comprehensive Problem 2—Special Journals Based, Part 2
(Requirement 5. Continued)

Comprehensive Problem 2—Special Journals Based, Part 2
(Requirement 5. Concluded)

Comprehensive Problem 2—Special Journals Based, Part 2

Requirement 6.

GENERAL JOURNAL

	DATE	DESCRIPTION	POST. REF.	DEBIT	CREDIT	
1						1
2						2
3						3
4						4
5						5
6						6
7						7
8						8
9						9
10						10
11						11
12						12
13						13
14						14
15						15
16						16
17						17
18						18
19						19
20						20
21						21
22						22
23						23
24						24
25						25
26						26
27						27
28						28
29						29
30						30
31						31
32						32
33						33
34						34

Comprehensive Problem 2—Special Journals Based, Part 2

Requirement 7.

GENERAL JOURNAL

PAGE 3

	DATE	DESCRIPTION	POST. REF.	DEBIT	CREDIT	
1						1
2						2
3						3
4						4
5						5
6						6
7						7
8						8
9						9
10						10
11						11
12						12
13						13
14						14
15						15
16						16
17						17
18						18
19						19
20						20
21						21
22						22
23						23
24						24
25						25
26						26
27						27
28						28
29						29
30						30
31						31
32						32
33						33
34						34

Comprehensive Problem 2—Special Journals Based, Part 2

Requirement 8.

ACCOUNT	DEBIT BALANCE	CREDIT BALANCE

Exercise 1-1A

1. _____ Owners

2. _____ Managers

3. _____ Creditors

4. _____ Government
                     agencies

a. Whether the firm can pay its bills on time

b. Detailed, up-to-date information to measure business performance (and plan for future operations)

c. To determine taxes to be paid and whether other regulations are met

d. The firm's current financial condition

Exercise 1-2A

<u>Order</u>	<u>Accounting Process</u>	<u>Definition</u>
_____	Recording	
_____	Summarizing	
_____	Reporting	
_____	Analyzing	
_____	Interpreting	
_____	Classifying	

Exercise 1-1B

<u>Users</u>	<u>Information</u>
Owners (present and future):	_____
	_____
	_____
Managers:	_____
	_____
	_____
Creditors (present and future):	_____
	_____
	_____
Government agencies:	_____
	_____
	_____

Exercise 1-2B

<u>Letter</u>	<u>Accounting Process</u>		<u>Definition</u>
_____	Analyzing	a.	Telling the results
_____	Recording	b.	Looking at events that have taken place and thinking about how they affect the business
_____	Classifying	c.	Deciding the importance of the various reports
_____	Summarizing	d.	Aggregating many similar events to provide information that is easy to understand
_____	Reporting	e.	Sorting and grouping like items together
_____	Interpreting	f.	Entering financial information into the accounting system

Exercise 2-1A

Item	Account	Classification
Money in bank	Cash	_____
Office supplies	Supplies	_____
Money owed	Accounts Payable	_____
Office chairs	Office Furniture	_____
Net worth of owner	John Smith, Capital	_____
Money withdrawn by owner	John Smith, Drawing	_____
Money owed by customers	Accounts Receivable	_____

Exercise 2-2A

Assets	=	Liabilities	+	Owner's Equity
_____	=	$27,000	+	$17,000
$32,000	=	$18,000	+	_____
$27,000	=	_____	+	$20,000

Exercise 2-3A

	Assets	=	Liabilities	+	Owner's Equity
(a)	_____		_____		_____
Bal.	_____		_____		_____
(b)	_____		_____		_____
Bal.	_____		_____		_____
(c)	_____		_____		_____
	_____		_____		_____
Bal.	_____		_____		_____
(d)	_____		_____		_____
Bal.	_____		_____		_____

Exercise 2-4A

Assets	=	Liabilities	+	Capital	–	Drawing	+	Revenues	–	Expenses	Description
						Owner's Equity					

Bal.
from
E 2-3A

(d)

(e)

(f)

(g)

(h)

(i)

(j)

(k)

Bal.